The Loire

Nicola Williams

D0778001

LONELY PLANET PUBLICATIONS
Melbourne • Oakland • London • Paris

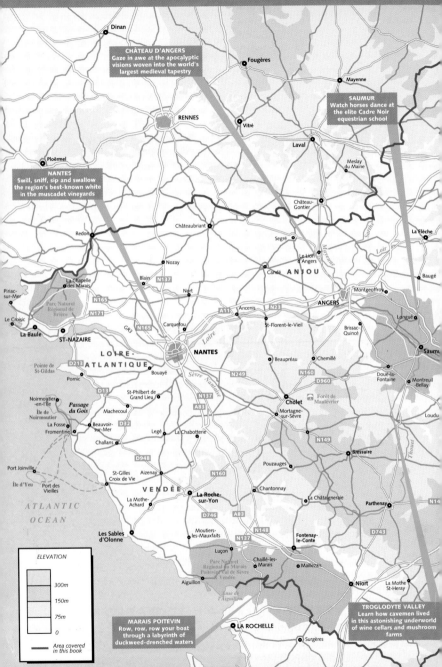

THE LOIRE

CHÂTEAU D'ANGERS
Gaze in awe at the apocalyptic visions woven into the world's largest medieval tapestry

SAUMUR
Watch horses dance at the elite Cadre Noir equestrian school

NANTES
Swill, sniff, sip and swallow the region's best-known white in the muscadet vineyards

TROGLODYTE VALLEY
Learn how cavemen lived in this astonishing underworld of wine cellars and mushroom farms

MARAIS POITEVIN
Row, row, row your boat through a labyrinth of duckweed-drenched waters

Dinan

Fougères

Mayenne

CHÂTEAU D'ANGERS

RENNES

Vitré

Laval

Meslay du Maine

Ploërmel

Château-Gontier

La Flèche

Redon

Châteaubriant

Segré

Le Lion d'Angers

Baugé

Piriac-sur-Mer

La Chapelle des Marais

Nozay

Blain **N137**

Candé

ANJOU

Montgeoffroy

Parc Naturel Régional de Brière

N165

N171

Niort

Ancenis **A11** **N23**

ANGERS

Longué

Le Croisic

GR3

N165

Carquefou

St-Florent-le-Vieil

Brissac-Quincé

Saum

La Baule

ST-NAZAIRE

LOIRE-ATLANTIQUE

NANTES

Beaupréau

Chemillé

Doué-la-Fontaine

Montreuil-Bellay

Pointe de St-Gildas

D213

Bouayé

Sèvre Nantaise **N249**

N160 **D960**

Forêt de Maulévrier

Pornic

D13

St-Philbert de Grand Lieu

N137

Cholet

Mortagne-sur-Sèvre

Loudu

Noirmoutier-en-l'Île

Île de Noirmoutier

Passage du Gois

Machecoul

D32

A83

La Fosse Fromentine

Beauvoir-sur-Mer

Legé

La Chabotterie

N149

Bressuire

Challans

D948

VENDÉE

Pouzauges

Port Joinville

St-Gilles Croix de Vie

Aizenay

N160

Chantonnay

La Châtaigneraie

Parthenay

N14

Île d'Yeu

Port des Vieilles

La Mothe-Achard

La Roche-sur-Yon

ATLANTIC OCEAN

D746

A83

D743

Les Sables d'Olonne

Moutiers-les-Mauxfaits

N148

Fontenay-le-Comte

La Mothe St-Heray

N137

Luçon

Chaillé-les-Marais

Maillezais

Niort

ELEVATION

Parc Naturel Régional du Marais Poitevin Val de Sèvre & Vendée

Aiguillon

Anse de l'Aiguillon

Surgères

300m

150m

75m

0

LA ROCHELLE

Area covered in this book

CHÂTEAU DE CHAMBORD
Marvel at the stunning Renaissance architecture and watch stags play in the forest

AMBOISE
Be amazed by Leonardo da Vinci's fabulous, far-fetched flying machines

CHÂTEAU DE VILLANDRY
Discover love in the amour-inspired Renaissance gardens

LA SOLOGNE
Explore soggy Sologne, a low-lying land of 11,000 lakes, criss-crossed by hiking paths and cycling trails

CHÂTEAU DE CHEVERNY
Be bewitched by the elegant white facade and the sumptuously furnished interior

FUTUROSCOPE
Step into the future and be dazzled at the moving-image theme park

Alençon

Chartres

Pithiviers

ORLÉANAIS

Nogent-le-Rotrou

Forêt d'Orléans

Bellegarde

N60

Montargis

N7

Châteaudun

N154

N157

ORLÉANS

N60

Jargeau

Châteauneuf-sur-Loire

GR3

D952

LE MANS

St-Calais

BLÉSOIS

Cléry-St-André

N20

Beaugency

La Ferté St-Aubin

A71

Sully-sur-Loire

Gien

Briare

Château du Loir

La Chartre-sur-le-Loir

Montoire-sur-le-Loir

Vendôme

N152

Chambord

Domaine National de Chambord

GR3c

Neung-sur-Beuvron

Nouan-le-Fuzelier

Argent-sur-Sauldre

Aubigny-sur-Nère

D940

Le Lude

D959

Château-la-Valière

TOURAINE

Neuillé-Pont-Pierre

N138

A10

Blois

Bracieux

Cheverny

SOLOGNE

Noyant

Onzain

GR3

Contres

Romorantin-Lanthenay

Sauldre

La Chapelle d'Angillon

Forêt d'Ivoy

Sancerre

TOURS

Vouvray

Loire

Amboise

Pontlevoy

Montrichard

Selles-sur-Cher

N76

N20

Vierzon

Langeais

N152

Villandry

Montbazon

Indre

St-Aignan

BOURGES

Parc Régional Loire-Anjou-Touraine

Chinon

Forêt de Chinon

A10

N143

Loches

Seuilly

Richelieu

Ste-Maure de Touraine

N10

Descartes

Issoudun

Cher

N147

Châtellerault

Mirebeau

POITOU

A10

Châteauroux

Parc Naturel Régional de la Brenne

OITIERS

Futuroscope

Chauvigny

Le Blanc

St-Savin

J11

N147

Gençay

Lussac-les-Châteaux

Montmorillon

Civray

Ruffec

0   20   40 km
0   12.5   25 miles

The Loire
1st edition – June 2000

Published by
Lonely Planet Publications Pty Ltd A.C.N. 005 607 983
192 Burwood Rd, Hawthorn, Victoria 3122, Australia

Lonely Planet Offices
Australia PO Box 617, Hawthorn, Victoria 3122
USA 150 Linden St, Oakland, CA 94607
UK 10a Spring Place, London NW5 3BH
France 1 rue du Dahomey, 75011 Paris

Photographs
Many of the images in this guide are available for licensing from
Lonely Planet Images.
email: lpi@lonelyplanet.com.au

Front cover photograph
The 16th-century Renaissance Château de Chambord
(Tony Stone Images)

ISBN 1 86450 097 2

text & maps © Lonely Planet 2000
photos © photographers as indicated 2000

Printed by The Bookmaker Pty Ltd
Printed in China

Although the authors
and Lonely Planet try
to make the informa-
tion as accurate as
possible, we accept
no responsibility for
any loss, injury or
inconvenience sus-
tained by anyone
using this book.

Contents – Text

Contents – Maps

MAP INDEX

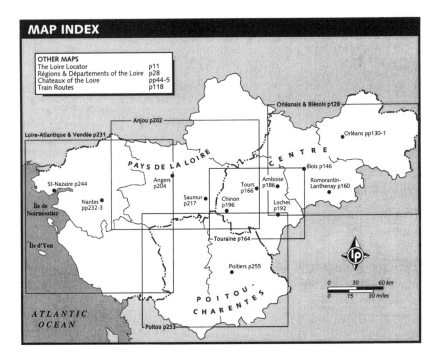

Orléanais & Blésois p128

Anjou p202

Loire-Atlantique & Vendée p231

Orléans pp130-1

PAYS DE LA LOIRE

CENTRE

St-Nazaire p244

Angers p204

Tours p166

Amboise p186

Blois p146

Romorantin-Lanthenay p160

Île de Noirmoutier

Nantes pp232-3

Saumur p217

Chinon p196

Loches p192

Île d'Yeu

Touraine p164

Poitiers p255

ATLANTIC OCEAN

POITOU-CHARENTES

Poitou p253

0   30   60 km
0   15   30 miles

The Author

Nicola Williams

Nicola lives in Lyon, crossroads to the Alps and the Mediterranean. A journalist by training, she first hit the road in 1990 when she bussed and boated it from Jakarta to East Timor and back again. Following a two-year stint at the *North Wales Weekly News*, she moved to Latvia to bus it around the Baltics as Features Editor of the English-language *Baltic Times* newspaper. Following a happy 12 months exploring the Baltic region as Editor-in-Chief of the *In Your Pocket* city-guide series, she traded in Lithuanian *cepelinai* for Lyonnaise *andouillette*.

Nicola graduated from Kent and completed an MA in Islamic Societies and Cultures at London's School of Oriental and African Studies. Previous Lonely Planet titles she has updated parts of include *Estonia, Latvia & Lithuania, Russia, Ukraine & Belarus* and *France*. Nicola authored *Romania & Moldova* and also wrote *Provence & the Côte d'Azur*, Lonely Planet's first regional France title.

FROM THE AUTHOR

A multitude of friendly faces from a multitude of chateaux assured I did not forget which was which when writing up. Fifty chateau visits or so later, particularly sincere thanks to Catherine Leroi from Château d'Angers, Yveline Galand from Château de Chenonceau, Carole Bracq from Chenonceau's *bureau de presse* in Paris, Laurent de Froberville from the Domaine de Cheverny, Louis Hubert from the Domaine de Chambord, Jean Saint-Bris from Le Clos Lucé in Amboise, Catherine Moulé from the École Nationale d'Équitation in equestrian Saumur, and Monsieur Morillon of Nantes Mairie. An equally *grand merci* to Léon Longepée in Port des Brochets for his giant-sized oysters and colourful explanation of *ostréiculture*; and to Monsieur and Madame Gaultier in St-Georges-sur-Loire for unveiling the secrets of Anjou's sweet Coteaux du Layon wine.

In London particular thanks to Claudia Martin, Paul Bloomfield, Katrina Browning, Marcel Gaston and his heroic team of cartographers for their enthusiasm and painstaking work on this book. Elsewhere on the Lonely Planet globe, thank you to Jen Loy (LP-US) and Leonie Mugavin (LP-Oz) for verifying the Getting There & Away chapter; and to fellow France fiends and authors Steve Fallon, Daniel Robinson, Julia Wilkinson and John King, whose texts formed an invaluable basis for parts of this book. Closer to home, sweet thanks to my *belle-mère* Christa Lüfkens for her tip-top chauffeuring and guiding skills; to my parents Ann and Paul Williams for a lifetime of support and encouragement; and to my husband Matthias Lüfkens for wining and dining his way around much of the Loire with me.

5

This Book

Nicola Williams researched and wrote this 1st edition of *The Loire*.

From the Publisher

This edition of *The Loire* was edited and proofed in Lonely Planet's London office by Claudia Martin, with help from Christine Stroyan and Anna Jacomb-Hood. Paul Edmunds coordinated the mapping, with assistance from Gadi Farfour, Ed Pickard, Angie Watts and Sara Yorke. Angie laid out the book and designed the colour pages and cover. The back-cover map was drawn by Jim Miller. The illustrations were drawn by Jane Smith, and photographs were supplied by Lonely Planet Images, Château de Cheverny, École Nationale d'Équitation and M Vimenet. Quentin Frayne produced the language chapter.

Foreword

ABOUT LONELY PLANET GUIDEBOOKS

The story begins with a classic travel adventure: Tony and Maureen·Wheeler's 1972 journey across Europe and Asia to Australia. Useful information about the overland trail did not exist at that time, so Tony and Maureen published the first Lonely Planet guidebook to meet a growing need.

From a kitchen table, then from a tiny office in Melbourne (Australia), Lonely Planet has become the largest independent travel publisher in the world, an international company with offices in Melbourne, Oakland (USA), London (UK) and Paris (France).

Today Lonely Planet guidebooks cover the globe. There is an ever-growing list of books and there's information in a variety of forms and media. Some things haven't changed. The main aim is still to help make it possible for adventurous travellers to get out there – to explore and better understand the world.'

At Lonely Planet we believe travellers can make a positive contribution to the countries they visit – if they respect their host communities and spend their money wisely. Since 1986 a percentage of the income from each book has been donated to aid projects and human rights campaigns.

Updates Lonely Planet thoroughly updates each guidebook as often as possible. This usually means there are around two years between editions, although for more unusual or more stable destinations the gap can be longer. Check the imprint page (following the colour map at the beginning of the book) for publication dates.

Between editions up-to-date information is available in two free newsletters – the paper *Planet Talk* and email *Comet* (to subscribe, contact any Lonely Planet office) – and on our Web site at www.lonelyplanet.com. The *Upgrades* section of the Web site covers a number of important and volatile destinations and is regularly updated by Lonely Planet authors. *Scoop* covers news and current affairs relevant to travellers. And, lastly, the *Thorn Tree* bulletin board and *Postcards* section of the site carry unverified, but fascinating, reports from travellers.

Correspondence The process of creating new editions begins with the letters, postcards and emails received from travellers. This correspondence often includes suggestions, criticisms and comments about the current editions. Interesting excerpts are immediately passed on via newsletters and the Web site, and everything goes to our authors to be verified when they're researching on the road. We're keen to get more feedback from organisations or individuals who represent communities visited by travellers.

Lonely Planet gathers information for everyone who's curious about the planet – and especially for those who explore it first-hand. Through guidebooks, phrasebooks, activity guides, maps, literature, newsletters, image library, TV series and Web site we act as an information exchange for a worldwide community of travellers.

Research Authors aim to gather sufficient practical information to enable travellers to make informed choices and to make the mechanics of a journey run smoothly. They also research historical and cultural background to help enrich the travel experience and allow travellers to understand and respond appropriately to cultural and environmental issues.

Authors don't stay in every hotel because that would mean spending a couple of months in each medium-sized city and, no, they don't eat at every restaurant because that would mean stretching belts beyond capacity. They do visit hotels and restaurants to check standards and prices, but feedback based on readers' direct experiences can be very helpful.

Many of our authors work undercover, others aren't so secretive. None of them accept freebies in exchange for positive write-ups. And none of our guidebooks contain any advertising.

Production Authors submit their raw manuscripts and maps to offices in Australia, USA, UK or France. Editors and cartographers – all experienced travellers themselves – then begin the process of assembling the pieces. When the book finally hits the shops some things are already out of date, we start getting feedback from readers, and the process begins again ...

WARNING & REQUEST

Things change – prices go up, schedules change, good places go bad and bad places go bankrupt – nothing stays the same. So, if you find things better or worse, recently opened or long since closed, please tell us and help make the next edition even more accurate and useful. We genuinely value all the feedback we receive. Julie Young coordinates a well-travelled team that reads and acknowledges every letter, postcard and email and ensures that every morsel of information finds its way to the appropriate authors, editors and cartographers for verification.

Everyone who writes to us will find their name in the next edition of the appropriate guidebook. They will also receive the latest issue of *Planet Talk*, our quarterly printed newsletter, or *Comet*, our monthly email newsletter. Subscriptions to both newsletters are free. The very best contributions will be rewarded with a free guidebook.

Excerpts from your correspondence may appear in new editions of Lonely Planet guidebooks, the Lonely Planet Web site, *Planet Talk* or *Comet*, so please let us know if you *don't* want your letter published or your name acknowledged.

Send all correspondence to the Lonely Planet office closest to you:

Australia: PO Box 617, Hawthorn, Victoria 3122
UK: 10A Spring Place, London NW5 3BH
USA: 150 Linden St, Oakland CA 94607
France: 1 rue du Dahomey, Paris 75011

Or email us at: talk2us@lonelyplanet.com.au

For news, views and updates see our Web site: www.lonelyplanet.com

HOW TO USE A LONELY PLANET GUIDEBOOK

The best way to use a Lonely Planet guidebook is any way you choose. At Lonely Planet we believe the most memorable travel experiences are often those that are unexpected, and the finest discoveries are those you make yourself. Guidebooks are not intended to be used as if they provide a detailed set of infallible instructions!

Contents All Lonely Planet guidebooks follow roughly the same format. The Facts about the Destination chapter or section gives background information ranging from history to weather. Facts for the Visitor gives practical information on issues like visas and health. Getting There & Away gives a brief starting point for researching travel to and from the destination. Getting Around gives an overview of the transport options when you arrive.

The peculiar demands of each destination determine how subsequent chapters are broken up, but some things remain constant. We always start with background, then proceed to sights, places to stay, places to eat, entertainment, getting there and away, and getting around information – in that order.

Heading Hierarchy Lonely Planet headings are used in a strict hierarchical structure that can be visualised as a set of Russian dolls. Each heading (and its following text) is encompassed by any preceding heading that is higher on the hierarchical ladder.

Entry Points We do not assume guidebooks will be read from beginning to end, but that people will dip into them. The traditional entry points are the list of contents and the index. In addition, however, some books have a complete list of maps and an index map illustrating map coverage.

There may also be a colour map that shows highlights. These highlights are dealt with in greater detail in the Facts for the Visitor chapter, along with planning questions and suggested itineraries. Each chapter covering a geographical region usually begins with a locator map and another list of highlights. Once you find something of interest in a list of highlights, turn to the index.

Maps Maps play a crucial role in Lonely Planet guidebooks and include a huge amount of information. A legend is printed on the back page. We seek to have complete consistency between maps and text, and to have every important place in the text captured on a map. Map key numbers usually start in the top left corner.

Although inclusion in a guidebook usually implies a recommendation we cannot list every good place. Exclusion does not necessarily imply criticism. In fact there are a number of reasons why we might exclude a place – sometimes it is simply inappropriate to encourage an influx of travellers.

Introduction

The River Loire is France's longest, most regal river. The fortresses and chateaux reflected in its waters are a spectacular testimony to the glories of Renaissance France and its pack of kings and queens who came to this beautiful region to play.

The earliest chateaux in this *Vallée des Rois* (Valley of Kings) were raised in the 9th century to fend off marauding Vikings. By the 11th century, fortified keeps, arrow slits, massive walls topped with battlements, and moats spanned by drawbridges were all the rage (as was boiling oil to pour on attackers). Five centuries on, the Renaissance introduced beauty. Whimsical and fantastical decoration covered everything from chimney pots to door knobs in a quest to create the king of all castles. The chateaux at Chambord, Chaumont, Chenonceaux and Azay-le-Rideau were the most resplendent extravaganzas. Then, in the 17th century, the king and his court deserted their chateaux and the nobility moved into the empty pleasure palaces.

Scores of these fairy-tale chateaux and their surrounding stag-rich forests remain in private hands today. The heady days of balls and ladies-in-waiting are now nothing more than an ancestral memory for most chateau dwellers, who face the awesome task of preserving the white stone edifices of these Renaissance rhapsodies for future generations. At the weekend, marauding Parisians flock to their second homes in the Loire, following in the footsteps of Joan of Arc (Jeanne d'Arc), Leonardo da Vinci, Gérard Depardieu and a host of other famous names who have left their mark on the chateau-studded landscape.

THE LOIRE LOCATOR

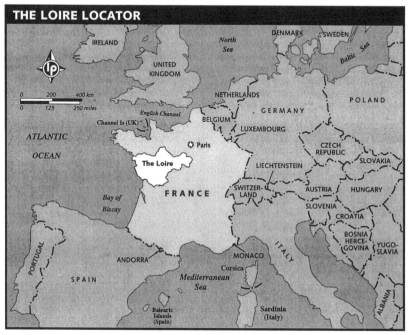

11

The Loire Valley proper follows the course of the river downstream from Sancerre to the sea. Vineyards and fruit orchards cloak the banks of the River Loire, from which a rash of other rivers – including the Cher, Indre and Loir (Le Loir, not the feminine La Loire) – flow. Wines produced here are famous the world over, and taking the time to sniff, swill, sip and swallow them is one of the greatest pleasures the region affords. Artichoke, asparagus and cherry yields are high in this well-watered land which Touraine-born author Rabelais called '*le jardin de France*' (the garden of France). Downstream, past the historical regions of Touraine and Anjou, the River Loire spills through the university city of Nantes and into the Atlantic Ocean. Here on the coast, muscadet vineyards meet mussel and oyster beds.

When tired feet spurn another chateau tour, alternative activities abound: balloon in blue skies, punt in green duckweed pools, cycle in the soggy Sologne, explore subterranean troglodyte dwellings, see wild animals at play or watch horses dance.

Facts about the Loire

HISTORY
Early Inhabitants
The Loire Valley has been inhabited since the Middle Palaeolithic period (about 90,000 to 40,000 BC), when Neanderthal people (thought to be early representatives of *Homo sapiens*) hunted animals, made crude flakestone tools and paddled along the River Loire in hollowed-out tree trunks.

Modern man followed in 30,000 BC. The Neolithic period (about 6000 to 4500 years ago), also known as the New Stone Age, witnessed the earliest domestication of animals, the cultivation of lands and the clearance of forests. Megaliths, chiselled from stone and used to worship the dead, were a predominant feature of this period, as were dolmens, which were constructed in unusually high numbers around Saumur and Baugé from 3500 BC (see Prehistoric under Architecture later in this chapter).

The history of these early inhabitants is best illustrated in the Musée Départemental de Préhistoire in the Château du Grand-Pressigny and the Musée des Tumulus de Bougon, near Poitiers. The latter's archaeological treasures demonstrate how early man hunted, caught fish and subsequently cultivated cereals, beans and lentils. The Bougon museum houses five megalithic tumuli built 2000 years before the Egyptian pyramids, making them the world's oldest funeraria. Discovered in 1840, the tumuli date from 4500 BC and shelter eight burial chambers. The human skulls found inside had small incisions on them which archaeologists believe were cut by early man, while the 'guinea pigs' were still alive, to learn about the brain.

The Gauls & the Romans
The arrival of the Gauls in the region between 1500 and 500 BC ushered in the Iron Age. The Carnutes settled in Cenabum (Orléans), navigated the River Loire both upstream and downstream, and built a bridge across it. The Turones took hold of Touraine and the Andes adopted Anjou as their own. By about 600 BC, the River Loire had become a major trading route between the Celts and the Greeks, who had established colonies such as Massilia (Marseille), on the Mediterranean coast.

Centuries of conflict between the Gauls and the Romans ended in 52 BC, when Julius Caesar's legions crushed a revolt led by the Gallic chief Vercingetorix and took control of the territory. Caesar met with particularly fierce opposition around Cenabum, since the Carnutes were fierce allies of Vercingetorix. Caesar eventually burned the city to the ground.

The Romans rebuilt Cenabum and renamed it Aurelianis (after Civitatis Aurelianorum, the administrative district of which it became capital). They settled Caesarodunum (Tours), farther downstream on the banks of the River Loire, and established the city of Juliomagus (Angers) in about AD 1. Roads linking these Roman strongholds were then constructed.

Christianity arrived in the 3rd century AD, bringing a host of saintly figures who converted the region's pagan population and cultivated its vineyards. St Gatien was recognised as bishop of Tours by 304 and was succeeded in 372 by St Martin, a soldier in the Roman army who converted to Christianity after a beggar inspired him to slash his cloak in two to share it. After his death in Candes (later renamed Candes St-Martin), followers rowed his relics down the River Loire to Tours. In Orléans, Christianity was preached by St Aignan, best known for saving the city from Attila, leader of the Huns, in 451. In St-Benoît-sur-Loire, St Benedict (480–547) established religious communities on the banks of the River Loire, which led to the emergence of the Benedictine Order. The abbey founded by Robert d'Arbrissel (1045–1116) in Fontevraud in 1101 ranked as one of the Order's most powerful.

The region remained under Roman rule until the 5th century, when the Franks (from whom the word 'France' comes) and the Alemanii, tribes from the Rhine area, overran the country from the east. With the fall of the Roman Empire, traffic along the River Loire also declined.

The Merovingians & the Carolingians

Two Frankish dynasties, the Merovingians and the Carolingians, ruled France from the 5th to the 10th centuries. The Frankish tradition by which the king was succeeded by *all* his sons led to power struggles and the eventual disintegration of the kingdom into a collection of small feudal states. The Visigoths, who originated in the Danube delta region in Transylvania, had penetrated France in the 5th century and Touraine was bitterly fought over by the Franks and the Visigoths at the start of the 6th century, culminating in the battle of Vouillé in 507, which saw Clovis, king of the Franks, defeat the Visigoth king, Alaric II. The bickering between Clovis' sons on his death is related in *Historia Francorum* (*History of the Franks*), written by Gregory, bishop of Tours from 573 to 594 (see the boxed text).

In 732 the Frankish ruler Charles Martel defeated the Moors at Poitiers, thus ensuring that France would not fall under Muslim rule as had Spain. Martel's grandson Charlemagne (747–814) significantly extended the power and boundaries of the kingdom and was crowned Holy Roman Emperor (Emperor of the West) in 800. On his request, the Abbaye de St-Martin in Tours became a royal abbey headed by the scholarly monk Alcuin, thus paving the way for the city's emergence as a brilliant religious and intellectual centre in the 8th and 9th centuries.

But in the 9th century Scandinavian Vikings – also known as Norsemen (Normans) – began raiding France's western coast. In 853 they invaded Tours, plundered its cathedral, destroyed its famous abbey and ruined the city. Angers suffered a similar fate in 854 and again in 872 until, after a long siege, Charles the Bald delivered the city and took control of it. Orléans remained under Viking attack until as late as 903.

The Middle Ages

The Anjou Counts The death of Charles the Bald in 877 marked the end of the Carolingian dynasty and prompted a battle for power in the Loire region which was eventually won in 898 by Foulques le Roux (Falcon the Red) of the House of Anjou. Under the Anjou counts, the Angevin capital of Angers entered a notable period in its history which would see the dynasty of fierce Falcons extend its territorial wings across

Gregory of Tours

Historia Francorum (*History of the Franks*) by Gregory of Tours is regarded as the sole authority on Frankish history, although the 10-volume work spans a much wider period than its title implies. Adam, Eve and their ghastly fall kick off the history, which races through time to AD 591.

A miracle cure prompted Gregory (538–94) to enter the Church. A sickly child, he was called Georgius Florentius and was born into a privileged Gallo-Roman family sporting a family tree riddled with eminent bishops. He was raised by his uncle, the bishop of Clermont, but moved to Tours after a prayer to St Martin for better health – in the form of dust from the saint's tomb which Gregory mixed with water and drank – was answered.

From 573 until his death he served as bishop of Tours. The city of Tours as the religious centre of Gaul – thanks to St Martin's relics, which created a cult following among sick, elderly or other miracle-seeking Christians – features strongly in Gregory's *Historia Francorum*, which he started in 573. Literary critics slam Gregory's grammatical use of Latin as nothing short of barbarian. Of the 10 volumes, the final five, which reflect ideas and events occurring in the bishop's own lifetime, are held in the highest esteem.

Toulouse, Gascony, Périgord and Limousin, as well as Anjou, Maine, Touraine and Poitou in the Loire region.

The most notable count of this dynasty was Foulques Nerra (Falcon the Black), who ruled between 987 and 1040. He served as a vassal of Hugues Capet, founder of the Capetian dynasty, when Capet was crowned king in Orléans cathedral. The king's domains were then quite modest, consisting mostly of the land around Orléans and Paris.

It was during this sweeping territorial expansion by the Anjou counts that the first feudal fortresses were constructed in the region. Foulques Nerra built a series of 20 keeps (*donjons*) in the region to defend his newly acquired lands. In 1044 Touraine became part of Anjou, prompting further fortresses to be constructed under Geoffrey II (ruled 1040–60), Foulques Nerra's son. Remnants of these early chateaux still stand in Langeais, Loches and Montrichard.

The Plantagenêts Geoffrey V (ruled 1113–51) governed Greater Anjou with an iron rod following the death of his father, Foulques V, 'the Young' (ruled 1109–13), who had absorbed Maine into the House of Anjou in 1109. Nicknamed 'Plantagenêt' after the customary sprig of broom (*genêt*) he wore in his cap, Geoffrey V wed Mathilda, daughter of Henry I of England, in 1110, thus securing Maine and pre-empting the absorption of Normandy by Greater Anjou in 1144. Their son, Henri Plantagenêt, was crowned King Henry II of England in 1154. The subsequent rivalry between France and England for control of the vast English territories in France would last for three centuries.

During the reign of Henry II (1154–89) the royal court was shifted from Angers to Chinon, where the chateau was fortified and substantially enlarged to host the king and defend the Vallée de la Vienne. Henry's clashes with the Church led to the murder of Thomas à Becket, archbishop of Canterbury, in Canterbury Cathedral, England, in 1170. The murder prompted the guilty construction of many of the Loire's monasteries and religious edifices by Henry II. Chartreuse du Liget (1176–89), a half-ruined Carthusian monastery in Touraine, and the Hôpital St-Jean (1175–80), in Angers, are notable examples.

Henry II's glory days ended in 1189, on the banks of the River Indre in Azay-le-Rideau, with his bitter defeat at the hands of his rebel son, Richard the Lionheart (Cœur de Lion), and the Capetian King Philippe-Auguste, who had inherited the French throne in 1180. Richard the Lionheart wore the English crown from 1189. Anjou and Touraine fell into Philippe-Auguste's hands in 1202 and 1205 respectively. Richard, wounded in battle in 1199, died in Chinon and was buried at the feet of his father in the Abbaye de Fontevraud, in Anjou. The Lionheart's heart was plucked out and taken to Rouen and his entrails were taken to an abbey in Charroux, in Vienne (Poitou).

France played a leading role in the Crusades (the First Crusade was preached at Clermont in 1095 by Pope Urban II), and most of France's major cathedrals and churches – including the superb Église Notre Dame la Grande, in Poitiers – were erected between the 11th and early 14th centuries.

The Hundred Years' War By the mid-14th century the struggle between the Capetians and England's Edward III (a member of the Plantagenêt family) over the powerful French throne had degenerated into the Hundred Years' War (1337–1453). The River Loire marked the border between the French and the English. The Black Death (bubonic plague), which ravaged the entire country between 1348 and 1349, killed about one-third of the population, but only briefly interrupted the fighting.

By the early 15th century things were not going well for the Capetians. French forces were defeated at Agincourt in 1415. The dukes of Burgundy, who were allied with the English, occupied Paris five years later. In 1422 John Plantagenêt, duke of Bedford, was installed as regent of France for England's Henry VI, then an infant. Henry was crowned king of France at Notre Dame less than 10 years later.

Joan of Arc (Jeanne d'Arc)

JANE SMITH

The Maid of Orléans, divinely inspired, was burned at the stake.

Never was there a more legendary virginal warrior than Joan of Arc, an illiterate peasant girl burned at the stake by the English in 1431 and made France's patron saint in 1920.

Scores of stories surround her origins, notably that she was the bastard daughter of Louis d'Orléans, Charles VI's brother, who lived at Château de Blois until his murder in 1407. The less glamorous, more accurate account pinpoints Domrémy, in north-eastern France (Domrémy-la-Pucelle today; *pucelle* means 'virgin'), as her place of birth in 1412. Her father was Jacques d'Arc, a pious God-fearing farmer who reared his children to clean, sew and tend livestock.

Divine revelations delivered by the Archangel Michael prompted Joan to flee the fold in 1428. Her mission was to raise the siege against the city of Orléans and see the dauphin, Charles, crowned king of France (Charles VII). In Vaucouleurs, 50km west of Nancy in Lorraine, the 16-year-old persuaded Robert de Baudricourt to arm her with a sword and two male escorts, with whom she rode to Chinon in February 1429. The fabled scene in which Joan plucks the dauphin out of his court at Château de Chinon has been immortalised on the silver screen countless times, most notably by Ingrid Bergman in 1948 (in Victor Fleming's *Joan of Arc*), and again in 1954 (in Rossellini's neorealist *Jeanne au bûcher*).

The consequent Poitiers Inquiry, which was conducted by clergy and university clerks in the Poitevin capital,

In 1429 a 17-year-old peasant girl known as Joan of Arc (Jeanne d'Arc) persuaded the French legitimist Charles VII that she had received a divine mission from God to expel the English from France and bring about Charles' coronation. Driven from Paris by the English in 1418, Charles VII had sought refuge at the royal Château de Chinon, in the Loire Valley, an exile that continued even after it was safe for French royalty to return to the capital. With Charles' support, Joan rallied the French troops and defeated the English near Orléans, after which Charles was crowned at Reims. He returned to Paris in 1437, but it was not until 1453 that the English were entirely driven from French territory (with the exception of Calais). With the end of the Hundred Years' War, the Loire Valley rapidly emerged as the centre of French court life, marking the most glorious chapter in its history.

The Renaissance

Having regained his crown, King Charles VII (ruled 1422–61) retired in an orgy of pleasure-seeking to his royal residence in Loches with his mistress, Agnès Sorel, whose breathtaking beauty and scandalous behaviour quickly became legendary. The return of peace, relative prosperity and assured royal authority in the aftermath of the Hundred Years' War was reflected in the decline of the medieval fortified fortresses and emergence of the less militaristic edifices that sprang up at this time. Medieval floor plans were scrapped in favour of more Italianate ideas that were slowly penetrating France. The king was wholly supported by the French nobility and bourgeoisie, all of

Joan of Arc (Jeanne d'Arc)

strived to establish if Joan of Arc was a fraud or a gift, as she claimed, from the king of Heaven to the king of France. At the same time, her virginity was certified. Following the six-week interrogation, Joan was sent by the dauphin to Tours, where she was equipped with companions, a horse, a sword (found in a church in the Vallée de la Vienne) and her own standard featuring God sitting in judgement on a cloud. The armour that was made for her disappeared following her capture in 1430 (to the delight of unscrupulous antique dealers who sporadically claim to have discovered the what-would-be-priceless suit). In Blois, the divine warrior collected her army, which was drummed up by the dauphin.

In April 1429 Joan started her attack on Orléans, which had been besieged by the English since October 1428. She entered the city on 29 April via Porte de Bourgogne (at the eastern end of today's rue de Bourgogne), rallying the city's inhabitants and gaining their support (she stayed at Jacques Boucher's house on place du Général de Gaulle). On 5, 6 and 7 May respectively, the French gained control of the Bastille St-Loup (in the suburb of St-Loup, on the right bank of the River Loire), Bastille des Augustins and the legendary Fort des Tourelles (at the southern end of Pont George V on quai Fort des Tourelles), a fort guarding the only access to the city from the left bank. This last shattering defeat prompted the English to lay down the siege on 8 May and was a decisive turning point in the Hundred Years' War.

From Orléans, Joan went on to defeat the English at Jargeau (12 June), Beaugency (16 June) and Patay (18 June). During this time, Charles stayed at chateaux in Loches and Sully-sur-Loire and prayed to St Benedict in the Abbaye de St-Benoît, in St-Benoît-sur-Loire. Despite Charles' coronation in July 1429, battles between the English and French carried on until 1453, by which time the young woman responsible for turning the war round had long been dead.

Joan was captured by the Burgundians, sold to the English, convicted of witchcraft and heresy by a tribunal of French ecclesiastics in Rouen in 1431, and burned at the stake.

In 1456 a trail of rehabilitation found the five-month trial of Joan of Arc to be fraudulent and calumnious, and overturned its verdict. The Church beatified her in 1909 and canonised her in 1920.

⚜ ⚜

whom had chateaux built to demonstrate their royal or seigniorial powers.

A treasure trove of sacred art works dates from this early Renaissance period, thanks to René d'Anjou (1409–80), a Provençal count who was a close companion of Charles VII and nicknamed Bon Roi René (Good King René). The first printing opened in the Loire Valley in Angers in 1477.

Under Louis XI (ruled 1461–83), work started on Château de Langeais, the last fortified chateau to be built in the valley intended to cut off the most likely invasion route from Bretagne (Brittany). In 1491 the chateau was the setting for the marriage of Charles VIII (ruled 1483–98) and Anne de Bretagne, which marked the unification of independent Brittany with France. Anne's heraldic symbol (a crowned 'A') came to be sculpted on many a chateau facade after her subsequent marriage to Louis XII (ruled 1498–1515).

The culture of the Italian Renaissance (French for 'rebirth') arrived in France during the reign of François I (1515–47), in part through a series of indecisive French military operations in Italy. For the first time, the French aristocracy was exposed to Renaissance ideas of scientific and geographic scholarship and discovery, and the value of secular over religious life. Under the patronage of François I, Leonardo da Vinci made Amboise his home in 1516 and worked there until his death (see the boxed text 'Fabulous Flying Machines' in the Touraine chapter). Evidence of a purely Renaissance architectural influence manifests itself in numerous chateaux in the region. Notable examples are in Azay-le-Rideau, Chenonceaux, Chaumont and Chambord,

Vallée des Rois (Valley of Kings): A Who's Who

Dates in brackets indicate reign

Charles VI (1380–1422)
Charles inherited the throne at the height of the Hundred Years' War, with the consequences that his reign turned into a farce and the king lost his mind. Under the Treaty of Troyes, his wife, **Isabeau de Bavière**, married their daughter to Henry V, king of England – their child was declared heir to the French throne.

Charles VII (1422–61)
Son of Charles VI and Isabeau, he was France's legitimate heir, who secured the throne in 1429 with the help of 17-year-old Joan of Arc. He held court at Chinon with his queen **Marie d'Anjou** and his scandalously sexy mistress, Agnès Sorel. Sorel was the first officially recognised royal mistress.

Louis XI (1461–83)
Son of Charles VII and Marie d'Anjou, he turned his childhood home at Loches into a prison and held court at Amboise. Authoritarian throughout his reign, he had two queens, **Marguerite d'Écosse** from 1436 and **Charlotte de Savoie**, whom he wed in 1457.

Charles VIII (1483–98)
Son of Louis XI and Charlotte, he was raised at Amboise. He wed the 15-year-old **Anne de Bretagne** in Langeais when he was 21. Both broke off relationships to wed: Anne was married by proxy to Maximilien de Habsburg, archduke of Austria, and Charles was engaged to Maximilien's four-year-old daughter. Charles and Anne's marriage contract decreed that, should something ghastly happen to the king, Anne would marry his heir. The unfortunate bride did so seven years later, when Charles died after hitting his head.

Louis XII (1498–1515)
Son of Charles d'Orléans and great grandson of Charles V, he persuaded the pope to annul his marriage to Jeanne de Valois so he could marry widowed **Anne de Bretagne**. The pair settled at Blois, where Anne commanded a highly revered court. Her guards consisted of 100 Bretons. Following Anne's death in 1514, Louis XII wed **Marie d'Angleterre**. He died a year later.

François I (1515–47)
Louis XII left no direct heir, so François, his second cousin, inherited the throne. He grew up at Amboise, where he studied Latin, poetry and chivalric romances. He realised his architectural

the latter having been built as a hunting lodge for François I. In Blois, François had a new wing designed for his queen, Claude de France. Its revolutionary spiral staircase became a potent symbol of all that the Renaissance embodied: harmony, beauty and balance.

This new architecture was meant to reflect the splendour of the monarchy, which was fast moving towards absolutism. But all this grandeur and show of strength by the Catholic monarchy was not enough to stem the tide of Protestantism.

In 1525 François I was captured during an Italian campaign at Pavia (his wife, Claude, had died the previous year) and he was married off by his captors to Eleonore d'Autriche.

The Reformation
By the 1530s the position of the Reformation sweeping Europe had been strength-

Vallée des Rois (Valley of Kings): A Who's Who

aspirations through a rash of Renaissance chateaux, extending Blois for his wife, **Claude de France**, after whom the *reine claude* plum (greengage) was named. He was widowed in 1524, taken captive at Pavia in 1525, and married to **Eleonore d'Autriche** in 1530.

Henri II (1547–59)

Son of François I and Claude, he sired 10 children with his queen, **Catherine de Médicis**, three of whom were raised at Blois and later became king. Diane de Poitiers was Henri II's best-known royal mistress – he gave her Chenonceau and Chaumont. Upon the king's death, Poitiers was obliged to cede Chenonceau to Catherine de Médicis, who outlived Henri II by 30 years.

François II (1559–60)

Eldest son of Henri II and Catherine de Médicis, he scarcely had a reign. He married **Mary Stuart (Queen of Scots)** in 1558, inherited the throne in 1559 and died – aged 17 – in Orléans in 1560.

Charles IX (1560–74)

Charles was 10 years old when François II died, so Catherine de Médicis took charge until her boy-king son reached teenage-hood. Charles IX's reign was dominated by the Wars of Religion and the St Bartholomew's Day massacres. The French court shifted from chateau to chateau at this time, but Chenonceau hosted many gatherings. Charles IX married **Elisabeth d'Autriche** at the age of 15.

Henri III (1574–89)

Third son of Henri II and Catherine de Médicis, and husband of **Louise de Lorraine**, he fled to Blois when the civil war between the Huguenots, Catholic League and Catholic monarchy threatened his overthrow. The king's assassination of the duke of Guise at Blois in 1588 led to his own assassination a year later. He left no direct heir, so the throne passed to his cousin.

Henri IV (1589–1610)

Henri de Navarre was the first king in the Protestant Bourbon dynasty. In 1600 he divorced his queen, **Marguerite de Valois**, sister of François I, in favour of **Marie de Médicis**. Henri IV had a dozen or so mistresses, including Gabrielle d'Estrées, who mothered three of his children and died pregnant with a fourth.

Louis XIII (1610–43)

Son of Henri IV and Marie de Médicis, and husband of **Anne d'Autriche**, he occasionally visited Amboise or Chambord to hunt. His reign marked the final collapse of the Loire as the *Vallée des Rois*.

ened in France by the ideas of John Calvin (1509–64), a Frenchman who studied at the university of Orléans from 1528 to 1533. Henri II (ruled 1547–59) tried to clamp down on the Protestantism that was rapidly making inroads in his kingdom, but to no avail. In 1560 Catholics captured hundreds of French Protestants and drowned them in the River Loire. The Edict of January (1562) afforded Protestants certain rights, but was met by ferocious opposition from ultra-Catholic nobles, whose fidelity to their religion was mixed with a desire to strengthen their power base in the provinces.

The Wars of Religion (1562–98) involved three groups: the Huguenots (French Protestants who received help from the English); the Catholic League, led by the House of Guise; and the Catholic monarchy. The fighting severely weakened the position of the French king, Charles IX (ruled 1560–74), and brought the French

State close to disintegration. Throughout the wars, Orléans served as a major Huguenot stronghold, with Protestants plundering the cathedral in 1568 and dynamiting it. In 1572, following the so-called St Bartholomew's Day massacres (23–24 August) in Paris which saw some 3000 Huguenots slaughtered while celebrating the wedding of the Protestant Henri of Navarre (the future Henri IV) to Marguerite de Valois, Catholic terrorists moved on to Angers, Saumur and other cities on the River Loire to kill hundreds more Huguenots.

On 24 May 1588, the so-called Day of the Barricades, the Catholic League rose up against Henri III (ruled 1574–89) and forced him to flee the royal court at the Louvre. The king ran to Blois, where he got revenge by ordering the assassination of the ultra-powerful duke of Guise – leader of the Catholic League – in Château de Blois on 23 December 1588. On the king's orders, Guise's brother, the cardinal of Lorraine, was arrested the same day and brought to Blois, where he was imprisoned and eventually executed. Both bodies were burned, after which Henri III sought refuge from angry Catholic nobles in Tours. Eight months later the Catholics won sweet revenge when a monk assassinated the king in Tours.

Henri III died without a direct heir and was succeeded by his cousin, the Protestant Henri IV (1553–1610), the first king of France in the Bourbon dynasty. In 1598 Henri IV decreed the Edict of Nantes, which guaranteed the Huguenots freedom of conscience and many civil and political rights, though the Edict was not universally accepted. However, the Edict opened the doors for the creation of a prestigious Protestant academy in the riverside town of Saumur. Founded by the theologian Philippe Duplessis-Mornay – slammed as the 'Huguenot Pope' by opposition Catholics in town – the academy established Saumur as a leading academic centre. This lasted until 1685, when Louis XIV, a Catholic, revoked the Edict of Nantes. He considered the Protestant community a threat to the unity of the State (and thus his power).

The accession of the Bourbon dynasty to the throne marked the end of the Loire region's privileged position as home of the royal court. By the start of the 17th century, the French monarchy had lost all interest in the grandiose pleasure palaces and royal dwellings built by its ancestors on the banks of the River Loire. Louis XIII (who succeeded Henri IV in 1610) occasionally visited Amboise or Chambord to hunt, but for no other reason. Several chateaux were sold or given away, while others were simply abandoned and left to rot.

Le Fleuve Royal

Trade boomed on the *fleuve royal* (royal river) from the 15th century, prompting the merchants' guild to start controlling it. The River Loire's banks were laid with *hausserées* (a type of path) to ease the towing of barges, and a channel was marked with buoys to prevent vessels grounding on one of the many sand banks. By the 16th century, merchants from 22 towns on the River Loire attended the guild's general meeting, held every three years in Orléans. A major gripe was the river tolls, dating from feudal times and collected at 120 toll stations by the mid-1500s.

Increased commerce prompted massive canalisation in the 17th century. In 1605 work started on the Briare canal, which would link the Rivers Loire and Seine and – upon completion in 1642 – meant that sugar, textiles and other trading goods could be transported easily between Orléans and Paris. Between 1676 and 1678 the Orléans canal was dug from Lorris to Montargis, ensuring that Paris had regular supplies of wood from the Forêt d'Orléans. The Loing canal was built between 1719 and 1724.

Cities such as Orléans, Tours and Nantes threw their energies into reaping the profits of the extended navigable waterway system. Wines that turned sour during river transportation prompted Orléans to open its first vinegar factory. Distilleries soon followed and on the eve of the French Revolution Orléans boasted 200 factories fed by 30-odd distilleries. Nantes' slave trade, meanwhile, fuelled the manufacture of various goods in the region. These were transported downstream to Nantes, then shipped to West Africa to be bartered for slaves. Between 1678 and 1780 there were calico (printed cotton) factories in Nantes, Angers, Tours and Orléans. Stockings, slippers and gloves (woven from wool imported from Spain) were produced in Orléans for export to Canada, while the city's oriental hosiery factory churned out Turkish caps to trade with the West Indies for unrefined sugar, tobacco, coffee and carpets. Throughout the 18th century, two-thirds of the West Indian sugar which sailed into Nantes was transported along the River Loire to Orléans to be refined. All along the river, factories making sweets, chocolates and preserves sprang up to take advantage of the ready availability of the sweet commodity.

The French Revolution & the Vendée War

Nowhere was the revolutionary cry for the scrapping of the monarchy more fiercely opposed than in the Loire Valley, traditionally a royalist and Catholic stronghold. Nevertheless, the mark left by the French Revolution (1789) on the region was indelible. Although few chateaux were actually destroyed during the Revolution, most were seized, plundered and damaged. The heraldic symbols sculpted on facades and above fireplaces were the first to be slashed by the revolutionary knife. The vaulted cellars of Château du Montreuil-Bellay and Abbaye de Fontevraud were turned into prisons. In Saumur, the royal cavalry school established by Louis XV in 1763 was closed, as were all national studs. Fearing for their lives, some 75% of the populations of Angers and Saumur sought refuge in troglodyte caves inside the tufa cliffs on the southern bank of the River Loire.

During the Reign of Terror (September 1793 to July 1794), use of the guillotine was deemed too slow by the Nantes representative of the Committee of Public Safety. Instead, suspected counter-revolutionaries were stripped, tied together in pairs and loaded onto barges that were then sunk in the middle of the River Loire. Religious freedoms were revoked, churches desecrated and closed and cathedrals turned into Temples of Reason. Notable examples include Orléans' Collégiale St-Pierre-le-Puellier and Église St-Aignan (which became a Temple of Gratitude and Victory); the Basilique St-Benoît, in St-Benoît-sur-Loire; and the Abbaye St-Julien and Basilique St-Martin, in Tours.

The Revolution was most fiercely opposed in the impoverished barren marshland of rural Vendée, where the public execution of Louis XVI in 1793 sparked off the Guerre de Vendée (Vendée War; 1793–6), a bitter civil war fought south of the River Loire between Catholic pro-Royalists, led by the peasant leader Charette (1763–96), and Protestant Republicans. Three years of brutal fighting and thousands of deaths culminated in March 1796 with the capture of Charette by Republican troops and his public execution three days later on place Viarme, in Nantes.

The Aftermath The Revolution's immediate aftermath inflicted the greatest damage on the Loire's treasure trove of royal chateaux. While a handful had scarcely been touched, thanks to either a foreign proprietor (such as at Château de Serrant) or a sympathetic owner well regarded by the local peasantry (Château de Chenonceau), the majority of chateaux stood empty and abandoned. Blois, which Louis XVI had ordered to be demolished in 1788, was turned into army barracks, while Château de Chambord served as a warehouse and, after that, as a prison until 1802, when the 440-room edifice was handed over to Maréchal Augereau to headquarter his 15th Légion d'Honneur in. In Orléans, Tours, Angers and Nantes, abandoned *hôtels particuliers* (private mansions) became salt cellars, horse stables and the like. Other edifices – such as the chateau built for Cardinal Richelieu, in Richelieu, and the Carthusian Chartreuse du Liget monastery, in the Forêt de Loches – were sold as building material and demolished stone by stone.

The Restoration saw Louis XVIII (1814–24) and Charles X (1824–30) hark back to the formalities of former regimes. In 1841 Louis-Philippe (1830–48) set up the

National Commission for Historical Monuments, aimed at restoring crumbling Loire chateaux such as Blois and Chambord.

19th- & 20th-Century Industrialisation

Trade on the River Loire witnessed a short revival with the arrival of the first steam boat, which puffed its way upstream from Nantes to Paimbœuf on 6 June 1822, and to Orléans the following year. In 1834 the *Vulcan* – capable of navigating shallow waters – set sail, but was replaced in 1837 by the *Emerald* after its high-pressure boiler exploded in Tours, killing six people. By 1840 steam boats made a return Nantes–Angers trip in a day, sailing at an average speed of 16/18km per hour down-/upstream and with 250 passengers on board.

The advent of the railway in the mid-1850s led to a dramatic drop in passenger activity on the River Loire. This, coupled with the abolition of slavery in 1848 – scrapped by the Revolution but reinstated by Napoleon in 1802 – prompted a similar drop in trade in sugar and textiles along the river. The estuary, meanwhile, had become practically impossible to navigate for the large ships that sailed from Nantes to the Atlantic and beyond. A new outer harbour was therefore built at the mouth of the Loire estuary, in St-Nazaire. In 1840 a transatlantic postal service was set up and by the 1860s transatlantic liners were making regular crossings between St-Nazaire, the West Indies, Mexico and Cayenne. On the coast, the *belle époque* (literally 'beautiful age') ushered in La Baule in 1879, one of the Atlantic Ocean's most glamorous coastal resorts.

By the start of the 20th century, the St-Nazaire shipyards employed around 5000 workers, who built France's most luxurious ocean liners. Among the most famed was *Le Normandie*, which took two years to build and immediately won prizes for the fastest Atlantic crossing (averaging 30 knots), only to be gutted by fire on arrival in New York in 1942.

Le Normandie was in fact one of the few pleasure palaces to be produced at the shipyards during the years immediately preceding WWII. These years were marked by the emergence of the trade union movement, mass unemployment and a series of strikes which saw some 10,000 shipyard workers march through the streets of St-Nazaire demanding bigger pay packets.

WWII

As French resistance to the German invasion collapsed in mid-June 1940, the French government briefly relocated to Tours, before moving on to Vichy. The Germans divided France into a zone under direct German occupation (in the north and along the western coast) and a puppet state based in the spa town of Vichy which was led by the ageing WWI hero of the Battle of Verdun, Maréchal Henri Philippe Pétain. From 1940 to 1942, the demarcation line between the two zones ran along the River Cher, with Château de Chenonceau – which straddles the Cher – being directly split between German-occupied and Vichy-ruled France. After the war, Pétain (1856–1951) was tried for treason and imprisoned for life in the citadel on Île d'Yeu.

The shipyards of St-Nazaire were a prime target for German forces, who marched into the port town on 21 June 1940 and turned the harbour into a fortified base for a German U-boat fleet. An Allied attack on St-Nazaire in February 1942 destroyed over 60% of the town. It was finally liberated in May 1945, almost a year after the Allied D-day landings. Orléans and Tours were also heavily bombed during WWII, though most smaller towns and villages in the region survived unscathed. Indeed, it was at Château de Cheverny that the *Mona Lisa* was hidden for the duration of WWII.

Modernity

Rapid industrialisation marked the 1960s: three nuclear power plants – the ugly face of modernity – were built, peering across the banks of the River Loire at Chinon-Avoine, St-Laurent des Eaux and Belleville-sur-Loire. The hydroelectric station at Dampierre-en-Burly followed in the 1980s. The four combined generate around 15% of France's energy today. The 1960s likewise witnessed the expansion of the petrochemical zone at Donges, built after WWII to adjoin the industrial port of St-Nazaire, overlooking the Loire estuary. By 1968 the shipyards here were constructing vessels of 500,000 tonnes.

In 1972 the French government created the new administrative *régions* (regions) of Pays de la Loire, Centre and Poitou-Charentes, intended to roughly adhere to historical divisions but – controversially – throwing the traditionally Poitevin département of Vendée into the Pays de la Loire région. Worse still, Nantes – the historical capital of Brittany – was crowned 'capital' of Pays de la Loire, despite its staunchly Breton soul. When neighbouring Brittany introduced bilingual – Breton–French – town-name signs in 1985, many villages around Nantes followed suit.

In the 1990s the TGV (*train à grande vitesse*) Atlantique train linked Tours and Poitiers with Paris by high-speed train track. The fabulous and daring geometric glass designs of innovative French architect Denis Laming erupted at Futuroscope, the world's only communication theme park, while 'cosmetic valley' (see Economy later in this chapter) transformed Orléanais into a metropolis on the move.

Chateau renovation and restoration remains a preoccupation for the region's numerous private proprietors, as well as the Caisse Nationale des Monuments Historiques, the body responsible for overseeing state-owned chateaux such as Angers and Chambord. The first *son et lumière* (literally 'sound and light') show lit up Château de Chambord in 1952.

Following the birth of the euro on 1 January 1999, the unknown village of Blancafort, 20km south-west of Briare, in Orléanais, promptly declared itself the geographical centre of Euroland (see the boxed text 'Euroland's Centre' in the Orléanais & Blésois chapter).

GEOGRAPHY

The Loire is the longest river in France. Its source is in Mont Gerbier de Jonc (1400m) in the southern Massif Central. From here it follows a 1020km-long course through Auvergne (central France), Bourgogne (Burgundy), Orléanais (south of the Paris basin), Blésois, Touraine and Anjou before spilling into the Atlantic. The river drains a total area of 115,120 sq km – equal to one-fifth of the size of France. Its flow is eight times greater in December and January than at the end of summer.

The Loire Valley is generally understood to refer to the western stretch of river between Orléans (south-west of Paris) and Nantes (56km east of the Loire estuary and the Atlantic). Several significant tributary valleys fall within the environs of this approximately 300km stretch. The Rivers Cher, Indre and Vienne join the River Loire from the south; the Sarthe, Mayenne and masculine Loir (not to be confused with feminine Loire) meet it from the north. The banks of these less-fabled rivers host as many chateaux as Mother Loire herself.

The tidal mouth of the Loire is 60km long, 3km wide and dominated by an oil refinery at Donges and the industrial port town of St-Nazaire. On the right (northern) bank of the estuary sits the Presqu'île du Guérande, at the centre of which lies the Marais Brière. This 40,000-hectare wetland of salt pans and marshes was formed after the sea flooded it in 7500 BC, following which sand deposited by the River Loire formed a protective dike, thus cutting the wetland off from the ocean. Sandy (and briefly oily after the tanker spill of late 1999) beaches at Le Croisic and La Baule hug the western and southern coastline respectively of the Presqu'île du Guérande.

Further fine sand beaches line the Atlantic coast immediately south of the Loire estuary. Two islands, Île de Noirmoutier and Île d'Yeu, form the region's westernmost point. The Marais Poitevin, which delineates the southernmost boundary of the area covered in this book, is another marshland, covering an area of 80,000 hectares. It was formed by alluvial deposits washed in by the Atlantic (to the west), the Rivers Lay, Vendée and Autise (to the north) and the River Sèvre Niortaise (to the east) to transform a gulf into a swamp, subsequently canalised by monks in the 11th century.

CLIMATE

The Loire Valley enjoys a temperate climate, hence its extraordinary bounty of fruit and vegetables. The Atlantic Ocean has a profound impact on the western part of the region, particularly around Nantes and St-Nazaire, whose weather is characterised by high humidity, although rainfall remains lower than the national average (134 days per year compared to the national average of 164). The area can be subject to persistent, and sometimes violent, westerly winds. The coast enjoys an annual average temperature of 13°C, dropping to around 12°C in the valley core around Angers, though the temperature has been known to soar as high as 33°C and drop as low as -11°C. The seawater temperature remains at a constant 13°C year round.

Spring and late summer are ideal months to visit the Loire Valley proper, thanks to warm and sunny days. The region records an annual precipitation of 690mm on the coast and 648mm inland, but rainfall patterns are erratic, meaning travellers are just as likely to be caught in a heavy spring or autumn downpour as in a sudden summer cloudburst.

To check the weather forecast call: Deux-Sèvres (☎ 02 36 68 02 79), Indre-et-Loire (☎ 02 36 68 02 37), Loire-Atlantique (☎ 02 36 68 02 44), Loiret (☎ 02 36 68 02 45), Loir-et-Cher (☎ 02 36 68 02 41), Maine-et-Loire (☎ 02 36 68 02 49), Sarthe (☎ 02 36 68 02 72), Vendée (☎ 02 36 68 02 85), Vienne (☎ 02 36 68 02 86).

For a marine forecast call ☎ 08 36 68 08 08 (national) or, for a more detailed departmental report, ☎ 08 36 68 08 plus the two-digit departmental number (for example ☎ 08 36 68 08 44 for Loire-Atlantique or ☎ 08 36 68 08 85 for Vendée). All reports are in French.

ECOLOGY & ENVIRONMENT
Energy

Since the late 1980s, the state-owned electricity company, Electricité de France (EDF), has produced about three-quarters of France's electricity using nuclear power produced in nuclear plants such as those at Chinon-Avoine (1963), St-Laurent des Eaux (1969), Dampierre-en-Burly (1980) and Belleville-sur-Loire (1960s), which sit on the banks of the River Loire. Since the 1980s, the Centre région has generated 15.3% of the country's energy (17.8% of its nuclear energy), making it the second-highest nuclear-energy-producing région in France (after Rhône-Alpes).

The environmental cost of the River Loire's four nuclear power stations is dear. Radioactive emissions spewed out by the plants represent more than 25% of rare gas emissions in France and double the atmospheric pollutants produced by the more nuclear-dependent Rhône-Alpes région.

EDF also controls France's hydroelectric programme. By damming rivers to produce electricity, it has created huge recreational lakes – limited in the Loire region to the Barrage d'Eguzon in the Indre département. The River Loire has never been dammed, thanks in the main to its shallowness and the irregularity of its water levels, which make any significant industrial development or navigation impossible (at times of low water, EDF is forced to pump water into the river to ensure there is sufficient water to maintain the cooling systems at its nuclear plants).

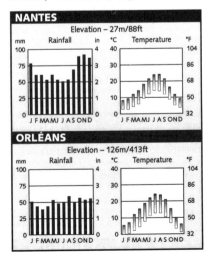

A high-voltage electricity line (225,000 volts) threatens to blight the rural landscape in the protected Parc Naturel Régional de Brière. Despite fierce opposition both locally and by environment minister Dominique Voynet, the EDF say that the 63,000-volt line currently linking St-Nazaire and the Presqu'île du Guérande with the Loire Valley power plants is insufficient to meet growing energy needs. It would cost five to eight times more to run the new 13km-long line underground from St-Malo de Guersac and Pontchâteau instead of atop eyesore pylons, 22 to 40m high.

The sinking of the *Erika* oil tanker off the Atlantic coast in December 1999 and the consequent oil slick that sludged its way across the region's coastal quarters was the nastiest environmental blow to strike the region in decades. See the boxed text 'Oil Spill' for details.

Tourism

The six million or so tourists that descend on the region are an annual environmental hazard.

The impact of this human locust storm is keenly felt by the region's centuries-old chateaux, many of which remain under constant renovation as part of an eternal battle against erosion. A 122 million FF project will see Château des Ducs de Bretagne in Nantes under renovation until 2008. Scaffolding, meanwhile, will ensnare part of the fragile tufa-stone facade of Château de Chambord until late 2000 as part of an ongoing restoration project that has seen 30 million FF ploughed into the 440-room chateau since 1996.

Particularly troublesome among Château de Chambord's 800,000 annual visitors are graffiti artists who carve their names in stone on the walls, scarring the historical monument and further exacerbating the soft stone's inevitable disintegration.

Industrial Development

The most notorious pocket of industrial development to menace the region devours the northern bank of the Loire estuary, around the industrial port town of St-Nazaire and the Elf oil refinery at Donges, 10km to the east. Petroleum products account for 53% of the 30 million tonnes of freight that pass through St-Nazaire port. Eleven million tonnes of petrol were refined at the refinery in 1998, totalling more than half of Elf's total production in France. Propylene,

Oil Spill

The *Erika* disaster in December 1999 was the worst oil spill to hit European waters since the Amoco Cadiz disaster in 1978. The Maltese-registered tanker, which was on its way from Dunkirk to Livorno, in northern Italy, snapped in two and sank 80km west of the French Atlantic coast. An estimated 8000 of the 25,000 tonnes of crude oil it was carrying for French oil giant TotalFina spewed into the sea. Ten days later, high winds washed the oil ashore, slicking 400km of French coastline – including Le Croisic and La Baule on the Presqu'île du Guérande, Île d'Yeu and Île de Noirmoutier – in the sticky black slime. Six thousand sea birds died and at least 6000 more had to be air-lifted to bird protection centres in France, Belgium and the Netherlands to be cleaned. In the Baie de Bourgneuf, the oil slick washed across oyster beds, destroying two years' oyster production. By February 2000, several rockier beaches, including Le Croisic, were still black.

Pumping the remaining oil from the wreck will cost an estimated US$150 million and take several years to complete, according to environment minister Dominique Voynet. Under the 1992 International Oil Pollution Compensation Fund Convention, France is eligible for a maximum of US$185 million in compensation, of which the Italian owners of the 25-year-old oil tanker are liable for US$11.8 million. The *conseil régional* (regional council) of the Pays de la Loire région, and the Loire-Atlantique département, pledged an immediate 5 million and 1 million FF respectively towards the clean-up operation.

butane, naphtha, petrol and aviation fuel are among the numerous products refined by Elf in Donges.

The creation of Futuroscope, a state-of-the-art technology theme park 10km north of Poitiers in Jaunay-Clan, has led to massive development in the immediate area. The future will also see a rash of new *autoroutes* (motorways) and *routes nationaux* (national roads) carved across the region, including the Angers–Cholet A87, which is scheduled to open in 2002 and is intended to assist the five million tourists who plough their way annually to Vendée. Plans are likewise afoot to extend the Paris–Nantes section of the A11 to four lanes by 2001 to alleviate traffic congestion, and to build a new autoroute (A82) between Nantes and Brest in Brittany.

Forest & Hedgerow

The region is among the most heavily forested in France. The Centre région alone – one-fifth of which comprises forest (809,350 hectares) – is home to the country's largest forest (the 38,234-hectare Forêt d'Orléans) and the largest forested park (the 5440-hectare Forêt de Chambord). Both forests are managed by the Office National des Forêts (ONF; Web site www.onf.fr) and are state owned; a staggering 86% of forest in Centre still remains in private hands.

Irresponsible walkers and cyclists, forest fires and hunters pose the greatest threats to the region's fauna-rich forests. Consequently, just 22% of the forest surrounding Château de Chambord is open to the public. Despite large-scale reforestation since the 1960s, in some areas, such as Poitou-Charentes, forest has decreased by 5.8% since 1991.

The freak storms that swept across Europe in December 1999 destroyed an estimated 270 million trees in France, including at least one million in Poitou-Charentes, 240,000 in Centre and 110,000 in Pays de la Loire. In Pays de la Loire, 16.1 million FF was ploughed into the region's forests in 1997 – a sum that was anticipated to triple or quadruple in 2000 to compensate for the storm damage. Protecting and replanting

forests that stabilise shifting sand dunes is a particularly strong concern in this coastal area. Inland, efforts have already been made to restore the *bocage* (a grid of hedgerows to facilitate water drainage) on the flood-susceptible plains in Vendée. In the last four decades, farmers – keen to make use of more sophisticated, larger farm machinery – have ripped up 8000km of hedgerows, comprising some eight million trees.

FLORA & FAUNA

Nuclear power plants, oil refineries and age-old dikes aside, the River Loire and its valley continue – against all odds – to shelter and protect an exceptional ecosystem of natural habitats.

Flora

Forest – predominantly oak, beech and pine – covers 20.4, 14 and 17% of the Centre, Pays de la Loire and Poitou-Charentes régions respectively. Ash, alder and willow trees are common in the marshy Marais Poitevin, whose waters are well oiled with a slick of duckweed.

Salicorne is an aquatic herb common on the Presqu'île du Guérande, on the Atlantic coast. It grows on the banks of the Presqu'île's salt pans, is renowned for its diuretic qualities and has become an ingredient much sought-after by the region's top chefs.

Vines were brought to the region by the Greeks around the 4th century BC. The Romans brought melons. Apples, cherries, quinces and pears have been cultivated around Orléans since the Middle Ages, as has the purple crocus, from which saffron is produced. By the 16th century, greengage (*reine claude*) trees had been firmly planted in most chateau gardens. Asparagus arrived in the region from north-western France in the 1870s.

Fauna

The River Loire is full of bream, small catfish, roach, pike and pike-perch. Closer to the coast, schools of eels slip through the water. Carp and perch are more commonplace in the Rivers Loir, Aubance and

Layon. All these river fish can be viewed at close quarters in the Aquarium de Touraine, near Amboise.

The Loire's riverbanks shelter an extraordinarily rich and diverse bird life, including 15 and 25% respectively of France's protected common tern and little tern populations, which nest on the sandy gravel banks of the River Loire and its tributaries. Île de Cuissy, near Gien (see the Orléanais & Blésois chapter), is home to one of the region's largest tern colonies. The northern bank of the River Loire near Orléans is the only place in France to shelter nesting osprey. South of the river, in La Sologne, whiskered and black terns build their nests afloat water lilies on the lakes. Birds such as grey herons, dabbling ducks, buzzards and cranes come to the wetland in the autumn. The largest colonies of grey heron hide in the marshes around the Loire estuary and in the muddy waters of the Marais Poitevin.

Deer and the nocturnal wild boar roam wild in the Forêt de Chambord, which has been protected as a national hunting reserve since 1947 (see Chambord in the Orléanais & Blésois chapter). The red deer is a flourishing species in France, though it is seldom seen outside forests. Some 30 wild sheep, natives of Corsica and Sardinia's rocky mountain scrub, were introduced to Chambord by the High Commission for Hunting in 1949 as part of a breeding programme. Other forest-loving mammals include the fox, badger, hare and rabbit, as well as several birds of prey (such as the great osprey, short-toed eagle and honey buzzard).

In all, France's 113 species of mammal (more than any other country in Europe), 30 kinds of amphibian, 36 varieties of reptile and 72 kinds of fish are well represented in the region.

Endangered Species

The stone curlew and lapwing are among a rash of nesting birds threatened with becoming an endangered species in the Loire Valley. However, the white spoonbill, which had almost disappeared in the 1980s, has started once more to feed on the banks of the Loire estuary.

At the end of the 19th century, the Atlantic salmon population in the River Loire numbered several tens of thousands. Today, fewer than 100 adults remain in the river as a result of the dams, which prevent the salmon from accessing their natural spawning grounds. Large-scale silting up of the Loire estuary coupled with the construction of nuclear power plants in the 1960s, which warm the river water, pose further threats to the Atlantic salmon.

Nature Parks

Three *parcs naturels régionaux* (regional nature parks) fall within the area of the Loire Valley and its surrounds. The largest is the Parc Naturel Régional Loire-Anjou-Touraine, formed in 1996 to protect 260,000 hectares in the western half of southern Touraine and the south-eastern section of Anjou. The chateaux of Azay-le-Rideau, Villandry, Ussé, Chinon, Montreuil-Bellay and Saumur are within the park, as are numerous Angevin and Tourangeau vineyards, and the stretch of the River Loire

JANE SMITH

Red deer stags can be seen rutting in the Domaine National de Chambord.

between Tours and Gennes. Approximately 40% of the park comprises riverbed.

The Parc Naturel Régional de Brière is among the oldest and smallest of France's parcs naturels régionaux. Since 1970 it has covered 40,000 hectares of the Presqu'île du Guérande, a ball of land wedged between the Atlantic Ocean and the Loire estuary in the west of the region. Its swamps and reed-beds form part of a substantially larger wetland that stretches north to the Vilaine estuary (in neighbouring Brittany) and west to Pointe du Castelli.

In the south of the region is the Parc Naturel Interrégional du Marais Poitevin, Val de Sèvre and Vendée, created in 1979. The marshland of the Marais Poitevin covers 80,000 hectares of the 200,000-hectare park, which sprawls as far south as La Rochelle (on the Atlantic coast in Charente-Maritime). The park protects a fragile area of wet and drained marshes and the Anse de l'Aiguillon, a bay sheltering a rich and diverse bird population.

Unlike national parks, which receive state funding, parcs naturels régionaux are created and financed by local régions, départements and *communes* (the smallest unit of local administration).

GOVERNMENT & POLITICS

The area covered by this book is split between three of the 22 régions in France: Centre (east), Pays de la Loire (centre) and Poitou-Charentes (south-west).

Each région has an elected *conseil régional* (regional council) with limited powers, based in Orléans, Nantes and Poitiers respectively. The régions are split into several départements (departments), known by their two-digit code, which are included in postcodes and on car number plates registered there. France (including Corsica) has 96 départements in all, six of which fall within Centre, five within Pays de la Loire and four in Poitou-Charentes.

Those covered by this book are:

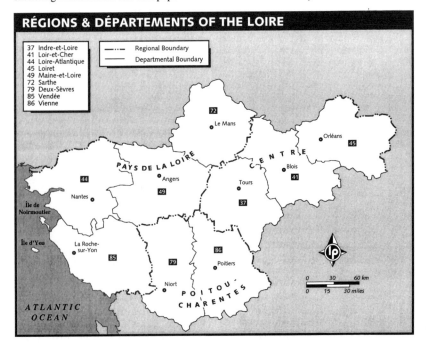

RÉGIONS & DÉPARTEMENTS OF THE LOIRE

37 Indre-et-Loire
41 Loir-et-Cher
44 Loire-Atlantique
45 Loiret
49 Maine-et-Loire
72 Sarthe
79 Deux-Sèvres
85 Vendée
86 Vienne

----- Regional Boundary
——— Departmental Boundary

72
Le Mans
Orléans 45

PAYS DE LA LOIRE
Angers
44
Nantes
49

CENTRE
Blois
Tours
41
37

Île de Noirmoutier

Île d'Yeu
La Roche-sur-Yon
85
79
86
Poitiers

Niort
POITOU-CHARENTES

ATLANTIC OCEAN

0   30   60 km
0   15   30 miles

Centre
  Indre-et-Loire (37), Loir-et-Cher (41), Loiret (45)
Pays de la Loire
  Loire-Atlantique (44), Maine-et-Loire (49), Sarthe (72), Vendée (85)
Poitou-Charentes
  Deux-Sèvres (79), Vienne (86)

Each département has a *préfet* (prefect) – based in a *préfecture* (prefecture) – who represents the national government, and an elected *conseil général* (general council). There is a préfecture in Tours (37), Blois (41), Nantes (44), Orléans (45), Angers (49), Le Mans (72), Niort (79), La Roche-sur-Yon (85) and Poitiers (86).

During the 1980s and 90s, a handful of noteworthy politicians emerged. One such was Socialist Jack Lang (1939–), culture minister under Mitterrand, who created the international Fête de la Musique (Music Festival) in 1983, since celebrated in 80 countries on 21 June. Lang has been mayor of Blois since 1989, but in early 2000 he announced his intention to stand as mayor of Paris in the 2001 municipal elections and will therefore have to stand down in Blois.

The other end of the political spectrum is dominated by Vendée-born Philippe de Villiers (1949–), whose traditionalist right-wing party, Rassemblement pour la France et l'Indépendance de l'Europe (Movement for France and Independence from Europe) – in alliance with former interior minister Charles Pasqua – landed 13.1% of the nationwide vote in the June 1999 European elections. Villiers, a staunch Catholic, has served as president of the conseil général of Vendée since 1988. In 1995 he unsuccessfully ran in presidential elections.

In recent years the pro-hunting lobby has made significant inroads in local politics (see Treatment of Animals under Society & Conduct later in this chapter).

ECONOMY

Tourism provides a steady source of income (an annual turnover of more than 20 million FF in Pays de la Loire, for example) for the Loire Valley – the eighth most popular spot in France after régions such as Île de France

and Provence-Côte d'Azur. Despite its abundance of chateaux, half of each franc spent in the area is spent on the coast. Almost 90% of the tourists visiting the region are domestic; foreign tourists account for 11% (one-third of whom are from the UK).

Nantes (Pays de la Loire) and Orléans (Centre) respectively sit at the helm of France's fourth and fifth largest industrial régions. The Pays de la Loire is one of Europe's largest manufacturers of shoes (with 40% of French shoe production) and children's clothing, and ranks top in France for shipbuilding. Agriculturally, it leads France's bovine-meat industry, while its fishing ports reaped a catch of 34,000 tonnes of fresh fish, worth 592 million FF, in 1997.

The perfume and cosmetics industry in 'cosmetic valley' (around Orléans) accounts for 23% of employment in the Loiret and is represented by such sweet-smelling giants as Christian Dior, Novartis, Séphora and Shiseido.

In Poitou-Charentes, Futuroscope ranks among Europe's leading centres in image-technology research and special media production. The Poitiers-based European image park employs 1300, supports 15,000 in the service industry and has an annual turnover of 670 million FF. Its adjoining Teleport houses some 80 research institutes and companies.

France's thriving aeronautical industry – ranked top in Europe and second in the world after the USA – also has a foot in the Loire Valley. At the Airbus factories in St-Nazaire (Aérospatiale) and Nantes, composite Airbus A340 parts are manufactured and sections of the fuselage assembled, both of which are flown to Airbus factories in Toulouse or Hamburg for final assembly. Not surprisingly, Aérospatiale is among the region's biggest employers, with a cast of 4000. Other large employers include Philips and Renault in Le Mans, Blois-based Lucas (car accessories), Matra Automobile (cars) in Romorantin-Lanthenay, Alcatel (telecommunications) near Orléans, SKF (ball-bearings) in St-Cyr-sur-Loire and Michelin (car tyres) in Cholet and Joué-lès-Tours.

Exports overall for the Pays de la Loire and Centre – the ninth and tenth régions in France for exports – valued 73.9 billion FF and 70.5 billion FF respectively in 1997, around 8% of total exports from France.

Despite the Loire Valley's abundance of fresh fruit and vegetables, only 2% or so of its workforce is employed in agriculture. This is in keeping with the national trend, which has seen 50% of French farms close in the last 25 years. Centre nevertheless ranks among Europe's leading cereal producers: almost half of its agricultural land supports cereal crops, totalling 14% of French production. It also cultivates 18% of France's oil-producing plants, such as sunflowers and rape. Its vineyards account for 3% (compared to 4.7% in Pays de la Loire) of the wine produced in France. Almost all (90%) of France's *mâche* (lamb's lettuce) is grown in Loire-Atlantique.

Meat production, a traditional industry in Pays de la Loire, remains fragile. Even prior to the outbreak of BSE ('mad cow disease') in 1996, which saw cattle breeding in the region drop by 3%, French beef sales fell by 14% between 1990 and 1997. Nevertheless, in 1997 Pays de Loire continued to produce 22.2% of France's poultry meat, 23.1% of its rabbit meat, 18.2% of the country's cattle meat (such as beef), 8.8% of its veal and 8% of its horse meat. Over 30% of French goats are bred in Poitou-Charentes.

France Champignon, in Saumur, is the world's leading producer of *champignons de Paris* (button mushrooms), which are cultivated in caves and yield an annual turnover of 1.7 billion FF.

Unemployment in the Poitou-Charentes, Pays de la Loire and Centre regions clocked in at 12.6%, 10.8% and 13.2% in 1997 (compared to a national average of 12.5%). In St-Nazaire alone, unemployment has steadily risen from 14.7% in 1995 to 17.2% in 1997.

POPULATION & PEOPLE

Pays de la Loire, Poitou-Charentes and Centre have a combined population of 7,208,809; the area covered by this guide is inhabited by 5,124,670 people. Just over 20% of the latter are packed into Loire-Atlantique, where Nantes is the largest centre (home to 16.2% of Loire-Atlantique's population).

Poitou-Charentes is the least populated area in the Loire Valley: the population density per square kilometre (sq km) is just 54 and 58 people respectively in Deux-Sèvres and Vienne, compared to 61 inhabitants per sq km in Centre and 98 in Pays de la Loire (107 per sq km in France and 117 in the European Union).

Approximately 5.5% of Centre's total population and 2% of the population of both Pays de la Loire and Poitou-Charentes are immigrants. Of this immigrant population in all three régions, approximately 60% are European and 25% are of North African origin (Moroccan, Algerian or Tunisian). Of the European population, some 35% in all three régions are Portuguese.

SCIENCE & PHILOSOPHY

The region has produced several scientists, including Antoine Becquerel (1788–1878), winner of the 1903 Nobel Prize for Physics, who discovered the radioactivity of uranium; and Louis Pasteur (1822–95), inventor of pasteurisation and the first rabies vaccine, who studied the fermentation of vinegar in Orléans.

The founder of modern philosophy and the greatest thinker since Aristotle, René Descartes (1596–1650), was born in La Haye (since renamed Descartes), in southern Touraine. The son of a middle-class family, he was small in stature and poor in health, but an intellectual giant who used a rigorous method of wholesale doubt and sought mathematical-like certainty in all things. Descartes' famous phrase '*Cogito, ergo sum*' (I think, therefore I am) is the basis of modern philosophical thought. His method came to be known as Cartesianism. Having completed his studies at a Jesuit college in La Flèche, Descartes fought as a soldier, then lived in Holland (1629–49) until being beckoned to Stockholm by Queen Christine of Sweden. He died 12 months later of pneumonia.

ARTS
Literature
Middle Ages As a region famed for the purity of its spoken 'king's' French, it is not surprising that the Loire should have nurtured the earliest written French literature. The 10-volume *Historia Francorum* (*History of the Franks*) by Gregory of Tours (538–94) was one of the first historical documents to emerge, contributing to Tours' standing as a leading centre of learning. Other bishops, such as Baudri of Bourgueil (1046–1130), also put pen to paper. The latter is best known for the homosexual overtones in the poems he wrote. The 11th-century epic poem *Chanson de Roland* (*Song of Roland*) is the earliest secular work in French literature; it recounts in verse the heroic death of Roland, the nephew of Charlemagne (747–814), who was ambushed on the way back from a campaign against the Muslims in Spain in 778.

Lyric poems of courtly love composed by troubadours dominated medieval literature. The new genre of the *roman* (literally 'the romance') often drew on Celtic stories such as those of King Arthur and his court, the search for the Holy Grail and Tristan and Iseult. The *Roman de la rose* (*Romance of the Rose*), a 22,000-line didactic poem started by Guillaume de Lorris (1200–40) and finished by Jean de Meung (1240–1305), was a new departure. The 18,000 lines written by the Loire-born de Meung (born Jean Chopinel) manipulated allegorical figures such as Pleasure and Riches, Shame and Fear, and broke new ground with a satirical attack on the clergy, nobility and women.

Charles d'Orléans (1391–1465), nephew of Charles VI, found expression in poetry after being taken prisoner by the English during the Battle of Agincourt (1415). Following his release 25 years later, he returned to his family home, Château de Blois, where he headed a sparkling court famed for its literary soirees and poetic jousts.

Among the elite circle who frequented the Blésois court was François Villon (1431–63). In 1461 the poet was imprisoned in Château de Meung-sur-Loire, south of Orléans, where he wrote *Épistre à mes amis* (*Epistle to my Friends*). As well as a long police record, Villon left a body of poems charged with a highly personal lyricism, among them the *Ballade des femmes du temps jadis* (*Ballad of Ladies from Yonder*) and *Le testament* (*The Testament*), which refers to his imprisonment in 1461 by the Bishop of Orléans. He was condemned to death in 1462 for stabbing a lawyer. His sentence was subsequently commuted to banishment from Paris.

Renaissance The great landmarks of French Renaissance literature are the works of Rabelais and La Pléiade, two products of the Loire Valley. Seuilly-born François Rabelais (1494–1553), son of a Chinon lawyer, composed a farcical epic about the adventures of the giant Gargantua and his son Pantagruel. His highly exuberant narrative blends coarse humour with encyclopaedic erudition in a vast panorama that seems to include every kind of person, occupation and jargon to be found in mid-16th-century France. The first book in Rabelais' epic was published in 1532 under the pen name Alcofribas Nasier (an anagram of the author's true name) and was promptly censored by Sorbonne theologians. The second volume (1534) was likewise slammed for its outrageous satire and was also censored, as were the two volumes that followed. Several towns and landscapes in Touraine feature throughout the Rabelaisian epic, as do the River Loire and its traditional fishermen. It was Rabelais who coined the phrase '*le jardin de France*' (the garden of France) to describe Touraine.

La Pléiade was a group of highly influential poets active in the 1550s and 60s chiefly remembered for their lyric poems, which looked to Italian and classical literature for inspiration. Its leading light was Pierre de Ronsard (1524–85), born near Couture-sur-Loir. In 1545 Ronsard stayed at the 13th-century Château de Talcy, where he fell in love with and wed the 15-year-old daughter of a Florentine banker, to whom he dedicated his sonnets *Les amours de Cassandre* (*The Loves of Cassandra*; 1552).

Ronsard spent the last 20 years of his life at the 11th-century Prieuré de St-Cosme, where he succeeded his brother as prior. Despite wanting to be buried on Île Verte near the confluence of the Rivers Braye and Loir, Ronsard was laid to rest at the priory near Tours. Other poets of this era include the Maine-et-Loire-born Joachim du Bellay (1522–60) and Nicolas Rapin (1538–1608), a native of Fontenay-le-Comte in the Vendée.

At the royal court in Amboise, the reform-minded sister of François I – Marguerite d'Angoulême (1492–1549), known as Marguerite de Navarre after her marriage to Henri II, king of Navarre – wrote a collection of prose entitled *L'Heptaméron* (*The Heptameron*) and the poem collection *Les Marguerites de la Marguerite des princesses*.

The wife of Marguerite d'Angoulême's grandson Henri IV, Marguerite de Valois (1553–1615) was likewise a keen writer. Her memoirs revealed a stash of shockingly scandalous secrets about life at a 17th-century French court. She is best known as *la reine Margot* (Queen Margot), subsequently immortalised on the silver screen (see Films in the Facts for the Visitor chapter).

Classicism Molière (1622–73) was an actor who became the most popular comic playwright of his time. Plays such as *Tartuffe* are staples of the classical repertoire, and they are still performed in translation around the world. From 1668, Louis XIV hunted at Château de Chambord and called on Molière to entertain his court. In 1669 the controversial playwright stayed for a month at the chateau and premiered what would become one of his most famous plays, *Monsieur de Pourceaugnac*. Molière returned to Chambord the following year to stage *Le bourgeois gentilhomme*, during a state visit by the Turkish ambassador to France. Despite its satirical nature and staunch ridicule of the king's courtiers, the darkly comic play won instant approval from Louis XIV.

Château d'Ussé was supposedly a great source of inspiration for Parisian-born writer Charles Perrault (1628–1703), who wrote the much-loved fairy tale *La belle au bois dormant* (*Sleeping Beauty*) while staying at the turreted castle.

Romanticism The literature of the 18th century is dominated by philosophers, among them Voltaire and Jean-Jacques Rousseau, both of whom were frequent visitors to the Loire Valley. Voltaire (1696–1778) stayed at Château de Sully-sur-Loire in 1719 after being banished from Paris for his licentious prose. Remnants of the small theatre the philosopher created are still visible in the upper great hall.

In the 1750s and 60s Rousseau spent much time at Château de Chenonceau, where he served as secretary to Louise Dupin (1706–99), tutored her son and frequented her glittering literary salon. Rousseau's time at Chenonceau, where he worked on *Emile* (1762), features in his *Les confessions* (*Confessions*; 1764–70). Rousseau's insistence on his own singularity makes *Les confessions* the first modern autobiography.

The region's best-known Romantic poet, novelist and dramatist was Alfred de Vigny (1797–1863). Born in Loches, he spent most of his life in Charentes, which is famously depicted in his poem *La maison du berger* (*The Shepherd's House*). An idyllic Touraine is brought to life in his historical novel *Cinq mars* (*5 March*).

The Balzac Era Touraine's most outstanding literary hero is Honoré de Balzac (1799–1850). His vast series of novels, known under the general title of *La comédie humaine* (*The Human Comedy*), are almost a social history of France. His novel *Eugénie Grandet* (1833) is set in Saumur and brilliantly evokes small-town life through the tale of a miser and his beautiful daughter. Other novels set in his home region include *Le curé de Tours* (*The Priest of Tours*), published in 1832, and *Le lys dans le vallée* (*The Lily in the Valley*; 1835), which describes the countryside around Château de Saché. The latter was home to Jean de Margonne, the lover of Balzac's mother, who warmly welcomed the impoverished writer into his castle, encouraging Balzac to write part of his most famous novel, *Le père*

Goriot (*Old Goriot*; 1834), while staying there. All Balzac's novels are as tragic in parts as the Tours-born writer's own life, which ended five months after his marriage in Ukraine to a Polish countess, with whom he had had an affair for 18 years.

Parisian-born Aurore Dupain (1804–76), better known as George Sand, spent much of her controversial literary career at Château de Nohant on the fringe of the Loire region. She combined the themes of romantic love and social injustice in her work.

Born in Nantes, the prolific Jules Verne (1828–1905) wrote a staggering 63 novels, many of which have been translated into English and numerous other languages. The adventure novel *Le tour du monde en quatre-vingts jours* (*Around the World in Eighty Days*; 1873) sees the pedantic Phileas Fogg whizz round the world with his freshly hired, scatty French servant Passepartout. His best-known works include *De la terre à la lune* (*From the Earth to the Moon*; 1865) and *Vingt mille lieues sous les mers* (*Twenty Thousand Leagues under the Sea*; 1869).

20th Century Orléans-born Charles Péguy (1873–1914) immortalised Joan of Arc in his trilogy *Jeanne d'Arc* (1897) and subsequent religious poem *Le mystère de la charité de Jeanne d'Arc* (*The Mystery of the Charity of Joan of Arc*; 1909).

Le grand Meaulnes (1912) by Alain Fournier, born Henri Alban (1886–1914) in La Chapelle d'Anguillon, is a haunting and dreamy tale of an adolescent boy's passage to manhood and his eternal quest for the fabulous chateau (and a beautiful girl) he stumbled on by accident as a young boy. Fournier's potrayal of rural Sologne and adolescent woes was a smash hit on publication and remains an absolute classic. Fournier grew up in Épineuil-le-Fleuriel, upon which the fictitious village of Ste-Agathe is based. He died in action in WWI in September 1914.

Parisian-born novelist and story-teller Anatole France (1844–1924) spent the last 10 years of his life living in St-Cyr-sur-Loire with the former maid of a famous Paris salon hostess (with whom he had also had a romantic entanglement). While living

there, France was awarded the Nobel Prize for Literature (1921). His historical novel *Les Dieux ont soif* (*The Gods will have Blood*; 1912) evokes the French Revolution and is a classic in its field.

Former newspaper vendor Jean Rouaud (1952–) had his first novel, *Les champs d'honneur* (*Fields of Glory*), published in 1990; it immediately scooped the Prix Goncourt (the first novel ever to do so). The novel depicts life in Loire-Atlantique prior to, and during, WWI.

Architecture

Prehistoric The earliest monuments made by humans in France are stone megaliths erected during the Neolithic period, from about 4000 to 2500 BC. Although these prehistoric monuments are mainly found in Brittany, noteworthy examples of dolmens (prehistoric burial chambers) include the Dolmen de la Madeleine, near Gennes, and the Dolmen de Mettray, north of Tours. The Grand Dolmen de Bagneux, outside Saumur, is 20m long, 7m wide and is considered Europe's most spectacular megalithic monument. A 3m-high roof composed of 16 boulders, some weighing up to 500 tonnes, shelters the largest dolmen chamber in France. Numerous other dolmens pepper the barren, pancake-flat plateau of Les Mauges (in Vendée) and the coastal quarters to the north, including the Dolmen de la Jorelière and Dolmen des Mousseaux (near Pornic), and the 4000 BC Tumulus de Dissignac (7km west of St-Nazaire). The richest collection of dismantled remnants of prehistoric architecture can be viewed at the Musée des Tumulus de Bougon, near Poitiers.

Gallo-Roman The Romans constructed a large number of public works all over France from the 1st century BC: aqueducts, fortifications, marketplaces, temples, amphitheatres, triumphal arches and bathhouses. They established regular street grids at many settlements and built roads to connect their cities. Despite this prolific output, few traces of the period remain in the Loire.

Vestiges of the Roman wall built around Caesarodunum (Tours) remain today, as does an impressive Gallo-Roman amphitheatre in Gennes which was built in the 2nd century for chariot races and bloodthirsty gladiator fights. Roman archaeological exhibits can be viewed in Angers' Musée Pincé, in Cherré in the Vallée du Loir and at Poitier's Musée Ste-Croix, which stands atop Gallo-Roman walls that have been excavated and left *in situ*.

Dark Ages Although quite a few churches were built during the Merovingian and Carolingian periods (5th to 10th centuries), very little remains of them. However, the Loire is graced with what many consider to be France's finest example of Carolingian art. Église de Germigny des Prés, 4km south-east of Châteauneuf-sur-Loire, in Orléanais, dates from 806 and was built in the shape of a Greek cross. The mosaic in its eastern apse is stunning (see the boxed text 'Germigny des Prés: France's Oldest Church' in the Orléanais & Blésois chapter).

Further rare remnants of the Dark Ages can be seen in Poitiers. The 4th- to 6th-century Baptistère St-Jean, rebuilt in the 10th century, is one of the oldest Christian structures in France; the octagonal well used for total-immersion baptisms until the 7th century remains. The baptistry houses a museum of Merovingian sarcophagi (6th to 8th centuries). Nearby, there's a Merovingian funerary chapel (Hypogée des Dunes).

The Loire is studded with keeps (*donjons*) that took root in the 10th century. The most notable of these defensive constructions were built between 987 and 1040 by the Anjou count Foulques Nerra (Falcon the Black), who had a series of 20 keeps built in Touraine and Blésois to defend his recently acquired territory. The ruined Donjon de Foulques Nerra, in Langeais, dates from 944 and is considered to be the oldest such structure in France.

Romanesque A religious revival in the 11th century led to the construction of a large number of Romanesque churches, so called because their architects adopted many architectural elements (such as vaulting) from Gallo-Roman buildings still

standing at the time. Romanesque buildings typically have rounded arches, heavy walls whose few windows let in very little light, and a lack of ornamentation that borders on the austere.

Some of the most breathtaking examples of this era are showcased in Poitiers: Église St-Hilaire has a beautiful fresco-decorated choir, while the fabulously carved western facade of Église Notre Dame la Grande illustrates tales from the Old and New Testaments. The basilica in St-Benoît-sur-Loire, with its monumental porch tower and ornamented capitals featuring the Book of Revelations, is another beautiful example of Romanesque architecture that richly blends the austere with exquisite decoration. It is unusual in that its floor plan sports a double transept.

The majestic but sober Chartreuse du Liget (1176–89) near Loches, Abbaye Ronceray (1028) in Angers, Ancienne Abbaye de la Trinité (1040) in Vendôme and Abbaye de Fontevraud (1101) are examples of the fortress-like sacred buildings that also characterised this era. The kitchens at Fontevraud, built in the first half of the 12th century, are the only remaining example in France of kitchens built around a central fireplace and centred plan. Chateaux at this time – such as those at Langeais, Loches, Chinon and Beaugency – likewise tended to be sturdy, heavily fortified structures, built around a core keep and affording no luxuries to their inhabitants.

Gothic In the 11th and 12th centuries a new school of architecture emerged in western France, centred around the Angevin vault. Angevin vaulting, which added a new lightness and suppleness to both sacred and secular architecture, pre-empted the emerging Gothic style when premiered in 1149 under Henri (Plantagenêt) II at Cathédrale St-Maurice in Angers. The nave here boasts three convex vaults which form a perfect square.

Other outstanding examples of the Angevin vault are inside Angers' Abbaye St-Serge (1059) and the Ancien Hôpital St-Jean (1175–80), an old hospital built under

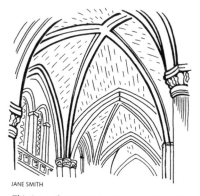

JANE SMITH

This type of Angevin (or Plantagenêt) vault dates from the mid-12th century.

Henri II and since transformed into a contemporary tapestry museum. Traces of the original Angevin vaulting of the 11th-century Abbaye Toussaint (today the David d'Angers Gallery) are also evident in the glass roof that tops the former abbey in Angers. In Poitiers, the vast Cathédrale St-Pierre (1162–1271) is a prime example of Angevin vaulting.

Gothic structures are characterised by ribbed vaults carved with great precision, pointed arches, slender verticals, chapels (often built by rich people or guilds) along the nave and chancel, refined decoration and large, stained-glass windows.

Edifices built in the early Gothic style, which lasted until about 1230, were majestic but still lacked lightness and airiness compared with later works. Since the stained-glass windows could not support the roof, thick stone buttresses were placed between them. It was soon discovered that reducing the bulk of the buttresses and adding outer piers to carry the thrust created a lighter building without compromising structural integrity.

This discovery gave rise to flying buttresses – such as those at Cathédrale St-Gatien in Tours or Cathédrale Ste-Croix in Orléans – which helped lift the Gothic style to its greatest achievements between 1230 and 1300. During this period, when French architecture dominated the European scene for the first time, Gothic masterpieces were decorated with ornate tracery (the delicate stone rib-work on stained-glass windows) and huge, colourful rose windows. In secular architecture, this period produced huge structures such as the Salle des États Généraux – France's largest Gothic civil hall – at Château de Blois. By the end of the 13th century, Gothic technology had reached its limits and architects became less interested in sheer size and put more energy into ornamentation.

During the 14th century the Rayonnant (Radiant) Gothic style – named after the radiating tracery of the rose windows – developed, with interiors becoming even lighter thanks to broader windows and more translucent stained glass. The Rayonnant style is well demonstrated in Tours' Cathédrale St-Gatien, whose stained glass forms a sheer curtain of glazing in both transepts. The stunning rose windows in the north and south transepts of Angers' Cathédrale St-Maurice depict scenes from the Apocalypse.

By the 15th century, decorative extravagance led to Flamboyant Gothic, so named because its wavy stone carving was said to resemble flames. Beautifully lacy examples of Flamboyant architecture are Basilique Notre Dame de Cléry in Cléry St-André, Orléans' Salle des Thèses and Cathédrale Ste-Croix, Cathédrale St-Louis in Blois, the facade of Vendôme's Ancienne Abbaye de la Trinité, Chapelle St-Hubert at Château d'Amboise, Oratoire d'Anne de Bretagne at Château de Loches and Cathédrale St-Pierre et St-Paul in Nantes.

Despite this surge towards the decorative and extravagant in religious architecture, the region's medieval chateaux remained steadfastedly staid and solid. Fortified castles dating from this period – such as Chinon, Loches, Langeais, Montreuil-Bellay and Plessis Bourré – were commonly built atop a rocky promontory or safeguarded by a drawbridge and Loire-fed moat, and served a purely defensive and military purpose. Château d'Angers, with its 17 grizzly towers, remains one of the finest examples of feudal architecture.

Renaissance The Renaissance, which began in Italy in the early 15th century, set out to realise a 'rebirth' of classical Greek and Roman culture. It had its first impact on France at the tail-end of the 15th century, when Charles VIII began a series of invasions of Italy.

The French Renaissance is divided into two periods: early Renaissance and Mannerism. During the first period (late 15th to mid-16th century), a variety of classical components and decorative motifs (columns, tunnel vaults, round arches and domes) were blended with the rich decoration of Flamboyant Gothic, a synthesis best exemplified by Tours' Cathédrale St-Gatien, which beautifully fuses a Flamboyant Gothic facade with Renaissance ornamented bell towers, and by Château de Chambord. The transition from late Gothic to Renaissance is most clearly seen, however, in Château de Blois, whose Flamboyant section (1498–1503) was built only 15 years before its early-Renaissance wing (1515–24). The Gothic-inspired Collégiale (1520–41) in Montrésor, with Renaissance ornamentation, dates from the same period.

It was during the early Renaissance period that the region's chateaux were used, for the first time, as pleasure palaces rather than defensive fortresses. Numerous edifices dating from the 15th and early 16th centuries – such as Château du Moulin near Romorantin-Lanthenay, Château de Villesavin near Chambord, Château d'Azay-le-Rideau and Château de Villandry – were built as summer or hunting residences for royal financiers, chamberlains and courtiers. Red patterned brickwork – such as that on the Louis XII wing of Château de Blois – adorns the facade of most chateaux dating from Louis XII's reign (1498–1515).

As towns and cities started to grow around the king's court, so an urban architecture sprang up. Timber-framed houses, built with wood from the region's plentiful forests, were constructed. The early plaster or wattle-and-daub nogging used to support the wooden framework was quickly superseded by a more ornate brick nogging, often reflecting the same criss-cross or herringbone pattern of light- and dark-red bricks as seen in Louis XII's chateaux. Many edifices, such as Maison Rouge in Chinon, were corbeled, while others – notably Angers' Maison d'Adam, and Maison des Acrobates in Blois – featured ornate wooden carvings on their facades. At the same time, the richest nobility and bourgeoisie had opulent hôtels particuliers built, such as the exquisite Hôtel Groslot (1550–2) and Angers' Hôtel Pincé (1530–8). Timber-framed houses were outlawed in the 17th century, due to their susceptibility to fire.

Mannerism began to emerge around 1530, when François I (who had been so deeply impressed by what he'd seen in Italy that he brought Leonardo da Vinci to Amboise) hired Italian architects and artists – many of them disciples of Michelangelo or Raphael – to design and decorate a new chateau for him at Chambord and a new wing at Château de Blois. The resultant spiral staircases are a potent symbol of the incredible Italian influence on French architecture. In the following decades, French architects who had studied in Italy took over from their Italian colleagues.

Baroque During the Baroque period, which lasted from the end of the 16th century to the late 18th century, painting, sculpture and classical architecture were integrated to create structures and interiors of great subtlety, refinement and elegance. Parisian François Mansart (1598–1662) designed the symmetrical classical wing of Château de Blois (1635). The stunningly classical Château de Cheverny was the work of Blois-born architect Jacques Bougier. In 1636 Guillaume Bautru redesigned Château de Serrant, the westernmost chateau to grace the Loire Valley.

Despite the return of the king and his court to Paris in the 17th century, the Loire Valley continued to lure a chateau-seeking set whose desire to outdo their neighbours, coupled with a craze for all things 'exotic', resulted in a rash of architectural follies – such as the Pagode de Chanteloup (1773–8), near Amboise.

Rococo, a derivation of Baroque, was likewise popular during the period of Enlightenment (the 18th century), though it was confined almost exclusively to the interiors of private residences and had a minimal impact on the architecture of churches and chateaux, which continued to follow the conventional rules of Baroque classicism. Rococo interiors were lighter, smoother and airier than their 17th-century predecessors and favoured pastels over vivid colours.

Neoclassical Neoclassical architecture, which emerged around 1740, had its roots in the renewed interest in classical forms. Although it was in part a reaction against the excesses of rococo, it was more profoundly a search for order, reason and serenity through the adoption of the forms and conventions of Graeco-Roman antiquity: columns, simple geometric forms and traditional ornamentation.

Two notable Loire chateaux exemplify the grace and elegance of neoclassicism. Château de Ménars (1760–4) was the work of Jacques-Ange Gabriel (1698–1782), the royal architect under Louis XV, who is credited with ushering rococo out and neoclassicism in. Gabriel was a model for numerous architects, including the Angevin architect Bardoul de la Bigottière, whose Château de Pignerolle, near Angers, is a blatant replica of Gabriel's Le Petit Trianon in Versailles.

Gabriel's work anticipated the *style Louis XVI*, an architectural trend that saw the opulent neoclassicism under Louis XV become more disciplined and formal under Louis XVI (1774–92). Château de Montgeoffrey, reconstructed on the site of a 16th-century chateau by Parisian architect Jean Barré, is a good example of this late-18th-century neoclassicism.

Contemporary Few contemporary architects have succeeded in stamping their mark on a region so riddled with historical architectural gems. A bold example of modern architecture is the breathtaking Galerie David d'Angers, an art gallery in Angers

housed in an 11th-century abbey (1040). In ruins until 1980, the abbey was transformed over a four-year period by Pierre Prunet – chief architect for historical monuments in France – into a gallery topped with a steel-and-glass roof. The resultant contrast between past and present is dramatic, complementary and beautiful.

Contemporary architect Jean Nouvel, noted for his penchant for modern technology, reflected in Paris' Insitut du Monde Arabe, designed the Centre International de Congrès Vinci in Tours and the Lycée Pilote Innovant Universitaire at Futuroscope, near Poitiers. The neo-futurist architecture of Denis Laming at the Futuroscope theme park is daring, bold and a perfect embodiment of the park's thrust towards the cutting edge of image, design and technology.

Painting
Medieval to Renaissance Illuminated manuscripts were an early form of artistic expression. Many – such as *Les très riches heures du duc de Berri* (*The Very Rich Hours of the Duke of Berry*), commissioned by Jean, duke of Berry, in the early 15th century – featured medieval chateaux. The above manuscript depicts Berry's own chateau and the opulent residences of his rival brothers, Charles V (who lived in Paris' Louvre) and Louis I of Anjou (who acquired Château de Saumur in 1360).

Jean Fouquet (1420–81) was a manuscript illuminator and portrait artist who evoked the Loire Valley in many of his works. Perversely, the Tours-born artist, who earned a living as a court artist for Charles VII (hence his well-known portrait of the king's mistress, Agnès Sorel, as the Virgin with one bare breast), did not achieve fame or fortune during his lifetime. His portraits, several of which are displayed in the Louvre in Paris (such as that of a long-nosed François I), were not sought after until the 19th century. The only Fouquet masterpiece to remain in the region is *La Pietà* (*Pity*; 1455), a panel painting displayed in the church of Nouans-lès-Fontaines (see Vallée de l'Indrois in the Touraine chapter), where it was unexpectedly discovered behind the altar in 1931. In Amboise, there's a Fouquet-illuminated manuscript at Château de Clos Lucé. In Château de Loches, a triptych (1485), originally displayed in the nearby Chartreuse du Liget (Carthusian monastery), is believed to belong to the Fouquet School of Tours.

In 1516 François I invited Leonardo da Vinci (1452–1519) to Amboise, where the great artist lived until his death. Travelling from Rome, he crossed the Alps by donkey, carrying the *Mona Lisa*, plus portraits of St Anne and John the Baptist, in leather saddle bags. In Amboise, da Vinci painted little, dedicating his time to the study of geometry and physics (see the boxed text 'Fabulous Flying Machines' in the Touraine chapter).

Between 1530 and 1560, François I's court at Fontainebleau drew many Italian artists, including Francesco Primaticcio (1504–70) and Rosso Florentino (1495–1540). They worked for the king and travelled with his court to the royal chateaux in the Loire. Through this early School of Fontainebleau, Mannerism was introduced to French painting and hence adopted by French artists such as Tourangeau artist François Clouet (1520–72). Portraits, many royal commissions, from this period can be viewed in bulk in the Portrait Room of the Musée des Beaux Arts in Blois and in Château de Beauregard, a former hunting lodge of François I, where there are 327 portraits of notable faces from the 14th to the 17th centuries. A copy of one of the best-known portraits produced by the School of Fontainebleau – featuring a bare-breasted Gabrielle d'Estrées, mistress of Henri IV, with her nipple-pinching sister – can be seen at Château de la Bourdaisière, where Gabrielle d'Estrées was born; the original is in the Louvre.

17th Century to Contemporary Blindman's buff, stolen kisses and other such courtly frivolities were the subject matter of the French school of artists that emerged in the late 17th and early 18th centuries during the Enlightenment. With the return of the royal court to Paris, however, few French works featured the Loire Valley. The English landscape artist Turner (1775–1851) frequented the region from 1802, immortalising the River Loire both in oil and watercolour. Landscape painting evolved further under the Barbizon School: Parisian-born Theodore Rousseau (1812–67) captured the light and liquidity of France's longest river in works which pre-empted the Impressionist movement of the 19th century.

French painting in the 20th century was characterised by a bewildering diversity of styles, swiftly moving from fauvism to cubism, to expressionists such as Orléans-born Roger Toulouse (1918–94). Prior to WWII, Toulouse was a staunch friend of Jewish French author Max Jacob, of whom he painted several portraits now displayed in the Musée des Beaux Arts in Orléans.

The Musée de l'Objet in Blois showcases works by contemporary artists who have worked in the region, such as Arman, Yves Klein, Christo, César and Agullo Thierry (1945–80), who died in a car accident near Poitiers.

Sculpture

At the end of the 11th century, sculptors began to decorate the portals, capitals, altars and fonts of Romanesque churches, illustrating Bible stories and the lives of the saints for the illiterate. Two centuries later, when the cathedral became the centre of monumental building, sculpture spread from the central portal to the whole facade, whose brightly painted and carved surface offered a symbolic summary of Christian doctrine.

As well as adorning cathedrals, sculpture was increasingly commissioned for the tombs of the nobility. From his workshop in Tours, sculptor Michel Colombe (1430–1514) was commissioned by Anne de Bretagne in 1502 to sculpt what is now considered a masterpiece of Renaissance art – the royal tomb of François II and his wife Marguerite de Foix in Nantes' Cathédrale St-Pierre et St-Paul. Justice, Prudence and Temperance all feature in the monumental piece, carved from Italian marble. Another example of funerary art sculpted by Colombe is in Château de Montrésor.

The 18th century was dominated by the Romantic and ardent republican sculptor David d'Angers (1788–1856). The works of the Angers-born artist encapsulated the heroism of the individual and sent clear republican messages. D'Angers' sculpted pediment for the Panthéon in Paris featured a series of revolutionary figures and was entitled *Nation Distributing Crowns to Genius*; a maquette of the model eventually realised in 1834–7 is displayed in the Galerie David d'Angers in Angers, as are several portrait busts and medallions for which d'Angers was well known. The funerary monument atop the tomb of Bonchamps in St-Florent-le-Vieil (see Les Mauges in the Anjou chapter) is considered one of d'Angers' best works. It encapsulates the violence and bitterness of the Vendée War.

Several pieces by the region's earliest female sculptor, Julie Charpentier (1770–1845), are in Blois' Musée des Beaux Arts.

In the 19th century, memorial statues in public places started to replace sculpted tombs. Joan of Arc has been immortalised in stone several times across the region.

Tapestry

Tapestries in the Loire Valley have their origin in one cold fact: the region's lumbering stone chateaux were too damn chilly. Woven from wool as early as the 8th century, tapestries covered walls, benches and chairs to create warmth in what would otherwise have been a very cold, dank room.

By the 13th century, tapestries were a status symbol. A nobleman's wealth was measured by the quality, weight, colour, pattern and number of tapestries hung in his residence: Louis I of Anjou owned sufficient tapestries to illustrate 76 different (very lengthy) tales, while the duke of Berry's tapestries could cover 400m of wall. Each time a nobleman changed his residence, he had the interior hung with a different set of woven pieces to demonstrate his affluence.

Paris served as Europe's leading tapestry centre until the Hundred Years' War (1337–1453), when chateaux were pillaged and their woven treasures stolen or destroyed.

Many weavers moved their workshops to Flanders, but still secured contracts in France through a handful of Parisian merchants – Nicolas Bataille, Jacques Doudin and Pierre de Beaumetz – who negotiated with weavers on behalf of aristocracy and royalty.

Between the 13th and 16th centuries, Gothic art forms penetrated the woven medium. Intensely religious and spiritual motifs, often derived from an illuminated manuscript, were reproduced by medieval weavers in sombre wools of brown, red and ochre interwoven with gold or silk threads. *L'Apocalypse* (*The Apocalypse*; 1373–83) – now in Château d'Angers – is a masterpiece from the period. Commissioned in 1375 by the Anjou duke Louis I, the monumental 103m-long tapestry illustrates the last book of the Bible according to St John. It remains the largest tapestry of its kind in the world.

During the Renaissance, tapestry flourished. Louis XI's royal court at Amboise saw the Loire and Cher Valleys emerge as textile strongholds in the 1460s. In support of French workshops, Henry IV banned foreign tapestry imports in 1601 and established lucrative privileges for weavers in order to lure Flemish craftsmen to France.

Religious stories (such as the creation of Adam and Eve and the murder of Abel) and expressions of Christian virtue still featured in 16th-century Renaissance works. However, it is hunting scenes, family crests, seigniorial symbols, astrology and other representations of aristocratic or courtly life that are the predominant trademarks of tapestries from this golden period. Château de Langeais' late-15th-century tapestries of a deer hunt – the slaughter of the deer, the giving away of its front right foot to the guest of honour and the feeding of the less noble pieces of game to the pack – are a marvellous (and gory) example of the extraordinary detail with which tapestries were woven.

Dramatic images of bravery and chivalry, such as knights on horseback, are likewise common; the *Neuf preux* (*Nine Valiant Knights*; 1531) series which hangs in Château de Langeais is a fine example.

Particularly prevalent in the Loire Valley at this time was *millefleurs* (literally 'a thousand flowers'), a style typified by a repetitive background smothered with flowers, green vegetation, birds and animals. Millefleurs tapestries hang in most Loire chateaux; the finest are at Angers, Cheverny, Langeais and Serrant. The fascination with the Orient, which did not express itself in architecture until the 17th century, was evident in tapestries as early as the 16th century. Fantastical monkeys, lions and other animals added an exotic touch to traditional flower-filled textiles.

Picardy wool, Italian silk, linen and gold or silver threads were the primary materials used in tapestry. In the 16th century, illuminated manuscripts were superceded as patterns by *cartons* (cartoons), full-sized drawings reproduced exactly by the tapestry workshop. Laurent Guyot, who designed the cartons (1610–18) for *La chasse du Roi François I* (*The Hunt of François I*) featuring Château de Chambord, was one of France's best-known 'cartoonists'. These templates were replaced by paintings in the late 17th century.

A century on, tapestry lost all value as a prized art form; *L'Apocalypse* was used to protect orange trees against the winter frost in 1792 and recycled as stable rugs in 1844.

Tapestries today are produced with computerised Jacquard weaving looms. Monumental tapestries woven by artist Jean Lurçat (1892–1966), known for his use of natural dyes, are displayed in the Musée Jean Lurçat et de la Tapisserie Contemporaine, in Angers. Château de Langeais' tapestry collection remains one of the Loire Valley's finest; a wealth of contemporary tapestries are sold in the chateau's shop (8400FF to 18,650FF).

Cinema

Very few film directors have actually been born in the Loire (but for information on the many films that have been shot or set in the Loire, see Films in the Facts for the Visitor chapter).

In the late 1950s a large group of new directors burst onto the cinema scene with a new genre, the so-called *nouvelle vague* (new wave). The basic premise of this genre was that a film should be the conception of the film-maker rather than the product of a studio or producer, hence giving rise to the term *film d'auteur*. The nouvelle vague crowd included Henri Georges Coulzot (1907–77), a native of Niort, in Poitou. His *La salaire de la peur* (*The Wages of Fear*; 1953) won Best Film at Berlin and Cannes that year.

In 1975 local film director and jazz musician Alain Corneau (1943–) produced *Police Python 357*, starring French actor Yves Montand and using Corneau's home town – Orléans – as a film set.

SOCIETY & CONDUCT
Dos & Don'ts

As in every part of France, people from the Loire are staunchly proud of their region's natural treasures and rich cultural heritage. Most have an equally staunch loyalty to the hamlet, village, town or city where they live. Food is also an extremely serious matter. Many people live, dream and sleep food – a topic that miraculously wangles its way into the most unrelated of conversations.

Offences warranting social ostracism include expressing even so much as a mild dislike for a traditional culinary dish such as *andouillette* (tripe sausage of grotesque proportions) or *fressure vendéenne* (pig parts stewed in wine and eaten cold); admitting you're a vegetarian; declining a tasting (*dégustation*) session, regardless of time, day or circumstance; or failing to show as enthusiastic an interest in food as your next-door neighbour.

Definite dining dos and don'ts include never *ever* asking for ice cubes to drop into warm wine or ketchup/mayonnaise to douse over food. When tasting wine, be sure to mimic the series of facial contortions required as well as the traditional sniff, sip, and swallow or spit action. If invited to lunch, don't make any plans for the ensuing afternoon: you can rest assured that lunch will last at least three hours and will leave you feeling so blissfully full that it is doubtful you will be able to move. Skipping lunch (or indeed any meal) altogether is seen as the ultimate sin, while a quick snack standing up is severely frowned on.

Handy little tricks to make friends quickly include always saying 'Bonjour, monsieur/madame/mademoiselle' with a smile when you sail into a shop/cafe/restaurant – or saying it with flowers when visiting someone's home. Never buy/offer chrysanthemums unless you intend laying them on a gravestone. Exchanging kisses (*bises*) upon a first meeting is a charming norm that should be respected. The number of pecks can vary from one on each cheek to an exhausting four (frighteningly common in Tours). Money and time are taboo subjects.

Treatment of Animals

Hunting Since the region served as the hunting ground of France's kings from the 13th to the 18th centuries, it is inevitable that hunting traditions in the Loire are among the strongest in the country.

Hunting was reserved exclusively for royalty and the aristocracy by Charles VI in 1397 and enjoyed its glory days under François I, who riddled the region with grandiose hunting 'lodges' such as Château de Chambord and Château de Beauregard. The 1789 French Revolution firmly entrenched hunting as a considered right of the common man.

Out of the country's 1.5 million hunters and 7000 hounds, approximately 20% hunt in the Pays de la Loire, Centre and Poitou-Charentes régions. In rural Poitou-Charentes, 14% of the male population hunts, despite the number of hunting permits issued falling by 23% between 1985 and 1995. Game-rich La Sologne rings with gunshots during the hunting season, which – depending on the département – runs from some time between the end of September until the end of February; wild boar and fox hunts start as early as mid-August.

Château de Cheverny and Château de Champchevrier both have a working pack of hounds which hunt foxes and deer in the forests and woodlands twice weekly. In season, venison is as likely to end up on your plate as pheasant, rabbit, hare, skylark and partridge.

Presidential hunts traditionally take place at the Domaine National de Chambord, a national hunting reserve since 1947, kept for presidential use. Since his election in 1995, President Jacques Chirac has chosen not to exercise this right. Some 14 annual culls are thus organised by the Office National des Forêts (ONF) and Office National de la Chasse (ONC) to keep down Chambord's boar population, which sports an almost 100% growth rate: 500 boars each year are hunted by a pack of 24 to 36 dog-assisted hunters who shoot the boar as the dogs chase it into a tree-cleared alleyway in the forest. Chambord's 600-strong stag population is likewise controlled: 100 are currently withdrawn annually, with 4000 stags being driven into nets, captured and released elsewhere since 1947.

Unfortunately, the hunting lobby remains strong: the political party Chasse Pêche Nature Tradition (Hunting and Fishing Natural Tradition), which supports hunting practices, made notable inroads in the June 1999 European elections, winning 11.96 and 6.94% of votes in Loir-et-Cher and Loire-Atlantique respectively (compared to 5.38 and 4.99% in 1994 elections). This trend was reflected across the board in the Loire Valley départements.

Despite a 1979 EU directive to protect wild birds in member states, France has yet to make the directive's provisions part of French law.

Foie Gras Vendée is the fourth-largest foie gras-producing département in France (after Gers, Pyrénées-Atlantique and Landes, in south-western France), producing 1200 tonnes annually. *Le gavage* – the force-feeding of geese to make foie gras (fattened goose liver) – rouses strong feelings only among foreign visitors.

RELIGION

Countrywide, 80% of people identify themselves as Catholic, though few ever attend church. Protestants (Huguenots) account for less than 2% of today's population. Despite bloody clashes between Catholics and Protestants in the past – the St Bartholomew's Day massacres (1572), the Edict of Nantes (1598) and its subsequent revocation (1689), and the Vendée War (1793–6) – the two live together harmoniously now. Traditional Catholic/Protestant strongholds in the Loire include the Vendée/Saumur respectively.

Other religions represented in the region include Islam and Judaism.

LANGUAGE

French is, naturally, the main language spoken in the Loire region. The Tours accent is considered to be the purest in the country. Although many French people speak some English, any effort to speak French is generally appreciated. Staff at most hotels and restaurants usually speak English. For more information on French, a list of useful words and phrases and a food glossary, see the Language chapter at the back of this book.

CHATEAUX OF THE LOIRE

Five centuries of royal architecture are mirrored in the glassy waters of the River Loire. Blue-blooded counts and kings built military fortresses in the 12th to 14th centuries, pleasure palaces in the 15th and 16th centuries, and classical creations from the 17th century on.

The medieval fortified castle (*château fort*) was designed to be impregnable. Its central keep (*donjon*) and enclosure (*enceinte*) were hidden from the world by a 2- to 3m-thick defensive wall, studded with towers and machicolated ramparts from which boiling oil or missiles could be dropped on attackers. The early-13th-century Château d'Angers is a good example of a fortified castle.

A duel between military practicality and aestheticism resulted in the creation of the moated castle of the early 15th century. The interior keep was replaced by a chateau, built in a quadrangular form that was more suited to residential comfort. The exterior defensive wall – safeguarded with a portcullis and licked by moat waters which were crossed by a drawbridge – remained. Château du Moulin, near Romorantin-Lanthenay in La Sologne, is a grand example of this style of chateau fort.

The Renaissance chateau showcased wealth, ancestry and refinement. Defensive towers – a historical seigniorial symbol – were incorporated into a new, decorative architecture, typified by its three-dimensional use of pilasters and arcaded loggias, terraces, balconies, exterior staircases, turrets and gabled chimneys. Heraldic symbols were sculpted on soft stone facades, above doorways and fireplaces and across coffered ceilings. Symmetrical floor plans broke new ground and heralded a different style of living: Château de Chambord contained 40 self-contained apartments, arranged on five floors around a central axis. This ensured easy circulation in a vast edifice which many rank as the first modern building in France.

A king's bedroom (*chambre du roi*) was a standard feature of seigniorial chateaux until the mid-17th century. The bedroom remained unslept in, reserved for the king in the rare case that he should drop in for a visit.

In the royal chateaux, the king and queen each had an apartment comprising – at the very least – two antechambers where different ranks of nobility could seek a royal audience, a chamber for the valet or lady-in-waiting, plus the king's or queen's private chamber. Royal mistresses, barred from the king's chamber, had their own apartment to receive royal visits. The queen enjoyed little privacy: she even gave birth before a very large audience.

Top: The forbidding stone walls of Château d'Angers (1228–38), a typical 13th-century fortress

JANE SMITH

INTERIORS
Furnishings

Contrary to popular belief, the vast majority of *grands châteaux* (major chateaux) are empty. Until the 17th century many royal chateaux had no permanent furnishings. When King François I (ruled 1515–47) decided to hunt at Château de Chambord, his court traipsed on foot or horse-back from Blois. Furnishings accompanied the cortege and were assembled in the chateau prior to the king's arrival. Upon his departure, the chateau would be emptied until the next royal visit, courtiers being forbidden to remain without a king present. Chambord was hence inhabited for just 42 days during François I's 32-year reign. The French Revolution later inflicted a devastating blow on these royal and aristocratic properties. Château de Blois was turned into army barracks in 1788, for example, while the entire contents of Chambord (finally given a permanent set of furniture in 1782) were auctioned off in 1792.

Many chateaux enjoyed massive facelifts in the late 19th and early 20th centuries, during which attempts were made to reconstruct original furnishings. The interior of Château de Langeais, for example, was almost entirely returned to its late-15th-century state by the chateau proprietor in the early 1900s. Langeais apart, most furnished chateaux showcase an eclectic mix of styles and periods, reflecting the contrasting decorative trends – Renaissance through to Louis XVI or Empire style – that influenced different proprietors.

Given the royal court's mobility, wooden chests – in which gold and silver plates, goblets, candlesticks and so on could be transported with ease – were a vital commodity in the 16th century. Several **early-**

Left: The mythical salamander, François I's emblem, adorns the facades and interiors of the chateaux at Blois and Chambord.

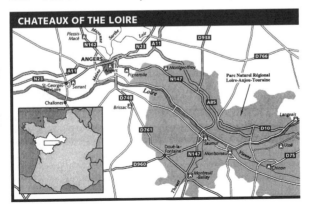

CHATEAUX OF THE LOIRE

JANE SMITH

Renaissance-style chests are displayed in Château de Blois. Their facades were often panelled or intricately carved with heroic images from antiquity. Similar carved images smothered the facades of two-tiered cupboards (*armoires*), which were popular at this time. Château de Beauregard houses some fine pieces of early-Renaissance furniture and furnishings.

The so-called **Louis XIII style** which dominated the latter part of the 16th and first half of the 17th centuries saw a revival in the use of tapestry as wall hangings, seat covers and bed drapes. An exceptional example of the canopied, four-poster bed prevalent at this time is in the king's bedroom in Château de Cheverny. The bed – original and never slept in because a king never stayed at Cheverny – is richly hung with exquisite 16th-century Persian silk.

Ceilings – coffered or beamed – were richly painted *à la française* (French style) with elaborate floral and seigniorial motifs. Examples abound, including in Châteaux de Blois, Brissac, Chaumont and Montpoupon. Decorative floor tiling – such as the Italian tiles depicting a stag hunt in the council chamber at Chaumont – were another important feature of the 17th century. Fine Dutch tiles carpet the floor of Beauregard's portrait gallery.

Right: The crowned-ermine emblem of Anne de Bretagne can be seen in all its furry glory at Château de Langeais.

The late-17th-century **Louis XIV style** exhibited a taste for the exotic – distinctive red tortoise-shell desks and cabinets with brass inlays became its signature. Created by André Charles Boulle, the royal cabinet maker, this exemplary marquetry was inspired by the Florentine cabinets of the 16th century, which bore pearl or ivory inlays (and concealed 49 secret drawers); Château d'Ussé has examples of both.

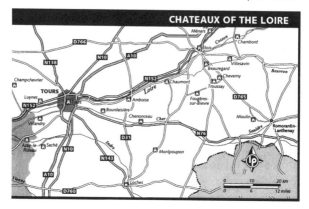

Boulle created the first chest of drawers (*commode*) at the close of the 17th century; by 1710 practically every chateau had one. Lacquered pieces inspired by the Orient appeared around this time and remained fashionable until the century's close.

The region shelters two outstanding works of art from this period. In Château de Serrant the stunning 17th-century ebony cabinet by Dutch cabinet maker Pierre Gole is one of four in the world, while the 327 historical portraits that form a mural in Château de Beauregard are unique.

Regency style furniture dates from 1715–30. Decor from this era can be viewed in the Regency suite at Château d'Ussé, which, with the change of each season, was decorated with a different fabric.

From 1730 the **Louis XV style** abandoned the straight line in favour of more curvaceous and comfortable forms. Chest corners became round, table legs spelt the letter 'S', and comfort became a priority in chair design: the *duchesse* – a cross between a bed and a chair – allowed ladies to read or receive people in a horizontal position while being protected from draughts by a 'bed head' at one end.

Tables designed for specific purposes multiplied. The concept of chateau inhabitants dining in unison *à la Anglaise* (English-style) round the same table did not take off until 1750, when the portable tressel table (*table mobile*) was superseded by a dining-room table (*table de salle à manger*), designed to fill the dining room created at the same time. Three-sided tables designed for card games requiring three players were created. There was even a special type of table (*table gibier*) to display game before a feast. On a different note, the bidet was invented in 1751.

From 1774 to the end of the 18th century, **Louis XVI style** celebrated a return to sober, geometric forms. Chair legs were tapered and semi-circular forms became popular. Wall panelling (*boiserie*) was painted pale grey, and decorative carvings of lion heads, paws, olives and so on heralded a return to antiquity for inspiration. In the sitting room (*salon*), the *voyeuse* – a chair allowing one to sit back to front, one leg either side of the seat and elbows resting on a cushioned arm that topped its upright back – was among the new pieces of furniture designed. It eased the art of watching a card game.

JANE SMITH

One of the most important designers to emerge at this time was Georges Jacob. Examples of Jacob pieces are in Château de Montpoupon and Château de Serrant, where a giant Jacob mahogany

Left: The *voyeuse*, designed to be sat on back to front, was an essential aid in every 18th-century *salon*.

table with lion paws sits in the dining room. The best chateau to see genuine 18th-century furnishings, however, is Château de Montgeoffroy. It is one of the few to sport its original neoclassical furnishings.

Cheverny, also sumptuously furnished, reflects the post-Revolution **Directory** and **Empire styles**, as well as their predecessors.

Staircases

Renaissance architecture stamped chateaux with a new artistic form: the monumental staircase. The most famous of these splendid ceremonial (and highly functional) creations are at Azay-le-Rideau, Blois, Chambord and Serrant.

The medieval staircase – traditionally cork-screwed – had already been remodelled to grandiose proportions at Amboise, where a brick ramp had been spiralled five times round a hollow core in the massive, 40m-tall **Tour des Cavaliers** (Knights' Tower; also known as Tour des Minimes) in 1495, and was subsequently echoed in the **Tour Hurtault** (Hurtault Tower).

However, it was not until 1515–24 that the spiral staircase as a monumental exterior form (*hors œuvre*) was realised in the famous **Escalier François I**, at Château de Blois. Reflecting that same Italian influence that stamped all François I's architectural dreams, the spiralling staircase was the only access from the *cour d'honneur* (central courtyard) to the king's apartment. It snakes up an octagonal tower which is semi-submerged in the wing's facade and cut with open galleries so that the king and his guards could see whoever entered the royal chambers. The stone balustrades are fabulously carved with François I's insignia, a capital 'F' and a salamander.

The spiral was further revolutionised by architects at Château de Chambord in 1545. Of the castle's 77 staircases, one, known as the **Grand Staircase**, is unique: two equal spiral ramps cork-screw their way up a central hollow, allowing the king to scale one set of stairs and his queen to descend by the other. Openings in the central core ensured the pair could peek at each other. This double-revolution staircase sports 157 steps, is 9m in diameter and is encircled by eight pillars. A lantern,

Right: Watch your step at the fabulous Escalier François I, Château de Blois.

JANE SMITH

crowned with the traditional royal *fleur de lys* (lily), lit the top.

At Château d'Azay-le-Rideau, built around the same time as the François I wing at Blois, the spiral staircase was straightened. The **Central Staircase** was laid out in a zigzag Italianate form, escalating in a straight ramp that doubles back on itself. The flight is completely enclosed in the building interior, but a triple set of galleries allowed stair users to peer out into the courtyard. Its ribbed roofing incorporates a Gothic element, interspersed with traditional Renaissance coffers featuring coats of arms and other seigniorial insignia. This form of staircase was subsequently mimicked in Château de Serrant and other chateaux.

GARDENS

The concept of chateau as pleasure palace was mirrored in the Renaissance garden, which, from the mid-16th century, became an integral part of chateau design. Architects lavished equal attention to detail on both interior and exterior. Thus, the random sensuality of the traditional medieval garden – with its sweet-smelling herbs, roses and aromatic plants – was forced into a new symmetry.

Cabbages, carrots, the rarer artichoke and other vegetables were allotted to the **kitchen garden** (*potager*), itself a work of art with its carefully planned rows and geometric patterns. The borders of each vegetable bed were planted out with pansies, petunias, blue sage and other blooms to add colour. Renaissance kitchen gardens have been reconstructed at Château de la Bussière, Château de la Bourdaisière and Château de Villandry.

Formal paths intersected with fountains and statues formed the backbone of the **ornamental garden**, in which courtly romance played a key role. Every twist and turn of a box hedge, flower bed or yew tree was loaded with symbolism. Lyres, lutes and harps were hidden in the intricate patterns carved in green. Nowhere is this Renaissance quest for love more explicit than in the 52km of landscaped plant rows and 1150 lime trees at Château de Villandry. Its ornamental gardens were replaced by English gardens in the 19th century but returned to their Renaissance glory from 1906. Other exemplary gardens, likewise restored, are those created by Diane de Poitiers and Catherine de Médicis at Château de Chenonceau.

DIANA MAYFIELD

CHRISTOPHER WOOD

DIANA MAYFIELD

DIANA MAYFIELD

Top: The ornamental gardens of Chenonceau, created by Diane de Poitiers, mistress of Henri II, in the 16th century

Middle left: The *cour d'honneur* (central courtyard) at Blois

Middle right: The stylised 16th-century drawbridge at Chenonceau was never used for defence.

Bottom: The Great Hall in medieval Loches, where Joan of Arc, in 1429, begged the dauphin, Charles VII, to be crowned at Reims

DIANA MAYFIELD

MICHELLE LEWIS

CHÂTEAU DE CHEVERNY

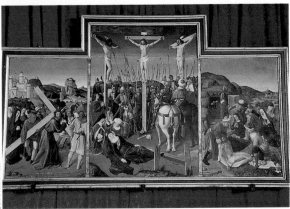

DIANA MAYFIELD

Top: The magnificent dining room at Cheverny, with walls covered by embossed Cordova leather

Middle left: Renaissance stained glass in unmissable Chambord

Middle right: The elegant drawing room at Cheverny, with the original 17th-century painted ceiling

Bottom: This rare triptych in Loches dates from 1485 and is believed to belong to the School of Tours, of which Jean Fouquet (1420–81) was master.

DIANA MAYFIELD

DIANA MAYFIELD

Top: The perfectly proportioned neoclassical facade of 17th-century Cheverny

Middle: A mosaic, showing the royal pastime of hunting, in the Salle des Trophées, Cheverny, where the antlers of over 2000 stags are displayed

Bottom left: The River Indre flows past fairy-tale 16th-century Azay-le-Rideau.

Bottom right: The famous rooftop at 16th-century Chambord can be viewed any way you want.

DIANA MAYFIELD

MATTHIAS LÜFKENS

DIANA MAYFIELD

MICHELLE LEWIS

MICHELLE LEWIS

DIANA MAYFIELD

Top: The intricate geometric patterns of the reconstructed Renaissance kitchen gardens at Villandry

Middle left: The fabulous lantern tower at the top of the Italianate double-spiral staircase (1545) at Chambord

Middle right: The elegant Henri II spiral staircase at Chambord, one of 77 stairways in the chateau

Bottom: The ornamental gardens at Villandry are loaded with romantic symbolism: hunt for tender, tragic, passionate and fickle love among the manicured hedges.

Facts for the Visitor

HIGHLIGHTS

The obvious highlight for travellers who make their way to the *Vallée des Rois* (Valley of Kings) is the extraordinary collection of chateaux that peppers its riverbanks. Spanning the course of history from medieval to Renaissance and beyond, these monumental masterpieces evoke the brilliance of a bygone era. Coffered ceilings dressed in Cordova leather, dimly lit Flemish tapestries, facades carved with the coats of arms of kings and queens, spiral staircases and Italianate galleries are among the dazzling array of structural and decorative gems offered to travellers.

The famous chateaux of Chambord, Chaumont, Chenonceau, Cheverny, Blois, Amboise and Azay-le-Rideau are indisputable highlights of any chateau tour, although a trip to some of the less grandiose edifices – Serrant, Saché or Ussé – can be equally rewarding (as well as less crowded). Smaller chateaux that warrant a trip include Château du Moulin and Château de la Bourdaisière, plus those that dominate Sully-sur-Loire, Langeais and Montreuil-Bellay. Attending a *son et lumière* (sound and light) show at a chateau is a mesmerising and illuminating affair, allowing you to view the chateaux of the Loire from a magical perspective. Alternatively, take to the skies in a hot-air balloon for an aerial view (see the boxed text 'Hot-Air Ballooning' later in this chapter).

Highlights for the green-fingered include the beautiful Renaissance-inspired gardens of Château de Villandry, the annual International Garden Festival which transforms the grounds of Château de Chaumont into an amazing collection of avant-garde horticultural creations, the kitchen garden at Château de la Bussière, and the tomato crops of Château de la Bourdaisière.

Equally invigorating is a short hike at dawn or dusk to one of Chambord's wildlife observatories, where, come the rutting season in September and October, silent observers can see stags performing. Chambord's

thick forests and its soggy southern neighbour, La Sologne, are fabulous to explore on foot or by bicycle year round.

Highlights around Tours include Leonardo da Vinci's fabulous flying machines in Amboise, and the crisp white wines of Vouvray and Montlouis. A visit to the École National d'Équitation in Saumur provides a fascinating insight into France's strong equestrian tradition and its elite riding core, the Cadre Noir. The valley stretching east and west of Saumur is strewn with troglodyte caves.

Farther west, the serpentine river takes travellers to Loire-Atlantique. Unmissable sights and smells include the oyster beds of Baie de Bourgneuf, the salt pans of the Presqu'île du Guérande, the Îles de Noirmoutier and Yeu, and the unusual wetlands of the Marais Poitevin and Parc Naturel Régional de Brière. Cities include the university town of Nantes, with its muscadet vineyards, and the architecturally rich stronghold of Poitiers, home to some of France's finest Romanesque churches.

The definitive Loire Valley lowlight is to trail around a chateau at a snail's pace, with (what feels like) the rest of the world's populace. Chateau fatigue is an infectious disease unique to the region. Travellers most at risk include those who fail to balance chateau visits with other activities or who attempt to cram in too many chateaux in a day/week/month.

PLANNING
When to Go

May and June are the best times to visit, followed by September. Spring is a cocktail of brilliant sunflower fields, golden wheat fields and colourful wild flowers. The red and yellow pansies, forget-me-nots and crimson tulips planted in strict symmetrical patterns in Villandry's Renaissance gardens burst into bloom at this time. Cabbages, tomatoes and other summer vegetables are planted out in June, while July and August see 20,000 dahlias bathe in the summer sun.

Son et Lumière

The first *son et lumière* (literally 'sound and light') show lit up Château de Chambord in 1952. Since then, a wildly varied and imaginative host of these night-time shows have been projected at chateaux throughout the Loire Valley. Most son et lumières conform to traditional theatre protocol in that the sound and light projections start at a pre-scheduled time. Some, however, such as those at Chambord or Azay-le-Rideau, are less formal affairs: there is no central stage and guests can arrive and depart at any time during the evening, being left to uncover at their own pace the magical sights and sounds enveloping the chateau facade and its interior. In a *cinéscénie*, real people – usually inhabitants of the village or town – mime to voices that are projected overhead.

Tickets are generally sold in advance and can be pre-booked by telephone. Some chateaux, such as Blois, sell tickets only on the actual day. Performances start when it's dark, varying from some time around 8 pm in June or October to 9.30 or 10 pm in August. Seating can be on bum-numbing cobblestones; bring a cushion or deck chair.

Abbaye de Fontevraud Rencontres Imaginaires. Evening spectacle recounting the history, architecture and intrigue surrounding this royal abbey.
Every evening in August
Information: ☎ 02 41 38 18 17
85/50FF adults/those aged 12 to 25; free for children aged under 12

Château d'Amboise À la Cour du Roy François. Extravagant cinéscénie: 300 actors play 450 roles to re-enact the court of King François I, from his childhood at Amboise to his eventual coronation. Wednesday and Saturday evenings from mid-June to end of August, plus Monday evening from 7 to 14 August
Information: ☎ 02 47 57 14 47
75/35FF adults/children (plus 5FF reservation fee)

Château d'Azay-le-Rideau Les Imaginaires. Evening promenades of the chateau and park, which are transformed into a shimmering mirage of lights and music evoking the Renaissance spirit.
Every evening from mid-May to mid-September
Information: ☎ 02 47 45 42 04
60/35FF adults/those aged 12 to 15; free for children aged under 12

Age-old vines grow heavy with plump red grapes in early September and pumpkin fields turn deliciously orange. Come October, the grape harvests (*vendanges*) are well under way, the apple trees pruned and the delicate orange trees taken inside until another year. From mid-October until March the region sleeps: the leaves drop from the lime trees and many smaller chateaux slam shut their doors to visitors.

All the major chateaux (see the map in the Chateaux of the Loire special section) are open year round, with the exception of Saché (closed December and January), Langeais (closed October to March), Serrant (closed mid-November to March) and Montreuil-Bellay (closed December to March). At the larger chateaux, however, autumn and winter are very much second seasons: the frequency of guided tours is severely reduced (or they're nonexistent), horse-and-carriage rides and other attractions do not operate and opening hours are shorter.

Son et lumière shows and other chateau-hosted spectacles run from around mid-May to mid-September; some happen only in July and August (see the boxed text above). Château de Blois hosts its English-language show only on Wednesday in May, June and September. The region's rich pageant of other festivals can also be a deciding factor as to

Son et Lumière

Château de Blois Traditional son et lumière illustrating the chateau's history.
Every evening from early May to mid-September; in English on Wednesday evening in May, June and September
Information: ☎ 02 54 78 72 76
60/30FF adults/students and those aged seven to 20; free for children aged under seven

Château de Chambord Les Métamorphoses de Chambord. Evening promenades around the dimly lit chateau interior, aflutter with music, sounds and lights to conjure up images of celestial divinities.
Every evening from mid-July to mid-September; weekends only from mid- to end of September
Information: ☎ 02 54 50 40 00
80/50FF adults/students; free for children aged under 12

Château de Chenonceau Au Temps des Dames de Chenonceau. Traditional son et lumière recounting the history of the chateau and the women who made it what it is.
Every evening in July and August
Information: ☎ 02 47 23 90 07
50/40FF adults/students and those aged seven to 17; free for children aged under seven

Château de Loches Le Chevalier au Loup. Traditional son-et-lumière-cum-cinéscénie, with 100 actors.
Friday and Saturday evenings in July and August
Information: ☎ 02 47 59 01 76
70/40FF adults/children aged under 12

Château du Puy du Fou La Bataille du Donjon. Gigantic cinéscénie extravaganza at the chateau that premiered France's first cinéscénie in 1977; each show stars 850 actors, 50 (real) animals, 4500 different characters and 400 fireworks.
Friday and Saturday evenings in June, July and August, plus two or three weekend shows in late May and early September
Information: ☎ 02 51 64 11 11, ✉ info@puydufou.tm.fr
Web site: www.puydufou.com
125/50FF adults/children aged five to 12; free for children aged under five

---

when you go (or don't go): see the boxed text 'Feasts & Festivals' later in this chapter.

On the Atlantic coast, sun worshippers bare their bodies from June to September. Easter to the end of August sees beach resorts such as La Baule and Les Sables d'Olonne buzz with activity round the clock, while a steady stream of ferries goes back and forth to Île de Noirmoutier and Île d'Yeu. Boat excursions on the Loire, Cher and other rivers are likewise restricted to the summer period, from April or May to early or mid-October. July and August see hordes of tourists and French holiday-makers descend upon the region, clogging up roads, hotels and camp sites. One tasty

reason for visiting the coast or its islands out of season is to feast on oysters and mussels, which are abundant from September until March.

Maps

Michelin (www.michelin-travel.com) and IGN (www.ign.fr) have Internet boutiques where you can purchase maps. IGN Sologne (☎ 02 54 94 13 40, fax 02 54 88 14 66, ✉ ign-sologne@ign.fr), 41200 Romorantin-Lanthenay, mails maps abroad.

Locally, an outstanding selection of maps is sold in the Géothèque travel bookshops in Tours and Nantes and the FNAC stores in Orléans and Nantes.

Regional & Thematic Maps Quality regional maps are widely available outside France and are invaluable in planning a trip to the region. The Loire region is best covered by Michelin's yellow-jacketed maps (1:200,000). *Centre Berry-Nivernais* (No 238, 32FF), *Pays de Loire* (No 232, 32FF) and *Poitou-Charentes* (No 233, 32FF) cover the entire stretch from Orléans to the Atlantic coast. IGN publishes equivalents (1:250,000, 35FF) in its Découvertes Régionales and TOP 250 series.

IGN's 1:1,000,000, grey-jacketed No 903 (29FF), entitled *France: Grande Randonnée*, shows the region's GR (*grande randonnée*, literally 'long walk') trails and is useful for strategic planning of a cross-country trek through the region. Map No 906 (29FF), in the same series, called *France: VTT & Randonnées Cyclos*, indicates dozens of bicycle tours around rural France. Hiking and cycling trails are likewise marked on IGN's *Sologne* map in its Plein-Air series, ideal if you intend exploring the Domaine National de Chambord in any depth. Another handy IGN title is *Jardins de France* (No 917), which pinpoints France's most fabulous gardens, many of which are in the Loire.

Nautical Maps Waterway maps are sold at the Île d'Yeu branch store of Librarie Nautique St-Nicolas (☎ 05 46 50 20 92, in La Rochelle), a nautical bookshop. On-line, try www.shom.fr.

IGN's *France Tourisme Fluvial* (No 913, 29FF) highlights navigable rivers and canals in the region. Its *France: Canoë-Kayak et Sports d'Eau Vive* (No 905, 29FF) is useful for water-sports enthusiasts wanting to ply the River Loire by oar power.

Navicarte maps and guides published by Éditions Grafocarte are the best investment for serious boaties. The chartbooks detail the canals and navigable rivers in the region, marking locks and where you can buy food supplies or make boat repairs and so on. No 13 charts *Les Rivières des Pays de la Loire* (including the Bassin de la Maine and the Rivers Loire and Erdre), and No 12 covers *Bretagne* (including northbound waterways from Nantes). Seafaring maps include *Le Croisic-Nantes-Pornic-l'Herbaudière* (No 547) and *Pornic-Île de Noirmoutier, Île d'Yeu, St-Gilles Croix de Vie* (No 549). Navicarte maps cost 135FF and are available from Éditions Grafocarte (☎ 01 41 09 19 00, fax 01 41 09 19 22), 125 rue Jean Jacques Rousseau, BP 40, 92132 Issy-les-Moulineaux.

Another French waterways series is Guides Vagnon, published by Éditions du Plaisancier. Titles include *Bretagne et Loire-Atlantique* (115FF) and *Pays de Loire et Cher* (99FF).

City Maps City maps are easily found within France at the large newsagencies (*maisons de la presse*) in most towns and cities, stationery shops (*papeteries*), tourist offices, travel bookshops and many mainstream bookshops. The free street maps (*plans*) distributed by tourist offices range from the superb to the useless.

Michelin's *Guide Rouge* (Red Guide; see Food & Wine under Books later in this chapter) series includes maps for larger cities, towns and resorts that show one-way streets and have numbered town entry points that are coordinated with Michelin's yellow-jacketed 1:200,000 road maps.

Kümmerly+Frey's Blay-Foldex Plans-Guides series covers Orléans, Blois, Tours, Saumur, Angers, Nantes and St-Nazaire. The orange-jacketed street maps cost 19FF to 31FF and are sold on-line (www.geoshop.com/Blayfoldex). Éditions Grafocarte (see Nautical Maps) also publishes city maps under its Plan Guide Bleu & Or series; it covers Orléans, Blois, Tours, Angers, Nantes and St-Nazaire-La Baule.

What to Bring

Bring as little as possible: forgotten items can be picked up practically anywhere in the region. If you intend travelling around or doing any walking with your gear – even from the train station to your hotel – opt for a backpack. The type with an exterior pouch that zips off to become a daypack is most useful.

Hostellers have to provide their own towel and soap. Bedding is almost always provided or available for hire; sheets cost around 17FF per night. Bring a padlock to secure your backpack by day and your storage locker (provided by most hostels) at night.

Other handy little numbers include a torch (flashlight), Swiss army knife, adapter plug for electrical appliances, universal bath/sink plug (a plastic film canister sometimes works) and several clothes pegs.

In July and August include a water bottle and pre-moistened towelettes. Beach-bound travellers should not forget sunglasses, sun block and after-sun cream. A warm sweater can be useful on early- and late-summer evenings, as can a waterproof garment to protect against spring and autumn showers.

Those heading into the wetlands of the Marais Poitevin, Parc Naturel Régional de Brière or Presqu'île du Guérande need a pair of binoculars and an excess of mosquito repellent. Binoculars are also invaluable for anyone intending to bird-watch on the banks of the Loire or visit Chambord during the rutting season.

RESPONSIBLE TOURISM

When touring the region's chateaux, never ever graffiti your name on the soft stone walls. Respect signs telling you not to walk on the grass (*pelouse interdite*), picnic (*pique-nique interdit*), scale a staircase or enter private property (*propriété privée*). In some chateaux, be prepared to don soft slippers to flop along polished floors. Flash photography is forbidden in some chateau interiors.

Rules of the forest include sticking to marked tracks and paths, not littering, not camping, not smoking, not picking flowers or disturbing bird nests, and not lighting camp fires. See also Dos & Don'ts under Society & Conduct in the Facts about the Loire chapter.

TOURIST OFFICES
Local Tourist Offices

Every city, town, village and hamlet has an *office du tourisme* (tourist office run by one of the units of local government) or a *syndicat d'initiative* (tourist office run by an organisation of local merchants). Both are

an excellent resource and can almost always provide a local map and information on accommodation possibilities. Some change foreign currency. Many make local hotel reservations.

Tourist information for the *régions* is available from the *comités régionaux du tourisme* (regional tourist boards) listed below. For information about the Poitou-Charentes région contact the Maison Poitou-Charentes in Paris.

Centre (☎ 02 38 70 32 74, fax 02 38 70 33 80, @ crtl.centre@wanadoo.fr) 9 rue St-Pierre Lentin, 45041 Orléans
Web sites: www.loirevalleytourism.com, www.regioncentre.com
Pays de la Loire (☎ 02 40 48 24 20, fax 02 40 08 07 10, @ crt.promo@wanadoo.fr) 2 rue de la Loire, 44204 Nantes
Poitou-Charentes (☎ 01 42 22 83 74, fax 01 45 49 18 84) 68–70 rue du Cherche-Midi, 75006 Paris

Within each région, there are *comités départementaux du tourisme* (departmental tourist offices):

Deux-Sèvres (☎ 05 49 77 19 70, fax 05 49 24 90 29, @ tourisme.2.sevres@wanadoo.fr) 15 rue Thiers, BP 8510, 79025 Niort
Indre-et-Loire (☎ 02 47 31 47 48, 02 47 31 42 52, fax 02 47 31 42 76, @ tourisme.touraine@wanadoo.fr) 9 rue de Buffon, 37032 Tours
Web site: www.tourism-touraine.com
Loire-Atlantique (☎ 02 51 72 95 30, fax 02 40 20 44 54, @ info@cdt44.com) 2 allée Baco, 45005 Nantes
Web site: www.cdt44.com
Loiret (☎ 02 38 78 04 04, fax 02 38 78 04 12, @ tourisme.loiret@wanadoo.fr) 8 rue d'Escures, 45000 Orléans
Web sites: www.loiret.com, www.tourismloiret.com
Loir-et-Cher (☎ 02 54 78 55 50, fax 02 54 74 81 79, @ tourisme.41@wanadoo.fr) 5 rue de la Voûte du Château, 41005 Blois
Web site: www.chambordcountry.com
Maine-et-Loire (☎ 02 41 23 51 51, fax 02 41 88 36 77, @ anjou.cdt@wanadoo.fr) 11 place du Président Kennedy, 49021 Angers
Sarthe (☎ 02 43 40 22 50, fax 02 43 40 22 51) 40 rue Joinville, 72000 Le Mans
Vendée (☎ 02 51 47 88 20, fax 02 51 05 37 01) 8 place Napoléon, 85006 La Roche-sur-Yon

euro currency converter   10FF = €1.52

Vienne (☎ 05 49 37 48 48, fax 05 49 37 48 49,
✉ cdt@vienne.org) 15–17 rue Carnot, 86007
Poitiers
Web site: www.vienne.org

French Tourist Offices Abroad

Australia (☎ 02-9231 5244, fax 9221 8682,
✉ ifrance@internetezy.com.au, frencht@
ozemail.com.au) 22nd Floor, 25 Bligh St,
Sydney, NSW 2000

Belgium (☎ 02-513 32 14, fax 514 33 75,
✉ maisondelafrance@pophost.eunet.be) 21
ave de la Toison d'Or, 1050 Brussels

Canada (☎ 514-288 4264, fax 845 4868,
✉ mfrance@mtl.net) Suite 490, 1981 ave
McGill College, Montreal, Que H3A 2W9

Germany (☎ 069-580 131, fax 745 556,
✉ maison_de_la_France@t-online.de)
Westendstrasse 47, D-60325 Frankfurt
Web site: www.maison-de-la-france.com

Ireland (☎ 01-679 0813, fax 679 0814,
✉ frenchtouristoffice@tinet.ie) 10 Suffolk St,
Dublin 2

Italy (☎ 02 584 86 57, fax 02 584 86 222,
✉ info@turismofrancese.it) Via Larga 7,
20122 Milan
Web site: www.turismofrancese.it

Netherlands (☎ 0900 112 2332, 020-638 3883,
fax 620 3339, ✉ informatie@fransverkeers
bureau.nl) Prinsengracht 670, NL-1017 KX
Amsterdam
Web site: www.fransverkeersbureau.nl

Spain (☎ 91 548 97 40, fax 91 541 24 12,
✉ mad@maisondelafrance.es) Gran Via 59,
28013 Madrid
Web site: www.maisondelafrance.es

Switzerland (☎ 01-211 3085, fax 212 1644,
✉ tourismefrance@bluewin.ch) Löwenstrasse
59, CH-8023 Zürich
Web site: www.doucefrance.ch

UK (☎ 0891 244 123, 020-7399 3500, fax 7493
6594, ✉ piccadilly@mdlf.demon.co.uk) 178
Piccadilly, London W1V 0AL
Web site: www.franceguide.com

USA (☎ 212-838 7800, fax 838 7855,
✉ info@francetourism.com) 16th Floor, 444
Madison Ave, New York, NY 10022
Web site: www.francetourism.com

VISAS & DOCUMENTS
Passport

Your most important travel document is
your passport, which should be valid for
three months beyond the date of your departure from France. Applying for or re-

newing your passport can take anything
from a few days to several months, so don't
leave it until the last minute. First check
what is required: passport photos, birth certificate, exact payment in cash and so on.

By law, everyone in France, including
tourists, must carry ID on them at all times.
For foreign visitors, this means a passport
or national ID card.

Visas

Tourist France is one of the 15 countries
that have signed the Schengen Convention,
an agreement whereby all European Union
(EU) member countries (except the UK and
Ireland) plus Iceland and Norway have
agreed to abolish checks at common borders by the end of 2000. The other EU
countries involved are Austria, Belgium,
Denmark, Finland, Germany, Greece, Italy,
Luxembourg, the Netherlands, Portugal,
Spain and Sweden. Legal residents of one
Schengen country do not require a visa for
another Schengen country. Citizens of the
UK and Ireland are also exempt from visa
requirements for Schengen countries. In addition, nationals of a number of other countries, including Canada, Japan, New
Zealand and Switzerland, do not require
visas for tourist visits of up to 90 days to
any Schengen country.

In practice, however, it is not recommended to travel without a passport, as sig-
natories reserve the right to implement both
temporary and more permanent border controls (your passport is also necessary as a
form of ID in France; see the previous passport section for details). The French government has chosen to exercise this right
and passport controls at its borders with
Belgium and Luxembourg are still in place
(the differing drug laws made France ner-
vous about removing border controls).

Individual Schengen countries may also
impose additional restrictions on certain
nationalities. It is, therefore, worth checking visa regulations with the consulate of
each country you plan to visit. For up-to-
the-minute information, call the EU information office in Brussels on ☎ 02-295
1780.

The standard tourist visa issued by French consulates is the Schengen visa. To obtain a visa you must present your passport, air or other tickets in and out of France, proof of finances and possibly accommodation, two passport-size photos and the visa fee in cash. A 30-day tourist visa generally costs around US$31, while a three-month single/multiple-entry visa is US$37/44. Visas are usually issued on the spot.

Rules for obtaining Schengen visas have been tightened and it's now mandatory that you apply in your country of residence. You can apply for no more than two Schengen visas in any 12-month period and they are not renewable inside France. If you are going to visit more than one Schengen country you are supposed to apply for the visa at a consulate of your main destination country or, if you have no main destination, the first country you intend to visit. It's worth applying early for your visa, especially in the busy summer months.

Tourist visas cannot be extended except in emergencies (such as medical problems). If you have an urgent problem, you should first consult your own nearest consular office in France or call the nearest *préfecture* (see Carte de Séjour later in this section).

Long-Stay, Student & Au Pair If you'd like to work or study in France or stay for over three months, apply to the French embassy or consulate for the appropriate sort of *séjour* (long-stay) visa. Unless you are an EU citizen, it is difficult to get a séjour allowing you to work in France. People with student visas can apply for permission to work part-time (inquire at your place of study).

Au pair visas likewise have to be arranged before leaving home (unless you're an EU citizen).

Carte de Séjour If you intend to stay in France for longer than three months, you'll have to apply for a *carte de séjour* (residence permit) within eight days of arrival in France. For details, inquire at your place of study or the local prefecture (*préfecture*), sub-prefecture (*sous-préfecture*), city hall (*hôtel de ville*), town hall (*mairie*) or police station (*commissariat de police*). The prefectures in Orléans (☎ 02 38 81 40 00) and Tours (☎ 02 47 60 46 15) issue cartes de séjour.

Travel Insurance
Travel insurance covers you for medical expenses (EU citizens holding an E111 form do not need to pay for medical insurance; see Health Insurance under Health later in this chapter) and luggage theft or loss, as well as for cancellation or delays in your travel arrangements. Cover depends on your insurance and sometimes on your type of airline ticket, so be sure to ask your insurer and ticket-issuing agency where you stand.

Driving Licence & Permits
A driving licence from an EU country is treated as a French one. Most non-EU driving licences are valid in France, but it's still a good idea to bring along an International Driving Permit. This is a multilingual translation of the vehicle class and personal details noted on your local driving licence and is not valid unless accompanied by your licence. An IDP can be obtained for a small fee from your local automobile association.

Hostel Card
A Hostelling International (HI) card is necessary only at official *auberges de jeunesse* (youth hostels). You can become a member by joining your national Youth Hostel Association (YHA). For details, look at HI's Web site at www.iyhf.org. Alternatively, you can buy a card at most official French hostels for 70/100FF if you're aged under/over 26. One-night membership (where available) costs between 10FF and 19FF; a family card costs 100FF.

Student, Youth, Teachers & Journalists Cards
An International Student Identity Card (ISIC; www.istc.org) can pay for itself through half-price admissions, discounted air and ferry tickets, and cheap meals in student cafeterias. Many stockists (which are generally student travel agencies) stipulate a maximum age, usually 24 or 25. In France, ISIC cards

(60FF) are issued by student travel agencies such as Accueil des Jeunes en France (AJF).

If you're aged under 26 but are not a student you can apply for a GO25 card (60FF), issued by the Federation of International Youth Travel Organisations (FIYTO), which entitles you to much the same discounts as an ISIC. It is also issued by student unions or student travel agencies.

A Carte Jeunes (120FF; www.cartejeunes .fr) is available to anyone aged under 26 who has been in France for six months. It gets you discount air tickets, car rental, sports events, concerts, movies and so on. In France, call ☎ 08 03 00 12 26. Teachers, professional artists, museum conservators, journalists and certain categories of students are admitted to some museums free of charge. Bring along proof of affiliation, such as an International Teacher Identity Card (ITIC).

Seniors Card

Reductions are available for people aged over 60 at most cultural centres, including chateaux, museums, galleries and public theatres. You may be asked to show proof of age. The Societé Nationale des Chemins de Fer (SNCF) has an annual Carte Senior (285FF) for those aged 60 and over. It gives reductions of 25, 30 or 50% on train tickets.

Camping Card International

The Camping Card International (CCI) is a camp site ID that can be used instead of a passport when checking into camp sites and includes third-party insurance for damage you may cause. As a result, many camp sites offer a small discount if you sign in with one. CCIs are issued by automobile associations, camping federations and, sometimes, on the spot at camping grounds. In the UK, the AA (☎ 0870 5500 600) issues them to its members for UK£4.

La Clé des Temps

La Clé des Temps costs 130FF and gives 'key holders' 10 entrances to a choice of 15 national monuments in the Loire region. Passes are valid for one year and are not restricted to one key holder: the 10 entrances can be shared between several people.

Passes are sold at participating monuments (including the chateaux in Angers, Chambord, Chaumont and Azay-le-Rideau, plus the Abbaye de Fontevraud in Anjou) and the FNAC stores in Orléans and Nantes. Further information is available from the Caisse Nationale des Monuments Historiques et des Sites (☎ 01 44 61 21 50), Hôtel de Sully, 62 rue St-Antoine, 75186 Paris. Also have a look at the Web site at www.monuments-france.fr.

Billets Jumelés

Several museums and monuments sell combination tickets which include admission to more than one sight and can offer a considerable saving. Some chateaux – including Azay-le-Rideau, Blois and Chambord – offer a *billet jumelé* that entitles the ticket holder to visit the chateau during the day and return in the evening to attend the son et lumière.

In Indre-et-Loire, the Billet des Maisons des Écrivains covers admission to three writers' houses in the *département* (department). It is sold at the participating monuments: Prieuré de St-Cosme outside Tours, Château de Saché, or the Maison de la Devinière in Seuilly.

Several cities (such as Angers and Tours) have a museum pass which cuts the cost of visiting sights in the city. Details are listed in the respective city chapters.

Copies

All important documents (passport data page and visa page, credit cards, travel insurance policy, air/bus/train tickets, driving licence etc) should be photocopied before you leave home. Leave one copy with someone at home and keep another with you, separate from the originals.

There is another option for storing details of your vital travel documents before you leave – Lonely Planet's on-line Travel Vault. Keeping details of your documents here is safer than carrying photocopies. It's a good option if you're travelling in a country such as France with easy Internet access. You can create your own Travel Vault for free at www.ekno.lonelyplanet.com.

EMBASSIES & CONSULATES
French Embassies & Consulates

France's diplomatic and consular representatives abroad include:

Australia
Embassy: (☎ 02-6216 0100, fax 6216 0127) 6 Perth Ave, Yarralumla, ACT 2600
Consulate: (☎ 03-9820 0944, fax 9820 9363) Level 4, 492 St Kilda Rd, Melbourne, VIC 3004
Consulate: (☎ 02-9262 5779, fax 9283 1210) 20th Floor, St Martin's Tower, 31 Market St, Sydney, NSW 2000
Web site: www.france.net.au

Belgium
Embassy: (☎ 02-548 8711, fax 513 6871) 65 rue Ducale, B-1000 Brussels
Consulate: (☎ 02-229 8500, fax 229 8510) 12a place de Louvain, B-1000 Brussels
Web sites: www.ambafrance.be, www.consulfrance-bruxelles.be

Canada
Embassy: (☎ 613-789 1795, fax 562 3704) 42 Sussex Drive, Ottawa, Ont K1M 2C9
Consulate: (☎ 514-878 4385, fax 878 3981, ✆ fsltmral@cam.org) Bureau 2601, 26th Floor, 1 place Ville Marie, Montreal, Que H3B 4S3
Consulate: (☎ 416-925 8041, fax 925 3076, ✆ fsltto@idirect.com) Suite 400, 130 Bloor St West, Toronto, Ont M5S 1N5
Consulate: (☎ 604-681 4345, fax 681 4287, ✆ consulat_france_bc@mindlink.bc.ca) Suite 1100, 1130 West Pender St, Vancouver, BC V6E 4A4

Germany
Embassy: (☎ 030-206 390 00, fax 206 390 10) Kochstrasse 6–7, D-10969 Berlin
Consulate: (☎ 030-885 902 43, fax 885 5295) Kurfürstendamm 211, 10719 Berlin
Consulate: (☎ 089-419 4110, fax 419 411 41) Möhlstrasse 5d, D-81675 München
Web sites: www.botschaft-frankreich.de, www.consulfrance-munich.de
Other consulates are in Düsseldorf, Frankfurt, Hamburg and Stuttgart.

Ireland
Embassy: (☎ 01-260 1666, fax 283 0178, ✆ consul@ambafrance.ie) 36 Ailesbury Rd, Ballsbridge, Dublin 4
Web site: www.ambafrance.ie

Italy
Embassy: (☎ 06 68 60 11, fax 06 686 01 360, ✆ france-italia@france-italia.it) Piazza Farnese 67, 00186 Rome
Consulate: (☎ 06 688 06 437, fax 06 686 01 260) Via Giulia 251, 00186 Rome
Web site: www.france-italia.it
Other consulates are in Florence, Milan, Naples and Turin.

Netherlands
Embassy: (☎ 070-312 5800, fax 312 5854) Smidsplein 1, NL-2514 BT Den Haag
Consulate: (☎ 020-530 6969, fax 530 6988) Vijzelgracht 1, NL-1017 HA Amsterdam
Web sites: www.ambafrance.nl, www.consulfrance.nl

New Zealand
Embassy: (☎ 04-384 2555, fax 384 2577) 34–42 Manners St, Wellington

Spain
Embassy: (☎ 91 423 8900, fax 91 423 8901) Calle de Salustiano Olozaga 9, 28001 Madrid
Consulate: (☎ 91 700 7800, fax 91 700 7801) Calle Marques de la Enseñada 10, E-28004 Madrid
Consulate: (☎ 93 270 3000, fax 93 270 0349) Ronda Universitat 22b, E-08007 Barcelona
Web site: www.ambafrance.es
Other consulates are in Alicante, Bilbao, Malaga and Seville.

Switzerland
Embassy: (☎ 031-359 2111, fax 352 2192, ✆ ambassade@iprolink.ch) Schosshaldenstrasse 46, 3006 Bern
Consulate: (☎ 022-310 0000, fax 319 0072) 11 rue Imbert Galloix, 1205 Geneva
Consulate: (☎ 01-268 8585, fax 268 8500) Mühlebachstrasse 7, 8008 Zürich
Web site: www.consulat-france-zurich.ch
Other consulates are in Lausanne and Bale.

UK
Embassy: (☎ 020-7201 1000, fax 7201 1004, ✆ tourisme@ambafrance.org.uk) 58 Knightsbridge, London SW1X 7JT
Consulate: (☎ 020-7838 2000, fax 7838 2001) 21 Cromwell Rd, London SW7 2DQ
Visa Section: (☎ 020-7838 2051, 0891 887 733 for general visa information, fax 7838 2001) 6a Cromwell Place, London SW7 2EW
Web site: www.ambafrance.org.uk

USA
Embassy & Consulate: (embassy ☎ 202-944 6000, fax 944 6166; consulate ☎ 202-944 6195, fax 944 6148, ✆ visas-washington@amb-wash.fr) 4101 Reservoir Rd NW, Washington, DC 20007
Consulate: (☎ 212-606 3600, fax 606 3620, ✆ info@franceconsulatny.org) 934 Fifth Ave, New York, NY 10021
Consulate: (☎ 415-397 4330, fax 433 8357, ✆ cgsfo@best.com) 540 Bush St, San Francisco, CA 94108

Web sites: info-france-usa.org, www.france-consulat.org, www.franceconsulatny.org
Other consulates are in Atlanta, Boston, Chicago, Houston, Los Angeles, Miami and New Orleans.

Embassies & Consulates in France

It's important to realise what your own embassy – the embassy of the country of which you are a citizen – can and can't do to help you if you get into trouble. Generally speaking, it won't be much help in emergencies if the trouble you're in is remotely your own fault. Remember that you are bound by the laws of the country you are in. Your embassy will not be sympathetic if you end up in jail after committing a crime locally, even if such actions are legal in your own country.

In genuine emergencies you might get some assistance, but only if other channels have been exhausted. For example, if you need to get home urgently, a free ticket is exceedingly unlikely – the embassy would expect you to have insurance. If you have all your money and documents stolen, it might assist with getting a new passport, but a loan for onward travel is out of the question.

There are no consulates in the Loire. The nearest foreign representations are in Paris:

Australia (☎ 01 40 59 33 00) 4 rue Jean Rey, 15e, Paris. The consular section, which handles all matters concerning Australian nationals, opens 9.15 am to noon and 2 to 4.30 pm on weekdays.
Belgium (☎ 01 44 09 39 39) 9 rue de Tilsitt, 17e, Paris
Canada (☎ 01 44 43 29 00) 35 ave Montaigne, 8e, Paris. The consular section, which handles matters concerning Canadian nationals, opens 9.30 to 11 am and 2 to 4.30 pm on weekdays.
Germany (☎ 01 53 83 45 00) 13–15 ave Franklin D Roosevelt, 8e, Paris
Ireland (☎ 01 44 17 67 00 for 9.30 am to 1 pm and 2.30 to 5.30 pm on weekdays, 01 44 17 67 67 for after-hours emergencies) 4 rue Rude, 16e, Paris. Opens 9.30 am to noon on weekdays (or by appointment).
Italy (☎ 01 49 54 03 00) 51 rue de Varenne, 7e, Paris
New Zealand (☎ 01 45 00 24 11 for 24-hour voicemail and emergencies) 7ter rue Léonard de Vinci, 16e, Paris. Opens 9 am to 1 pm for routine matters and 2 to 5.30 pm for emergencies, on weekdays.
Spain (☎ 01 44 43 18 00) 22 ave Marceau, 8e, Paris
Switzerland (☎ 01 49 55 67 00) 142 rue de Grenelle, 7e, Paris
UK (☎ 01 44 51 31 02, 01 42 66 29 79 for emergencies 24 hours) 18 rue d'Anjou, 8e, Paris. Opens 9.30 am to 12.30 pm and 2.30 to 5 pm on weekdays (except public holidays).
USA (☎ 01 43 12 22 22) 2 ave Gabriel, 8e, Paris. Opens 9 am to 3 pm on weekdays (except French and US holidays).

CUSTOMS

The usual allowances apply to duty-free goods purchased at airports or on ferries outside the EU: tobacco (200 cigarettes, 50 cigars or 250g of loose tobacco), alcohol (1L of strong liquor or 2L of less than 22% alcohol by volume; 2L of wine), coffee (500g or 200g of extracts) and perfume (50g of perfume and 0.25L of toilet water).

Do not confuse these with duty-paid items (including alcohol and tobacco) bought at normal shops and supermarkets in another EU country and brought into France, where certain goods might be more expensive. In that case, the allowances are more than generous: 800 cigarettes, 200 cigars or 1kg of loose tobacco; 10L of spirits (more than 22% alcohol by volume), 20L of fortified wine or aperitif, 90L of wine or 110L of beer.

MONEY
Currency

The French franc (FF) remains the national currency in France until January 2002, when it will be exchanged for the euro (€). See the boxed text 'Euroland' for more euro details.

One franc is divided into 100 centîmes. French coins come in denominations of 5, 10, 20 and 50 centîmes and 1FF, 2FF, 5FF, 10FF and 20FF; the two highest denominations have silvery centres and brass edges. French franc banknotes are issued in denominations of 20FF, 50FF, 100FF, 200FF and the less common 500FF.

Exchange Rates

The Universal Currency Converter gives the latest currency exchange rates on-line at

Euroland

Since 1 January 1999, the franc and the euro – the new currency for 11 European Union (EU) countries – have both been legal tender in France. Euro coins and banknotes have not been issued yet, but you can already be billed in euros and opt to pay in euros by credit card. Essentially, if there's no hard cash involved, you can deal in euros. Travellers should check bills carefully to make sure that any conversion has been calculated correctly (see the currency converter at the bottom of the page).

The whole idea behind this paperless currency is to give euro-fearing punters a chance to limber up arithmetically before euro coins and banknotes are issued on 1 January 2002. The same euro coins (one to 50 cents, €1 and €2) and bridge-adorned bills (€5 to €500) can be used happily in Euroland's 11 countries: Austria, Belgium, Finland, France, Germany, Ireland, Italy, Luxembourg, the Netherlands, Portugal and Spain. The French franc will remain legal tender alongside the euro until 1 July 2002, when the franc will be hurled on the scrapheap of history. Luckily, the euro should make everything easier. One of the main benefits will be that prices in the 11 participating countries will be immediately comparable.

Until then, one euro is A$13.7, BF40.3, 5.95 mk, 6.56FF, DM1.96, IR£0.79, L1936, flux40.34, f2.2, 200$00 and 166.4 ptas. You can log into Euroland on the Internet at europa.eu.int/euro/html/entry.html. The Lonely Planet Web site at www.lonelyplanet.com has a link to a currency converter and up-to-date news on the integration process.

The geographic centre of Euroland is allegedly in the Loire Valley (see the boxed text 'Euroland's Centre' in the Orléanais & Blésois chapter).

---

www.xe.net/ucc. At the time of going to press, some exchange rates were:

country	unit	€	FF
Australia	A$1	0.64	4.18
Canada	C$1	0.70	4.59
euro	€1	—	6.56
Germany	DM1	0.51	3.35
Japan	¥100	0.92	6.00
New Zealand	NZ$1	0.50	3.26
UK	UK£1	1.63	10.70
USA	US$1	1.02	6.66

Exchanging Money

France's central bank, Banque de France, can offer the best exchange rates. It does not accept Eurocheques or provide credit card cash advances. Most branches do not accept old US$100 notes due to the preponderance of counterfeits. Many branches, despite being open all day, only offer foreign currency exchange services for two or three hours in the morning.

Commercial banks usually charge between 22FF and 50FF per foreign currency transaction. The rates offered vary, so it pays to compare.

Many post offices change money for a middling rate and charge 2% commission (minimum charge 20FF). The commission for travellers cheques is 1.5% (minimum charge 25FF). Most accept cheques issued by American Express (Amex; in US dollars or French francs) or Visa (in French francs).

In cities such as Nantes and Orléans, bureaux de change are faster, easier, open longer hours and give better rates than the banks. When using bureaux de change, shop around. Familiarise yourself with rates offered by banks and compare them with those offered at bureaux (which are generally not allowed to charge commission). On relatively small transactions, even exchange bureaux with less than optimal rates may leave you with more francs in your pocket.

Cash Cash is not a safe way to carry money. The Banque de France pays about 2.5% more for travellers cheques than for cash, easily compensating for the 1% commission usually involved in buying them. Bring the equivalent of about US$100 in French francs in low-denomination notes for when you first arrive.

euro currency converter 10FF = €1.52

Travellers Cheques & Eurocheques Except at bureaux de change and the Banque de France, you have to pay to cash travellers cheques: at banks, expect a charge of 22FF to 30FF per transaction. A percentage fee may apply for large sums. Amex offices do not charge commission for their own travellers cheques, but holders of other brands must pay 3% on top (minimum charge 40FF) at Amex offices. Travellers cheques issued by Amex and Visa offer the greatest flexibility.

Eurocheques, available if you have a European bank account, are guaranteed up to a certain limit. When cashing them (at post offices or banks), you will be asked to show your Eurocheque card bearing your signature and registration number, and perhaps a passport or ID card. Many hotels and traders refuse to accept Eurocheques because of the relatively large commissions.

If travellers cheques issued by Amex are lost or stolen in France, call ☎ 08 00 90 86 00. For reimbursements, you have to go to the Amex offices in Paris (☎ 01 47 77 77 07), 11 rue Scribe (metro Auber or Opéra).

If you lose your Thomas Cook cheques, contact any Thomas Cook bureau; again, the nearest bureaux are in Paris. The company's customer service bureau can be contacted toll free on ☎ 08 00 90 83 30.

ATMs In French, ATMs (automatic teller machines) are called *distributeurs automatiques de billets* or *points d'argent*. ATM cards can give you direct access to your cash reserves back home at a superior exchange rate. Most ATMs give a cash advance through Visa or MasterCard. There are plenty of ATMs in the region linked to the international Cirrus and Maestro networks.

If you remember your PIN code as a string of letters, translate it back into numbers, as keyboards may not show letters.

Credit Cards This is the cheapest way to pay for things and to get cash advances. Visa (Carte Bleue) is the most widely accepted, followed by MasterCard (Access or Eurocard). Amex cards are not very useful except at upmarket establishments, but they

do allow you to get cash at certain ATMs. Taking along two different credit cards (stashed in different wallets) is safer than taking one.

If your Visa card is lost or stolen, call Carte Bleue (☎ 02 54 42 12 12). To replace a lost card you have to deal with the issuer.

Report a lost MasterCard, Access or Eurocard to Eurocard France (☎ 01 45 67 53 53) and, if you can, to your credit card issuer back home. For cards from the USA, call ☎ 001-314-275 6690.

If your Amex card is lost or stolen, call ☎ 01 47 77 70 00 or ☎ 01 47 77 72 00. In an emergency, Amex card-holders from the USA can call collect ☎ 202-783 7474 or ☎ 202-677 2442. Replacements can be arranged at any Amex office (the nearest office is in Paris). Report a lost Diners Club card on ☎ 01 47 62 75 75.

International Transfers Telegraphic transfers are not very expensive, but can be quite slow. It's quicker and easier to have money wired via Amex. Western Union's Money Transfer system (☎ 01 43 54 46 12) is available at most post offices.

Costs

Its promixity to Paris coupled with hefty chateau entrance fees makes travelling around the Loire an expensive business, but careful planning can save the odd centîme. Draw up a rough agenda of which sights you want to see, bearing in mind that entrance to three of the major chateaux is covered by La Clé des Temps (see Visas & Documents earlier in this chapter).

If you stay in a camp site, hostel or showerless/toiletless room in a budget hotel and have picnics rather than dining out, it's possible to travel around the region for about US$40 per day per person. You then need to add 23FF to 35FF to cover the entrance fee for each chateau you intend to visit; Château d'Ussé is the dearest in the region at 59FF per person.

Travelling with someone else cuts costs: few hotels in the region offer single rooms. Those that do charge the same price (or only marginally less) for singles as for doubles.

Triples and quads (often with only two beds) are the cheapest per person and can offer an amazing price/comfort ratio. Consider staying in one of the cities – Orléans, Tours, Nantes and so on – where accommodation is cheaper, and from where day trips can easily be made along the valley.

Dining-wise, hearty picnics of baguette and cheese on the riverbank will reduce costs dramatically. Carrying a water bottle instead of forking out an outrageous 15FF to 25FF for a poxy canned drink is another massive money saver. In restaurants, forget calorie-counting and opt for the *menu* – guaranteed to leave you stuffed and offering far better value than dining a la carte. When it comes to drinks, ask for a jug of tap water (*une carafe d'eau*) instead of bottled water, and order the house wine instead of beer.

Discounts Museums, cinemas, the SNCF, ferry companies and other institutions offer price breaks to those aged under 25 or 26, students with ISIC cards and those aged over 60 or 65. Look for the words *demi-tarif* or *tarif réduit* (half-price or reduced rate) on price charts and ask if you qualify. Those aged under 18 get an even wider range of discounts, including free or reduced entry to most museums.

For information on La Clé des Temps, Billets Jumelés and Billets des Maisons des Écrivains – each offering a cheaper way to visit the sights – see Visas & Documents earlier in this chapter.

A handful of sights (including Château de Saumur) offer family tickets, which can work out cheaper for families comprising two adults and two or more children.

Throughout the region, numerous galleries, museums, gardens and other historic or cultural places which usually demand an entrance fee are free for two days during France's Journées du Patrimoine (Heritage Days) on the second or third weekend in September. Details on what deals are on offer are listed on the Ministry of Culture's Web site at www.culture.fr.

For information on SNCF train passes, see the boxed text 'Train Passes & Discount Fares' in the Getting There & Away chapter.

Tipping

French law requires that restaurant, cafe and hotel bills include the service charge (usually 10–15%), so a tip (*pourboire*) is neither necessary nor expected. However, most people – dire service apart – usually leave a few francs in restaurants.

Taxes & Refunds

France's Value Added Tax (TVA in French) is 20.6% on most goods except food sold in shops, medicine and books, for which it's 5.5%; it goes as high as 33% on such items as watches, cameras and video cassettes. Prices are rarely given without VAT.

If you are not an EU resident, you can get a refund of most of the VAT you pay provided that: you're aged over 15, you'll be spending fewer than six months in France, you purchase goods (not more than 10 of the same item) worth at least 1200FF (tax included) at a single shop and the shop offers duty-free sales (*vente en détaxe*).

Present your passport at the time of purchase and ask for an export sales invoice (*bordereau de détaxe*). Some shops refund 14% of the purchase price on the spot rather than the full 17.1% you are entitled to in order to cover the time and expense involved in the refund procedure. When you leave France or another EU country, ensure that the country's customs officials validate all three pages of the invoice; the green sheet is your receipt.

You will receive a transfer of funds in your home country.

POST & COMMUNICATIONS
Post

Postal services in France are fast (next-day delivery for most domestic letters), reliable and expensive. Post offices are signposted La Poste; older branches may be marked with the letters PTT (Postes, Télégraphes, Téléphones). To mail things, go to a window marked *toutes opérations* (all services).

Postal Rates Domestic letters up to 20g cost 3FF. Postcards and letters up to 20g cost 3FF within the EU, 3.80FF to most of the rest of Europe and Africa, 4.40FF to the

USA, Canada and the Middle East and 5.20FF to Australasia.

Sending & Receiving Mail Most shops that sell postcards sell stamps (*timbres*) too. Stamps bought from coin-operated machines inside post offices come out as an uninspiring, pale-blue printed sticker.

When addressing mail to addresses in France, do it the French way: write the surname or family name in capital letters first, followed by the first name in lower-case letters. Insert a comma after the street number and don't capitalise rue, ave, blvd. 'Cedex' after the city or town name means mail sent to that address is collected at the post office rather than delivered to the door. Poste restante is available at larger post offices.

Telephone

France has one of the most modern and sophisticated telecommunications systems in the world. Most public telephones require a phonecard (*télécarte*), sold at post offices, tobacconists (*tabacs*), supermarket checkout counters and SNCF ticket windows.

French telephone numbers have 10 digits and need no area code. Telephone numbers starting with the digits 06 are mobile-phone numbers. To call anywhere in the Loire region from abroad, dial your country's international access code, followed by 33 (France's country code) and the 10-digit number, dropping the first 0. To call abroad from France, dial 00 (France's international access code), followed by the country code, area code (dropping the initial zero if there is one) and local number.

Collect Calls & Inquiries To make an international reverse-charge (collect) call (*en PCV*), dial 00-33, then the country code of the place you're calling (dial 11 instead of 1 for the USA and Canada). If you're using a public phone, you must insert a phonecard or, in the case of coin telephones, a 1FF coin to place operator-assisted calls through the international operator.

To find out a country code (*indicatif du pays*), call directory inquiries (☎ 12); it costs 2.94/4.50FF from a public/private phone. To find out a subscriber's telephone number abroad, call international directory inquiries (☎ 00-3312 plus relevant country code – dial 11 instead of 1 for the USA and Canada). This service costs 14.70/14.80FF per inquiry from a public/private phone.

Bizarrely, the above services are substantially cheaper if you call from a public phone using a 120-unit phonecard.

International Rates The cheapest time to call home is during reduced-tariff periods – weekday evenings from 7 pm to 8 am (until 1 pm to the USA and Canada), weekends and public holidays. Updated tariffs are published on France Télécom's Web site at www.francetelecom.fr.

A phone call to Europe costs 0.74FF for the first 20-odd seconds, then 1.85FF to 2.25FF per minute; reduced tariffs are 1.45FF to 1.8FF per minute. Calls to continental USA and Canada cost 0.74FF for the first 22 seconds and then 2FF per minute (reduced tariff 1.6FF per minute). To telephone Australia, New Zealand or Japan costs 0.74FF for the first 10 seconds then 4.5FF per minute (reduced tariff 3.60FF per minute). Calls to other parts of Asia, non-Francophone Africa and South America are 0.74FF for the initial 5 to 8 seconds then 5.90FF to 9.40FF per minute (reduced tariffs 4.70FF to 7.50FF per minute).

France Télécom's Ticket de Téléphone (a cheap telephone card available from tobacconists) is handy for those on the move. The Ticket de Téléphone International costs 100FF and, if used exclusively during reduced tariff periods, covers 80 minutes of calls to Europe, the USA and Canada; regular/reduced rates work out at 1.70/1.25FF per minute. An extra 0.35FF per minute is added to calls made from a public phone. To use a ticket, dial 3089 followed by the code written on the reverse side of your card, '#' and the subscriber's number.

Lonely Planet's eKno Communication Card (see the insert at the back of this book) is aimed specifically at independent travellers and provides budget international calls, a range of messaging services, free email and travel information (but for local calls you're usually better off with a local card). You can join on-line at www.ekno .lonelyplanet.com, or by phone from the Loire by dialling ☎ 0800 912 677. Once you have joined, to use eKno from France, dial ☎ 0800 912 066. Check the eKno Web site for joining and access numbers from other countries and updates on super budget local access numbers and new features.

Domestic Tariffs Local calls are quite cheap. The first three minutes costs 0.74FF, followed by 0.28FF per minute during peak *tarif rouge* (red tariff) periods (weekdays from 8 am to 7 pm) and 0.14FF per minute at off-peak times during *tarif bleu* (blue tariff) periods (weekdays from 7 pm to 8 am and at any time at the weekend). National calls cost 0.74FF for the initial 39 seconds, then 1FF per minute in tarif rouge periods and 0.50FF per minute in tarif bleu periods.

Minitel

Minitel is a telephone-connected computerised information service. It's expensive to use and being given a good run for its money by the Internet. Numbers consist of four digits and a string of letters. We have not included Minitel addresses in this book. However, France Télécom has an electronic directory which you can access in some post offices. 3611 is for general address and telephone inquiries. 3615 SNCF and 3615 TER give train information.

Fax

Virtually all town post offices can send and receive domestic and international faxes (*télécopies* or *téléfaxes*), telexes and telegrams. It costs 15/30FF to send an A4 page within France/to Europe.

Email & Internet Access

Travelling with a portable computer is a great way to stay in touch with life back home, but unless you know what you're doing it's fraught with potential problems. If you plan to carry your notebook or palmtop computer with you, remember that the power supply voltage in the countries you

visit may vary from that at home, risking damage to your equipment. The best investment is a universal AC adapter for your appliance, which will enable you to plug it in anywhere without frying the innards. You'll also need a plug adapter for each country you visit – often it's easiest to buy these before you leave home.

Also, your PC-card modem may or may not work once you leave your home country – and you won't know for sure until you try. The safest option is to buy a reputable 'global' modem before you leave home, or buy a local PC-card modem if you're spending an extended time in any one country. Keep in mind that the telephone socket in each country you visit will probably be different from the one at home, so ensure that you have at least a US RJ-11 telephone adapter that works with your modem. You can almost always find an adapter that will convert from RJ-11 to the local variety. For more information on travelling with a portable computer, see www.teleadapt.com or www.warrior.com.

Major Internet service providers such as AOL (www.aol.com), CompuServe (www .compuserve.com) and IBM Net (www .ibm.net) have dial-in nodes throughout Europe; it's best to download a list of the dial-in numbers before you leave home. If you access your Internet email account at home through a smaller ISP or your office or school network, your best option is either to open an account with a global ISP, like those mentioned above, or to rely on Cyberposte (see over the page), cybercafes and other public access points to collect your mail.

If you do intend to rely on cybercafes, you'll need to carry three pieces of information with you to enable you to access your Internet mail account: your incoming (POP or IMAP) mail server name, your account name and your password. Your ISP or network supervisor will be able to give you these. Armed with this information, you should be able to access your Internet mail account from any net-connected machine in the world, provided it runs some kind of email software (remember that Netscape and Internet Explorer both have mail modules). It pays to become familiar with the process for doing this before you leave home. A final option for collecting mail through cybercafes is to open a free eKno Web-based email account on-line at www .ekno.lonelyplanet.com. You can then access your mail from anywhere in the world from any net-connected machine running a standard Web browser.

La Poste operates Internet stations known as Cyberposte (www.cyberposte.com) at numerous post offices countrywide, including at post offices in Blois, Saumur, Angers, Loches and Nantes. A Carte Cyberposte – a rechargeable chip card – costs an initial 50FF, including one hour's on-line access; each hour thereafter costs 30FF. Private mail boxes to receive email messages can be set up at any Cyberposte station.

There are cybercafes where you can send emails and access the Internet in Orléans, Blois, Tours, Angers, Chinon, Nantes and Poitiers. Their addresses are given in the respective chapters. On-line access costs around 60FF per hour.

INTERNET RESOURCES

The World Wide Web is a rich resource for travellers. You can research your trip, hunt down bargain air fares, book hotels, check on weather conditions or chat with locals and other travellers about the best places to visit (or avoid!).

There's no better place to start your Web explorations than the Lonely Planet Web site (www.lonelyplanet.com). Here you'll find succinct summaries on travelling to most places on earth, postcards from other travellers and the Thorn Tree bulletin board, where you can ask questions before you go or dispense advice when you get back. You can also find travel news and updates to many of our most popular guidebooks, and the subWWWay section links you to the most useful travel resources elsewhere on the Web.

Loire-related Web sites are plentiful. Most tourist offices have their own Web site loaded with practical information (listed in the regional chapters). Addresses of numer-

ous other useful sites are embedded in this guide in the relevant sections. In addition, you might want to try:

Loire Valley Online (LVO) Weather, tourism, gastronomy, business and more.
www.loirevalley-online.com
Office National des Forêts (ONF; National Forests Office) Informative environmental facts and figures on the Loire's wealth of forests; sorted by région, with practical information on guided nature walks and so on.
www.onf.fr
Tourism in France Comprehensive Web resource courtesy of the Fédération National des Offices du Tourisme et Syndicats d'Initiative (FNOTSI; National Federation of Tourist Offices).
www.tourisme.fr
University Web Sites The universities of Nantes, Tours, Orléans and Poitiers on-line; crammed with in-depth background information, links and some tourist information.
www.univ-nantes.fr, www.univ-tours.fr,
www.univ-orleans.fr, www.univ-poitiers.fr

BOOKS

Most books are published in different editions by different publishers in different countries. Thus a book might be a hardcover rarity in one country while it's readily available in paperback in another. Fortunately, bookshops and libraries search by title or author, so your local bookshop or library is the best place for advice on the availability of the following recommendations.

Lonely Planet

If you intend to travel more widely in France or venture into the rest of Europe, check out Lonely Planet's *France*, *Western Europe*, *Mediterranean Europe* or *Europe on a shoestring*. You might also want to have a look at *Paris*, *Provence & the Côte d'Azur*, *South-West France* and *Corsica*. There's also the handy *French phrasebook*.

Guidebooks

Michelin, the huge rubber conglomerate which has published travel guides since the earliest days of motorcar touring, covers the region in its *Guide Vert* series. *Châteaux de la Loire* covers the Loire Valley between

Pick your season to visit the Loire: in spring, brilliant red poppies burst into bloom...

..while in summer, sunflowers jostle to catch a few rays.

DIANA MAYFIELD

INGRID RODDIS

SALLY DILLON

SALLY DILLON

CHRISTA LÜFKENS

Whether you're sailing, walking or just lazing, the well-watered valley that Touraine-born author Rabelais called 'le jardin de France' (the garden of France) never disappoints.

Orléans and Nantes, while the south-west of the region falls into its *Poitou Vendée Charentes* guide. In keeping with historical tradition, the cities of Nantes and St-Nazaire and the Presqu'île du Guérande are covered in a separate *Bretagne* guide. All three titles are available in English too. The advantage of Michelin is the mass of historical information. The downside is the perhaps conservative editorial approach.

Within the region, most chateaux have a boutique-cum-bookshop stocking a mind-boggling array of locally published guides. Amid this indiscriminate plethora of guidebooks (most of which cost around 100FF and provide little or no practical information), two series stand out: the Itinéraires des Découvertes series by Éditions Ouest-France and the Itinéraires du Patrimoine series, published by Éditions du Patrimoine. The latter is the publishing house of the Caisse Nationale des Monuments Historiques et des Sites (CNMHS), the body within the Ministry of Culture that is responsible for many heritage sites in France. Its publications are aimed at history buffs and art lovers and some are in English. The entire catalogue is on-line at www.cnmhs.cycnos.fr. The range is also sold at Libraire du Patrimoine (☎ 01 44 61 21 75), Hôtel du Sully, 62 rue St-Antoine, 75004 Paris.

The English Family Guide to the Vendée and Surrounding Area (1997) by Angela Bird is a hands-on, family-oriented guide covering what to see and do. For titles covering walking, canoeing, boating, birdwatching and other activities in the Loire, see Activities later in this chapter.

Travel & Literature

The following list contains fictional and factual outsiders' accounts of the Loire. For suggested works by French writers born and bred in the Loire (Balzac, Fournier, Rabelais and others) see Literature under Arts in the Facts about the Loire chapter.

L'Alouette (*The Lark*) by Breton literary figure Jean Anouilh (1910–87).

Dramatis Personae by Robert Browning (1812–89). A collection of poems inspired by Browning's lengthy stays in Le Croisic and Pornic in the 1860s.

A Little Tour in France by Henry James (1843–1916). Details a tour starting in Tours that the New York-born writer took in October 1882.

A Motor-Flight through France by Edith Wharton. An amusing account of the author's motor trip from Paris to Provence with fellow writer Henry James, journeying along the Rivers Loire and Indre and through the city of Poitiers en route to southern France.

La Pucelle (*The Virgin*) by the socially conscious thinker Verney-Voltaire (1694–1778).

Quatrevingt-Treize (*Ninety-Three*) by Victor Hugo (1802–85). Focuses on the Vendée War of 1793–6.

La Reine Margot (*Queen Margot*) by Alexander Dumas (1802–70). A compelling tale of murder and intrigue in a Renaissance royal French court. The lead character is based on the queen of King Henri IV.

Saint Joan by playwright George Bernard Shaw.

La Terre (*The Earth*) by Émile Zola. La Beauce's flat, agricultural plains are the backdrop for this classic novel in which the economic, political and social woes of a 19th-century rural community are portrayed.

Les Trois Mousquetaires (*The Three Musketeers*) by Alexandre Dumas. This outstanding adventure novel opens in Meung-sur-Loire.

Watersteps through France by Bill & Laurel Cooper. A colourful portrait of the highs and lows of the couple's canal journey through France.

History & Politics

Citizens by Simon Schama. A truly monumental work that examines the first few years after the French Revolution of 1789.

For Altar and Throne: The Rising in the Vendée by Michael Davies. Addresses the Vendée War (1793–6) from a staunchly Catholic viewpoint.

A History of Modern France by Alfred Cobban. A very readable, three-volume history that covers the period from Louis XIV to 1962.

Joan of Arc: By Herself and her Witnesses by Régine Pernoud, English translation by Edward Hyams. Detailed account of the meteoric rise and fall of Joan of Arc (Jeanne d'Arc), conveyed through 15th-century letters, testimonies and trial notes.

Pétain's Crime by Paul Webster. Examines the collaborationist Vichy government, which ruled France during WWII, and the crimes of Pétain, the Vichy leader who is buried on Île d'Yeu.

A Social History of the French Revolution by Christopher Hibbert. A highly readable social account of the period.

The Sun King by Nancy Mitford. A classic work on Louis XIV.

Women of the French Revolution by Linda Kelly. Provides a fascinating account of the French Revolution from a wholly female perspective.

Food & Wine

In the UK, specialist cook-book shop Books for Cooks (☎ 020-7221 1992, fax 7221 1517, ✉ info@booksforcooks.com), 4 Blenheim Crescent, London W11 1NN, stocks a superb range.

Food Lovers' Guide to France by American food critic Patricia Wells.

The Food of France by Waverley Root. Written by a foodie for foodies, this classic describes Tourangeau cuisine as 'pure French cooking in keeping with the pure spoken accent of the Garden of France'.

Guide Gault Millau France. Published annually, this restaurant guide is said to be quicker at spotting up-and-coming restaurants than Michelin's *Guide Rouge*.

Guide Rouge. Published annually by Michelin, this is a great guide to France's mid-range and top-end hotels and restaurants, using the famous starring system.

Hugh Johnson's Atlas of Wine. A solid wine reference.

Loire Gastronomique by Hilaire Walden. A delightful travel cook book, illustrated with stunning photography and enhanced by traditional recipes from the region.

Oxford Companion to Wine by Jancis Robinson (ed). A reliable reference tome with plenty of Loire-related entries.

Saveurs et Terroirs des Pays de Loire: 100 Recettes de Terroir par les Chefs. Published in 1998 by Éditions Philippe Lamboley, this is a superb cook book featuring recipes by local chefs.

The Sparkling Wine Houses of Saumur: Architecture & Skills. Part of the Itinéraires du Patrimoine series; available locally (45FF).

Touring in Wine Country: The Loire by Hugh Johnson (ed). Hubrecht Duijker's listings of chateaux where you can taste and buy wine.

A Wine & Food Guide to the Loire by Jacqueline Friedrich. Reviews of some 600 wine producers, recommended *fromageries* (cheese shops), market listings and insider tips on how to cook

up rustic *rillettes* (minced pork paste) make for a mouth-watering read.

Wines of the Loire by Roger Voss. A detailed account of the history, geography, grapes, appellations and producers of the Loire.

World Food France by Steve Fallon & Sophie Le Mao. A full-colour Lonely Planet guide covering everything to do with the culture of eating and drinking in France.

Art, Architecture & Photography

Artists, movements and decorative trends are covered by several titles in the World of Art series by Thames and Hudson (☎ 020-7636 5488, fax 7636 4799, ✉ sales@thbooks.demon.co.uk), 30–34 Bloomsbury St, London WC1B 3QP. Titles – including *Turner*, *Furniture: A Concise History* and *Art of the Renaissance* – are catalogued on its Web site at www.thesaurus.co.uk/thames andhudson.

Éditions du Patrimoine publishes books about the Loire aimed at art lovers (see Guidebooks earlier in this section).

The Age of the Cathedrals by Georges Duby. An authoritative study of the relationship between art and society in medieval France.

Chateaux of the Loire: Architectural Guides for Travellers by Marcus Binney. A Penguin-published architectural guide to a mind-boggling 50 or so chateaux in the Loire.

The Loire Valley by Jehan Despert, with photographs by Jaroslav Poncar. One of the numerous coffee-table picture albums worth the wallet-crunching investment. Poncar's awe-inspiring panoramic chateau shots were taken using a pre-WWII Russian panoramic lens camera (Lomo) and are breathtaking.

Turner on the Loire by Ian Warrell. This album features 120 black-and-white reproductions and 18 colour plates of works by the English landscape painter Joseph Mallord William Turner (1775–1851), who painted countless scenes of the River Loire.

Environment

Pour une Loire Vivante (*That the Loire might Live*). A novel picture book, published in 1996 by the Fondation des Artistes pour la Nature (Artists for Nature Foundation) and featuring the impressions and experiences of 16 artists who spent part of 1994–5 on the banks of the River Loire. Nuclear power plants, the degeneration of age-old dikes and the defiling of the

Loire estuary are among the environmental issues raised.

Troglodytes in the Saumur Area by Jacek Rewerski. Provides a fascinating glimpse into the Loire Valley's subterranean world.

FILMS

If you'd like to get in the mood for your holiday by watching films that are set in the Loire or use the region as a backdrop, have a look at some of the following. For films made by Loire-born directors, see Cinema under Arts in the Facts about the Loire chapter.

Jean Renoir went to the Loire Valley to film *La Règle du Jeu* (*Rules of the Game*; 1939), perhaps his best film. Set in a chateau and shot at La Ferté St-Aubin in La Sologne, the film exhibited the same poetic realism and strong narrative that stamped most of Renoir's work. *La Règle du Jeu* was promptly banned for its satirical attack on the French bourgeoisie and remained unacclaimed until its re-release in 1956.

In 1967 Jean-Gabriel Albicocco adapted Alain Fournier's novel *Le grand Meaulnes*. Entitled *The Wanderer*, it successfully conveyed the magic and mystery of a chateau in La Sologne. Claude Chabrol, one of the pioneers of *nouvelle vague* (new wave) cinema, used the Loire as a backdrop for several films, including *Les Noces Rouges* (*Red Wedding*; 1973).

The 1970s were kick-started by Jacques Demy's *Peau d'Âne* (*Donkey Skin*; 1971), an adaptation of Charles Perrault's 17th-century fairy tale and starring the incomparable Catherine Deneuve, generally considered one of France's leading actresses. The fantasy, filmed on location at Château du Plessis-Bourré, north of Angers, tells the tale of a widowed king who vows never to remarry until a queen as beautiful as the first is found. The same year, Steve McQueen raced into gear in *Le Mans*, directed by US film-maker Lee Katzin and rated the most powerful evocation of the thrills and scares of the world's only 24-hour motor race.

Parisian-born director Luc Besson made the historical drama *Jeanne d'Arc* (*Joan of Arc*; 1999), mainly shot in the Czech Republic. With a star-studded cast (John Malkovich as Charles VII, Ukrainian model Milla Jovovich as Joan of Arc, Dustin Hoffman and Faye Dunaway) and a budget of US$50 million (modest by Hollywood standards), the film was a guaranteed hit. The only scene to be filmed in the Loire (at Château de Blois) was part of the trial. Besson's is the seventh film to immortalise the 15th-century virginal warrior on the silver screen (see the boxed text 'Joan of Arc' under History in the Facts about the Loire chapter).

Patrice Chéreau's *La Reine Margot* (*Queen Margot*; 1994) is an equally stunning portrayal of historical events. Based on the novel by Alexandre Dumas, the film focuses on the arranged marriage of Marguerite de Valois (played by French actress Isabelle Adjani) and Henri of Navarre (the future Henri IV) in 1572 and the bloody St Bartholomew's Day massacres that ensued. The highly emotive film landed the Jury Prize and Best Actress (for Virna Lisi's portrayal of Catherine de Médicis) at Cannes in 1994, and Best Foreign Language Film and Best Costume Design at the 1995 Academy Awards.

NEWSPAPERS & MAGAZINES

One of the leading regional, daily newspapers is *Ouest France* (www.france-ouest.com), which covers western France and has a separate Nantes edition (4.40FF). *Presse Océan-Sud* and *Vendée Matin Océan* serve the Atlantic coast. In Poitou-Charentes, *Nouvelle République* is the leader in its field, sporting separate Deux-Sèvres and Vienne editions. The *Courrier de l'Ouest* is popular in Orléans.

English-language newspapers – the *International Herald Tribune*, *Washington Post*, *USA Today* and London's *Guardian* or *The Times* – are easy to pick up in Nantes and Orléans, but hellish to find elsewhere.

RADIO

The BBC World Service in English can be picked up on 6195, 9410, 11955, 12095 (a good daytime frequency) and 15575kHz, depending on the time of day.

VIDEO SYSTEMS

SECAM is used in France (unlike the rest of Western Europe and Australia, which use PAL). French videotapes can't be played on video recorders and TVs that lack SECAM capability.

PHOTOGRAPHY & VIDEO

Colour print and slide (*diapositive*) film is widely available in supermarkets, camera shops and FNAC stores, as are replacement video cartridges for your camcorder.

Photography is forbidden inside many chateaux and museums and some art galleries; others charge a camera or camcorder fee. Taking fine panoramic shots of a chateau exterior can be a tad troublesome due to box hedges or trees strategically planted to intersect a potential sweeping view, or due to fine meshing or chicken wire tacked across gates to ensure that even the smallest of cameras cannot sneak in between the iron railings (Château de Cheverny offers a classic example of the latter).

When photographing people, ask permission (basic courtesy). If you don't know any French, smile while pointing at your camera and they'll get the picture – as you probably will.

TIME

French time is GMT/UTC plus one hour, except during daylight-saving time (from the last Sunday in March to the last Sunday in October), when it is GMT/UTC plus two hours. The UK and France are always one hour apart – when it's 6 pm in London, it's 7 pm in Chambord. New York is generally six hours behind France. The Australian eastern coast is between eight and 10 hours ahead of France. France uses the 24-hour clock: 3.30 pm would be written 15h30 or 15:30.

ELECTRICITY

France runs on 220V at 50Hz AC. Old-type wall sockets take two round prongs. New kinds of sockets take fatter prongs and have a protruding earth (ground) prong. Adapters to make new plugs fit into the old sockets are said to be illegal but are available at electrical shops.

WEIGHTS & MEASURES

France uses the metric system. For a conversion table, see the inside back cover of this book. When writing numbers with four or more digits, the French use full stops or spaces (and not commas): one million is 1.000.000 or 1 000 000. Decimals, on the other hand, are written with commas, so 1.75 becomes 1,75.

LAUNDRY

Doing laundry while on the road is a straightforward affair. There is an unstaffed, self-service laundrette (*laverie libre-service*) in most towns.

Count on paying around 22/32/42FF to wash a 7/10/16kg machine load, plus 2/5FF for five/12 minutes of drying.

TOILETS
Public Toilets

Public toilets, signposted *toilettes* or WC, are surprisingly few and far between, meaning you can be left in a very desperate situation. In towns that have public toilets they are generally near the town hall. Expect to pay 2FF to 5FF in exchange for a wad of toilet paper (soft variety). Other towns have coin-operated, self-flushing toilet booths – usually in car parks and public squares – which cost 2FF to enter. Some places sport flushless, kerbside urinals reeking with generations of urine. Failing that, there's always McDonald's or a local cafe.

Most chateaux have a public toilet next to the souvenir shop or boutique. Restaurants, cafes and bars are often woefully underequipped with such amenities, so start queuing ahead of time. Bashful males be warned: some toilets are unisex, with the urinals and washbasins in a common area through which all and sundry pass to get to the closed toilet stalls.

Older establishments often sport *toilettes à la turque* (Turkish-style toilets) – squat toilets with a high-pressure flushing mechanism that can soak your feet if you don't step back in time.

Hall toilets in cheap hotels can be in an impossibly small room, with the nearest washbasin absolutely nowhere to be found.

Bidets

A bidet is a porcelain fixture that looks like a shallow toilet with a pop-up stopper in the base. Originally conceived to improve the personal hygiene of aristocratic women, its primary purpose is for washing the genitals and anal area, though its uses have expanded to include everything from hand-washing laundry to soaking your feet or peeing. Bidets are to be found in many hotel rooms.

HEALTH

The Loire Valley is a healthy place. Your main risks are foot blisters (from touring chateaux), insect bites (in the Marais Poitevin and Parc Naturel Régional de Brière), sunburn (on the Atlantic coast) and an upset stomach from eating and drinking too much (the entire region).

Predeparture Planning

Immunisations No jabs are required to travel to France. However, there are a few routine vaccinations that are recommended whether you're travelling or not: polio (usually administered during childhood and updated every ten years), tetanus and diphtheria (usually administered together during childhood, with a booster shot every 10 years), and sometimes measles.

All vaccinations should be recorded on an International Health Certificate, available from your doctor or government health department.

Health Insurance Make sure you have adequate health insurance if you are not a citizen of an EU country; see Travel Insurance under Visas & Documents earlier in this chapter. Citizens of EU countries are covered for emergency medical treatment throughout the EU on presentation of an E111 certificate, though charges are likely for medication, dental work and secondary examinations, including X-rays and laboratory tests. Ask about the E111 at your national health service or travel agency at least a few weeks before you go. In the UK you can get the forms at post offices. Claims must be submitted to a local *caisse*

primaire d'assurance-maladie (sickness insurance office) before you leave France.

Other Preparations Ensure you're healthy before you start travelling. If you are going on a long trip, make sure your teeth are OK. If you wear glasses take a spare pair and your prescription.

If you require a particular medication take an adequate supply, as it may not be available locally. Take part of the packaging showing the generic name, rather than the brand, which will make getting replacements easier. It's a good idea to have a legible prescription or letter from your doctor to show that you legally use the medication to avoid any problems.

Medical Treatment

Major hospitals are indicated on the maps in this book, and their addresses and phone numbers are given in the text. Tourist offices and hotels can give you the name and number of a doctor or dentist. For emergency phone numbers see Emergencies later in this chapter.

Public Health System Anyone (including foreigners) who is sick can receive treatment in the emergency room of any public hospital. Hospitals try to have people who speak English in casualty wards, but this is not done systematically. If necessary, the hospital will call in an interpreter. It's an excellent idea to ask for a copy of the diagnosis – in English, if possible – for your doctor back home.

Pharmacies French pharmacies are usually marked by a green cross, the neon components of which are lit when it's open. Pharmacists can often suggest treatments for minor ailments.

If you are prescribed medication, make sure you understand the dosage. Ask for a copy of the prescription (*ordonnance*) for your own records. During the mushroom-picking season (autumn), pharmacies act as a mushroom-identifying service.

Pharmacies coordinate their closure so that a town isn't left without a place to buy medication. Details of the nearest pharmacy on weekend/night duty (*pharmacie de garde*) are posted on the door of any pharmacy.

24-Hour Doctor Service If your problem is not sufficiently serious to call SAMU (see Emergencies later in this chapter) but you still need to consult a doctor at night, call the 24-hour doctor service, operational in most towns in the region, including:

Nantes	☎ 04 90 87 75 00
Orléans	☎ 04 93 52 42 42
Tours	☎ 04 42 26 24 00

The hospitals in all three cities also operate a 24-hour emergency service.

Basic Rules
Water Tap water all over France is safe to drink. River water is not drinkable, and nor is the water which spouts out of fountains. *Eau non potable* means 'undrinkable water'.

It's very easy to not drink enough liquids, particularly in summer on hot days. Don't rely on thirst to indicate when you should drink. Not needing to urinate or very dark-yellow urine is a danger sign. Carrying your own water bottle is a good idea.

Environmental Hazards
Fungal Infections Fungal infections occur more commonly in hot weather and are usually found on the scalp, between the toes or fingers, in the groin and on the body (ringworm). You get ringworm (which is a fungal infection, not a worm) from infected animals or other people. Moisture encourages these infections.

To prevent fungal infections wear loose, comfortable clothes, avoid artificial fibres, wash frequently and dry carefully. If you do get an infection, wash the infected area at least daily with a disinfectant or medicated soap and water, and rinse and dry well. Apply an antifungal cream or powder such as tolnifate (Tinaderm). Try to expose the infected area to air or sunlight as much as possible and wash all towels and underwear

in hot water, change them often and let them dry in the sun.

Hay Fever Hay fever sufferers can look forward to sneezing their way around more rural parts of the Loire in May and June, when the pollen count is highest.

Heat Exhaustion Dehydration and salt deficiency can cause heat exhaustion. Take time to acclimatise to the high temperatures, drink sufficient liquids and do not do anything too physically demanding.

Salt deficiency is characterised by fatigue, lethargy, headaches, giddiness and muscle cramps; salt tablets may help, but adding extra salt to your food is better.

Jet Lag Jet lag is experienced when a person travels by air across more than three one-hour time zones. It occurs because many functions of the human body (such as temperature, pulse rate and emptying of the bladder and bowels) are regulated by internal 24-hour cycles called circadian rhythms. When we travel long distances rapidly, our bodies take time to adjust to the 'new time' of our destination, and we may experience fatigue, disorientation, insomnia, anxiety, impaired concentration and loss of appetite.

These effects are usually gone within three days of arrival, but to minimise the impact of jet lag:

- Rest for a couple of days prior to departure
- Try to select flight schedules that minimise sleep deprivation: arriving late in the day means you can sleep soon after you arrive. For long flights, try to organise a stopover
- Avoid excessive eating (which bloats the stomach) and alcohol (which causes dehydration) during the flight. Instead, drink plenty of noncarbonated, nonalcoholic drinks such as fruit juice and water
- Avoid smoking
- To help you sleep on the flight, make yourself comfortable by wearing loose-fitting clothes and perhaps bringing an eye mask and ear plugs
- Try to sleep at the appropriate time for the time zone to which you're travelling

Motion Sickness Eating lightly before and during a trip will reduce the chances of motion sickness. If you are prone to motion sickness, try to find a place that minimises movement – near the wing on aircraft, close to midships on boats, near the centre on buses. Fresh air usually helps; reading and cigarette smoke don't. Commercial motion sickness preparations, which can cause drowsiness, have to be taken before the trip commences. Ginger (available as capsules) and peppermint (including mint-flavoured sweets) are natural preventatives.

Prickly Heat This is an itchy rash caused by excessive perspiration trapped under the skin. It usually strikes people who have just arrived in a warmer climate. Keeping cool, bathing often, drying the skin and using a mild talcum or prickly heat powder, or resorting to air-conditioning may help.

Sunburn On the coast you can get sunburned surprisingly quickly, even through cloud. Use a sunscreen, hat and barrier cream for your nose and lips. Calamine lotion and commercial after-sun preparations are good for mild sunburn. Protect your eyes with good-quality sunglasses, particularly if you will be near water, sand or snow.

Infectious Diseases
Diarrhoea Simple things such as a change of water, food or climate can cause a mild bout of diarrhoea, but a few rushed toilet trips with no other symptoms is not indicative of a major problem.

Dehydration is the main danger with any diarrhoea, particularly in children or the elderly, as it can occur quickly. Fluid replacement (at least equal to the volume being lost) is most important. Weak black tea with a little sugar, soda water, or soft drinks allowed to go flat and diluted 50% with clean water are all good. Keep drinking small amounts often. Stick to a bland diet as you recover.

AIDS & HIV The Human Immuno-deficiency Virus (VIH in French), develops into AIDS, Acquired Immune Deficiency Syndrome (SIDA in French), which is a fatal disease. Any exposure to infected blood, blood products or body fluids may put an individual at risk. The disease is often transmitted through sexual contact or dirty needles – acupuncture, tattooing and body piercing can potentially be as dangerous as intravenous drug use. HIV/AIDS can also be spread through infected blood transfusions, but in France all blood products are safe. Fear of HIV infection should never preclude treatment for serious medical conditions.

For information on free and anonymous HIV-testing centres (*centres de dépistage*) in France, ring the SIDA Info Service toll free, 24 hours (☎ 08 00 84 08 00). Information is available in Orléans at the Centre de Dépistage Anonyme et Gratuit inside CHRO d'Orléans la Source (☎ 02 38 51 43 61), 14 ave de l'Hôpital. In Tours, Tours Elisa 2000 (☎ 02 47 20 08 99), 22 ave de Grammont, provides information and advice on the prevention of AIDS (open from 9 am to noon and 2 to 6 pm).

AIDES is a national organisation that works for the prevention of AIDS and assists AIDS sufferers. It has offices in Orléans (☎ 02 38 53 30 31), 11 rue de la République, and in Tours (☎ 02 47 64 30 88) at the Centre des Halles (open 2.30 to 6.30 pm on weekdays).

Sexually Transmitted Diseases Gonorrhoea, herpes and syphilis are among these diseases; sores, blisters or rashes around the genitals, discharges, or pain when urinating are common symptoms. With some STDs, such as wart virus or chlamydia, symptoms may be less marked or not observed at all, especially in women. Syphilis symptoms eventually disappear completely but the disease continues and can cause severe problems in later years. While abstinence from sexual contact is the only 100% effective prevention, using condoms is also effective. The treatment of gonorrhoea and syphilis is with antibiotics. The different sexually transmitted diseases each require specific antibiotics. There is no cure for herpes.

All pharmacies sell condoms (*préservatifs*) and many have 24-hour automatic condom dispensers outside the door. Some brasseries, discotheques, metro stations, and WCs in cafes and petrol stations are also equipped with condom machines. Condoms that conform to French government standards are marked with the letters NF (*norme française*) in black on a white oval inside a red-and-blue rectangle.

Rabies This is a fatal viral infection found in many countries, but it is not widespread in France. Animals can be infected and it is their saliva that is infectious. Any bite, scratch or even lick from a warm-blooded, furry animal should be cleaned immediately and thoroughly. Medical help should be sought promptly to receive a course of injections to prevent the onset of symptoms and death.

Bites & Stings

Bee and wasp stings are usually painful rather than dangerous. However, in people who are allergic to them severe breathing difficulties may occur and the victim may require urgent medical care.

Calamine lotion or a sting-relief spray will give relief under normal circumstances, and ice packs will reduce any pain and swelling. Remember to wear mosquito repellent in areas such as the Marais Poitevin and Parc Naturel Régional de Brière.

Women's Health

Antibiotic use, synthetic underwear, sweating and contraceptive pills can lead to fungal vaginal infections when travelling in hot climates. Maintaining good personal hygiene and wearing loose-fitting clothes and cotton underwear will help to prevent them. Fungal infections, characterised by a rash, itch and discharge, can be treated with a vinegar or lemon-juice douche, or with yogurt. Nystatin, miconazole or clotrimazole pessaries or vaginal cream are the usual treatment.

WOMEN TRAVELLERS

French men have clearly given little thought to the concept of sexual harassment. Most still believe that staring suavely at a passing woman is paying her a compliment. Women need not walk around the region in fear, however. Suave stares are about as adventurous as most French men get, with women rarely being physically assaulted on the street or touched up in bars at night. However, in the dizzying heat of the high season, things can hot up on the Atlantic coast. Apply the usual 'woman traveller' rules and, chances are, you'll emerge from the circus unscathed.

In general, remain conscious of your surroundings, avoid going to bars and clubs alone at night and be aware of potentially dangerous situations: deserted streets, lonely beaches, dark corners of large train stations and night buses in certain districts of Orléans, Tours and Nantes.

The national rape-crisis hotline (☎ 08 00 05 95 95) is staffed by SOS Viol, a voluntary women's group based in Paris.

GAY & LESBIAN TRAVELLERS

France is one of Europe's most liberal countries when it comes to homosexuality, in part because of the long French tradition of public tolerance towards groups of people who have chosen not to live by conventional social codes. There are large gay and lesbian communities in Orléans, Tours, Angers and Nantes (which organises a colourful Lesbian and Gay Pride march each year in June). The lesbian scene is less public than its male counterpart.

In Tours, the Maison des Homosexualités (☎ 02 47 20 55 30), 1ter rue des Balais, 37000 Tours, has contact details for other groups in the region. Its drop-in centre opens 6 to 8 pm on weekdays. Women's night is Tuesday from 6 to 11 pm, Monday is aimed at younger gay men, and a cafe open to all is staffed on Wednesday from 7.30 pm.

In Nantes, Lesbian and Gay Pride (LPG; ☎ 02 40 08 04 54), 42 rue des Hauts Pavés, 44000 Nantes, is an excellent information source. The centre is home to Gays Randonneurs Nantais (☎ 02 40 75 25 65), a hiking association which organises weekend hikes and walks for members in Loire-Atlantique, Vendée, Brittany and Anjou; and to the advisory association Si Maman

Savait (If Mummy Knew; ☎ 02 40 35 53 91). The latter staffs an information centre (☎ 02 40 74 08 68) on the second and fourth Friday of the month between 6 and 8 pm at 42 rue des Hauts Pavés, and on the third Friday of the month at 8.30 pm at Nantes' Gay and Lesbian Centre at 49–51 rue du Maréchal Joffre.

On the Internet, hot links to gay and lesbian bars, clubs and pubs in the region can be found at www.loirevalley.fr, while a scant list of gay-friendly places to stay is at www.gayplaces2stay.com. Gay & Lesbian (www.france.qrd.org) is a queer resources directory. *Guide Gai Pied* (www.gaipied.fr) is a French- and English-language annual guide to France with bits on the Loire Valley. *Le Guide Ouest*, published twice a year, lists gay establishments in Brittany and the Nantes area.

DISABLED TRAVELLERS
The region is not particularly user-friendly for disabled people: kerb ramps are few and far between, older public facilities and budget hotels lack lifts, while the turrets and spiral staircases typical to the region's medieval fortresses and Renaissance pleasure palaces are almost impossible to navigate.

But all is not lost. Many two- or three-star hotels are equipped with lifts; Michelin's *Guide Rouge* indicates hotels with lifts and facilities for disabled people. Most of the larger chateaux are also equipped to deal with wheelchairs, allowing disabled travellers to at least get a glimpse of the main courtyard (*cour d'honneur*) and other ground-level sights. At Château d'Angers, a lift transports people to the basement gallery to view the *Apocalypse* tapestry. In Amboise, discounted tickets are offered (60FF instead of 100FF) to disabled travellers wanting to attend the son et lumière show at the chateau.

Nantes airport offers assistance to wheelchair users. At Aéroport International Nantes-Atlantique, contact the Service Handicapés GIS (☎ 04 93 21 44 58). The SNCF's TGVs (*trains à grande vitesse*) and regular trains are also accessible to passengers in a wheelchair, provided they make a reservation by phone or at a train station at least 48 hours in advance. Details are available in SNCF's booklet *Le Mémento du Voyageur à Mobilité Réduite* (one page in English). Alternatively, contact SNCF Accessibilité Service (☎ 08 00 15 47 53).

Particularly useful is *Gîtes Accessibles aux Personnes Handicapées*, an accommodation guide (60FF) listing *gîtes ruraux* (country cottages) and *chambre d'hôtes* (B&Bs) with disabled access in the region. It's published by Gîtes de France (see Gîtes Ruraux under Accommodation later in this chapter).

Local organisations can handle specific requests and respond to any queries disabled travellers may have. Try the Association pour la Promotion des Handicapés du Loiret (APHL; ☎ 02 38 74 56 26), 58 bis blvd de Châteaudun, 45000 Orléans.

SENIOR TRAVELLERS
Senior citizens are entitled to discounts on public transport, museum and chateaux admission fees and so on, provided they show proof of their age. See Seniors Cards under Visas & Documents earlier in this chapter.

TRAVEL WITH CHILDREN
Successful travel with young children requires planning and effort. Don't overdo things: trying to see too much can cause problems. Include the kids in the trip planning. Balance a day spent traipsing around chateaux with time on the beach (if by the Atlantic coast) or an outing to a theme park such as Futuroscope (in Poitou). The Parc de Mini-Châteaux et Aquarium de Touraine, near Amboise, which also hosts a donkey farm, is guaranteed to thrill children, as is the Parc des Labyrinthes – a giant labyrinth cut in a corn field – in the Vallée de l'Indrois. After visiting Château d'Amboise, escape to the Pagode de Chanteloup, where children can run wild across vast stretches of lawn or cool off with a fascinating selection of medieval children's games – irresistible to children and adults alike.

Many chateaux cater to children. Chenonceau and Villandry both have a *jardin des enfants* (play area), equipped with swings, a slide and see-saw; the latter also has a small boxed-hedge maze. Several tourist offices run organised tours for children in summer; the office in Tours has a particularly impressive range aimed at six- to 12-year-olds. Most comités départementaux du tourisme (see Tourist Offices earlier in this chapter) offer nature workshops for children as well as adults.

Practically every bicycle rental outlet has kids' bikes and children's seats to hire. On Île d'Yeu, adults keen to explore the island by pedal power can hire a kiddies' trailer (complete with hood in case of rain) to attach to your own bicycle, allowing your children to be pedalled along in style.

Car rental·firms likewise have children's safety seats for hire at a nominal cost; book in advance. The same goes for highchairs and cots; they're standard in most restaurants and hotels, but numbers are limited. The choice of baby food, infant formulas, soya and cow's milk, disposable nappies (diapers) and the like is as great in French supermarkets as it is back home, but the opening hours may be quite different. Run out of nappies on Saturday afternoon and you're facing a very long and messy weekend. Most tourist offices have a list of baby-sitting services (gardes d'enfants) and creches.

Lonely Planet's Travel with Children is a good source of information.

DANGERS & ANNOYANCES

The region poses few dangers or annoyances beyond chateau fatigue and blistered heels.

Theft – from backpacks, pockets, cars, trains, laundrettes and beaches – is a serious problem. Keep an eagle eye on your bags, especially at train and bus stations, on overnight train rides, in tourist offices, in fast-food restaurants and on beaches.

Always keep your money, credit cards, tickets, passport, driver's licence and other important documents in a money belt worn inside your trousers or skirt. Keep enough money for the day in a separate wallet. Theft from hotel rooms is less common but it's still not a great idea to leave your valuables in your room. In hostels, lock your

non-valuables in a locker provided and cart your valuables along. Upmarket hotels have safes. When swimming on the beach or by the pool, have members of your party take turns sitting with everyone's packs and clothes. At the train station, if you leave your bags at a left-luggage office or in a luggage locker (where available), treat your claim chit (or locker code) like cash. Daypack snatchers have taken stolen chits to the train station and taken possession of the rest of their victim's belongings.

Nonsmokers with a vehement dislike of sitting in smoke-filled restaurants should maybe holiday elsewhere. Even in places where smoking is supposedly prohibited (of which there are very few), people still light up.

EMERGENCIES

The following numbers are toll free:

Emergency medical treatment/ambulance	☎ 15
Police	☎ 17
Fire Brigade	☎ 18
Rape Crisis Hotline	☎ 08 00 05 95 95

When you dial ☎ 15, the 24-hour dispatchers of the Service d'Aide Médicale d'Urgence (SAMU; Emergency Medical Aid Service) take down details of your problem and send out a private ambulance with a driver (250FF to 300FF) or, if necessary, a mobile intensive care unit. For less serious problems, SAMU can dispatch a doctor for a house call. If you prefer to be taken to a particular hospital, mention this to the ambulance crew, as the usual procedure is to take you to the nearest one. In emergency cases (ie, those requiring hospitalisation in an intensive care unit), billing will be taken care of later. Otherwise, you need to pay in cash at the time.

LEGAL MATTERS

The police are allowed to search anyone at any time, regardless of whether there is an obvious reason to do so or not. Importing or exporting drugs can lead to a 10- to 30-year jail sentence. The fine for possession of drugs for personal use can be as high as 500,000FF. If you litter, you risk a 1000FF fine. See also Road Rules under Car in the Getting Around chapter for information on the dangers of drinking and driving.

BUSINESS HOURS

Museums, shops and some smaller chateaux (but not cinemas, restaurants or *boulangeries*) are closed on public holidays. On Sunday, apart from chateaux, a boulangerie is usually about all that is open (in the morning only), and public transport services are less frequent. In villages, shops (including the boulangerie) close for a long lunch every day between 1 and 3 pm. Many hotels, restaurants, cinemas, cultural institutions and shops close for a period in winter. Commercial banks are generally open from 8 or 9 to sometime between 11.30 am and 1 pm and from 1.30 or 2 to 4.30 or 5 pm on weekdays.

PUBLIC HOLIDAYS & SPECIAL EVENTS

Festivals (*fêtes*) and fairs (*foires*) are very much a way of life, with every city/town/village/hamlet throwing a street party at least once a year (usually more often) to celebrate everything from a good grape or tomato harvest to the annual feast of their patron saint or the size of the local sausage. An unimaginable abundance of food, a *boule de fort* (see Spectator Sports later in this chapter) championship and dancing late into the night are guaranteed to stir the soul of any traveller lucky enough to witness such a joyous occasion. See the boxed text 'Feasts & Festivals' for information.

French National Holidays

National public holidays (*jours fériés*) are often a cue for festivities to spill into the streets.

New Year's Day (Jour de l'An) 1 January
Easter Sunday and Monday (Pâques and lundi de Pâques) March/April
May Day (Fête du Travail) 1 May – buy a lily of the valley (*muguet*) from a street vendor for good luck
Victory in Europe Day (Victoire 1945) 8 May – celebrates the Allied victory in Europe that ended WWII
Ascension (L'Ascension) May – celebrated on the 40th day after Easter Sunday
Pentecost/Whit Sunday and Whit Monday (Pentecôte and lundi de Pentecôte) mid-May to mid-June – celebrated on the seventh Sunday after Easter
Bastille Day/National Day (Fête Nationale) 14 July
Assumption (L'Assomption) 15 August
All Saints' Day (La Toussaint) 1 November
Remembrance Day (Le onze novembre) 11 November – commemorates the armistice of WWI
Christmas Day (Noël) 25 December

Feasts & Festivals

Regional and departmental tourist offices (see Tourist Offices earlier in this chapter) publish annual entertainment guides for their area. Information on the *son et lumière* (sound and light) shows which light up the Loire chateaux in a kaleidoscope of colour and pattern is provided in a separate boxed text earlier in this chapter. Wine fairs are mentioned in the Food & Wine of the Loire special section.

January
Festival Premier Plans Short and full-length films are screened during this annual European cinema festival hosted by cinemas and the Centre des Congrès in Angers.
Salon Musical de la Bourdaisière Classical-music concerts inside Château de la Bourdaisière, outside Tours.

February
Foire au Miel Honey festival on blvd Maréchal Foch, Angers.

Feasts & Festivals

March/April

Fête de la Batellerie Traditional Loire boat and boating festival in St-Jean de Braye, Orléanais.

Fête des Œufs Easter-egg treasure hunts in and around the Pagode de Chantaloup, near Amboise; Easter Monday.

May

Festival Cinéma d'Afrique African film festival, every two years in Angers.

Fête du Goût et du Patrimoine Walking, mountain-bike expeditions and wine-tasting in and around the vineyards of Savennières mark this celebration of 'taste and heritage' in Savennières; early May.

Fête Johanniques Festival to mark Joan of Arc's (Jeanne d'Arc) liberation of Orléans, held in Orléans; 7 and 8 May.

June

Festival International de Musique International music festival in and around the medieval Château de Sully-sur-Loire; June weekends.

Festival de Jazz Orléans; end of June.

Fête Nationale de la Pêche A two-day fishing festival.

Les Fêtes Musicales en Touraine A classical-music festival dating from 1964 in Tours; last two weeks of June.

July

Angers l'Été Open-air music concerts aimed at all tastes every Tuesday and Thursday in the lovely Cloître Toussaint, Angers; July and August.

Festival d'Anjou Major theatre festival (www.angers.ensam.fr/festanjou) which brings plays and theatrical events to theatres and historical sites throughout Anjou; first three weeks of July.

Festival des Arts de la Mer A summer-long cultural festival showcasing photography and contemporary art exhibitions, concerts and theatrical performances across Île de Noirmoutier; July and August.

Festival de la Tomate Tomato festival at the Chateau de la Bourdaisière, Montlouis-sur-Loire; July and August.

Fête au Son des Orgues A four-week organ festival with classical and choral concerts in the cathedral in Orléans; July or August.

Fête des Vins et de l'Andouillette A two-day wine and *andouillette* (tripe sausage) festival with wine-tasting, andouillette-tasting and walks in the Coteaux du Layon vineyards, St-Lambert du Lattay; early July. It's followed by a wine and omelette festival in neighbouring Beaulieu-sur-Layon at the end of the month.

Foire à l'Ail et au Basilic Garlic and Basil Fair, Tours; end of July.

Heures Musicales de Cunault A series of Sunday-evening classical-music concerts in Cunault or Trèves village church; July and August.

Journées de la Rose Rose festival and exhibition, Doué-la-Fontaine; mid-July.

Marché Médieval Medieval market with fireworks and other son et lumière-style animations in Meung-sur-Loire; mid July.

Marché Renaissance A two-day Renaissance market with costumed venders and street cabarets, in Amboise; first weekend of July.

Nuits des Mille Feux Fabulous, four-day Nights of a Thousand Fires festival, which sets the Renaissance gardens of the Château de Villandry ablaze with thousands of candles each evening from 9 pm; mid-July.

Feasts & Festivals

August

Festival de Musique Baroque 'Musique et Jardins' A three-day Baroque music festival, with concerts held in the 17th- and 18th-century *cour d'honneur* (main courtyard) of Château de Villandry; mid-August.

Festival de Noirmoutier-en-l'Île An open-air, two-week festival that showers theatrical and musical spectacles on the courtyard of Château de Noirmoutier, which dominates place d'Armes in Noirmoutier-en-l'Île, Île de Noirmoutier; mid-August.

Fête aux Tripes Tasty, two-day tripe fair, St-Georges des Sept Voies, Anjou; around 29 August.

Heures Musicales du Haut Anjou A month of jazz concerts in a variety of venues, Angers.

Marché à l'Ancienne Re-creation of a 19th-century farmers' market with wines and traditional food products from the Loire region on sale, Chinon; third weekend of August.

Marché Rabelais Musicians, dancers and locals dress up in period costume for the Rabelais market, which sees crafts and local products for sale in Chinon; first weekend in August.

September

Festival International de Musique et Folklore International Music and Folklore Festival held in Angers.

Grand Bal Renaissance Grand Renaissance Ball (tickets 100FF) held by the Centre de Musique Ancienne (☎ 02 47 38 48 48), 7 bis rue des Tanneurs, 37000 Tours, in the fabulous Château d'Azay-le-Rideau to celebrate the Journées du Patrimoine (see below).

Jazz en Touraine Joyous, two-week jazz festival in Tours, Montlouis and Joué-lès-Tours; mid-September.

Journées de la Loire Days of the Loire festival organised by the environmental Association pour la Loire which brings fluvial and nautical events to the riverside villages and towns of Saumur, Le Thoureil, Gennes, St-Florent-le-Vieil, Nantes and St-Nazaire during a two-day festival at the end of September.

Journées du Patrimoine The Heritage Days sees chateaux and other historical monuments open their doors for free (or with reduced entrance fees) to the public during a two-day festival throughout the region in mid- to late September.
Web site: www.culture.fr

Journées du Potager The Days of the Kitchen Garden sees chateau gardeners share their green-fingered tips, tricks and *savoir-faire* (know-how) with the public, Château de Villandry; 25 and 26 September.

Nuits du Cinéma A three-day film festival at Château d'Angers; early September.

October

Le Festival Rockomotives Four-day rock festival in Vendôme; tickets cost 80/250FF for one/four days.
Web site: www.multimania.com/rockomotives

La Semaine du Goût Eat, drink and be merry during this week-long gastronomic festival aimed at promoting regional food and wine, Angers.

Sonates d'Automne Chamber-music festival in Tours.

November

Journées Cinématographiques Cinema Days film festival, Orléans.

Foire au Miel Honey Fair, blvd Maréchal Foch, Angers.

Though not official public holidays, numerous festivals fall on Shrove Tuesday (Mardi Gras), Maundy (or Holy) Thursday, Good Friday and Boxing Day (26 December).

ACTIVITIES
The region offers a wealth of outdoor pursuits guaranteed to fulfil the most adventurous – or lazy – of travellers. Numerous travel agencies abroad arrange thematic tours of the region (golfing, cycling, walking, ballooning and so on); see Organised Tours in the Getting There & Away chapter for details.

Bird-Watching
The Loire's riverbanks and its numerous sand banks lure ornithologists, as do the Marais Poitevin, in Poitou, and the coastal Parc Naturel Régional de Brière, north of St-Nazaire. In Vendée, the Association de Défense de l'Environnement en Vendée (ADEV) organises bird-watching and botany trails on Île d'Yeu, in the Marais Poitevin and along the Vendéen coast; local ADEV branches have details (Île d'Yeu ☎ 02 51 59 47 33, Pays d'Olonne ☎ 02 51 33 12 97, Sud Vendée ☎ 02 51 27 23 92).

On Île de Noirmoutier ask for the excellent *Découvrez les Oiseaux* (*Discover Birds*) brochure which details birding trips on the island (30FF per person) organised by the Ligue pour la Protection des Oiseaux (League for the Protection of Birds; ☎/fax 02 51 35 81 16), based at the Maison de la Réserve in Fort Larron, Noirmoutier-en-l'Île.

The string of Maisons de la Loire are an excellent source of information on local flora and fauna, and can assist with arranging bird-watching sprees and expeditions with or without a guide. Contact the Maison de la Loire du Loir-et-Cher (☎ 02 54 81 65 45, fax 02 54 81 68 07), 73 rue Nationale, 41500 St-Dyé-sur-Loire; the Maison de la Loire du Loiret (☎ 02 38 59 76 60, fax 02 38 59 97 96), La Chanterie, blvd Carnot, 45150 Jargeau; or the Maison de la Loire d'Indre-et-Loire (☎ 02 47 50 97 52, fax 02 47 45 15 75), 60 quai Albert Baillet, 37270 Montlouis-sur-Loire.

The spotters' guide *Where to Watch Birds in France* (1989), published by the French League for the Protection of Birds, includes maps and marked itineraries that are cross-referenced to the text.

Canoeing & Kayaking
Paddling down the River Loire is an obvious way of getting to the true heart of this valley region, although not all the river is navigable. Places that offer canoe hire and expeditions include: Beaulieu-sur-Loire, Briare and Gien (east of Orléans); Meung-sur-Loire, Beaugency and Muides-sur-Loire (between Orléans and Blois); Blois, St-Dyé-sur-Loire and Saumur. Sections of the Rivers Cher and Loir around Blois also attract canoeists galore.

Numerous boat clubs – such as the Base de Loisirs de Millocheau, in Saumur (see the Anjou chapter) – arrange guided river expeditions. The latter runs half-day trips from Saumur to Chouzé (17km) and Candes-sur-Martin (13km), and full-day trips to La-Chapelle-sur-Loire (25km) and Chinon (25km). Half-day/day trips start at 80/120FF per person and include equipment hire.

The Ligue Pays de la Loire de Canoë-Kayak (☎ 02 41 73 86 10, fax 02 41 73 25 66), 75 ave du Lac de Maine, 49000 Angers, can supply information on clubs in the region. Most are affiliated to the Fédération Française de Canoë-Kayak (FFCK; ☎ 01 45 11 08 50), 87 quai de la Marne, 94340 Joinville-le-Pont. The Maisons de la Loire (see Bird-Watching) also provide information on routes; some have canoes to rent and offer expeditions with or without a local guide.

Cycling
Pedalling in the Loire is tremendously popular. There are few killing hills to climb, and charmingly narrow, picturesque country roads link most chateaux, making it an ideal region to two-wheel in for a day, week or month. Most tourist offices in the region are geared up for cyclo-tourism: many publish brochures and leaflets outlining short day tours. Amateur cyclists should count on clocking up no more than 50km per day –

often just enough mileage to cover a return trip to a chateau.

You can hire a mountain bike (*vélo tout-terrain*; VTT) in most towns. Some GR trails (see Walking later in this section) are open to mountain bikes. A *piste cyclable* is a cycling path; many are along the banks of the River Loire, such as the 360km-long trail that links Briare with Beaugency. Useful cycling maps are listed under Maps under Planning earlier in this chapter.

Didier-Richard publishes Les Guides VTT, a series of cyclists' 'topoguides' (in French) that are widely available in France. Each département publishes excellent guides (also in French) for cyclo-tourists, detailing trails. Many tourist offices also sell cycling itineraries (some in English) compiled by local cycling clubs.

Each département also has a Comité Départemental du Cyclo-tourisme to assist cyclists, including:

Loiret (☎ 02 38 63 16 53) 61 rue de Maupassant, 45100 Orléans
Loir-et-Cher (☎ 02 54 42 95 60, fax 02 54 42 17 07) 32 rue Alain Gerbault, 41007 Blois
Maine-et-Loire (☎ 02 41 59 02 30) 97 rue St-François, 49700 Doué-la-Fontaine

Lonely Planet's *Cycling France* has a five-day, 233km ride from Saumur to Blois, together with suggestions for shorter trips and all the information a cyclist in France needs, including advice on health and bike maintainance, places to eat and stay, and maps.

Fishing

A lone fisherman propped atop a fold-up stool on the riverbank is an integral part of the Loire Valley landscape. Fishing in any river in the region is forbidden without a fishing licence (*carte de pêche*), sold for around 35FF per day at local fishing shops. Fishing licences issued in Pays de la Loire, Centre and Poitou-Charentes account for almost 25% of the 1.7 million issued annually in France.

For information on the latest rules and regulations, contact a comité départemental du tourisme (see Tourist Offices earlier in this chapter). The Fédération de Pêche du Maine-et-Loire (☎ 02 41 87 57 09), 14 allée du Haras, 49100 Angers, or the Fédération d'Indre-et-Loire pour la Pêche et la Protection du Milieu Aquatique (☎ 02 47 05 33 77, fax 02 47 61 69 42), 25 rue Charles Gille, BP 0835, 37008 Tours, are also useful.

Many privately owned chateau hotels have lakes where guests can cast their rods.

The region celebrates a two-day Fête Nationale de la Pêche (National Fishing Festival) in early June.

Golf

A round of golf is one of life's simple pleasures in the Loire. For details on the 26 manicured greens in Pays de la Loire, contact the Ligue de Golf des Pays de la Loire (☎ 02 40 08 05 06, fax 02 40 08 40 03, @ golfpdl@aol.com), 9 rue Couëdic, 44000 Nantes. Formule Golf (☎ 02 40 12 55 99, fax 02 40 20 38 12), 1 place de la Garne, BP 36213, 44262 Nantes, is a golfing association that organises three/four/five-day golfing packages in western Loire and sells a Pass Formule Golf for 765FF, entitling its holder to three days of unlimited golf at specified courses. Information is on-line at www.formule-golf.com.

Golf du Sancerrois (☎ 02 48 54 11 22, fax 02 48 54 28 03, @ golf.sancerre@wanadoo.fr), St-Thibault, 18300 Sancerre, is a prestigious course in south-eastern Loire; daily green fees start at 60/230FF for a six/18-hole course in the high season. In the heart of chateau-land, golfers head to the 18-hole Golf du Château de Cheverny (☎ 02 54 79 24 70, fax 02 54 79 23 02), amid 350 acres of former hunting estate at Château de Cheverny.

Greens throughout the region are listed in the *Golf in France* guide, published by the Maison de la France and available (free) at tourist offices abroad. Alternatively, contact the Fédération Française de Golf (☎ 01 41 49 77 00, fax 01 41 49 77 01), 68 rue Anatole France, 92309 Levallois-Peret.

Horse Riding

Saumur is the obvious place to saddle up. The town's highly prestigious École Nationale d'Équitation is open only to professional riders, but there are plenty of smaller schools in the vicinity, where anyone can ride. The Centre Équestre Saumur-Petit Souper (☎ 02 41 50 29 90), near the entrance to the École Nationale on ave de l'École Nationale d'Équitation in St-Hilaire-St-Florent, is one of many riding schools; hourly rates start at 125FF.

Contact the Fédération Française d'Équitation (FFE; ☎ 01 53 67 43 43), 30 ave d'Iéna, 75116 Paris, for a list of *comités départementaux du tourisme équestre* (regional equestrian tourist boards) in the Loire.

Rollerblading

Rollerblading has taken off in a big way in recent years. Blades are a tip-top way to cruise around town. A set can easily be hired in larger cities, such as Nantes, as well as in most resorts on the Atlantic coast. Rates are around 80FF per day; blades for children are available at most hire outlets.

The promenade in La Baule, 17km west of St-Nazaire, and Le Remblai, which runs the 3km length of the golden sandy beach in Les Sables d'Olonne, are two excellent spots to rollerblade.

Sailing, Boating & Barging

The Base de Loisirs de Millocheau, in Saumur (see the Anjou chapter), runs a half-day sailing trip from Saumur to Montsoreau or Gennes (450FF for a boat and five people) and a full-day voyage to Le Toureil (700FF for five people). On the coast,

---

Hot-Air Ballooning

Viewing the Loire from the air is a fabulous way of experiencing the chateau-studded landscape. A handful of hot-air-ballooning specialists organise flights across the region.

France Montgolfière (☎ 02 54 71 75 40, fax 02 54 71 75 78, ❿ dlabeaume@teaser.fr) is run by a group of English, Welsh and Americans and is based at La Riboulière in Monthou-sur-Cher (about 30km south of Blois). Weather permitting, they run hot-air-balloon flights year round from almost anywhere in the Loire Valley. A one- to 1½-hour flight, including a round of champagne at the end, costs 1600FF per person (1100FF for children aged six to 12) for a fully flexible ticket which can be reimbursed should your flight be cancelled due to adverse weather conditions; cheaper non-refundable weekday/weekend fares (cancelled flights can only be rescheduled) cost 1250/1450FF, and a ticket for a stand-by flight (48 hours' notice) is 950FF. They also offer a variety of other deals. Make reservations several days ahead for weekday flights, and four weeks ahead for weekend (especially Saturday night) flights. France Montgolfière accepts reservations via its Web site at www.franceballoons.com.

Aérocom (☎ 02 54 33 55 00, fax 02 54 33 55 04, ❿ aero.com@wanadoo.fr), 27 route de St-Sulpice, 41330 Fossé, likewise organises balloon flights. Departures are usually from Blois or Cheverny. A one- to 1½-hour flight, including a celebratory glass of champagne, costs 1250FF per person; a group of four to 10 pays 1150FF per adult, and groups of more than 10 pay 1000FF per person. Flights that are cancelled due to bad weather (winds of more than 20km/h or rain) will be rescheduled; fares are reimbursed if no other date is possible. Reservations are essential, must be made in advance and require a 500FF deposit. Aérocom has a Web site at www.aerocom.fr.

Between mid-March and mid-October it is possible to jump aboard a helium-filled balloon without any advance reservation at **Château de Cheverny** (☎ 02 54 79 25 05), where a balloon takes to the skies every 20 minutes or so during chateau opening hours. The 10-minute flight costs 47FF (84FF including admission to the chateau).

Most of the luxurious chateau hotels, such as Château d'Artigny (see Azay-le-Rideau in the Touraine chapter), can organise a balloon flight for their guests, whom they allow to take off and land in the hotel grounds.

⚜ ⚜

leading sailing centres include Île de Noirmoutier, La Baule and Les Sables d'Olonne. Inland, there are numerous artificial lakes – such as Lac de Maine, in Angers – where you can sail or windsurf.

Boating and barging are popular in the swampy marshlands of the Marais Poitevin (see the boxed text 'Boating & Cycling in Green Venice' in the Poitou chapter) and in the Parc Naturel Régional de Brière, where you can hire a flat-bottomed boat on an hourly basis. The best place for information on thematic boat tours (fauna, flora, local food products and so on) is the Maison du Tourisme de Brière (☎ 02 40 66 85 01) at 38 rue de la Brière, in La Chapelle des Marais.

Details of the touristy river trips and cruises operated along the River Loire in summer are included in the relevant regional chapters. Information on navigating the River Loire and other rivers by canal or river boat can be found under Boat in the Getting Around chapter.

Hugh McKnight's *Cruising French Waterways* and *Slow Boat through France* are two absolutely indispensable titles written by Europe's leading authority on inland waterways. *Barging in Europe* by Roger Van Dyken is likewise crammed with practical information and essential background reading.

Walking

The region is criss-crossed by a maze of marked walking paths. No permits are needed for walking but there are restrictions on where you can camp, particularly in the national parks (see Nature Parks under Flora & Fauna in the Facts about the Loire chapter for details).

The best-known trails are the *sentiers de grande randonnée* (long-distance footpaths), whose alphanumeric names begin GR and whose track indicators are red and white stripes on trees, rocks, walls, posts and so on. Some are many hundreds of kilometres long, including the GR3 – also known as the Sentier Historique de la Vallée des Rois (Valley of Kings Historic Footpath). The GR3 is the main trail in the Loire

Valley and snakes along the Loire riverbanks for much of its 368km course. The shorter GR41 and GR46 shadow the Rivers Cher and Indre respectively.

Less challenging, and hence suited to the more casual walker, are the many forest trails that cut through the region's thick and numerous forests. A section of the forested Domaine National de Chambord is open to hikers, as is most of the Forêt d'Orléans in Orléanais and the Forêt de Loches and Forêt de Chinon in Touraine. Forest trails and walking itineraries are detailed (in French only) in the Promenons-Nous series of guides (49FF) published by the Office National des Forêts. IGN's (see Maps under Planning earlier in this chapter) *Guide du Promeneur en Forêt d'Orléans* is a handy resource for those keen to delve into forest wildlife. For information on botanical forests walks organised by local ONF branches contact:

Centre (☎ 02 38 65 47 00, fax 02 38 81 76 21) 100 blvd de la Salle, BP 18, 45760 Boigny-sur-Bionne
Pays de la Loire (☎ 02 40 73 79 79, fax 02 40 73 00 07) 4 place Eugène Livet, BP 20501, 44105 Nantes
Poitou-Charentes (☎ 05 49 58 21 59, fax 05 49 37 91 87) 389 ave de Nantes, 86020 Poitiers

Each département has a *comité de la randonnée pédestre* (rambling committee) – affiliated to the Fédération Française de Randonnée Pédestre (FFRP; French Ramblers' Association) – which arranges organised hikes, publishes guides and so on. The Touraine branch (☎ 02 47 70 37 35) staffs an information desk at the tourist office in Tours (see Information under Tours in the Touraine chapter for details) and is the most accessible to Anglophone hikers.

Numerous hiking guides cover the region – mostly in French. Some tourist offices produce English-language guides. Essential reading for anyone intending to trek the GRs is Brian Spencer's *Walking in the Loire Valley* (Bartholomew, 1996), which outlines 15 circular walks in the region. Each walk is accompanied by a large-scale colour map.

COURSES

French-language and cookery courses aside, workshops in the medieval arts of calligraphy, illumination, heraldry and tapestry are but some of the more unusual courses available in the region. The downside? Few courses are conducted in English.

French Language

All tourist offices stock information on language schools in the region, which include:

ACTeam Langues (☎ 02 38 77 05 36) 8 bis rue Faubourg Madeline, Orléans. Semi-intensive or intensive courses, from 4876FF per week (15 hours' tuition per week).

Alliance Française du Val de Loire (☎ 02 54 73 13 20, fax 02 54 73 23 20) 21 place St-Martin, 41100 Vendôme. Week- or month-long courses costing 1900FF per week (20 hours' tuition per week).

Centre International de Langues (CIL; ☎ 02 40 14 10 10, @ patrick.lemoine@humana.univ-nantes.fr) Université de Nantes, Nantes. Term-long French-language courses aimed at foreigners.

Centre Linguistique pour Étrangers (CLE; ☎ 02 47 64 06 19, fax 02 47 05 84 61) 7–9 place Châteauneuf, Tours. One/two-week courses costing 3150/4100FF in groups of 20, or one-month courses with seven students a class costing 7300FF (20 hours' tuition per week).

Institut de Touraine (☎ 02 47 05 76 83, fax 02 47 20 48 98) place 14 Juillet, 37100 Tours. Courses costing upwards of 4750FF per week (20 hours' tuition per week).

Tours Langues (☎/fax 02 47 66 01 00) 36 rue Briçonnet, Tours. A language school off place Plumereau in Tours old town.

Cookery

Most culinary courses for globe-trotting gourmets revolve around markets, vineyards and the kitchen table. The annual *Guide to Cooking Schools* (Shaw Guides, www.shaw guides.com) and the *Guide to Cookery Courses of the British Isles and Beyond* (1998), compiled by London's Books for Cooks (see Food & Wine under Books earlier in this chapter), have exhaustive listings.

Domaine de la Tortinière (☎ 02 47 34 35 00, fax 02 47 65 95 70) Les Gués de Veigné, 37250 Montbazon en Touraine. Five-day initiation courses into the gastronomic joys of traditional Touraine cuisine; cook all morning in the kitchen of a 19th-century manor and visit surrounding chateaux in the afternoon. Courses cost upwards of 11,500FF per person, including accommodation, meals, classes and chateau excursions.

Hostellerie Le Castel de Bray et Monts (☎ 02 47 96 70 47, fax 02 47 96 57 36) Bréhemont, 37130 Langeais. Housed in an 18th-century manor house, morning cooking classes (three hours) with chef Maxime Rochereau are followed by afternoon tours into the countryside. Weekend and five-day courses are available, starting at 4900FF per person including accommodation in the manor house.
Web site: www.frenchhotels.com

Jean Bardet (☎ 02 47 41 41 11, fax 02 47 51 68 72) 57 rue Groison, 37100 Tours. Top chef Jean Bardet opens his kitchen to amateur cooks keen to learn a trick or two – and concoct a delicious lunch into the bargain. One-day cooking classes are held every Thursday between 9 am and 3 pm, and cost 800/3800FF per person for one/five sessions (including lunch, prepared during the class).

Tapestry & Medieval Arts

The Centre Régional d'Art Textile (☎/fax 02 41 87 10 88), 3 blvd Daviers, 49100 Angers, organises tapestry classes for amateurs and professionals. A course comprising 30/60/90 hours of tuition split across 5/10/15 days costs 1500/2500/3700FF; each additional day thereafter costs 250FF. Bring along a translator if you don't understand French.

In Blésois, Château de Fougères-sur-Bièvre (☎ 02 54 20 27 18) hosts medieval-inspired workshops. Stone masonry, calligraphy, architecture and heraldry are among the one-week workshops organised (370FF per person per week). Courses must be booked in advance.

The Centre Culturel de l'Ouest (☎ 02 41 51 73 52), at the Abbaye de Fontevraud in Anjou, arranges various workshops, including Gregorian chant sessions for amateur musicians.

Art, Archaeology, Nature & Photography

The Musée des Tumulus de Bougon (☎ 05 49 05 12 13, fax 05 49 05 14 05), 79800 Bougon, runs half- and full-day workshops for individuals in summer. Courses (in French only) focus on everything from neolithic ceramics and weaving to pottery, stone polishing and the neolithic use of bones; some of the workshops are aimed at children aged as young as five.

In Loire-Atlantique, the Parc Naturel Régional de Brière runs watercolour painting and drawing courses in the park. The six-day courses are led by a naturalist painter and cost 2300FF per person.

Equally fascinating are the seven-day nature courses (from 2050FF) that the park runs in association with biologists from the university of Rennes. For further information contact the Maison du Parc (☎ 02 40 91 68 68, fax 02 40 91 60 58) 177 Île de Ferdun, 44720 St-Joachim.

The Domaine National de Chambord organises animal photography 'safaris' in the elk-rich forest surrounding Château de Chambord (see the boxed text 'Le Brame du Cerf' in the Orléanais & Blésois chapter for details).

WORK

To work legally you need a carte de séjour (see Visas & Documents earlier in this chapter).

Illegal work ('in the black') is very occasionally possible during the grape harvests in October, although picking is increasingly being done mechanically, meaning there are fewer opportunities for the casual grape picker. The start date is announced up to one week before picking – which lasts about two weeks. The most effective way of securing work is to approach the different wine-producing estates directly from May onwards. Tourist offices in the region have a list of producers.

Under the au pair system, single young people (aged 18 to about 27) who are studying in France live with a French family and receive lodging, full board and a bit of pocket money in exchange for taking care of the kids, doing light housework and perhaps teaching English to the children. Many families want au pairs who are native English speakers, but knowing at least some French may be a prerequisite.

ACCOMMODATION

Accommodation varies from the refreshingly good-value to the luxuriously expensive. It is by no means the cheapest in France, due in part to the region's proximity to Paris. But with a bit of careful planning and consideration of all the options (live like a queen in a chateau or like a caveman in a cave), accommodation is both affordable and inspiring.

Local authorities impose a *taxe de séjour* (tourist tax) on each visitor in their jurisdiction. This is enforced only between Easter and September or October, and makes prices charged about 1FF to 7FF per person higher than the posted rates.

Reservations

All the large cities have an abundance of hotels and accommodation options, meaning you can turn up without a reservation at most times of year and easily find a bed for the night. For the more discerning traveller, however, who tends to opt for mid-range accommodation, reservations are essential in the high season (June to mid-September).

Year round, calling just a couple of days before to reserve a room, or even early in the morning (8 or 9 am) on the day you intend to arrive, can save you a back-breaking hike around town upon arrival. Budget accommodation is usually snapped up by 11 am but almost never booked up weeks in advance (unlike mid-range and top-end accommodation).

If you do arrive in town without a place to stay, your best starting point is the tourist office. All tourist offices stock a comprehensive list of accommodation and have information on vacancies. For a small fee, they will make a hotel reservation for you. The going rate is generally no more than 5/10FF per reservation in the town/département, although some tourist offices – such as the one in Blois – take advantage of the huge number of tourists and charge more (it's 12FF for a reservation in Blois). You have to stop by the office to take advantage of reservation services.

A deposit (*des arrhes*) in French francs is usually required to confirm an advance reservation at a hotel or upmarket *chambre d'hôte* (see later in this section). Some places ask for your credit card number instead, or for a confirmation of your plans by letter or fax in clear, simple English (receipt of which is rarely acknowledged by French hoteliers). Deposits can easily be sent by postal money order (available from any post office) made payable to the hotel.

Camping

The region has hundreds of camp sites. Most are open from March or April to September or October. Some hostels allow travellers to pitch tents in the back garden; others have furnished tents or mobile homes to rent on a weekly basis.

Camp sites have stars to reflect their facilities and amenities which, along with location and seasonal demand, influence the nightly rate. Separate tariffs are usually charged for people, tents or caravans (the latter are charged extra for electricity), and cars, motorcycles or bicycles. Some places have fixed-price deals for two or three people, including tent and car. Children aged up to about 12 enjoy significant discounts. Receptions are often closed during the day: the best time to call for reservations is early morning or evening.

Camping on a farm (*camping à la ferme*) can be arranged through Gîtes de France (see Gîtes Ruraux below). Wilderness camping (*camping sauvage*) is illegal, although it is tolerated to some degree in places (*never* ever in any of the national parks or in the grounds of a chateau). Pitching your tent on the beach or in a meadow makes you an immediate – and easy – target for thieves.

The comités régionaux du tourisme for all three régions (Centre, Pays de la Loire and Poitou-Charentes; see Tourist Offices earlier in this chapter) publish an annual booklet listing all the camp sites in the région. Several comités départementaux du tourisme also publish camping booklets.

Gîtes Ruraux

Some of the region's most sought-after accommodation – farms, former monasteries, regal chateaux, manor houses and mills – is represented by Gîtes de France, a 'green' organisation that liaises between owners and renters. These idyllic little nests are off the public-transport track and are suitable only for travellers with a vehicle.

Amenities in a *gîte rural* (a self-catering holiday cottage in a village or on a farm) or a *gîte communal* (owned by the commune rather than an individual) include a kitchenette and bathroom facilities. In most cases there is a minimum rental period – usually one week.

Gîtes de France annual guides – *Centre-Val de Loire*, *Pays de la Loire* and *Poitou-Charentes* – include a listing (complete with a photograph of the property) of gîtes ruraux, chambre d'hôtes and camp sites in the areas covered by the respective guidebook. Guides can be ordered over the Internet from www.gites-de-france.fr. Advance bookings and information are available directly from the property owner or a Gîtes de France branch. These include:

Deux-Sèvres (☎ 05 49 24 00 42, 05 49 77 15 90, fax 05 49 77 15 94) 15 rue Thiers, 79025 Niort
Indre-et-Loire (☎ 02 47 27 56 10, 02 47 48 37 13, fax 02 46 48 13 39, ✉ info@loire-valley-holidays.com) Accueil Rural en Touraine, 38 rue Augustin Fresnel, Chambray-lès-Tours Web site: www.loire-valley-holidays.com
Loire-Atlantique (☎ 02 51 72 95 65, fax 02 40 35 17 05) 1 allée Baco, 44032 Nantes
Loiret (☎ 02 38 62 04 88, fax 02 38 62 98 37) 8 rue d'Escures, 45000 Orléans
Loir-et-Cher (☎ 02 54 58 81 63, 02 54 58 81 64, fax 02 54 56 04 13, ✉ gites41@wanadoo.fr) Association Vacances Vertes, 5 rue de la Voûte du Château, 41001 Blois
Maine-et-Loire (☎ 02 41 23 51 23, 02 41 23 51 42, fax 02 41 88 36 77, ✉ anjou.cdt@wanadoo.fr) 11 place du Président Kennedy, 49021 Angers
Sarthe (☎ 02 43 40 22 50, 02 43 40 22 60, fax 02 43 40 22 61) 40 rue Joinville, 72000 Le Mans
Vendée (☎ 02 51 37 87 87, fax 02 51 62 15 19) 124 blvd Aristide Briand, 86007 La Roche-sur-Yon
Vienne (☎ 05 49 37 48 54, fax 05 49 37 48 61) 15–17 rue Carnot, 86007 Poitiers

During holiday periods, it is vital to reserve rural accommodation well in advance; most places require a deposit.

Homestays

Students, young people and tourists can stay with French families under an arrangement known as *hôtes payants* (literally 'paying guests') or *hébergement chez l'habitant* (lodging with the occupants of private homes). In general, you rent a room .and have access (sometimes limited) to the family's kitchen and telephone.

Most language schools (see Courses earlier in this chapter) arrange homestays for their students.

Hundreds upon hundreds of agencies in the US and Europe arrange homestay accommodation in the Loire; the comités régionaux du tourisme have lists, as do most French tourist offices abroad (see Tourist Offices earlier in this chapter).

Hostels

There are *auberges de jeunesse* (youth hostels) in Amboise, Angers, Blois, Chinon, Montlivault (4km north of Chambord), Nantes, Orléans, Saumur and Tours. Expect to pay around 50FF to 75FF per night; this does not include a sometimes-optional continental breakfast (about 20FF).

Fédération Unie des Auberges de Jeunesse (FUAJ) and Ligue Française pour les Auberges de Jeunesse (LFAJ) affiliates require HI or similar cards (see Hostel Card under Visas & Documents earlier in this chapter). Check out their Web sites at www.auberges-de-jeunesse.com and www .fuaj.fr. Privately owned hostels charge more than HI-affiliated hostels.

Some hostels do not accept telephone reservations, so turn up early, especially in July and August, if you want to ensure you get a bed for the night. Most places have kitchen facilities, and many have an excellent range of facilities, including bicycles to hire.

In some places the hostels are a good hike out of town: the Blois hostel is 4.5km out of town, in Les Grouëts, and the one in Tours is 5km from the centre. If there are two of you it can be as cheap (or cheaper) – and a lot less hassle – to stay in a budget hotel in town. Some hostels open only in high season.

Chambre d'Hôtes

A *chambre d'hôte* (French-style B&B) is a room in a private house rented to travellers by the night; breakfast is always included in the price, while a delicious homemade evening meal is often available for an extra charge (about 100FF). Many chambre d'hôtes are housed inside chateaux and offer the most stunning accommodation in the Loire Valley (see Chateaux later in this section). Chambre d'hôtes are often listed in Gîtes de France guides (see Gîtes Ruraux earlier in this section).

Hotels

Hotels have between one and four stars. Few no-star hotels (ie, hotels that have not been rated) exist.

Breakfast (*petit déjeuner*) is almost never included in the room price. Count on paying an extra 25FF to 40FF (up to 100FF in four-star joints) for the privilege. Breakfast at a nearby cafe can be cheaper and is invariably more pleasant.

Some hotels in the region only operate, deplorably so, on a half-board basis in July and August, meaning that you are obliged to fork out the hefty prices they set for breakfast and an evening meal in a stuffy, cramped hotel restaurant (invariably inside).

A room with a bath is usually more expensive than a room with a shower. Most places supply neck-ache-inducing hot-dog-shaped bolsters (*traversins*) rather than pillows (*oreillers*). It is substantially cheaper to travel with someone you're happy to share a bed with; few hotels offer single rooms and most charge a fixed rate for a double (with twin beds or a double), irrespective of how many beds are actually used. Places that do have singles usually charge only marginally less for it than for a double. Triples and quads normally have one or two beds.

Budget Hotels Budget hotels are widespread in cities such as Orléans, Tours and Nantes, but nonexistent in wealthier villages in the exclusive heart of the Loire Valley, where the big chateaux are. In those cities where there are budget hotels, the cheapest rooms rock in at a bargain 150FF for a double with washbasin (and sometimes bidet) in your room, and a shared toilet and shower in the corridor. A shower in the hall bathroom is sometimes free but usually costs 10FF to 25FF. Most places have slightly more expensive rooms equipped with shower (starting at around 180FF) or shower and toilet (about 200FF) and other amenities. Prices stay the same year round at budget hotels.

Most cheap hotels demand pre-payment for the room. Make sure you see the room before parting with any cash. Do not expect a refund if you pay first, only to discover the room is an uninhabitable hovel prompting immediate departure. Few budget hotels serve breakfast.

There are postmodern, pressboard-and-plastic hotels on the outskirts of most towns in the region. They're run by hotel chains and are remarkably cheap (159FF for a room for up to three people). These ugly boxes (not listed in this guide) sport revolting views of busy roads and are convenient only for travellers with a car. Chains include Formule 1, Fimôtel and Campanile.

Mid-Range Hotels Expect to pay 200FF to 400FF for a room in what this guide considers 'mid-range' hotels. These hotels usually have three sets of seasonally adjusted prices. Low season applies from October/November to February/March. The middle season is usually March/April/May and September/October. High season is July and August (occasionally June and September too). Hotels usually close for several weeks in winter. Some places close straight through from September/October to March/April.

A reliable option in this price bracket are the family-run places that belong to Logis de France, an organisation whose affiliated establishments meet strict standards of service and amenities. The Association des Logis de France de Touraine (☎ 02 47 47 20 47, fax 02 47 61 62 38, ✉ info@logis-de-france.fr), 4 bis rue Jean Favre, 37000 Tours, or its counterpart in the Loiret (☎ 02 38 61 51 72, fax 02 38 61 72 75), 21 quai de Prague, 45000 Orléans, can put you in touch with other Logis de France offices in the region. Each office publishes an annual guide to the properties in its département. Complete hotel listings also feature on the Logis de France Web site at www.logis-de-france.fr.

Several mid-range hotels in Orléans, Blois, Tours, Saumur and Angers participate most years in Bon Weekend en Ville. This money-saving scheme offers weekend guests two nights' accommodation for the price of one. The deal is valid only if you arrive Friday or Saturday night and have booked your hotel accommodation at least eight days in advance; reservations have to be confirmed in writing. The tourist office in each city has details of which hotels participate in the scheme.

Chateaux

Sleeping in a centuries-old chateau, framed by beautifully manicured gardens and sprawling vineyards, is one of the Loire's greatest pleasures. Even more pleasurable is the price, which, contrary to popular belief, does not break the bank. Numerous privately owned chateaux have opened their doors to guests in recent years, offering accommodation on a refreshingly informal chambre d'hôte basis. Doubles with period furnishings and private bathroom start at 500FF, including a wholesome breakfast of home-grown products served in the family kitchen or more grandiose dining room. Evening meals are usually available for an additional 150FF or so. Many chateaux are part of a working wine-growing estate and will happily sell guests bottles of wine produced on their land.

Bienvenue au Château (✉ info@bienvenue-au-chateau.com) is a fabulous association of individual chateau owners in western France who offer chambre d'hôte accommodation in their even more fabulous homes. The annual Bienvenue au Château catalogue features English and French descriptions of property, maps and detailed instructions on how to get to each chateau, as well as line drawings of the respective chateaux. Bookings can be made directly through the property owner. The free catalogue is available from larger tourist offices. Alternatively, contact a comité regional du tourism (see Tourist Offices earlier in this chapter), or consult the association's Web site at www.bienvenue-au-chateau.com.

Several exclusive hotel chains offer upmarket accommodation in historic chateaux transformed into sumptuous five-star hotels, with a price tag to match. Relais et Châteaux (☎ 08 25 32 32 32, fax 01 45 72 96 69, ✉ resarc@relaischateaux.fr) has several top-of-the-range hotels in the Loire, featured in its annual catalogue. You can order the catalogue via the Web site at www.relaischateaux.fr. Châteaux et Hôtels Indépendants likewise publishes an annual guide to its small, pricey hotels in France; reservations can be made through its Paris office (☎ 01 40 07 00 20, fax 01 40 07 00 30, ✉ chatotel@chatotel.com), 12 rue Auber, 75009 Paris, or via the Web site at www.chatotel.com.

Grandes Étapes Françaises (☎ 01 43 66 06 40, fax 01 43 66 43 33, ✉ etapes@wanadoo.fr), 140 rue Belleville, 75020 Paris, boasts four beautiful estates in the Loire Valley. As part of its attempt to evoke 'avec élégance la vie de château' (chateau life with elegance), its properties host romantic, cocktail-fuelled soirées musicales (musical evenings; 180FF per person) and offer musical weekends (from 1080FF per guest). Expect to pay at least 1000FF to 1500FF per night for a basic double room in all these hotels; breakfast is an additional 100FF or so per person.

Abroad, most travel agencies that organise tours in the region can also arrange accommodation in chateaux (for details see Organised Tours in the Getting There & Away chapter).

Caves
Despite the high number of private cave dwellings which riddle this region, 'troglodyte' accommodation is still in its infancy. Les Hautes Roches, near Tours (see the boxed text 'Cave Dwellings' in the Touraine chapter), has four stars and is the only cave hotel in the Loire Valley; doubles start at 520FF. A cheaper option, though one

that needs to be booked several months in advance, is the Centre des Perrières (see Places to Stay & Eat under Doué-la-Fontaine in the Anjou chapter), a subterranean gîte in an abandoned quarry, open in summer only and equipped with 55 dorm beds.

A scanty handful of troglo chambre d'hôtes are listed in the practical, English-language guide Troglodytes Strange World (1993) by Suzanne Quéré and Roger Gaborieau; the publisher is Éditions CMD (☎ 02 41 38 70 76, fax 02 41 38 35 20), 396 rue de la Salle, 49260 Montreuil-Bellay.

Manors, Mills & Monasteries
The Loire has a wealth of upmarket hotels housed in traditional properties: mills (moulins), manor houses (manoirs), priories (prieurés) and pretty country homes (jolies demeures). Many are listed in the regional chapters of this book. Bienvenue au Château (see Chateaux earlier in this section) offers B&B accommodation in manor houses and priories too (or, in short, any other very old and very large property). Details of monasteries that accept guests are listed in the Guide St-Christophe (120FF), published by La Procure (☎ 01 45 48 20 25), 3 rue de Mézières, 75006 Paris. The annual Moulin Étape (www.moulin-etape .com) catalogue includes old mills in France where you can stay.

FOOD
For information on regional specialities, see the Food & Wine of the Loire special section. For more on French cuisine, including that of the Loire, have a look at Lonely Planet's World Food France (see Food & Wine under Books earlier in this chapter).

Vegetarian Cuisine
While most locals will stare at you as if you are downright crazy if you admit to not eating juicy slabs of practically raw meat, vegetarians will not starve when dining out. Few menus (set menus) feature vegetarian dishes, but there are usually a couple of vegetarian entrées (starters) to titillate the tastebuds, while salads alone can be huge.

Cardon is rare member of the artichoke family, found in abundance in the Loire region and usually dished up with *beurre blanc* (a traditional white sauce). *Pâté de citrouille* is a delicious pumpkin terrine-cum-pâté. Traditional *pain aux noix* (walnut bread), *boules aux châtaignes* (chestnut rolls) and *pain de fromage* (cheese bread) add a bite to the blandest of meals.

Restaurants & Cafes

Eating out can mean spending anything from 50FF (in a village bistro) to 250FF or more (in one of the region's multi-starred gastronomic temples). Regardless of price, most places have a menu pinned up outside, allowing for a quick price and dish check for those not wanting to end up washing the dishes or dining on *fressure vendéenne* (stewed pig parts).

The most authentic places to eat are often in tiny hamlets off the beaten track or languishing in the grounds of a chateau (such as Restaurant St-Michel inside the former kennels of Château de Chambord, or the rustic, 17th-century Auberge du XII Siècle opposite Château de Saché). These places invariably offer a *menu du terroir* (regional cuisine menu) or *menu saveur* (local specialities menu) – the ideal choice for those wanting to sample traditional regional fare. Upmarket spots often sport a *menu dégustation* (sampling or tasting menu) or *menu plaisir gourmand* (gourmet menu) – a gastronomic feast of fresh produce, kicking off with an *amuse-bouche* (appetiser, literally 'mouth-pleaser') followed by a succession of courses, each accompanied by a different glass of regional wine.

In cheaper restaurants and auberges, you might be expected to use the one set of eating utensils for the duration of your meal. Upon finishing your entree, replace your knife and fork (a subtle wipe clean with bread is allowed; licking is less cool) on the table either side of your dirty plate. If you don't do it, the waiter will do it for you. The waiter is likely to add up the bill (*addition*) on your paper tablecloth.

The cafe is an integral part of French society, with many doubling as the village bar and bistro. Most serve simple baguettes filled with cheese (around 25FF), *charcuterie* (cold meats) or *rillettes* (a minced pork paste). Others have select terraces hidden out back, where you can dine in the shade of overhead vines.

Fermes Auberges

A *ferme auberge* is a small, family-run inn attached to a working farm or chateau. They are among the most delightful places to dine. Traditional regional fare is guaranteed. Dining is around shared tables with wooden benches. Portions are sufficiently hearty for those with the largest of appetites to leave in a merry state of stuffed bliss. A *menu*, comprising four courses and often wine too, can cost 100FF to 180FF.

Salons de Thé & Crêperies

Salons de thé (tearooms) are trendy and expensive establishments that offer quiches, salads, cakes, tarts, pies and pastries in addition to tea and coffee.

Crêperies serve up ultra-thin pancakes (*crêpes*) with a variety of sweet or savoury fillings. *Galettes* (made with savoury wheat from wheatbuck or black Breton flour) are abundant in the historically Breton area around Nantes and St-Nazaire.

Self-Catering

When shopping, do as the locals do: spurn the supermarket and buy fresh local products from the market, then stroll to the local *boulangerie* (bread shop) for a baked-that-hour baguette (long stick of white bread) or some pain aux noix; then to the *pâtisserie* (cake shop) for *tartes tatins* (caramelised apple tarts), *pâte des fruits* (sweet fruits boiled with sugar), *gâteau de pithiviers* (an almond-filled pastry) and other yummy cakes and pastries. Margarine-based croissants can be identified by their almost-touching tips; buttery ones have their tips facing outwards.

Purchase cheese in the *fromagerie*, and ask how to best preserve the cheeses you buy, which wines are best served with them and so on. If you don't know a cheese type, ask to taste (*goûter*) it. Prewrapped cheese sold in supermarkets is unripe and utterly tasteless by comparison. Shop for slices of cold meats and salads at a *charcuterie* (delicatessen). The catch of the day is sold at a *poissonnerie* (fishmonger), general meat at a *boucherie* (butcher), poultry at a *marchand de volaille* (poultry seller), horse meat at a *chevaline* and tripe at a *triperie*.

Chèvreries (goat farms) are the place to buy the freshest, driest or most mature *chèvre* (goat's cheese). Most goat farmers are happy to give you a quick tour of the goat farm, prior to your tasting and buying some of the end product. Tourist offices in cheese-making towns – such as Sancerre, Ste-Maure de Touraine and Selles-sur-Cher – stock lists of goat farms that welcome tourists.

Any titbits you still need are probably sold at the local *épicerie* (literally 'spice shop', but actually a grocery store) or *alimentation générale* (general food shop). Backpackers wanting to stock up on shedloads of beer, bottled water and the like will – of course – find it cheaper to shop at a supermarket (Casino, Monoprix and so on) in town or at one of the giant *hypermarchés* (hypermarkets; Leclerc, Intermarché and so on) on the outskirts of most towns.

Every village, town and city also has a weekly or daily market, which sprawls across the central square and a nearby patchwork of streets. Farmers flock into town from the outlying farms and villages to sell their fresh produce and chat with friends. No bargaining is allowed. Some cities, such as Tours, host a weekly *marché gourmand* (gourmet market), an upscale version of a daily market, which showcases regional wines and other, more gourmet, products.

DRINKS
Alcoholic Drinks
The region's rich fruit yield is reflected in its sweeter-than-sweet alcoholic liqueurs, most of which are served as a *digestif* to ensure that appropriately 'plump and contented' feeling following a deliciously long and lazy meal.

Pears are turned into Poire d'Olivet, a strong pear liqueur, in Orléans. Triple Sec

and Cointreau are distilled from orange peel in Saumur and Angers respectively. The latter is a popular ingredient in a whole host of raunchily named cocktails. A lighter alternative to end a meal is an *eau de vie* (literally 'water of life'). Eaux de vie is the generic name for brandies distilled from the region's many fruits.

Beer is not a local drink and is priced accordingly.

For information on the region's wines, wine-tasting and so on, see the Food & Wine of the Loire special section.

Nonalcoholic Drinks
Tap water is safe to drink. In restaurants it is perfectly acceptable to order a carafe of tap water (*une carafe d'eau*) instead of a pricier soft drink, mineral water (*eau de source*) or wine. Soft drinks are generally 15FF per glass (wine can be cheaper). You don't get ice cubes (*glaçons*) unless you ask.

Coffee costs about 10FF a cup. Unless you specify otherwise, you get a small, strong, black espresso. Those requiring a bigger caffeine fix should ask for *un grand café* (a double espresso). Milky versions include *un café crème* (espresso with steamed milk or cream) and *un café au lait* (hot milk with a dash of coffee). Coffee is never served with cold milk.

Tea (*thé*) and hot chocolate (*chocolat chaud*) are widely available. Most salons de thé serve a choice of herbal teas (*infusions*).

ENTERTAINMENT
Local tourist offices are the best source of information on what's on where. In addition, there are a host of regional entertainment journals and newspapers – most of which are free – which contain comprehensive cinema, theatre and festival listings. Try *Orléans Poche* (monthly), *Angers Poche* (fortnightly) and *Nantes Poche* (weekly). In Nantes, there are several student-targeted magazines, including *Pulsomatic*.

FNAC (☎ 08 36 68 93 39) is the hub for tickets and reservations for everything from theatre, opera and exhibitions to rock concerts, football matches and festivals. Most stores have a ticket desk where a calendar of events is posted, advance bookings made and tickets sold. There are FNACs in Orléans and Nantes. Have a look at the Web site at www.fnac.fr.

Pubs & Bars

Lively pubs and bars catering to a boisterous student clientele are best represented in university cities such as Orléans, Tours, Nantes and Poitiers. Bars claiming to be Irish are particularly rife in Tours and Orléans. Many of these drinking holes host live bands at the weekend. By contrast, the local bar in villages and smaller towns is a humble affair, doubling as the village cafe-cum-gossip-shop by day.

Discos & Clubs

Discos and clubs (*discothèques* or *boîtes* in French) where you can strut your stuff on the dance floor are few and far between outside Orléans, Tours, Angers, Nantes and Poitiers; the last two cities enjoy the most eclectic clubs and nightlife due to their substantial student populations. The crowd can be gay, lesbian, straight or mixed. *Tenue correcte exigée* means 'appropriate dress required'.

Gay & Lesbian Venues

Orléans, Tours and Angers have a small but active gay and lesbian scene, but Nantes is the only city to openly market its gay and lesbian venues. See Gay & Lesbian Travellers earlier in this chapter for details on who to contact to uncover gay and lesbian venues in the valley.

Music

A colourful cross-spectrum of musical genres is performed in the region. Rock and pop concerts take to the stage in Orléans and Tours. Choral and organ concerts are a dime a dozen in city cathedrals and some rural churches, while the Grands Théâtres in Angers and Tours, and Nantes' Théâtre Graslin are the region's leading opera venues. Classical music is performed across the region, with some smaller chateaux – such as Château de la Bussière, Château de Fougères-sur-Bièvre and Château de

Montsoreau – hosting classical concerts under the starry night skies in summer.

Music festivals (jazz, classical, chamber music) are plentiful, particularly in summer; see the boxed text 'Feasts & Festivals' earlier in this chapter for details. The countrywide Fête de la Musique brings live music to every nook and cranny of the valley each year on 21 June.

Cinemas

You can see films in their original language (with French subtitles) in selected cinemas in Orléans, Tours and Nantes. Look for the letters VO (*version originale*) on cinema billboards. Prices vary, but you can expect to pay between 30FF and 50FF in most places. Some places (such as Orléans) have outside screenings in summer, which are a joy to attend, regardless of language.

Theatre

Angers, Tours and Nantes enjoy a lively theatre season, although the theatres break for summer each year in May or June until September or October. Tickets usually cost between 30FF and 200FF, depending on seating. Seniors and students often get discounted tickets. Tours has a handful of alternative cafe-theatres.

SPECTATOR SPORTS
Cycling

The three-week Tour de France (www.le tour.fr), which hits the road each year in July, often passes through the region. In 1998, 1999 and 2000 it kicked off at Futuroscope, the technology theme park outside Poitiers. Poitiers, Nantes and Tours are *villes étapes* – towns in which one of the 21 stages often starts or ends.

Equestrian Sport

Saumur is the arena for several national and international equestrian sporting events. Hot dates in the equestrian calendar include the Championnat de France de Voltige (French 'Trick' Riding Championships) in July; the European and International Pony and Trap Championships, also in July; and the Concours de Dressage International

Motor Racing

Les 24 Heures du Mans (Le Mans 24 Hours) ranks among the raciest dates in motorsports. It sees drivers from all over the world converge on Le Mans each year in June to lap the 13.605km-long Circuit de la Sarthe for 24 hours straight – the ultimate endurance test for man and machine.

Few succeed in completing the course, which has been modified several times since Le Mans was put into gear in 1923. Most recently, in 1990, two chicanes were added to the Hunaudières straight to slow down its notoriously fast pace; cars were reaching dizzying speeds of 350km/h. The worst accident in motor-racing history took place at Le Mans in 1955, when French driver Pierre Levegh crashed into a packed enclosure, killing some 80 spectators. Much of the Circuit de la Sarthe runs along regular roads, including sections of the N138 and D140 south of Le Mans.

Pre-qualifying and qualifying time trials precede the big weekend event, which draws some 200,000 spectators. Pits are open to all (at a price) on Friday to allow race-goers to drool over the latest speed machines created by Mercedes, Porsche, Toyota and the rest. During the race – Saturday 4 pm to Sunday 4 pm – 48 cars consume an estimated 130,000L of fuel. In 1999 triumphant Italian driver Pierluigi Martini clocked up a giddying 4967.99km at an average speed of 207km/h (compared to 2209km and 92km/h by the winners of the first Le Mans). That year also marked the first Le Mans victory for BMW.

Models that have raced in Les 24 Heures du Mans across the decades are displayed in the **Musée Automobile de la Sarthe** (☎ 02 43 72 72 24), a museum dedicated to the world's longest motor race. It's behind the start-finish straight of the Circuit de la Sarthe (admission 40FF).

Tickets for the race must be reserved in advance by fax or mail (until the end of May) from Le Mans International Circuit (☎ 02 43 40 24 75, 02 43 40 24 77, fax 02 43 84 47 13), Reservations Department, 72019 Le Mans. In 1999 tickets cost 320FF, plus 250FF to 470FF for a grandstand place. Race-goers can camp in specially designed areas around the circuit; pitch tickets cost 200FF to 450FF and must be reserved in advance. Check out the Web site at www.lemans.org.

(International Dressage Competition) in mid-September. Tickets and information for all these events are available from the tourist office in Saumur (www.saumur.org) or from the Comité Équestre de Saumur (☎ 02 41 67 36 37, fax 02 41 67 64 91), 8 quai Mayaud, 49400 Saumur.

The Mondial du Lion, an international three-day event (dressage, endurance, cross-country, show jumping), is held each year in mid-October in the grounds of the Haras National d'Isle Briand, in Le Lion d'Angers. Information and tickets, which cost 30FF to 50FF, are available from the stud farm (*haras*; ☎ 02 41 95 82 46, fax 02 41 95 69 69, ✉ mondial@lelion-hn.com). It has a Web site at www.lelion-hn.com.

Sailing

The Vendée Globe Challenge is a round-the-world yacht race that sets sail from the Atlantic coast resort of Les Sables d'Olonne every two or three years in early November. Skippers have to complete the tough voyage around three capes single-handedly and without stopping. Just 13 sailors successfully completed this mission in the first Global race-against-time in 1989.

Boule de Fort

Boule de fort is Loire Valley *boules* (bowls). From the 15th century, bargemen played the game aboard their river barges, and from 1700 it drifted ashore in the western half of the valley – around Angers, as far east as Tours, south to Saumur and north to La Flèche. Despite the seemingly informal nature of the game, boule de fort has a definitive set of rules that must be followed.

Two to six people, comprising two teams, can play. Each player has a set of wooden boules. Boules are not round, but rather flat and squat. The best are made of a hard wood such as box or ash, though boules are increasingly made of plastic today. Personal initials, a name or family coat of arms can be crafted onto made-to-measure boules.

Boule de fort revolves around the jack (*maître*, literally 'master'), a small wooden ball. Each team takes it in turn to aim a boule at this marker, the idea being to land the boule as close as possible to the jack. The team with the closest boule wins the round. Throughout the match, only the scorekeeper (*couvreur*) is allowed to walk across court; all other players must remain behind the throwing line. Underarm throwing is compulsory. Beyond that, players can opt between rolling the boule in a dribble along the ground or hurling it high in the air in the hope of its landing smack-bang on top of an opponent's boule, sending it flying out of position. This flamboyant tactic can turn an entire game round in a matter of seconds.

Three Angevin *sociétés de boule de fort* welcome novices. Société la Cure (☎ 02 41 67 31 76), place Jeanne d'Arc (off place de la Senatorerie, near the church), 3km west of Saumur in St-Hilaire-St-Florent, opens its doors to the public year round on Sunday from 10 am to noon; in July and August it hosts initiation evenings on Thursday, start-ing at 6 pm. Playing fees are negotiable with the club president. In the centre of Angers, try Société Champ de Bataille (☎ 02 41 48 98 76), 4 rue du Champ Bataille, or Société La Trinité (☎ 02 41 87 56 93), place du Tertre.

SHOPPING
The distinctive blue and terracotta pottery (*bleu de Gien*) that has been turned in Gien since 1821 is one of the few crafts typical to the region. Beyond that, toy-size models of chateaux reign supreme.

Practically every village, town and city hosts at least one weekly market. Most tend to be of the mouthwatering variety, al-though Orléans, Tours and Angers all host flea markets (*marchés aux puces*) crammed with a jumble of clothes, saucepans, furni-ture, the occasional antique, and second-hand goods of all shapes, sizes and uses. Tours hosts several weekly and monthly an-tiques markets (see Shopping under Tours in the Touraine chapter for details). Every city has a contemporary commercial centre strewn with fashion shops; the Passage Pommeray in Nantes – a beautiful shopping arcade dating back to 1843 – is best suited to those who enjoy shopping in style.

FOOD & WINE OF THE LOIRE

FOOD

The Tourangeau author Rabelais' phrase '*le jardin de France*' (the garden of France) has been exploited nationwide since he coined it in the 16th century to describe his native Touraine. Yet it is the Loire that remains most true to his image of a green and succulent, well-watered landscape laden with lush fruits, flowers, nuts and vegetables.

JANE SMITH

Appropriately, countless culinary dishes traditional to the region are considered quintessentially French. *Coq au vin* (chicken in red wine), *cuisses de grenouilles* (frog's legs) and the famous *tarte tatin* (upside-down caramelised apple tart) were all cooked up in this riverside region. Mushrooms galore – chanterelles and boletus mushrooms (*bolets*) – abound in the region's forests, while button mushrooms (*champignons de Paris*) are cultivated in beds in the Loire's unique troglodyte caves. Fresh fish – from both the River Loire and the Atlantic Ocean – is an equally major player in regional gastronomy.

Dining at a *bon table* (good restaurant; literally 'good table') is of the utmost importance to most inhabitants of the Loire. See Food in the Facts for the Visitor chapter for general information on places to eat.

Fruits, Nuts & Vegetables

Around Tours, plums are dried and stuffed to create *pruneaux farcis* (stuffed prunes) or baked to make *noisette de porc aux pruneaux* (roast pork with prunes). Game dishes, particularly wild boar, are invariably sweetened with a garnish of *confiture de marrons* (chestnut paste) and *purée de pommes* (apple sauce). Apples also feature in tarte tatin, that ubiquitous upside-down apple tart that features on menus around the globe today. Green cabbage (*chou vert*), artichoke (*artichaut*) and the closely related *cardon*, asparagus (*asperges*), cherries (*cerises*), quince (*coing*; from which *cotignac*, a sweet quince jelly is made) and walnuts (*noix*) are likewise rife in Rabelais' jardin de France.

Beans and lentils from Vendée contribute to the region's reputation for hearty 'peasant fare'. *Mojettes* are white, flat and resemble the better-known broad bean. They are dressed in *beurre blanc* (see Fish, next) or dried and dunked in a *pot au feu* (stew). Carrots (*carottes*), cabbages (*choux*) and pumpkins (*citrouilles*) are other stock vegetables that can be thrown in a pot au feu or used to decorate Renaissance gardens: few of the thousands of ornamental red- or white-hearted cabbages at Château de Villandry are eaten – most are recycled as compost.

ght: You can take your pick of mushrooms in the Loire.

93

Pays Nantais (the region around Nantes) enjoys rich crops of different lettuces, notably lamb's lettuce (*mâche*) and dandelion leaves (*pissenlits*). At the start of spring, marsh samphires (*salicornes*) are picked from around salt pans. They can be boiled and eaten fresh with a light coating of butter, or pickled. Top chefs go wild over this marine herb.

Fish

Pike-perch (*sandre*) and pike (*brochet*) are traditionally served in beurre blanc, a buttery white sauce concocted in the 19th century by the fabled chef Mère Clémence of Nantes. Melted butter, vinegar (traditionally from upstream Orléans), shallots and white pepper are the primary ingredients of the sauce, which is considered a perfect and honourable accompaniment to most freshwater fish.

Countless beurre blanc recipes have evolved. Cooks tend to respect culinary protocol à la Clémence, which requires the shallots to be finely chopped, laced in wine and vinegar, and simmered over a hot flame to reduce the liquids. Cube by cube, cold butter is whisked into the sauce, and then pepper is added for spice. Local muscadet wine must be used. Contentious issues include the ratio of wine to vinegar and the type of butter (salted or unsalted); some cooks add cream.

Eel (*anguille*) is eaten near the coast. The fish market at Aiguillon-sur-Mer is a prime spot to buy eels or grey mullet (*mulet*), a silvery fish that local fishermen catch with large nets from the footbridge next to the port. Shellfish (*coquillage*) – including mussels (*moules*) and oysters (*huîtres*) in season – is equally abundant at the port market. Washed

JANE SMITH

Left: Feast on local wine, fruit and goat's cheese the 'garden of France'.

and beardless, ready-to-cook mussels are called *moules prêtes à cuire*. Whelks (*bulots*), periwinkles (*bigorneaus*) and clams (*palourdes*) are among the thumbnail-sized shellfish that amateur fishermen seek beneath rocks and in the sand; during low tide the causeway (Passage du Gois) to Île de Noirmoutier is riddled with these *pêcheurs à pied* (literally 'fishermen on foot').

Meat

Poultry and game dishes were the pride of the medieval kitchen. Once or twice a year, villages in the valley slaughtered a fattened pig, from which a highly enterprising range of porky products were made.

Meat from the pig's neck was traditionally minced up and fried in fat to make *rillettes*, a cold paste ranked as the region's signature dish. Traditionally typical to Touraine, it is equally widespread in Anjou today. Several cave restaurants around Saumur serve rillettes with *fouaces*, a type of bread baked in huge wood-fired ovens since the Middle Ages. *Rillons* are crispy, crunchy cubes of fat-fried pork which, unlike rillettes, can be eaten hot or cold.

Every last pig part is used. Offal is transformed into meaty tripe sausages: *andouillettes* are soft, fleshy and bought in a raw state, while *andouilles* are firm, hard and ready to eat upon purchase. The glories of andouilles are sung by the Confrérie des Chevaliers du Goûte Andouille (Tripe Sausage Brotherhood) in Jargeau. The Jargeau charcutier, Monsieur Guibet, makes and sells authentic andouilles (see Jargeau in the Orléanais & Blésois chapter). Pig blood gives the *boudin noir* (blood sausage) its distinctive dark colour (*boudin blanc* is a sausage made from veal, chicken or turkey).

Gérard Girardeau's Saumur shop supplies the presidential Elysée Palace with pigs' trotters (*pieds de cochon*). They come stuffed or unstuffed and have twice taken the gold in the Concours Européen du Meilleur Pied du Cochon (European Championships for the Best Pigs' Trotters). Girardeau makes andouillettes and *cailles farcies* (stuffed quail) as well, and his *terrine de grand-mère*, a type of pâté adhering to an old family recipe, is legendary. Chez Girardeau (☎ 02 41 51 30 33, fax 02 41 50 29 99) is in the centre of Saumur at 51–53 rue St-Nicholas, 49400 Saumur.

Cheese

Chèvre (goat's cheese) reigns supreme in the Loire, and the region churns out some of France's best known: Crottin de Chavignol, Selles-sur-Cher, Ste-Maure de Touraine and Poligny St-Pierre have each carried their own *appellation d'origine contrôlée* (AOC; guarantee of origin and quality) since the mid-1970s, and are moulded in a distinctive trademark shape.

Crottin de Chavignol and Selles-sur-Cher come in traditional round pats. Ste-Maure de Touraine is in the form of a 15- to 20cm-long cylinder, and Poligny St-Pierre is pyramid shaped. Each cheese is best tasted

MATTHIAS LÜFKENS

with wine from the same region – thus drink a Sancerre with Chavignol.

Chèvre originates in a *chevrière* (goat farm), is ripened by an *affineur* (refiner) and is sold at a *fromagerie*. The flavour of chèvre depends on whether it is *frais* (fresh or young) or *sec* (dried or ripened with age).

WINE

The Loire's wine-growing tradition dates from the 5th century AD, although the Romans planted vines around Nantes as early as 600 BC. By the 6th century AD, vineyards carpeted much of the valley, as is illustrated in Gregory of Tours' *Historia Francorum* (*History of the Franks*), in which the bishop expresses great concern for his diocese's vineyards. Today the Loire's 75,000 hectares of vineyards rank the region as the third in France for the production of *appellation d'origine contrôlée* (AOC) wines (2.5 million hectolitres annually, or 250 million litres, 23% of which is exported). AOC wines comply with stringent government regulations governing where, how and under what conditions they are grown, fermented and bottled.

The region is best known for its dry whites, which account for 55% of annual AOC production. Gros Plant du Pays Nantais is known as being the cheapest white wine in France. The most widely drunk whites, however, are muscadets – the vineyards of which cover 13,000 hectares of rolling hills south of Nantes – and Sancerre, which is produced across 2300 hectares at the eastern end of the valley. Between these two geographical extremes, the fertile banks of the River Loire yield an astonishing variety of appellations and vintages. Irrespective of age, colour or sparkle, Loire wine tends to be light and delicate. *Vins de garde* (wines best drunk after several years in storage) are few.

As in the rest of France, wine is drunk with almost every meal in the Loire. In bistros, brasseries and restaurants, house wine – always drinkable but never startling – is the cheapest. It can be served in a *carafe* (glass jug); a *pichet* (pottery jug), which can be *quart-* (quarter), *demi-* (half) or *litre-* (litre) sized; or a *bouteille* (bottle). The rarer half-bottle is called a *fillette* (literally 'little girl').

Come the first grape harvests in September or October, signs reading *vin nouveau* (new wine) or *vin bourru* (literally 'surly wine') spring up in cafe and bar windows. This new wine is unfermented, made from the first grapes harvested that year. It is murky in colour and would taste rather like grape juice were it not for its distinctive yeasty flavour.

Wines of the region can be bought direct from the estate of the wine producer (*producteur*) or grower (*vigneron*) at a lower price than in

Left: Goats are put out to grass at a cheese-producing farm, Chavignol.

SALLY DILLON

NICOLA WILLIAMS

MATTHIAS LOFKENS

MATTHIAS LOFKENS

Top left: A picnic with a view

Top right: Pick boletus mushrooms fresh from the forest at the market in medieval Loches.

Middle left: The pick of the bunch in the Vouvray vineyards

Middle right: It's pure cheese: preparing the famed Crottin de Chavignol goat's cheese in Chavignol

Bottom: Window shopping is all too tempting in Amboise.

DIANA MAYFIELD

FOOD HIGHLIGHTS AND WINE REGIONS

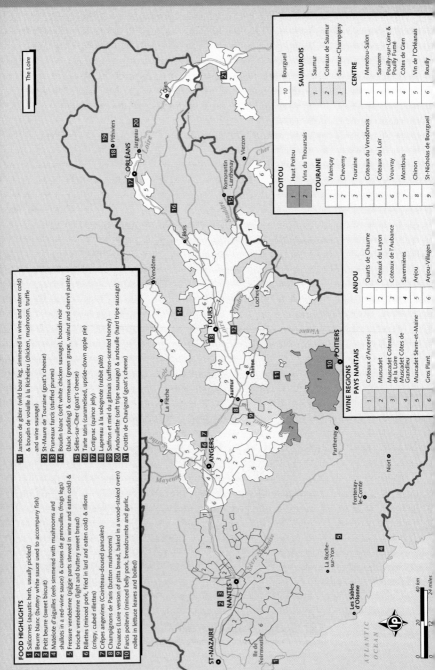

FOOD HIGHLIGHTS

1. Salicornes (aquatic herb, usually pickled)
2. Beurre blanc (buttery white sauce used to accompany fish)
3. Petit beurre (sweet biscuit)
4. Matelote d'aiguilles (eels simmered with mushrooms and shallots in a red-wine sauce) & cuisses de grenouilles (frog's legs)
5. Fressure vendéenne (piggie parts stewed in wine and eaten cold) & brioche vendéenne (light and buttery sweet bread)
6. Rillettes (minced pork, fried in lard and eaten cold) & rillons (crispy, cubed rillettes)
7. Crêpes angevines (Cointreau-doused pancakes)
8. Champignons de Paris (button mushrooms)
9. Fouaces (Loire version of pitta bread, baked in a wood-stoked oven)
10. Farcis poitevin (minced belly pork, breadcrumbs and garlic, rolled in lettuce leaves and boiled)
11. Jambon de gibier (wild boar leg, simmered in wine and eaten cold) & boudin de volaille à la Richelieu (chicken, mushroom, truffle and wine sausage)
12. St-Maure de Touraine (goat's cheese)
13. Pruneaux farcis (stuffed prunes)
14. Boudin blanc (soft white chicken sausage), boudin noir (black pudding) & cerneaux (green grape, walnut and chervil paste)
15. Selles-sur-Cher (goat's cheese)
16. Tarte tatin (caramelised, upside-down apple pie)
17. Cotignac (quince jelly)
18. Lapereau à la sologne (rabbit pâté)
19. Saffron et miel du gâtinais (saffron-scented honey)
20. Andouillette (soft tripe sausage) & andouille (hard tripe sausage)
21. Crottin de Chavignol (goat's cheese)

WINE REGIONS

PAYS NANTAIS

1. Coteaux d'Ancenis
2. Muscadet
3. Muscadet Coteaux de la Loire
4. Muscadet Côtes de Grandlieu
5. Muscadet Sèvre-et-Maine
6. Gros Plant

ANJOU

1. Quarts de Chaume
2. Coteaux du Layon
3. Coteaux de l'Aubance
4. Savennières
5. Anjou
6. Anjou-Villages

POITOU

1. Haut Poitou
2. Vins du Thouarsais

TOURAINE

1. Valençay
2. Cheverny
3. Touraine
4. Coteaux du Vendômois
5. Coteaux du Loir
6. Vouvray
7. Montlouis
8. Chinon
9. St-Nicholas de Bourgueil
10. Bourgueil

SAUMUROIS

1. Saumur
2. Coteaux de Saumur
3. Saumur-Champigny

CENTRE

1. Menetou-Salon
2. Sancerre
3. Pouilly-sur-Loire & Pouilly Fumé
4. Côtes de Gien
5. Vin de l'Orléanais
6. Reuilly

— The Loire

ATLANTIC OCEAN

0   20   40 km
0   12   24 miles

shops. Most places offer tasting (*dégustation*), which allows you to sample two or three of their vintages, with no obligation to buy. At a Maison du Vin (in Angers and Saumur; see those towns in the Anjou chapter for details), you can taste and buy wine by scores of different growers – often easier and quicker than traipsing from estate to estate. Purchasing one or two bottles or one to 20 boxes (six or 12 bottles per box) at either is equally acceptable.

Gérard Girardeau (see Meat under Food earlier in this special section) is one of the country's few antique wine dealers (*antiquaires de vins*). His awe-inspiring cellar has vintages dating back to 1855. In mid-1999 you could buy a 1900 Chinon here for 1500FF.

The primary centres for wine-tasting are Sancerre (Orléanais); neighbouring Vouvray and Montlouis (outside Tours, in Touraine); Angers and the Coteaux du Layon and Savennières vineyards (near Château de Serrant, in Anjou); Saumur and nearby Souzay-Champigny, where wine is stored in troglodyte caves; and in and around Nantes. Complete lists of *caves* (wine cellars) open to travellers are available from:

Bureau Interprofessionnel des Vins du Centre (BIVC; ☎ 02 48 78 51 07, fax 02 48 78 51 08, ◙ bivc@wanadoo.fr) 9 route de Chavignol, 18300 Sancerre
Comité Interprofessionnel des Vins d'Anjou et de Saumur (CIVAS; ☎ 02 41 87 62 57, fax 02 41 86 71 84) Hôtel des Vins, La Godeline, 733 rue Plantagenêt, 49100 Angers
Comité Interprofessionnel des Vins de Touraine et du Val de Loire (CIVTL; ☎ 02 47 05 40 01, fax 02 47 66 57 32) 19 square Prosper Mérimée, 37000 Tours
Fédération Interprofessionnelle des Vins du Val de Loire (FIVAL; ☎ 02 47 64 18 19, fax 02 47 64 48 00, ◙ fival@creaweb.fr) 47 rue Jules Simon, 37000 Tours
Web site: www.vins-valdeloire.com

Another excellent source of information is the English-language *Découvertes en Terroir* series published by the *comités régionaux du tourisme* (regional tourist offices; see Tourist Offices in the Facts for the Visitor chapter). Touraine, Anjou and Pays Nantais are covered in three separate guides (50FF); each maps out around 100km of marked walking trails that take travellers from *cave* to *cave* and vineyard to vineyard, and also lists some 145 growers who will help your taste buds discover one of the region's noblest treasures.

Centre

Viticulture in the upper Loire (east of Orléans) is dominated by the sauvignon blanc grape variety, from which the world's most commercial dry white wines are made. The soil ranges from chalky *terres blanches* (literally 'white earth') around Sancerre to the limestone slopes of Menetou-Salon and the gravel-sand soils of Reuilly. Of the four appellations produced, AOC Menetou-Salon, AOC Reuilly, AOC

INGRID RODDIS

Coteaux du Giennois and AOC Sancerre, the last is the best known. Sancerre vineyards sprawl for 2300 hectares. Some 25,000 hectolitres of subtle Sancerre rosés and cherry reds are produced annually from a small pocket of pinot noir vineyards, but the whites – yielded from sauvignon vines carpeting 1800 hectares – are legendary. Alphonse Mellot, Jospeh Mellot, Lucien Crochet and Henri Bourgeois are names to look out for.

Touraine

After Pays Nantais, this is the valley's largest vineyard. Embracing 11,000 hectares from Blois in the east to Saumur in the west, Touraine produces over 600,000 hectolitres of wine annually. Of its 11 appellations, Vouvray and Montlouis are the dominant whites. Both can be dry, semi-dry or sweet and are made exclusively from the chenin blanc grape, a native of the Loire Valley, known as Pineau de la Loire by local growers. Vouvray hosts annual wine fairs (*foires aux vins*) in January and August.

Vouvray and Montlouis both lend their name to sparkling wines, not to be confused with Crémant de Loire, which the valley has produced since 1975. Four million bottles of white or rosé Crémant de Loire were produced by 340 producers across Touraine, Saumurois and Anjou in 1998. Grapes – usually chenin blanc – must be picked by hand and pressed in bunches. The wine gets its champagne-like sparkle from a second (year-long) fermentation in the bottle, during which time bottles are stored in the troglolodyte *caves* around Saumur. Crémant de Loire should be served chilled to between 5 and 7°C; add a dash of Cointreau for an unusual aperitif.

Chinon and Bourgueil reds are notable for being the Loire's richest and most full-bodied reds. Ruby-red Chinons are made from the cabernet franc grape (known as the 'Breton') and vary considerably; wines grown on chalky soil are better suited to ageing than those cultivated on gravel terraces on the Vienne riverbanks. AOC Bourgueil and AOC St-Nicolas de Bourgueil are among the Loire's most sought-after appellations. The former can be stored for five years or so, but St-Nicolas matures at a younger age. Both are delicious served with Ste-Maure de Touraine (see Cheese under Food earlier in this special section) and are honoured at the annual wine fair in Le Bourgueil on the first Saturday in February.

Chinon

Chinon wine has been sold under its own AOC since 1937. Its vineyards cover 1850 hectares, worked by some 200 wine producers who

Left: Grapes crop up everywhere in the Loir

have an annual production – predominantly red – of 80,000 hectolitres. Since 1961, Chinon wine has been promoted by the Confrèrie des Bons Entonneurs Rabelaisiens (Brotherhood of Rabelaisian Singers; ☎ 02 47 93 30 44), a brotherhood of 30,000 *chevaliers* (honorary brothers, literally 'knights') named after Rabelais, the hedonistic novelist born in Chinon and famed for his penchant for the local vintage.

The brotherhood's five annual chapters – solemn and ceremonial occasions – mark key dates in the viticulture calendar; for example, the Chapitre des Ven-

JANE SMITH

danges celebrates the annual harvest. Chapters are held in the Caves Paintes, painted caves at the foot of Château de Chinon. In Rabelais' epic *Gargantua et Pantagruel*, Pantagruel drinks chilled wine at these caves tucked away in a former tufa quarry. Indeed, Rabelais' fictional *'temple de la dive bouteille'* (temple of the holy bottle), where Pantagruel ends his long quest for the holy bottle, is said to be based on these mysterious caves.

The yellow vests and red caps of the Confrèrie des Bons Entonneurs Rabelaisiens are a distinctive feature at Chinon's annual wine fair on the second weekend in March.

Saumurois & Anjou

The Saumur vineyards kiss Touraine but are twinned with Anjou. Average annual production of Saumur-Anjou wines is almost 600,000 hectolitres, the yield of a vast, 10,000-hectare vineyard sprawled across three départements. Reds and rosés account for 75% of production, but it is Anjou whites – notably Savennières, Coteaux du Layon and Quarts de Chaume – that have gained the most respect among wine specialists (*sommeliers*).

Vins d'Anjou et de Saumur are split between 27 different appellations, including Rosé de Loire, which is the premier rosé in the Loire. Light and fruity Saumur-Champigny – best served between 13 and 16°C – is the leading Saumur red, followed closely by the lighter Anjou-Villages, which is matured in a cask for one year prior to bottling. Saumur-Champigny makes a great accompaniment to game or red meat and Anjou-Villages goes well with grilled or cold meats and other summer dishes.

The startlingly dry, full-bodied Savennières (unfortunately with a minute annual production of 2500 hectolitres) makes a magnificent

ight: A member of the belaisian brotherhood looks for inspiration at e bottom of his glass.

contrast to the seductively sweet Coteaux du Layon or Quarts de Chaume. The latter are grown on pebble-clay soils, can be laid down and are best served between 8 and 10°C as an aperitif, accompanied by foie gras or blue cheese. Their annual productions total 50,000 and 700 hectolitres respectively. Local Coteaux du Layon wine makers celebrate their annual Fête des Vins et de l'Andouillette in St-Lambert du Lattay in early July.

In addition to Crémant de Loire (see Touraine earlier in this section), sparkling Saumur Brut is another sparkling wine native to the region. It's produced on 1300 hectares of tufa soil around Saumur and also laid to ferment in troglodyte *caves*.

Pays Nantais

The muscadet vineyards around Nantes are the valley's largest, spanning 13,000 hectares of schist soil north and south of the River Loire. Muscadet was one of the first wines to win its own AOC (1936), which requires the wine to be made solely from the melon de Bourgogne grape. Of the three sub-regional production areas, AOC Muscadet Sèvre-et-Maine (south of Nantes) accounts for 85% of production.

Gros Plant du Pays Nantais is produced from the folle blanche grape, a hardy native of south-western France which grows on almost any soil and was cultivated in Pays Nantais in the 16th century. It is credited with a *vin délimité de qualité supérieure* (VDQS; literally 'demarcated wine of superior quality'), the second rank of quality control, after AOC, and cashes in on its national reputation as being France's cheapest white.

Of the two white wines, muscadet is undoubtedly the better accompaniment to the region's wealth of seafood.

Getting There & Away

AIR
Airports & Airlines

Paris – next-door neighbour to the Loire – is the primary gateway to the region. The Paris airports of Roissy Charles de Gaulle and Orly are served by most major international carriers, including the national carrier, Air France (www.airfrance.com). Within the region, Nantes-Atlantique is the only airport that bills itself as an international transport hub, although few destinations are actually conected with Nantes by direct flights. Most short- and long-haul flights advertised to/from Nantes-Atlantique (www.nantes.aeroport.fr) require a change of plane in either Paris, Brussels or another regional airport such as Bordeaux, Clermont-Ferrand, Le Havre, Lyon or Nice.

In Angers, Tours and Poitiers there are small airports, served by flights to/from Paris and elsewhere in France. The leading carriers on these domestic routes are Regional Airlines (www.regionalairlines .com), the British Airways-owned Air Liberté (www.air-liberte.fr) and Air Littoral. For details of these airports and how to travel to/from the town centres, see Air under Getting There & Away and To/From the Airport under Getting Around in the relevant chapters.

Buying Tickets

An air ticket alone can gouge a great slice out of anyone's budget, but you can reduce the cost by finding discounted fares. Stiff competition has resulted in widespread discounting – good news for travellers. The only people likely to be paying full fare these days are travellers flying in 1st or business class. Economy passengers can usually manage some sort of discount.

The only way to find the best deal is to shop around. Before parting with any cash, always check the total fare, stopovers required (or allowed), the journey duration, the period of validity, cancellation penalties and any other restrictions.

It sometimes pays to approach the airline direct, particularly if you intend flying from a European airport to Paris with a no-frills carrier such as Ryanair or KLM's Buzz. These cut-price airlines all accept on-line bookings. On-line ticket sales work well if you are doing a simple one-way or return trip on specified dates. However, on-line super-fast fare generators are no substitute for a travel agency that knows all about special deals, has strategies for avoiding layovers and can offer advice on everything from which airline has the best vegetarian food to the best travel insurance to bundle with your ticket.

Student and Youth Fares

Full-time students and people aged under 26 have access to better deals than other travellers. The better deals may not always be cheaper fares, but can include more flexibility to change flights and/or routes. You

Air Travel Glossary

Cancellation Penalties If you have to cancel or change a discounted ticket, there are often heavy penalties involved; insurance can sometimes be taken out against these penalties. Some airlines impose penalties on regular tickets as well, particularly against 'no-show' passengers.

Courier Fares Businesses often need to send urgent documents or freight securely and quickly. Courier companies hire people to accompany the package through customs and, in return, offer a discount ticket which is sometimes a phenomenal bargain. However, you may have to surrender all your baggage allowance and take only carry-on luggage.

Full Fares Airlines traditionally offer 1st class (coded F), business class (coded J) and economy class (coded Y) tickets. These days there are so many promotional and discounted fares available that few passengers pay full economy fare.

Lost Tickets If you lose your airline ticket, an airline will usually treat it like a travellers cheque and, after inquiries, issue you with another one. Legally, however, an airline is entitled to treat it like cash and if you lose it then it's gone forever. Take good care of your tickets.

Onward Tickets An entry requirement for many countries is that you have a ticket out of the country. If you're unsure of your next move, the easiest solution is to buy the cheapest onward ticket to a neighbouring country or a ticket from a reliable airline which can later be refunded if you do not use it.

Open-Jaw Tickets These are return tickets with which you fly out to one place but return from another. If available, this can save you backtracking to your arrival point.

Overbooking Since every flight has some passengers who fail to show up, airlines often book more passengers than they have seats. Usually excess passengers make up for the no-shows, but occasionally somebody gets 'bumped' onto the next available flight. Guess who it is most likely to be? The passengers who check in late.

Promotional Fares These are officially discounted fares, available from travel agencies or direct from the airline.

Reconfirmation If you don't reconfirm your flight at least 72 hours prior to departure, the airline may delete your name from the passenger list. Ring to find out if your airline requires reconfirmation.

Restrictions Discounted tickets often have various restrictions on them – such as needing to be paid for in advance and incurring a penalty for alteration. Other restrictions are on the minimum and maximum period you must be away.

Round-the-World Tickets RTW tickets give you a limited period (usually a year) in which to circumnavigate the globe. You can go anywhere the carrying airlines go, as long as you don't backtrack. The number of stopovers or total number of separate flights is decided before you set off and they usually cost a bit more than a basic return flight.

Transferred Tickets Airline tickets cannot be transferred from one person to another. Travellers sometimes try to sell the return half of their ticket, but officials can ask you to prove that you are the person named on the ticket. On an international flight, tickets are compared with passports.

Travel Periods Ticket prices vary with the time of year. There is a low (off-peak) season and a high (peak) season, and often a low-shoulder season and a high-shoulder season as well. Usually the fare depends on your outward flight – if you depart in the high season and return in the low season, you pay the high-season fare.

have to show a document proving your date of birth, or a valid International Student Identity Card (ISIC) when buying your ticket and boarding the plane. There are plenty of places around the world where nonstudents can get fake student cards, but if you get caught using a fake card you could have your ticket confiscated.

Travellers with Special Needs

If you have special requirements – you're on crutches, vegetarian, terrified of flying – let the airline know when you book, again when you reconfirm, and again when you check in. It may even be worth ringing round the airlines before you book.

With advance warning, most international airports can provide escorts from check-in to the plane, and most have ramps, lifts, wheelchair-accessible toilets and telephones. Aircraft toilets, on the other hand, present problems for wheelchair users, who should discuss this early on with the airline and/or their doctor.

In general, children aged under two travel for 10% of the standard fare (or free on some airlines), as long as they don't occupy a seat. They don't get a baggage allowance. Bassinets or 'skycots' – for children weighing up to about 10kg – can usually be provided by the airline if requested in advance. Children aged between two and 12 can usually occupy a seat for half to two-thirds of the full fare and do get a baggage allowance. Pushchairs (strollers) can often be taken as extra hand luggage.

Other Parts of France

Air Liberté and Air France are the leading carriers on the domestic route between Paris and Nantes-Atlantique. To/from Paris there are nine daily flights (six on Saturday and seven on Sunday) year round to/from Nantes-Atlantique. Air France uses Paris Roissy Charles de Gaulle and Air Liberté flies in and out of Paris Orly Sud.

From the rest of France, there are flights to Nantes from Bordeaux (up to three daily), Brest (up to three daily), Clermont-Ferrand (up to two daily), Le Havre (up to two daily), Lille (up to three daily), Metz-

Nancy (two daily on weekdays), Montpellier (up to three daily), St-Etienne (two daily on weekdays) and Toulouse (up to three daily).

Other domestic routes include flights between Angers and Clermont-Ferrand with Regional Airlines. From the airport at Tours, there is a daily flight to/from Lyon with Air Liberté, while Poitiers is served by daily flights to/from Clermont-Ferrand (Regional Airlines), Lyon (Air Liberté) and Figari, in Corsica (Air Méditerranée).

Fares vary dramatically depending on when you make the reservation and which days you intend staying. Unless you are eligible for a youth/student fare, it is substantially cheaper to train it from Paris or other cities in France to the Loire.

Air France (☎ 08 02 80 28 02) has four regular fare levels, ranging from full fare with no restrictions to reduced fares that require advance booking and have various restrictions. Travellers aged over 60, families and couples who are married or have proof of cohabitation (eg a French-government-issued *certificat de concubinage*) are entitled to some discounts. A cheaper youth/student fare (with no restrictions or advance-booking requirements) is available to those aged under 25 and student-card holders aged 26 or under. The cheapest Paris–Nantes return with Air France cost around 840FF at the time of writing (you had to reserve the ticket 14 days in advance and stay a weekend). The return fare leaps to an expensive 2300FF for those not staying a weekend. The youth/student fare currently costs around 650FF return. Air Liberté has similar fares.

France has a network of student travel agencies which can supply discount tickets to travellers of all ages. OTU Voyages (www.otu.fr) has a central Paris office (☎ 01 40 29 12 12) at 39 Ave Georges Bernanos (5e), and 42 other offices around the country. Accueil des Jeunes en France (☎ 01 42 77 87 80), 119 rue St-Martin (4e), Paris, is another popular discount travel agency. In the Loire region, there are Voyages Wasteels offices in Tours (☎ 02 43 62 30 00, fax 02 47 61 89 83), 8 place du

Grand Marché, and Nantes (☎ 08 03 88 70 65, fax 02 40 89 90 88), 6 rue Guépin.

Continental Europe

Direct flights between the Loire region and Continental Europe do not exist. To/from Paris there are regular daily flights, operated by a number of different airlines, to/from almost every European capital, plus most major cities. All the big airlines usually offer some sort of deal and travel agencies generally have a number of deals on offer.

Across Continental Europe, there are many agencies with ties with STA Travel where cheap tickets can be purchased and STA-issued tickets altered (usually for a US$25 fee). Outlets include: STA Travel (☎ 030-311 0950, fax 313 0948), Goethestrasse 73, D-10625 Berlin, and Passaggi (☎ 06 474 09 23, fax 06 482 74 36), Stazione Termini FS, Galleria di Tesla, Rome.

In Belgium, Connections (☎ 02-550 01 00), part of the usit group, has several offices, including one at 19–21 rue du Midi, Brussels. Have a look at the Web site at www.connections.be. In Switzerland, SSR Voyages (☎ 01-297 11 11) specialises in student, youth and budget fares (www.ssr.ch). In Zürich, there is a branch at Leonhardstrasse 10, and there are also branches in most major cities. In the Netherlands, NBBS Reizen is the official student travel agency. You can find them in Amsterdam (☎ 020-620 50 71) at Schilphoweg 101, 2300 AJ Leiden. In Spain, try Barcelo Viajs (☎ 91 559 18 19) at Princesa 3, Madrid 28228.

Once in Paris, the quickest, cheapest and most efficient way of getting to the Loire is to hop aboard a train (see Other Parts of France under Land later in this chapter).

The UK & Ireland

Direct flights between the UK and the Loire are – predictably – thin on the ground. From Nantes, Air France operates three daily flights (two daily at the weekend) to/from London. An adult return fare, including a Saturday-night stay in France, cost around UK£160 at the time of writing.

Flying to Paris from the UK or Ireland can be a sensible alternative – particularly since the advent of no-frills, low-fare airlines, such as Buzz (KLM-Royal Dutch Airlines' budget airline), which have dramatically slashed air fares. At the time of writing, London Stansted–Paris fares with Buzz (☎ 0870 240 7070) cost UK£60 to UK£120 for a restricted return (two nights in France) and upwards of UK£200 for a fully flexible equivalent. Have a look at the Web site at www.buzzaway.com. Dublin-based Ryanair (☎ 01-609 7800 in Ireland, 0870 333 1231 in the UK) operates daily low-fare flights to Paris from Prestwick (near Glasgow) and Dublin. At the time of writing, returns from Prestwick/Dublin started at UK£45/70. No-frills airlines operate on a first-come-first-served basis, meaning the earlier you book your ticket, the cheaper the fare will be. Look out for sporadic ticket sales, when some great bargains can be scooped up.

At the time of writing, Air France (☎ 0845 0845 111) was offering a Saturday-night-away flight from London to Paris (departing in July) for as little as UK£95 return (booked 14 days in advance). Air France's fully flexible returns start at around UK£280. At the same time, British Airways (BA; ☎ 0845 722 2111) were offering a Saturday-night-away flight for around UK£90 return (booked three days in advance) and its fully flexible equivalent for around UK£280. BA's unrestricted London–Paris youth fares were as low as UK£160. Check out the Web site at www.british-airways.com.

The UK's best-known bargain ticket agencies are STA (☎ 020-7361 6161), with a Web site at www.sta-travel.co.uk, Trailfinders (☎ 020-7937 5400), with a Web site at www.trailfinder.com, and usit Campus (☎ 020-7730 3402), with a Web site at www.usitcampus.co.uk. All have branches in London and throughout the UK.

The USA & Canada

The flight options across the North Atlantic, the world's busiest long-haul air corridor, are bewildering. The *New York Times, LA Times, Chicago Tribune* and *San Francisco Chronicle* have weekly travel sections in which you'll find any number of travel agencies' ads. Council Travel (☎ 800 226 8624), with a Web site at www.council-travel.com, and STA (☎ 800 777 0112), with a Web site at www.sta-travel.com, have offices in major cities.

Canada's best bargain-hunting agency is Travel CUTS (☎ 888 835 2887), with a Web site at www.travelcuts.com, which has offices in major Canadian cities. You might also scan the budget travel agencies' ads in the *Toronto Globe and Mail, Toronto Star* and *Vancouver Province*.

Any journey to the Loire entails a flight to Paris, London or another European transport hub, from where there are train/ferry/plane connections to the region. A New York–Paris round trip can cost anything from US$560 in the low season to US$820 with Air France or British Airways in the high season. Airhitch (☎ 212-864 2000), with a Web site at www.airhitch.org, specialises in cheap stand-by fares.

Australia & New Zealand

Saturday's travel sections in the *Sydney Morning Herald* and *Melbourne Age* have many ads offering cheap fares to Europe. One of Australasia's best discount air fare shops is Flight Centre (☎ 03-9650 2899), 19 Bourke St, Melbourne. STA Travel (www.sta-travel.com) has offices in Sydney (☎ 02-9212 1255) and Auckland (☎ 09-309 0458). Both agencies have branch offices nationwide. Trailfinders (www.trailfinder.com) has branches in Sydney (☎ 02-9247 7666), Brisbane (☎ 07-3229 0887) and Cairns (☎ 07-4041 1199).

Airlines such as Thai Airways International (THAI), Malaysia Airlines, Qantas Airways and Singapore Airlines (SIA) have frequent promotional fares. At the time of writing, low/high-season return fares to Paris started at around A$1500/1900 from Melbourne or Sydney, and NZ$2310/2510 from Auckland. A round-the-world ticket from New Zealand will cost about NZ$2300.

LAND
Other Parts of France

Bus Forget even attempting to catch a bus from Paris to the Loire: French transport policy is completely biased in favour of its state-owned train system, meaning the country has an extremely limited inter-regional bus service. Take a train.

Train France's highly efficient train network, run by the state-owned SNCF (Société Nationale des Chemins de Fer), reaches almost every part of the country. The network is very Paris-centric, with key lines radiating from the capital like the spokes of a wheel. While travel between towns on different 'spokes' can be tricky and tedious, getting almost anywhere from Paris is fast and easy.

SNCF's pride and joy is the TGV (pronounced 'teh-sheh-veh'), short for *train à grande vitesse* (high-speed train). The western Loire region is served by the TGV Atlantique service, which links Paris with Nantes, Tours and beyond to Bordeaux, in south-western France. On this route, the TGV races at a lightning speed of 310km/h. In Paris, TGV Atlantique trains use Gare Montparnasse. From here there are regular daily trains to/from Villiers-sur-Loir (Vendôme; 229FF, 42 minutes, five daily), St-Pierre des Corps (Tours; 211FF, 1¼ hours, 10 to 15 daily), Nantes (291FF to 349FF, two hours, 10 to 15 daily) and Angers (243FF to 302FF, 1½ hours, 10 to 15 daily). The TGV Atlantique has a direct link with Paris' Roissy Charles de Gaulle airport.

In addition to these speedy TGV trains, there are slower services which are usually (but not always) cheaper. Both *grande ligne* (mainline) trains and those operated by TER (Transport Express Régional) link smaller cities and towns with the TGV network. Many towns not on the SNCF network are linked to nearby stations by SNCF or TER buses (see Bus in the Getting Around chapter for details). For scheduling and fare information for grande ligne trains call ☎ 08 36 67 68 69 (2.23FF per minute).

From Paris, these slower, non-TGV services to the Loire – including to Aubrais-Orléans (linked to Orléans, 2km south, by shuttle trains), Tours and Vendôme – use Gare d'Austerlitz. The non-TGV services are ideal for budget travellers with time on their hands.

At the time of writing, there were non-TGV trains between Paris Austerlitz and Amboise (142FF, two hours, five or six daily), Angers (243FF, 1¾ hours, at least eight daily), Aubrais-Orléans (91FF, 1¾ hours, 10 to 15 daily), Blois (123FF, 1½ to two hours, at least 11 daily, some with a change at Orléans), Tours (152FF, two to 2¾ hours, five to eight daily) and Vendôme town centre (123FF, two hours, two or three daily).

Sample fares for TGV and non-TGV trains to other cities in France are: Angers–Avignon (445FF to 620FF, six hours), Nantes–Bordeaux (237FF, four hours), Nantes–Lille (395FF to 450FF, four hours), Nantes–Lyon (394FF to 449FF, five hours), Nantes–Marseille (531FF to 622FF, 7½ to 8½ hours), Nantes–Quimper (186FF, 2¾ to four hours), Orléans–Toulouse (91FF, 1¾ hours), Poitiers–La Rochelle (117FF, 1½ hours) and Saumur–Marseille (448FF to 548FF, 8¾ to 12 hours).

Reservations & Tickets Most trains, including TGVs, have 1st- and 2nd-class sections. In this book, we quote fares for 2nd-class travel, which works out at about 50FF to 70FF per 100km for longer cross-country trips and 70FF to 100FF per 100km for shorter hops (compare this with autoroute tolls and petrol, each costing about 40FF to 50FF per 100km). A return ticket is twice the price of a single ticket. Travel in 1st class costs 50% more than in 2nd class.

A 25FF reservation fee is obligatory for TGV travellers (automatically included in the ticket price) and for non-TGV passengers on some trains that run during holiday periods. Most overnight trains are equipped with couchettes (sleeping berths), which have to be reserved. A couchette costs 105FF. Second-class couchettes have six berths; 1st class have four.

Reservations can be made by telephone (☎ 08 36 35 35 35), via the SNCF's Web site (www.sncf.com), at any SNCF ticketing office, or by using a ticket vending machine at any SNCF train station (tickets issued by machines are valid for two months). Advance reservations can be changed by telephone, or up to one hour before departure if you are actually at your departure station.

Tickets bought with cash can be reimbursed for cash (by you or a thief – keep them in a safe place). Alternatively, pay with a credit card at the ticket counter, one of the automatic, touch-screen ticket vending machines found at every SNCF station (touch the screen to activate it and the UK flag for English), or on-line at www.sncf.com. Prohibitive tariffs theoretically apply for tickets bought direct from the conductor on board trains, although most tend to be pretty lenient and charge ticketless passengers the regular station fare.

For information on useful train passes and fare reductions, see the boxed text 'Train Passes & Discount Fares' later in this section.

Validating Your Ticket You risk an on-the-spot fine if you fail to validate your train ticket before boarding: time-stamp it in a *composteur*, a bizarre-looking orange post situated at the platform entrance. If you forget, find the conductor on board so he/she can punch it for you. Tickets are usually checked and punched by the conductor midway through a journey.

SNCF Hotlines

SNCF (Societé Nationale des Chemins de Fer; www.sncf.com) information lines are open from 7 am to 10 pm. Calling from abroad, dial the international access code followed by 33 and then drop the initial zero. Domestic calls are charged at 2.23FF per minute. Languages offered include:

English ☎ 08 36 35 35 39
French ☎ 08 36 35 35 35
German ☎ 08 36 35 35 36
Italian ☎ 08 36 35 35 38
Spanish ☎ 08 36 36 35 37

Tickets are valid for 24 hours after they have been time-stamped, meaning you can break your journey briefly mid-way providing you are not on a line (such as a TGV) requiring a reservation. Time-stamp your ticket again before you reboard.

Unused tickets costing over 30FF can be reimbursed (90% of the original ticket price) up to two months after the date of issue. Refunds are available from any train station ticket window.

Transporting a Bicycle A bicycle can be brought along free of charge as hand luggage on most trains in France, provided it is either folded or enclosed in a cover that measures no more than 120 by 90cm. You are responsible for loading and unloading your bicycle from the luggage section of the train. The SNCF won't accept any responsibility for your bike's condition. You can also register a boxed bicycle as checked baggage to any destination in the region (and many places in Europe) for 195FF (295FF for door-to-door delivery), plus 15FF for a bike box. It will probably take three or four days to arrive; call ☎ 08 03 84 58 45 between 7 am and 10 pm on weekdays for details.

Car & Motorcycle Number one rule when motoring in France: traffic in July and August can be hellish and should be avoided if possible. If impossible, be prepared to sit in some mighty long traffic jams, both on and off the *autoroute* (motorway/highway).

The main route from Paris is along the A10 autoroute – called L'Aquitaine – which links the French capital with Orléans and Tours. The north-west of the Loire region is better served from Paris by the A11 – called L'Océane – which passes through Le Mans, Angers and Nantes.

Road tolls are imposed on most stretches of autoroute, the exception being around major cities such as Paris and Angers. Count on paying about 40FF per 100km (see the boxed text 'Autoroute Tolls' later in this section). Some parts of the autoroute have toll plazas every few dozen kilometres; most have a machine which issues

On the Road

FM 107.7 MHz broadcasts traffic reports in English every 30 minutes at peak times. Useful phone numbers for on the road include:

Autoroute! (autoroute info)	☎ 08 36 68 09 79
Intinerary Planning	☎ 01 47 05 90 01
National Traffic Updates	☎ 08 36 68 10 77
Regional Traffic Information	☎ 01 48 99 33 33
Road Toll Information	☎ 04 90 32 90 05

a little ticket that you hand over at a toll booth when you exit. You can pay in French francs or by credit card.

With the exception of the Le Mans–Angers stretch of the A11, autoroutes in the region are managed by Cofiroute (☎ 01 41 14 70 00), 6–10 rue Troyon, 92310 Sèvres, which has a Web site at www.cofiroute.fr. ASFA (Association des Sociétés Françaises d'Autoroutes; ☎ 01 47 53 39 41, ❷ asfa@auto routes.fr) has an excellent Web site (www .autoroutes.fr) with oodles of traffic-related information. See the boxed text 'On the Road' for info available when on the road.

IGN's *Routes: Autoroutes* (No 901, 22FF) is a handy map source for motoring it around France; a smaller-sized version is also available (No 951, 22FF).

For information on road rules, petrol costs, car hire and so on, see Car in the Getting Around chapter.

Hitching Hitching is never entirely safe anywhere in the world, and we don't recommend it. Travellers who hitch should understand that they are taking a small but potentially serious risk. A woman hitching on her own is particularly vulnerable. Two men together may have a harder time getting picked up than a man travelling alone. The best (and safest) combination is a man and a woman. Never get in a car with someone you don't trust. Keep your belongings with you on the seat rather than in the boot

Road Distances (km)

	Angers	Blois	Calais	Le Havre	Le Mans	Nantes	Niort	Orléans	Paris	Poitiers	St-Malo	Tours
Angers	---											
Blois	160	---										
Calais	625	462	---									
Le Havre	302	353	277	---								
Le Mans	88	139	484	234	---							
Nantes	91	251	716	400	159	---						
Niort	125	279	637	486	267	168	---					
Orléans	214	54	408	299	139	305	286	---				
Paris	263	150	288	198	175	354	392	96	---			
Poitiers	148	205	623	402	183	180	74	212	308	---		
St-Malo	268	346	496	308	207	177	345	346	382	357	---	
Tours	103	57	522	301	82	194	185	111	207	101	289	---

(trunk). Dedicated hitchers may wish to invest in the *Hitch-Hiker's Manual for Europe* by Simon Calder (Vacation Work, 1993).

In France, two organisations put people looking for rides in touch with drivers going to the same destination. Allostop Provoya (☎ 01 53 20 42 42 in Paris, 01 53 20 42 43 from outside Paris and abroad, ✉ allostop@ecritel.fr), with a Web site at www.ecritel.fr/allostop, is based at 8 Rue Rochambeau, 75009 Paris. Association Pouce (☎/fax 02 99 08 67 02, ✉ allopouce@infonie.fr), with a Web site at www.idonline.net/pouce, is Brittany based.

With Allostop, passengers pay 22 centîmes per kilometre to the driver, plus a fee to cover administrative expenses: 30/40/50/60FF for trips under 200/300/400/500km and 70FF for trips over 500km. Association Pouce has no cover charges.

Continental Europe

Bus Eurolines (☎ 08 36 69 52 52, fax 01 49 72 51 61, ✉ info@eurolines.fr), with a Web site at www.eurolines.fr, an association of companies that together form Europe's largest international bus network, links major cities in the region with points all over Western and Central Europe, Scandinavia and Morocco.

Eurolines' main offices in the Loire are at the bus station in Nantes (☎ 02 51 72 02 03) and in Tours (☎ 02 47 66 45 56), at 76 rue Bernard Palissy. Orléans, Angers, Le Mans and Poitiers are the other cities in the region served by Eurolines buses.

Buses are slower and less comfortable than trains, but they are cheaper, especially if you qualify for the 10 to 20% discount available to people who are aged under 26 or over 60. Children aged four to 12 also get discounts. In summer, book tickets well in advance. Return tickets cost substantially less than two one-way tickets. In addition to the standard fare, Eurolines offers cancellation insurance (20FF) and a change-date option (25FF), which enables you to change the date on which you intend travelling after the ticket has been issued. Passengers are allowed to transport two pieces of luggage per person; a 50FF fee is charged for each additional bag.

To Tours or Poitiers, sample youth/adult single fares from the following destinations are: Amsterdam f200/220, Frankfurt

Autoroute Tolls (FF)

Angers	---										
Blois	57	---									
Calais	237	180	---								
Le Havre	116	13*	67	---							
Le Mans	37	0*	200	79	---						
Nantes	42	99	279	158	79	---					
Niort	117	116	301	167	159	50	---				
Orléans	84	25	155	89	0*	126	143	---			
Paris	131	77	106	40	94	173	200	49	---		
Poitiers	87	86	266	71	124	85	35	113	58	---	
St-Malo	42	47	297	41	47	0*	50	47	141	0*	---
Tours	29	28	208	13*	66	71	88	55	112	58	71	---
	Angers	Blois	Calais	Le Havre	Le Mans	Nantes	Niort	Orléans	Paris	Poitiers	St-Malo	Tours

* All or the majority of the route does not include an autoroute

DM170/190, Madrid 18,500/20,800 ptas and Prague 3700/4100 Kč. Destinations serving Nantes include Barcelona 20,800/3,100 ptas and Brussels BF3100/3500.

Eurolines-affiliated companies can be found in cities across Europe, including Amsterdam (☎ 020-560 87 87), with a Web site at www.eurolines.nl; Barcelona (☎ 93 490 40 00), with a Web site at www.travel com.es/juliavia; Berlin (☎ 030-86 09 60), with a Web site at www.deutsche-touring .com; Brussels (☎ 02-203 07 07); Madrid (☎ 91 528 11 05); Prague (☎ 02-2421 3420), with a Web site at www.eurolines .cz; Rome (☎ 06 442 33 928), with a Web site at www.eurolines.it; and Vienna (☎ 01-712 04 35), with a Web site at www.euro lines.at.

Busabout (☎ 020-7950 1661, fax 7950 1662, 🅲 info@busabout.co.uk), with Web sites at www.busabout.com and www.bus about.co.uk, is a UK-based company that runs coaches round several loops covering a wide variety of destinations in Western and Central Europe, Scandinavia and Morocco. Two loops that include France go to northern Europe and to Spain and Portugal. A Busabout Pass – valid for 15 consecutive

days, 10 days in two months, or 30 days in four months – lets you get on and off whenever you choose, at designated pick-up points. Pick-up points (which include Paris and Tours) are often convenient for youth hostels and camp sites. Busabout operates year round, with services every two or three days at each pick-up point.

Passes are sold through major youth-travel agencies. At the time of writing, a 15-consecutive-day pass cost 1530/1700FF for those aged under 26/adults and a pass valid for 10/30 days over two/four months cost 2600/6600FF for adults and 2300/6000FF for those aged under 26.

Train Paris abounds with connections from all over Europe. The Loire is linked by direct TGV services with Bordeaux, from where there are train links (with a change at Irún/Hendaye) to Spain and Portugal. All other international connections to the region are via Paris.

Sample 2nd-class return fares from major European cities to Nantes are: Amsterdam f355, Brussels BF6100, Geneva SF275, Madrid 33,000 ptas, Milan L400,000 and Munich DM545.

euro currency converter 10FF = €1.52

Train Passes & Discount Fares

All the following passes are available from student travel agencies, major train stations within Europe, and the SNCF (Societé National des Chemins de Fer) subsidiary Rail Europe (☎ 0870 5848 848), 179 Piccadilly, London W1V 0BA. In the USA, contact Rail Europe on toll-free ☎ 800 438 7245, fax 800 432 1329; in Canada on toll-free ☎ 800 361 7245, fax 905 602 4198. Alternatively, have a look at the Web site at www.raileurope.com.

SNCF Discount Fares & Passes

Children aged under four travel free of charge; those aged four to 11 travel for half-price. Discounted fares (25% reduction) automatically apply to travellers aged 12 to 25, seniors aged over 60, one to four adults travelling with a child aged four to 11, two people travelling a return journey together or anyone taking a return journey of at least 200km and spending a Saturday night away.

Purchasing a one-year travel pass can yield a 50% discount (25% if the cheapest seats are sold out): a **Carte 12–25** aimed at travellers aged 12 to 25 costs 270FF, the **Carte Enfant Plus** for one to four adults travelling with a child aged four to 11 costs 350FF, and seniors aged over 60 qualify for a 285FF **Carte Sénior**.

The **France Railpass** entitles non-residents of France to unlimited travel on the SNCF system for three to nine days over a one-month period. In 2nd class, the three-day version costs around 1200FF (990FF each for two people travelling together); each additional day of travel costs around 200FF. There is also a cheaper youth version.

European Train Passes for European Residents

The **Euro Domino Pass**, available to those who have been resident in Europe for at least six months, can be used in France (and 28 other participating countries) for three to eight consecutive days, or non-consecutive days over a one-month period, of 2nd-class travel. The adult versions cost

---

You can book tickets and get information from Rail Europe (www.raileurope.com) up to two months ahead. Ring ☎ 02-534 45 31 in Belgium and the Netherlands, ☎ 069-97 58 46 41 in Germany, ☎ 02 725 44 370 in Italy, ☎ 01 547 84 42 in Spain, and ☎ 031-382 99 00 in Switzerland. Direct bookings through SNCF (☎ 08 36 35 35 35 in French, 08 36 35 35 39 in English) are possible, but SNCF won't post tickets outside France. For more on SNCF see Train under Other Parts of France earlier in this Land section.

If you intend to do a lot of train travel, consider purchasing the *Thomas Cook European Timetable*, updated monthly with a complete listing of schedules, plus information on reservations and supplements. Single issues cost about UK£11 from Thomas Cook Publishing (☎ 01733-503571, fax 503596, ✉ publishing-sales@ thomascook.com) in the UK.

For information on European train discount passes, see the boxed text 'Train Passes & Discount Fares'.

The UK

Bus Eurolines operates direct bus services year round (one to four times weekly) from London's Victoria Coach Station, via the Dover–Calais Channel ferry crossing, to Tours or Poitiers for around UK£65/70 youth/adult return, and Angers or Nantes for around UK£70/75 youth/adult return.

Bookings can be made in London at the Eurolines office (☎ 020-7730 8235), 52 Grosvenor Gardens, London SW1 0AU; by telephone through the main Eurolines office (☎ 01582-404511, 0870 5143 219) in Luton; on-line at www.eurolines.co.uk; or at any National Express office, whose buses link London and other parts of the UK with the Channel ports of Dover and Folkestone.

Train Passes & Discount Fares

UK£119/139/189/239 for three/four/six/eight days, and versions for those aged under 26 cost UK£99/119/149/189 for three/four/six/eight days. The pass covers supplements on TGV trains, but does not include seat or couchette reservations.

With the **InterRail Pass**, you can travel in 29 European countries organised into eight zones; France is in Zone E, grouped with the Netherlands, Belgium and Luxembourg. For 22 days of unlimited 2nd-class travel in one zone, the cost is UK£159/229 for those aged under/over 26. You also get 50% off travel from your home country to your zone(s) and between non-adjacent zones, and a considerable discount on Eurostar tickets.

European Train Passes for Non-European Residents

If you are not a resident of Europe but are aged under 26 on your first day of travel and anticipate clocking up more than 2400km around the Loire, France and Europe, consider buying a **Eurail Youth Pass**, which entitles you to unlimited train travel for 15/21 days or one/two/three months. One/two/three months of unlimited travel costs around US$710/1000/1240; more expensive adult equivalents are also available.

A **Eurail Youth Flexipass** covers 10/15 non-consecutive days of travel in a two-month period, costing around US$520/680. There are adult equivalents costing around US$745/980.

In the USA and Canada you can purchase Eurail passes over the phone on ☎ 1888 667 9734 and have them sent to your home by courier. Eurail's Web site is at www.eurail.on.ca.

The **Euro Pass** allows you to travel in five European countries for between five and 15 non-consecutive days over a two-month period. The adult pass, good for 1st-class train travel within France, Germany, Italy, Spain and Switzerland, ranges from US$410 for five days to US$860 for 15 days (20% less for two adults travelling together with a saver pass). Cheaper **Euro Pass Youth** equivalents, available for those aged under 26, are only good for 2nd-class travel and cost around US$275/605 for five/15 days.

For Busabout services from London, see Bus under Continental Europe earlier in this Land section. If you're beginning your journey in London, Busabout charges an extra UK£15 for the Channel crossing.

Train The cheapest train route from the UK to the Loire is from London to Paris on a 'train-boat-train' ticket (crossing the Channel by ferry, hovercraft or SeaCat), with a change of train (and mainline station) in Paris (see Train under Other Parts of France earlier in this Land section). Connex South Eastern (☎ 0870 603 0405, fax 0870 603 0505), 3 Priory Rd, Tonbridge TN9 2AF, handles this London–Paris route and sells tickets for the onwards journey too. At the time of writing, a 2nd-class London–Tours youth/adult return fare cost around UK£100/115.

Eurostar, the much-heralded high-speed passenger service through the Channel Tunnel, takes just three hours from London (Waterloo) to Paris. There is no direct Eurostar service to the Loire, but you can take Eurostar to Lille and transfer to a direct TGV to Angers (5¾ hours from London) or Nantes (6½ hours from London). Full fares can be more than twice those for train-boat-train, but certain nonrefundable, non-exchangeable tickets are competitive: a 2nd-class London–Angers/Nantes adult ticket can cost around UK£90/110 (book at least a week ahead and stay a Saturday night). The under-26 fares are the same but are subject to no restrictions. Alternatively, take Eurostar to Paris Gare du Nord and change mainline station by metro (Montparnasse for TGV trains, Austerlitz for non-TGV trains) to pick up a train to the Loire; for information on prices and times from Paris to the Loire see Train under Other Parts of France earlier in this Land section.

InterRail Pass holders (see the boxed text 'Train Passes & Discount Fares') get substantial discounts on Eurostar tickets, a 2nd-class London–Paris/Lille return typically costing UK£80/65, irrespective of when you travel.

In the UK, both Eurostar and non-Eurostar tickets are available from travel agencies, many mainline train stations and SNCF subsidiary Rail Europe (☎ 0870 5848 848), 179 Piccadilly, London W1V 0BA. For contact details in the US and Canada, see the boxed text 'Train Passes & Discount Fares'. On-line bookings are also possible at www.raileurope.com.

For Eurostar information only (eg for London trains as far as Paris/Lille), contact Eurostar UK (☎ 0870 5186 186, 01233-617575 from outside the UK) or visit its Web site at www.eurostar.com. In France, contact SNCF (☎ 08 36 35 35 39 in English) or log in on-line at www.sncf.com. Eurostar tickets sold in the UK are more expensive than those sold in France.

Car & Motorcycle High-speed shuttle trains operated by Eurotunnel whisk cars, motorcycles, bicycles and coaches from Folkestone through the Channel Tunnel to Coquelles, 5km south-west of Calais, in air-conditioned and soundproofed comfort. Journey time is 35 minutes (open 24 hours, year round). Trains run three to four times an hour (one or two an hour from midnight to 6 am). Passport and customs control are cleared before boarding. Once aboard, passengers can sit in their cars or walk around the train.

For information and reservations, ask a travel agency or contact Eurotunnel (☎ 0990 353 535 in the UK, ☎ 03 21 00 61 00 in France). A fully flexible standard return ticket for a passenger car (and all passengers) averages around UK£220 (more in high season). Motorcycles cost around UK£120 return. Promotional fares for cars are almost always available: check the Internet at www.eurotunnel.com.

When calculating costs, be sure to include hefty French road tolls from Calais to the Loire in your budget (see the boxed text 'Autoroute Tolls' earlier in this chapter).

For information on driving in France, including car-hire costs and road rules, see Car in the Getting Around chapter.

Bicycle European Bike Express (☎ 01642-251440, fax 232209, ✉ bike@bikeexpress.co.uk) facilitates independent cycling holidays by transporting cyclists and their bikes by bus and trailer from the UK to places all over France, including Poitiers. Route details are on-line at www.bikeexpress.co.uk. Return fares start at around UK£160; UK£10 less for members of the Cyclists' Touring Club (☎ 01483-417217), Cotterell House, 69 Meadrow, Godalming, Surrey GU7 3HS. This UK-based cycling club supplies information to members on cycling conditions in parts of Europe, as well as detailed routes, itineraries, cheap cycle and third-party insurance and cycling holidays.

SEA

Although no direct international ferries serve the Loire, the region is sufficiently close to northern France's ferry ports – it's 177km from St-Malo to Nantes and 301km from Le Havre to Tours – to make a Channel crossing by ferry a feasible and pleasant way of getting to the Loire from the UK and Ireland.

Fares are wildly seasonal. Winter tickets can cost less than half as much as in high season (each company has its own complex definition of high season). Three- or five-day excursion return fares cost about the same as regular one-way tickets. Return fares generally cost less than two one-way tickets. Children aged four to 14 or 15 travel for half to two-thirds of an adult fare. Most crossings also have higher fares for lounge seats and cabins.

The main ferry companies are:

Brittany Ferries (☎ 02 98 29 28 00 in France, 0870 5360 360 in the UK, 021-277 801 in Ireland)
Web site: www.brittany-ferries.com
Condor Ferries (☎ 02 99 20 03 00 in France, 01305-761551 in the UK)
Web site: www.condorferries.co.uk
Hoverspeed (☎ 08 20 00 35 55 in France, 0870 5240 241 in the UK)
Web site: www.hoverspeed.co.uk

Irish Ferries (☎ 02 33 23 44 44 in Cherbourg, 02 98 61 17 17 in Roscoff, 0870 5171 717 in the UK, 053-33158 in Ireland, 01-661 0715 for 24-hour information in Ireland)
Web site: www.irishferries.ie

P&O Portsmouth (☎ 02 33 88 65 65 in Cherbourg, 02 35 19 78 50 in Le Havre, 0870 600 3300 in the UK)
Web site: www.poportsmouth.com

P&O Stena Line (☎ 08 03 01 30 13 in France, 0870 600 0612 in the UK)
Web site: www.postena.com

SeaFrance (☎ 08 03 04 40 45 in France during office hours, 03 21 46 80 00 in France weekends/evenings, 0870 5711 711 in the UK)
Web site: www.seafrance.co.uk

Unless stated otherwise, sample prices listed here are the summer 2000 prices for standard, weekend, high-season, one-way tickets for a car plus driver and one passenger/a motorcycle plus driver and passenger/a bicycle plus rider/a pedestrian.

The UK

Dover–Calais and Folkestone–Boulogne offer the shortest ferry crossings from the UK to France but the longest drive the other side (408/716km to Orléans/Nantes) for Loire-bound travellers. Longer ferry crossings to ports in Brittany or Normandy are most convenient for those wanting to access the western Loire (177km from St-Malo to Nantes). For road distances between the ports and cities in the Loire region, see the boxed text 'Road Distances' earlier in this chapter.

Train passes are not valid for UK–France ferry travel, but some discounts are available for students and young people.

Via Far Northern France Dover–Calais and Folkestone–Boulogne are very competitive routes, with frequent cheap promotional fares if you book well in advance.

SeaFrance and P&O Stena Line together run about 45 ferries daily from Dover to Calais (1½ hours). SeaFrance charges around UK£130/70/15/15 for departures any day of the week from April to June and UK£160/90/15/15 for departures on week-

days in August (the most expensive period). P&O Stena Line's more frequent, slightly faster ferries cost marginally more.

Dover–Calais on Hoverspeed's hovercraft (UK£170/100/30/30, 20 daily) takes 35 minutes. SeaCat catamarans take 55 minutes. Hoverspeed SeaCats also make the 55-minute Folkestone–Boulogne crossing (UK£155/85/30/30, four daily).

Via Normandy The UK's southern ports have numerous links with Dieppe, Le Havre, Ouistreham (Caen) and Cherbourg.

Hoverspeed's SuperSeaCats make the two-hour Newhaven–Dieppe crossing three times daily (UK£165/70/30/30).

P&O Portsmouth makes the six-hour trip (8¼ hours overnight) from Portsmouth to Le Havre three times daily year round. Fares range from UK£95/50/30/30 in the low season to UK£210/100/50/40 in the high season. The 5½-hour Portsmouth–Cherbourg connection (7½ hours overnight) goes six times daily (less frequently between October and March) and offers similar fares.

Brittany Ferries makes a four-hour Poole–Cherbourg crossing (UK£200/100/45/40) once or twice daily. Its six-hour Portsmouth–Ouistreham (Caen) connection goes two or three times daily.

Via Brittany Services to St-Malo and Roscoff in Brittany run less frequently than those across the Straits of Dover, particularly in winter.

Ferries to St-Malo include Brittany Ferries from Portsmouth (UK£220/110/50/45 for a reclining seat), a nine-hour night/day crossing on the outward/return journey. Berths are available on night crossings. From May to mid-October, Condor Ferries has daily catamarans to St-Malo via Guernsey and Jersey from Weymouth (UK£190/90/30/25, five hours) and from Poole (same fares, 5½ to 6½ hours).

From mid-March to mid-November, Plymouth–Roscoff (six hours) is served by one or two Brittany Ferries daily (UK£170/70/35/35); during the rest of the year there is only one per week.

Ireland

Irish Ferries links Rosslare with Roscoff (15 hours, every other day from April to August) and Cherbourg (17 hours, every other day from April to August and two or three times weekly the rest of the year) for around IR£120/75/45/45. Eurail Pass holders get a 50% discount if they book ahead.

From April to early October, Brittany Ferries has one weekly ferry linking Cork and Roscoff (IR£360/215/100/80, 14 hours); bookings can be made only through the Brittany Ferries office in Cork.

ORGANISED TOURS

In addition to the travel agencies listed below, numerous other agencies offer a mind-boggling range of general chateau tours in the Loire. French Travel Connection (☎ 02-9966 8600, fax 9966 5888), Level 6, 33 Chandos St, St Leonards NSW 2065, and Ya'lla Tours (☎ 03-9523 1988, fax 9523 1934, ✆ yallamel@yallatours.com .au), 661 Glenhuntly Rd, Caulfield, Victoria 3162, are two leading operators in Australia. For an excellent and exhaustive list of agencies worldwide offering Loire-based tours, check the French Government Tourist Office's Web site at www.fgtousa.org.

Art & Architecture

International Study Tours (☎ 800 833 2111, 212-563 1202, fax 594 6953) 225 West 34th St, New York 10122, USA. Cultural and educational tours designed for the independent traveller.

Martin Randall Travel Ltd (☎ 020-8742 3355, fax 8742 7766, ✆ info@martinrandall.co.uk) 10 Barley Mow Passage, Chiswick, London W4 4PH, UK. A nine-day tour which takes in the architectural and artistic treasures of Angers, Cunault, Fontevraud and Poitiers and costs around UK£1340, including flights and hotel accommodation.

Cruises

European Waterways (☎ 800 217 447, 212-688 9489, fax 688 3778, ✆ sales@europeanwaterways.com) 140 East 56th St 4C, New York, NY 10022, USA. A leading riverboat cruise operator offering luxury one-week cruises for eight passengers aboard *Bonne Humeur*, starting at US$34,500 (to charter the boat plus four-man crew). Dutch-barge cruises on the River Cher (US$16,000 for six passengers) are also available.
Web site: www.europeanwaterways.com

Cycling & Walking

Most cycling tour operators lighten the load by transporting cyclists' baggage by minibus between hotels. Many tours take in chateaux and other sights en route.

Adventure Sports Holidays (☎ 800 628 9655, 413-568 2855, fax 562 3621) 815 North Rd, Westfield, MA 01085, USA. Cycling tours of the Loire, averaging 25 miles of cycling per day.
Web site: www.advonskis.com/bike

Alyson Adventures (☎ 800 825 9766, ✆ andy@a-1travel.com) PO Box 180179, Boston, Mass 02118, USA. Offers biking trips (costing upwards of US$1600 for a 10-day tour, including accommodation, cycle hire and so on) for gay and lesbian travellers.
Web site: www.alysonadventures.com

Cyclists' Touring Club (CTC; ☎ 01483-417217, fax 426994, ✆ cycling@ctc.org.uk). The UK's biggest cycling organisation offers occasional tours to the Loire among its good-value, non-profit tours run by and for CTC members. These and scores of commercial cycle-holiday outfits are listed in CTC's *Cycle Holiday Guide*.
Web site: www.ctc-org.uk

Europeds (☎ 800 321 9552, 831-646 4920, fax 655 44501, ✆ europeds@aol.com) 761 Lighthouse Ave, Monterey, CA 93940, USA. Cycling and walking tours.

Explore Worldwide (☎ 01252-760000, fax 760001, ✆ info@explore.co.uk) 1 Frederick St, Aldershot, Hants GU11 1LQ, UK. Ten-day cycling tours by the adventure specialists, costing UK£545/575 in the low/high season, including train travel from London.
Web site: www.explore.co.uk

Inn Travel (☎ 01653-628811, fax 628741, ✆ inntravel@inntravel.co.uk). UK-based company offering weekend breaks, six-day discovery journeys and one-week chateau or cycling tours (costing upwards of UK£500/660 by self-drive/air); accommodation is in family-run inns or chateaux.
Web site: www.inntravel.co.uk

Sherpa Expeditions (☎ 020-8577 2717, fax 8572 9788, ✆ sales@sherpa-walking-holidays.co.uk) 131a Heston Rd, Hounslow, Middx TW5 0RF, UK. Eight-day, self-guided tours of the Loire, walking 15 to 27km per day along parts of GR3, GR41 and GR46 (costing upwards of UK£630).
Web site: www.sherpa-walking-holidays.co.uk

Susi Madron's Cycling for Softies (☎ 0161-248 8282, fax 248 5140, ✆ info@cycling-for-softies .co.uk) 2–4 Birch Polygon, Manchester M14 5HX, UK. Nine-, 10- and 14-day tours costing upwards of UK£590 for seven nights, including unique tours of the Marais Poitevin; all cycling abilities are catered for.

Web site: www.cycling-for-softies.co.uk

Food & Wine

Arblaster & Clarke Wine Tours (☎ 01730-893344, fax 892888, ✆ sales@winetours.co.uk) Clarke House, Farnham Rd, West Liss, Hants GU33 6JQ, UK. Loire wines and truffles and other viticulture programmes costing from UK£700 per week, including ferry and coach transport; tours are led by a wine expert or restaurateur.

Web site: www.winetours.co.uk

Espirit Libre (☎ 212-470 158, fax 473 4404) Suite 30A, 5 East 22nd St, New York, NY 10010, USA. Fine-wine and art tours.

Old Ipswich Tours (☎ 887 356 5163, fax 978 356 9540, ✆ ipswichtours@mediaone.net) 8 Herrick Drive, Ipswich, MA 01938, USA. Gourmet wine tours costing upwards of US$3499, including Boston–Paris return air fare, accommodation and tours.

Tanglewood Wine Tours (☎ 01932-348720, fax 350861, ✆ jean@tanglewoodwine.co.uk) Tanglewood House, Mayfield Ave, New Haw, Surrey KT15 3AG, UK. Four-day wine weekends based in Saumur, costing upwards of UK£340.

Web site: www.tanglewoodwine.com

Wine Trails (☎ 01306-712111, fax 713504, ✆ sales@winetrails.co.uk) Greenways, Vann Lake, Ockley, Dorking RH5 5NT, UK. Walking, cycling and chateau tours of the Loire with a strong focus on wine and gourmet cuisine; four/seven-day cycling tours cost upwards of UK£300/490, including half-board hotel accommodation.

Web site: www.winetrails.co.uk

Getting Around

AIR

Unless you are absolutely loaded (with either cash or baggage) or travelling on a corporate expense account, there is little reason (or opportunity) to take to the sky in a plane between Loire Valley destinations. However, hot-air ballooning is a popular (but expensive and unreliable) means of hopping between chateaux in the valley; see the boxed text 'Hot-Air Ballooning' under Activities in the Facts for the Visitor chapter for details.

There are scheduled inter-regional flights between two of the region's four airports – Aéroport de Tours-Val de Loire (www.tours-aeroport.com) and Aéroport Poitiers-Biard. Flights between Tours and Poitiers run twice daily (once daily from mid-July to mid-September) on weekdays, and are operated by Air Liberté. Flying time is 25 minutes and a return ticket (including a Saturday-night stay) costs around 600FF. A fully flexible single costs around a hefty 800FF. Have a look at Air Liberté's Web site at www.air-liberte.fr.

Year round, Oya Hélicoptères (www.iledyeu.com) operates scheduled helicopter flights between mainland France and the small island of Île d'Yeu, 35km off the Atlantic coast. There are six scheduled flights daily between Fromentine, on mainland France, and Port Joinville or Aérodrome d'Yeu on Île d'Yeu. A single ticket costs 400FF; islanders pay 280FF and the fare for children aged two to 12 is 240FF. Tickets and schedules are available from Oya Hélicoptères (☎ 02 51 59 22 22, fax 02 51 59 20 77), 5 rue Gabriel Guist'hau, BP 100, 85350 Île d'Yeu; at the heliports in Fromentine (☎ 02 51 49 01 01) or Port Joinville (☎ 02 51 58 78 72); or at Aérodrome d'Yeu (☎ 02 51 58 38 22).

Several companies operate aerial twirls of the Loire chateaux by helicopter. Most use the small aerodromes in Blois (Aérodrome de Blois-Le Breuil) or Amboise (Aérodrome d'Amboise-Dierre). Private jets can take off and land here too. Sign up for a sightseeing tour or charter your own helicopter from one of the following companies:

Air Centre Ouest (☎/fax 02 47 88 97 35) Aéroport de Tours-Val de Loire, 4 rue de l'Aérogare, 37100 Tours. This company offers chateau trips, aerial-photography excursions and charters on request.

Air Touraine Hélicoptère (☎ 02 47 24 81 44, fax 02 47 24 82 84) BP 14, 37370 Neuvy-le-Roi. The company offers year-round departures from Belleville Heliport: 10-minute to 1½-hour trips over the chateaux of your choice.

Jet Systems Hélicoptères (☎ 02 47 30 20 21, 06 08 69 41 96, fax 02 47 30 28 29, ✉ jet-systems@aol.com) Aérodrome d'Amboise-Dierry, 37150 Dierre. Scheduled *circuits touristiques* (tourist trips) are offered on Tuesday, Thursday, Saturday and Sunday in summer. Trips take in two or three major chateaux; the 50-minute Majestic trip includes Amboise, Blois, Chambord, Chaumont, Chenonceau and Cheverny and costs 1450FF per person; the Inédit (Original; three hours) includes Amboise, Chaumont and Chenonceau with a stopover at Château de Montpoupon for lunch (1370/1095FF per adult/child, including lunch). Classic 10- or 20-minute twirls cost 350/290FF (ten minutes) and 690/560FF (20 minutes) for adults/children. Gastronomic stopovers are available on request.
Web site: www.jet.systems.fr

Toulouse Envol (☎ 02 54 20 19 18, 06 12 86 61 35) Aérodrome de Blois-Le Breuil. The company offers aerial tours of key Loire chateaux, including Amboise, Blois, Chambord, Chaumont, Chenonceau, Cheverny, Ménars and Villesavin, in a four-seater plane. Departures are from Blois. Fares start at 230/450FF per person for a 30/55-minute trip.

To/From the Airports

All airports in the region are a few kilometres from their respective city centres. Information on shuttle-bus/public-transport links to/from the city centre is given under To/From the Airport in the Getting Around section of the respective city listings throughout this guide.

BUS

Buses are used for short-distance travel within *départements* (departments). Services and routes are extremely limiting – not to mention downright frustrating – for any traveller keen to pack in more than one chateau in a day. Throughout the valley, the départements' bus systems are designed purely to transports kids to school, meaning a scanty service during school hours and an even scantier – or nonexistent – service on Sunday and during school holidays. Between May and October, special summer buses are scheduled between Tours, Chenonceaux and Amboise (see Getting There & Away in those sections for details).

Regional buses (*autocars*) are operated by a muddling host of different bus companies, most of whom usually have an office at the bus station (*gare routière*) of the cities they serve. One bus company usually sells tickets for all the different companies operating from the same bus station.

Certain uneconomical SNCF train lines have been replaced by SNCF buses in recent years. The main difference between these buses and regular regional ones is that travellers can often (but not always) take advantage of any train pass they have on an SNCF service. Routes covered by SNCF buses include to/from Tours and Azay-le-Rideau, Chinon and Loches; and to/from Nantes and Pornic, St-Gilles Croix de Vie, Poitiers, Cholet, Île de Noirmoutier and Les Sables d'Olonne. Tickets and timetables for SNCF buses are available from SNCF train stations; buses usually depart from a bus stop (*halte routière*) in front of the train station or, in the case of Tours, from the bus station opposite the train station.

Few bus stations have left-luggage facilities but some (such as Tours) have an information desk that doubles as an informal luggage room; leave your bag with the information clerk for 10FF per day.

TRAIN

SNCF's regional train network is efficiently served by *trains express régionaux* (regional express trains; TER). The main route snakes downstream along the River Loire

from Orléans to Le Croisic on the Atlantic coast, making the Loire Valley easily accessible by train. Stops en route include (from east to west) Blois, Amboise, Tours, Langeais, Saumur, Angers, Nantes and St-Nazaire.

Other primary train routings in the region include a trio of southbound lines linking Tours with Loches (to the south-east), Poitiers (to the south) and Chinon (to the south-west). Northbound, the railway cuts across the Loir Valley (not to be confused with the Loire Valley), via Château du Loir, to Le Mans. From Angers, a southbound line runs to Cholet. Nantes has efficient southbound train links with St-Gilles Croix de Vie, and Les Sables d'Olonne (via La Roche-sur-Yon inland), on the Atlantic coast.

In addition to these SNCF routes, a narrow-gauge railway links Ligré with Richelieu in the Vallée de la Vienne in Touraine. Operated by Trains à Vapeur de Touraine (TVT; ☎ 02 47 58 12 97, fax 02 47 58 28 72), a steam train (*train à vapeur*) puffs its way 21km along the banks of the River Veude. The 1930s locomotive stops at Champigny-sur-Veude en route; in 1999 the train only ran between mid-July and mid-August, departing from Richelieu on Saturday and Sunday at 3 pm and departing from Ligré at 4 pm. The journey time is 45 minutes and a return ticket costs 60/30FF for adults/children.

Information

Most train stations have separate ticket windows (*guichets*) and information/reservation offices; opening hours and phone numbers are listed under Train in the Getting There & Away section of each relevant city or town section.

Indispensable for anyone intending to do a lot of train travel in the region is *Les Châteaux de la Loire en Train*, an SNCF pamphlet (free) issued each year in late May and available at train stations. Up-to-date travel options and schedules are also detailed in the *Guide Régional des Transports*, also issued in May and available for free at many train stations. For further details about train travel in the entire area covered by this

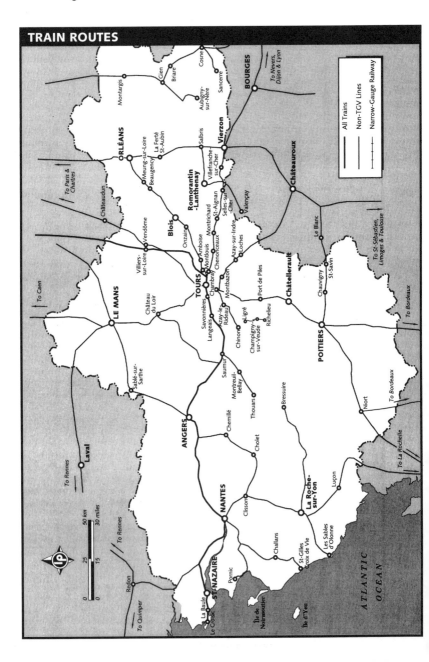

guide, pick up the TER guides for both the Pays de la Loire and Centre régions.

Left Luggage

Orléans, Tours, Nantes and other larger SNCF stations have either a *consigne manuelle* (left-luggage office), where you pay 30FF per bag or 35FF per bicycle for 24 hours; or a *consigne automatique*, a 72-hour computerised luggage locker that will issue you with a lock code in exchange for 15/20/30FF for a small/medium/large-sized locker. At many smaller stations (such as Blois) there is nowhere to leave luggage; luggage lockers at larger stations are sometimes out of service due to the security threat posed by terrorists. Check what time left-luggage counters close; many open around 8 am to noon and 2 to 6 or 7 pm. Locker rooms are often only accessible from around 6 am to 11 pm.

Schedules

SNCF's pocket-sized timetables (*horaires*), available for free at stations, are not that complicated to read, though French railway-speak can create a few obstacles. There is also an excellent multilingual 'Comment Lire un Tableau' (How to Read a Timetable) section in the *Guide Régional des Transports* (see Information, earlier).

Printed train timetables come in two types – those for regional TER trains (timetables are shiny sky blue or blood red in colour) and those for the *grandes lignes* (literally 'big lines') covering TGV and other mainline services. The two rows of boxed numbers that appear at the top of grande ligne schedules refer to the train number (*numéro de train*) and footnotes (*notes à consulter*). The train number is not listed in TER pocket timetables; CAR indicates an SNCF bus service (see Bus earlier in this chapter).

The footnotes at the bottom of both types of timetable explain when a particular train runs – often Monday to Friday or Saturday or only until (*jusqu'au*) a certain date. Alternatively, it may operate daily (*tous les jours*) except (*sauf*) Saturday, Sunday and/or holidays (*fêtes*).

SNCF generally issues two sets of timetables per year – a winter schedule valid from the end of September (or November on some routes) to the end of May, and a summer schedule which runs from the end of May to the end of September (occasionally November).

Train Passes

For details on train passes, see the boxed text 'Train Passes & Discount Fares' in the Getting There & Away chapter.

Between mid-June and mid-October during the Festival International des Jardins (International Garden Festival) at Château de Chaumont (see the Orléanais & Blésois chapter), SNCF teams up with the Centre région to offer discounted train fares and entrance tickets. Contact tourist offices in the région for details.

Tickets

In most stations, you can buy your ticket at a ticket window or from a machine. These touch-screen machines (*billetterie automatique*) accept credit cards for tickets of 15FF or more and issue all ticket types (except those for international destinations).

Return tickets cost exactly twice as much as a single. Count on paying 70FF to 100FF per 100km for short hops with 2nd-class travel. For more details on costs see Other Parts of France under Land in the Getting There & Away chapter. Train fares for specific routes are listed under Getting There & Away in the relevant town and city sections throughout this book.

Reservations are not mandatory – or necessary – on most regional trains. Tickets are valid for two months from the date of purchase; advance reservations (20FF) are possible for many trains, meaning you will be assured of a seat for the duration of the journey.

Tickets can be purchased on board but, unless the ticket window where you boarded was closed (often the case in pinprick-sized stations such as Azay-le-Rideau) *and* the station had no ticket machine (rarely the case), prohibitive tariffs apply: a flat 130FF for journeys under 75km, 90FF plus the price of a standard ticket for journeys of more than 75km. Finally, remember to timestamp your ticket before boarding (see Validating Your Ticket under Other Parts of France under Land in the Getting There & Away chapter) or you likewise risk an on-the-spot fine.

CAR

Having your own wheels is part of the secret to discovering a region which is absolutely impossible to discover in any depth by public transport. A car enables you to choose from a wider range of camp sites, hostels and hotels on city outskirts, as well as restored farmhouses, delightfully rambling old mills and chateaux. The downside? Driving between major chateaux in July and August can be mighty slow going when the rest of the world seems to be heading in precisely the same direction.

Away from the roads that snake along the northern and southern banks of the River Loire between Orléans and St-Nazaire – approximately 400km – traffic jams are rare. Two *autoroutes* (highways/motorways) slash across the region from north-east to south-west: the Paris–Le Mans–Angers–Nantes E50/A11, which is known as L'Océane (literally 'the road to the ocean'), and the Paris–Orléans–Tours E5/A10, which plummets south from Tours to Poitiers, Niort and beyond; the latter is called L'Aquitaine after the area around Bordeaux in which it terminates. Smaller stretches of autoroute include the E9/A71 (Orléans–Bourges) and the E60/A85 (Angers–Saumur–Bourgueil).

There are three types of road in addition to the autoroute. *Routes nationales* are highways whose names begin with N; these are generally wide, well signposted and lavishly equipped with reflectors. *Routes départementales* are local roads whose names begin with D. *Chemins communaux* are minor rural roads whose names sometimes begin with C.

All autoroutes and national roads are clearly marked on IGN's (Institut Géographique National) blue-jacketed *France Routes-Autoroutes* (No 951), indispensable

for motorists intent on getting around the region.

Documents

All drivers are required by French law to carry a national ID card or passport; a valid *permis de conduire* (driving permit or licence); car ownership papers, known as a *carte grise* (grey card); and proof of insurance, known as a *carte verte* (green card). If you're found by the police without one or more of these documents, you can be subject to a 900FF on-the-spot fine.

Equipment

A reflective warning triangle, to be used in the event of breakdown or accident, must be carried in the car. Recommended accessories – not mandatory in France but highly advisable in the interests of safety – are a first-aid kit, a spare-bulb kit and a fire extinguisher. In the UK, contact the RAC (☎ 0870 5275 600) or the AA (☎ 0870 5500 600) for more advice. In other countries, contact your automobile association.

Road Rules

In France, as throughout Continental Europe, people drive on the right side of the road and overtake on the left. Unless otherwise indicated, you must give way to cars coming from the right. North American drivers note: turning right on a red light (unless it is flashing) is illegal in France.

Speed Limits Unless otherwise posted, a speed limit of 50km/h applies in all areas designated as built up, no matter how rural they may appear. On intercity roads, you must slow to 50km/h the moment you pass a white sign with red borders on which a place name is written in black or blue letters.

Outside built-up areas, speed limits are 90km/h (80km/h if it's raining) on undivided N and D highways; 110km/h (100km/h in the rain) on dual carriageways (divided highways) or short sections of highway with a divider strip; and 130km/h (110km/h in the rain) on autoroutes. Speed limits are not posted unless they deviate from the above.

Alcohol French law is very tough on drunk drivers and the police do conduct random breathalyser tests to weed out drivers whose blood-alcohol concentration (BAC) is over 0.05% (0.50g per litre of blood). Fines range from 500FF to 8000FF and licences can be suspended.

Road Signs

Sens unique means 'one way' and *voie unique* means 'one-lane road'. If you come to a *route barrée* (closed road), you'll usually also find a yellow panel with instructions for a *déviation* (detour). Signs for *poids lourds* (heavy weights) are meant for lorries (trucks), not cars. The words *sauf riverains* on a no-entry sign mean 'except residents' – common in old historic areas of medieval towns. Road signs with the word *rappel* (remember) mean you should already know what the sign is telling you (such as the speed limit). Pictures of wild animals – common in forested areas such as Chambord – on a road sign are self-explanatory.

Expenses

Petrol *Essence* (petrol or gasoline), also known as *carburant* (fuel), is expensive in France, incredibly so if you're used to Australian or North American prices. In late 1999, unleaded (*sans plomb*) petrol (98 octane) cost around 7FF per litre. Filling up is cheapest at stations on city outskirts and at supermarkets, and most expensive on the autoroute; prices can fluctuate by as much as 20%.

Parking Finding a place to park in Nantes, Orléans and other largish towns can be an awesome task. Public parking facilities are marked by signs bearing a white letter 'P' on a blue background – many are underground. *Payant* written on the asphalt or on a nearby sign means you have to pay. Meters in above-ground car parks swallow 5FF to 10FF per hour. Most chateaux have giant, ugly purpose-built car parks (the record for the largest goes to Chambord) where you can park for a fee of 20FF or 30FF.

Rental

Most of the major international rental agencies, such as Hertz, Avis, Budget and Europcar have a desk at Aéroport International Nantes-Atlantique and in most large towns. Rates are outrageously expensive if you walk into one of their city offices and hire on the spot – up to 800FF per day for a Twingo (Renault's smallest model) with unlimited mileage (*kilométrage illimité*). Prebooked and prepaid promotional rates, by contrast, can be reasonable (weekly rates for Europe, as advertised in the USA, are as little as US$180). They sometimes have fly-drive combinations too, which are worth looking into.

Most rental companies require the driver to be aged over 21 (or, in some cases, over 23) and to have had a driving licence for at least one year. The packet of documents you are given should include a 24-hour number to call in case of a breakdown or accident. Check how many 'free' kilometres are – or are not – included in the deal you're offered.

For rentals not arranged in advance, domestic companies such as Rent-a-Car Système and Century have the best rates. Companies are listed under Getting There & Away in town and city sections.

Insurance Insurance for damage or injury you cause to other people is mandatory, but things such as collision-damage waivers vary greatly from company to company. The policies offered by some small discount companies may leave you liable for up to 8000FF – when comparing rates, the most important thing to check is the excess/deductible (*franchise*). If you're in an accident where you are at fault, or the car is damaged and the party at fault is unknown (for example, if someone dents your car while it's parked), or the car is stolen, this is the amount you are liable for before the collision-damage policy kicks in.

Forms of Payment All rental companies accept payment by credit card. They also require a deposit; most ask you to leave a signed credit card slip without a sum written on it as a deposit. If you don't like this arrangement, ask them to make out two credit card slips: one for the sum of the rental and the other for the sum of the excess. Make sure the latter is destroyed when you return the car.

Purchase-Repurchase Plans

Non-EU residents who want a car in Europe for between 17 days and six months will find that the cheapest option by far is to 'purchase' a new car from the manufacturer and then, at the end of your trip, 'sell' it back to them. In reality, you pay only for the number of days you use the vehicle, and the tax-free, purchase-repurchase (*achat-rachat*) aspect of the paperwork (none of which is your responsibility) makes this type of leasing much cheaper than renting, especially for longer periods. Eligibility is strictly restricted to people not resident in the EU.

Payment must be made in advance. If you return the car earlier than planned, you usually get a refund for the unused time (seven days minimum). From the USA, a Renault Twingo (the cheapest model available) costs around US$500 for the first 17 days and about US$16 for each additional day. In France, Twingo prices are around 3780/52FF respectively. Rates include unlimited kilometres, 24-hour towing and breakdown service (☎ 0800 051 515 in France) and comprehensive insurance with – incredibly – no excess (deductible).

Renault Eurodrive (☎ 212-532 1221 in the USA, 01 40 40 33 68 in Paris) and Peugeot Vacation (☎ 1800 572 9655 in the USA) get rave reviews. Their respective Web sites are www.eurodrive.renault.com and www.auto-france.com.

MOTORCYCLE

The Loire is superb country for motorcycle touring, with roads of good quality and lots of stunning scenery. Make sure your wet-weather gear is up to scratch in spring and autumn. Helmets are obligatory; easyriders caught bareheaded can be fined and have their bike confiscated. Bikes of more than 125cc must have their headlights on during

the day. No special licence is required to ride a motorcycle whose engine is less than 50cc.

To rent a scooter or motorcycle you have to leave a deposit of several thousand francs, which you forfeit – up to the value of the damage – if you're in an accident and it's your fault. Since insurance companies won't cover theft, you'll also lose the deposit if the bike is stolen. Most places accept deposits made by credit card, travellers cheques or Eurocheques.

BICYCLE

Cycling through the beautiful (and beautifully flat) Loire countryside is an excellent and thoroughly invigorating way to get around. The region sports an extensive network of local roads which carry relatively light traffic and serve as an ideal vantage point from which to view the Loire's celebrated rural landscapes, be it vineyards, sunflower fields or a chateau. Avoid the national roads that run along the River Loire: they get crammed with heavy traffic. Roads built on top of dikes, hence having steep sides which leave little room for verges (shoulders), and offering no protection against strong winds, are also worth avoiding.

Visiting more than one chateau by pedal power in a day is not recommended for the casual cyclist. Scheduling two or three chateaux per outing really clocks up the kilometres, though it is possible with careful advance planning. Covering, for example, Chambord, Cheverny and Villesavin in a day is feasible, although the 36km round trip leaves little time to visit each chateau interior. When planning a cycle trip, consider carefully the capabilities of each member of your party; the casual cyclist has an average pedal power of 40km per day (obviously variable depending on general fitness levels).

French law mandates that bicycles must have two functioning brakes, a bell, a red reflector on the back and yellow reflectors on the pedals. After sunset and when visibility is poor, cyclists must turn on a white light in front and a red one in the rear. When being overtaken by a car or truck, cyclists are required to ride in single file.

Bicycles are not allowed on most local or intercity buses or on trams; in Nantes cyclists can only travel on trams with their bicycles before 7.15 am and after 6.30 pm, Monday to Saturday, and all day Sunday. On some regional trains you can take a bicycle free of charge, allowing you to cycle either to or from your destination. On train timetables, a bicycle symbol indicates if a bicycle is allowed on particular trains or not. On some regional trains, bikes have to be stored in the luggage van (maximum capacity three bicycles). Further details are available from SNCF information offices; ask for its free *Guide du Train et du Vélo* (*Train and Bicycle Guide*).

The Comité Régional du Tourisme et des Loisirs Centre-Val de la Loire (☎ 02 38 70 32 74, fax 02 38 70 33 80, **✉** ctrl.centre@ wandoo.fr), 9 rue St-Pierre Lentin, 45041 Orléans, publishes the invaluable, English-language booklet *Bicycle Touring*, which lists camp sites and hotels in the Centre région that belong to the bicycle-friendly Vélotel-Vélocamp association. As members, they pledge to assist saddle-sore cyclists with overnight bike storage, route planning, map provision, bicycle repairs and other problems cyclists might encounter. On request (and for an extra fee) some hoteliers serve hearty 'Vélotel' breakfasts and supply packed lunches.

See Cycling under Activities and under Spectator Sports in the Facts for the Visitor chapter for more cycling-relevant information and contacts. See Train under Other Parts of France, or Bicycle under The UK, both in the Land section of the Getting There & Away chapter, for information on transporting your bicycle to the Loire from the rest of Europe.

Rental

Almost all towns, most small villages that sport a chateau, some chateaux and a handful of tourist offices (Vouvray and Romorantin-Lanthenay) offer bicycle rental. Most outlets rent out *vélos tout-terrains* (VTTs; mountain bikes), as well as classical road bikes, tandems and bicycles for children. *Vélos hollandais* – delightful Dutch bicycles with a sturdy frame designed to smoothly cruise across notably flat terrain – are also often available.

VTT and road bicycles cost around 40/80FF per half/full day. Longer rentals cut costs considerably; expect to pay around 300/450FF for one/two weeks. Tandems are more expensive (160/260FF for one/two hours). In addition, most places require a 1000FF or 2000FF deposit, which you forfeit if the bike is damaged or stolen. In general, deposits can be made in cash, with signed travellers cheques or by credit card (though a passport will often suffice). Never leave your bicycle outside overnight, even if it is locked up, if you want to see it again.

Rental shops are listed under Getting Around in city and town sections throughout this book.

HITCHING

See Hitching under Other Parts of France under Land in the Getting There & Away chapter for general advice and safety tips.

BOAT

See Canoeing & Kayaking under Activities, and Nautical Maps under Planning, both in the Facts for the Visitor chapter, for canoeing- and kayaking-relevant information.

River & Canal Boat

Contrary to popular belief, the legendary River Loire – with its numerous sand banks and unpredictable water levels – is practically impossible to navigate in anything larger than a kayak or canoe. Much of the river between Briare (upstream) and St-Nazaire (downstream) is protected, leaving powered river and canal boats with no more than a 90km stretch between Angers and Nantes to cruise.

The region does have plenty of other navigable rivers and canals to explore, however. From Angers, the northbound River Sarthe to Le Mans (approximately 100km) is accessible to all types of water craft, as is the canalised River Mayenne, which goes through 39 locks on its 80km Angers–Laval course. The River Erdre and Nantes–Brest Canal dominates western Loire. Eastwards, the key canal is the 57km-long Briare Canal, which crosses the River Loire in the town of Briare, courtesy of Europe's longest canal bridge. It forges through seven locks and 14 bridges en route to Montargis, from where the Loing Canal takes over its northbound course, thus providing a crucial link between the Rivers Loire and Seine. Finally, in the south-easternmost corner of the Loire region is the Canal Latéral à la Loire, which flows gracefully through the land of Sancerre wine and Chavignol goat's cheese to link the Rivers Seine and Rhône.

The tourist cruising season lasts from Easter to October. House boats (*bateaux habitables*) accommodate two to 12 passengers and can be hired on a weekly basis; the Rivers Mayenne and Sarthe (Anjou), the River Erdre (Loire-Atlantique) and the Canal Latéral à la Loire (Orléanais) are the most popular waterways. Anyone aged over 18 can pilot a river boat. Learning the ropes takes about 30 minutes; the speed limit is 6km/h on canals and 10km/h on rivers.

The region's major navigable waterways – including the stretch of the Loire between Angers and Nantes – are managed, maintained and controlled by Voies Navigables de France (VNF; Navigable Waterways of France). The VNF (www.vnf.fr) issues licences required for inland cruising and imposes river tolls at certain points on major waterways. Toll stickers must be displayed on the starboard side of the boat front.

The price of a licence depends on the size of your boat and the time spent on the water. For a craft of 12m or less in length, a single-day card costs 51FF, a Holiday Card valid for 16 consecutive days costs 104FF, a Leisure Card valid for 30 non-consecutive days costs 270FF, and a one-year card costs 467FF. Licences (issued in the form of a sticker) can be purchased in advance by post from the Librairie VNF (☎ 01 45 84 85 89), 18 quai d'Austerlitz, 75013 Paris; or from the Direction Régionale de VNF (☎ 02 40 44 20 20), Centre des Salorges, 18 quai Ernest Renaud, BP 3139, 44031 Nantes Cedex 4.

To get a boat in July and August, reservations must be made at least several months ahead. Information on house boats is available from, and reservations can be made through, Pays de la Loire Réservations (☎ 02 40 89 89 89, fax 02 40 89 89 85, @ tourisme@cr-pays-de-la-loire.fr), 2 blvd de la Loire, BP 20411, 44204 Nantes Cedex 2. The company publishes the excellent 90-page *D'Une Rive à l'Autre* (*From One River to Another*), which details the most beautiful sites on the region's navigable rivers and canals; it is free. For details on cruising the River Erdre north of Nantes, contact Formules Bretagne (☎ 01 53 63 11 53, fax 01 53 63 11 57), 203 blvd St-Germain, 75007 Paris.

You can hire a boat in France or from abroad through Crown Blue Line (www .crown-blueline.com). You can hop aboard either at Daon, 40km north of Angers, from where you can cruise northwards to Laval or southwards to Angers and beyond; or at Briare, 75km south-east of Orléans, from where you can cruise 133km south along the Canal Latéral à la Loire. Boats can be booked through Crown Blue Line's office in France (☎ 04 68 94 52 72, fax 04 68 94 52 73, @ boathols@crown-blueline.com); or in the UK (☎ 01603-630513, fax 664298, @ boating@crownblueline.co.uk), 8 Ber St, Norwich NR1 3EJ. Weekly rates for a boat for two/12 people start at UK£430/1180 in the low season, peaking at UK£720/1990 in the high season (July and August).

Boating in the Maine-Anjou area is handled by Rive de France (☎ 01 41 86 01 01, fax 01 41 86 01 02, @ rdf@i2m.fr), 55 rue d'Aguesseau, 92100 Boulogne-Billancourt. Have a look at the Web site at www.rive-de-france.tm.fr. In the UK, Farthing Holidays (☎ 0116-2793883), Holiday House, High St, Kibworth, Leicester LE8 0DN, is its agent.

Boating-holiday specialists abroad who can assist those wanting to sail their way around the Loire include:

France Afloat (☎/fax 020-7704 0700, @ boats@ franceafloat.com). The UK-based company provides house boats to rent in Anjou, starting at UK£658/1343 per week for a four/12-person

boat; weekly rates include a standard season return from the UK with Eurotunnel (car and up to eight passengers) or P&O Stena Line (car and up to five passengers).
Web site: www.franceafloat.com

French Country Cruises (☎ 01572-821330, fax 01571-821072) Andrew Brock Travel, 54 High St East, Uppingham, Rutland LE15 9PZ, UK. This company offers one- and two-week holidays in Anjou afloat the Rivers Mayenne and Sarthe with a *pénichette* (glass-fibre canal cruiser). Boat hire starts at UK£462 per week aboard a two-person pénichette, not including running costs.

Hoseasons Holidays Abroad (☎ 01502-500555, fax 500532) Sunway House, Lowestoft, Suffolk NR32 2LW, UK. The company provides cruisers to hire on a weekly, 10-day or fortnightly basis, costing upwards of UK£510 per week (two adults plus child).
Web site: www.hoseasons.co.uk

From Briare, Tours (Rochecorbon), Saumur, Angers, Nantes and St-Nazaire there are a multitude of river excursions in summer. Dinner cruises are available too. See regional chapters for details.

Ferry

Ferries ply the waters from the Atlantic coast to Île d'Yeu, an island from where boats also sail to/from Île de Noirmoutier farther north. Tickets for sailings in July and August – when early-morning and evening boats fill up quickly – should be reserved by telephone in advance. Sailing time is approximately 45 minutes. Bicycles can be taken on board for an extra fee.

There are scheduled departures year round from the Gare Maritime de Fromentine, on mainland France, but seasonal sailings only (April to October) from St-Gilles Croix de Vie and Île de Noirmoutier. Boat taxis service Île d'Yeu year round to/from St-Gilles Croix de Vie. For full details see Getting There & Away under Vendée in the Loire-Atlantique & Vendée chapter.

In season, soulless boat excursions aimed at tourists, often with blaring music and always with loud recorded commentaries, serve most hot spots along the Atlantic coast, including La Baule, Le Croisic and Les Sables d'Olonne.

LOCAL TRANSPORT

Getting around cities and towns in the Loire is a straightforward affair, thanks to excellent public transport systems.

Nantes is the only city in the region to have a tramway, although roads have already been dug up and rails laid in Orléans to pave the way for the first of two tram lines that will glide through the city streets by September 2000. A tramway is also planned for Le Mans. The tramway in Nantes – 27km long – is the longest in France. A new line expected to open in September 2000, plus planned extensions to the current two lines, will assure that the city retains this record.

Details of routes, fares and tourist passes are available at tourist offices and local-bus-company information counters. See Getting Around at the end of each city and town section throughout this book for information on local buses and so on.

Taxis are generally expensive. Most towns have a taxi rank in front of the train station. Count on paying between 3.50FF and 10FF per kilometre depending on the time of day and the distance you are travelling. Given the regional airports' out-of-town locations, don't even consider taking a taxi into town unless you have money to burn.

ORGANISED TOURS

Even veteran backpackers should consider an organised tour, given that touring the chateaux by public transport is such a horribly slow and pricey procedure. Far from being a regimental, sergeant-major affair, these interesting English-language tours are surprisingly relaxed and informal, allowing you to wander around each chateau independently (rather than as part of a restricted guided tour).

Aboard the bus, the 'English-speaking guide' advertised usually takes the form of a multilingual cassette recording, played at key moments during the journey. At each chateau the bus driver drops passengers off in a nearby parking lot, clearly stating at what time passengers need to reassemble (with the aid of a giant-sized clock face to overcome language barriers). Most tours give you between 45 minutes and one hour at each chateau on the agenda. Bus drivers generally have a fridge full of cold drinks on board; don't pay more than 10FF.

Several companies offer bus tours of the major Loire chateaux, with a different itinerary available on each day of the week. Many include wine-tasting too. Prices often include admission fees or entitle you to discounts (making it much cheaper than trying to do it on your own). If you can get five to seven people together, you can design your own minibus itinerary.

With the exception of Transports du Loir-et-Cher in Blois, most companies are based in Tours, with coaches usually departing from Tours bus station. Reservations can be made at the Tours tourist office. Companies include:

St-Eloi Excursions (☎ 02 47 37 08 04, fax 02 47 39 34 67, ✆ excursions@saint-eloi.com). This company runs minibus trips for up to eight people, costing 100FF (children aged under seven 50FF) for a half-day, and 135FF to 180FF (children aged under seven 75FF to 90FF) for a full day. Web site: www.saint-eloi.com

Services Touristiques de Touraine (STT; ☎/fax 02 47 05 46 09, ✆ info@stt-millet.fr). STT runs full-sized coaches aimed at individuals from April to mid-October. Morning tours of one chateau and a wine cellar in Vouvray or Montlouis cost 120FF, and an afternoon tour taking in three chateaux costs around 190FF. Exhausting all-day tours embracing four or five chateaux cost 300FF. All prices include admission fees. In July and August STT runs evening tours to the *son et lumière* (sound and light) shows at Amboise (140FF). STT's office is inside Tours train station opposite the Buffet de la Gare, though approaching the English-speaking staff in the tourist office is easier. Web site: www.stt-millet.fr

Transports du Loir-et-Cher (TLC; ☎ 02 54 58 55 55). This Blois-based public bus company operates chateau excursions from Blois to Chambord and Cheverny between mid-May and 31 August. There are two excursions daily, departing from in front of Blois train station, and tours cost 65FF (seniors, students and children 50FF); admission fees to the chateaux at Chambord and Cheverny are not included but tour participants are eligible for reduced tariffs. See Organised Tours under Blois in the Orléanais and Blésois chapter for details.

Orléanais & Blésois

The historical regions of Orléanais and Blésois are the gateway to the Loire Valley from Paris. Next-door neighbours on the arch of the River Loire, their proximity to Paris, coupled with the extraordinary rash of *grands châteaux* (major chateaux) they contain, ensures a steady stream of visitors year round.

The ancient Roman city of Orléans sits in all its splendour at this area's helm, its place in history having been secured in 1429 by a simple French peasant girl, Joan of Arc (Jeanne d'Arc). Upstream from Orléans, the sandy River Loire twists past a Romanesque basilica and France's oldest church to the rich vineyards of Sancerre, the source of one of the Loire Valley's most sought-after wines.

Downstream, Blésois is the fabled land of royal hunts, Renaissance chateaux and the pheasant-filled Sologne. Here, amid elk-rich forests, languish the historical hulks of the Châteaux de Chambord, Chaumont and Cheverny – three of the Loire's absolute greatest. French kings once held court in Blois, the historical capital of Blésois, which remains blessed with a fine chateau and some magical museums. The Rivers Loir (not to be confused with the Loire) and Cher – from which the Loir-et-Cher *département* (department) gets its name – flow past the city to the north and south respectively.

Orléanais

ORLÉANS

postcode 45000 • pop 112,600

Majestic Orléans straddles the mighty River Loire. It is the first city that weekend-cavorting Parisians hit on their route to the Loire chateaux. Despite being heavily bombed during WWII, historic Orléans survived more or less intact. Its streets hold a treasure trove of Romanesque churches and rich Renaissance *hôtels particuliers* (private mansions), while its museums and tech-

Highlights

- Marvel at spectacular Renaissance architecture and watch animal antics at Château de Chambord.
- Be bewitched by the white silhouette of richly furnished Château de Cheverny.
- See Château de Blois transformed at a night-time *son et lumière*.
- Tie the knot in the opulent bedroom in Hôtel Groslot in Orléans where King François II died aged 17.
- Follow in the footsteps of a 15th-century virgin warrior.
- Explore soggy Sologne, a low-lying land of 11,000 lakes, kissed by hiking paths and cycling trails.

nological parks have earned Orléans a reputation for innovation. A hi-tech tramway will grace the city's streets by September 2000. South of the centre is the lovely Parc Floral de la Source, source of the short River Loiret, a tributary of the River Loire after which the modern-day département of Loiret is named.

The residents of Orléans have one hero: the virgin warrior Joan of Arc, who stormed

ORLÉANAIS & BLÉSOIS

ORLÉANAIS & BLÉSOIS

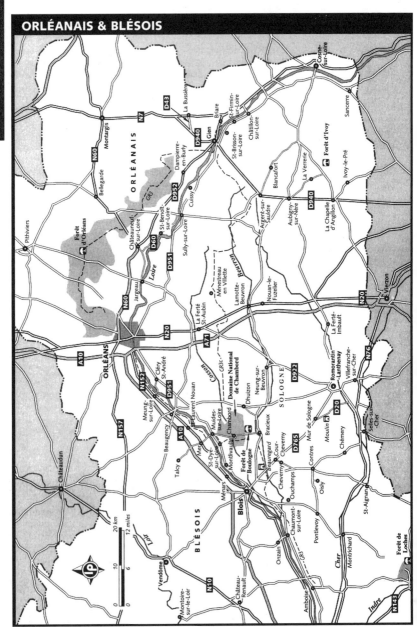

the city in 1429, smashed the English forces who had besieged it for seven months and then marched Dauphin Charles VII up north to be crowned king of France.

History

In pre-Roman times, Orléans, then called Cenabum, was inhabited by the Celtic Carnutes, who built a bridge across the River Loire, around which the settlement sprang up. In 52 BC Cenabum was conquered by Julius Caesar, who burned the town down. It was renamed Aurelianis (after Civitatis Aurelianorum, the administrative district of which it was capital) in the 3rd century.

A period of extraordinary prosperity followed Bishop Aignan's defeat of the Hun king Attila in 451. The city became a Roman Gaulish capital and two centuries later flourished as a religious and political centre during the Carolingian Renaissance. In 987 the nobles crowned Hugues Capet king in the cathedral in Orléans, after which the city served as a royal residence for the Capetian dynasty. In 1219 Pope Honorius banned the teaching of law in Paris – but not in Orléans, which consequently blossomed as a centre of intellectual learning. Its schools became a university in 1305. The victorious liberation of Orléans on 8 May 1429 was the turning point in the Hundred Years' War, which was bitterly fought between the Capetians and the English between 1337 and 1453.

Orléans' cathedral was blown up during the Wars of Religion (1562–98), but the city managed to profit from the French Revolution (1789) by amassing treasures that form the backbone of its eminent art collection today. The advent of the railway in the 19th century led to a rapid decline in the trade in sugar and textiles along the River Loire.

Since 1972, Orléans has served as the economic and administrative capital of the Centre *région* (region).

Orientation

The River Loire snakes from east to west along the southern fringe of Orléans city centre. Place du Martroi is the central square, linked by rue de la République to the central train station (Gare d'Orléans)

and adjoining Centre Commercial Place d'Arc (an indoor shopping complex), 400m north. Shop-lined rue Royale is the southern continuation of rue de la République. What remains of the old historic heart lies east of place du Martroi, along rue Jeanne d'Arc. Pedestrian rue de Bourgogne is the main shopping street in the old city.

The modern university district of La Source and surrounding Parc Floral de la Source are 3km south of the centre. The main station for trains to/from Paris, Aubrais-Orléans, is 2km north of the centre.

Maps Kümmerly+Frey's *Orléans, La Source et Agglomération* (Blay-Foldex, 1:10,000 scale) is a city map with a street index and detailed map of the centre. The tourist office sells a good-quality *Orléans Plan 1999* for 2FF.

An exhaustive range of hiking maps, city and regional maps are sold at La Maison du Style (☎ 02 38 53 27 74), 33–35 rue de la République.

Information

Tourist Offices The tourist office (☎ 02 38 24 05 05, fax 02 38 54 49 84, @ office-de-tourisme.orleans@wanadoo.fr), place Albert 1er, provides accommodation lists, sells city maps and tickets for most cultural events, and organises guided city tours (see Organised Tours later in this Orléans section). Opening hours are 9 am to 6 pm Tuesday to Saturday, and 10 am to 7 pm on Monday. On Sunday the smaller Espace Accueil Touristique (☎ 02 38 53 33 44), 6 rue Jeanne d'Arc, opens 10 am to 1 pm and 2.30 to 6 pm. On-line, have a look at www.ville-orleans.fr.

Tourist information about Loiret is available from the Comité Départemental du Tourisme (☎ 02 38 78 04 04, fax 02 38 78 04 12, @ tourisme.loiret@wanadoo.fr), 8 rue d'Escures. For regional information, go to the Comité Régional du Tourisme et des Loisirs de la Région Centre-Val de la Loire (☎ 02 38 70 32 74, fax 02 38 70 33 80, @ crtl.centre@wanadoo.fr), 9 rue St-Pierre Lentin. It has a Web site at www.loire valleytourism.com.

ORLÉANS

PLACES TO STAY
2 Hôtel de Paris
3 Hôtel Le Bannier
4 Hôtel St-Aignan
17 Hôtel de l'Abeille
18 Hôtel St-Martin
19 La Vieille Auberge
26 Grand Hôtel
32 Le Brin de Zinc
55 Hotel Jackotel
65 Hôtel Charles Sanglier

PLACES TO EAT
20 Café du Théâtre
23 La Martroi
24 Packman
27 Autobus Café
29 La Chancellerie
38 Le Lutetia
44 Nem+Ravioli
46 Le KT
50 La Petite Marmite
52 L'Estaminet
58 Le Gargantua
59 La P'tite Porte
60 Le Parisie
61 La Daride
62 Crêperie Bretonne
69 Espace Canal
74 Les Antiquaires
75 Le Mambassa
77 Auberge du Quai
80 L'Epicurien

OTHER
1 Intermarché Supermarket
5 Médiathèque
6 Rent-Van & Car Ecoto
7 Gare d'Orléans
8 Buses for La Source
9 Bus Station
10 Musée d'Orléans
11 Centre Commercial
   Place d'Arc
12 Tourist Office
13 Centre Régional
   d'Information Jeunesse

14 Cinéma Artistic
15 Maison du Style
16 Banque de France
21 Campo Santo
22 Comité Départemental
   du Tourisme
25 Café Jeanne d'Arc
28 Joan of Arc Statue
30 Espace Transport
31 Crédit Lyonnais
33 Hôtel Groslot
34 Town Hall
35 Musée des Beaux Arts
36 Synagogue
37 Cathédrale Ste-Croix
39 Espace Accueil Touristique
40 Centre Jeanne d'Arc
41 Central Post Office
42 Maison de Jeanne d'Arc
43 Musée Historique et
   Archéologique
45 Monté Cristo
47 Comité Régional du
   Tourisme et de Loisir
   de la Région Centre-
   Val de Loire
48 Salle des Thèses
49 Librairie Paes
51 Salon Lavoir
54 Lav'Club
56 Église St-Aignan
57 Collégiale St-Pierre-
   le-Puellier
58 Préfecture de Loiret
63 M@net
64 Post Office
66 Salon Lavoir
67 Hôtel Toutin
68 Ducs de Gascogne
70 Laundrette
71 Covered Market
72 Shannon Pub
73 Châtelet Tower
76 Marché de la Charpenterie
78 Cave de Marc et Sébastien
79 Église Notre Dame
   de Recouvrance

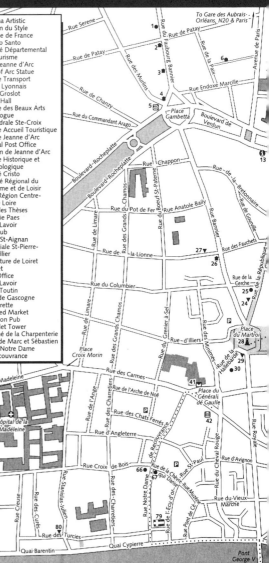

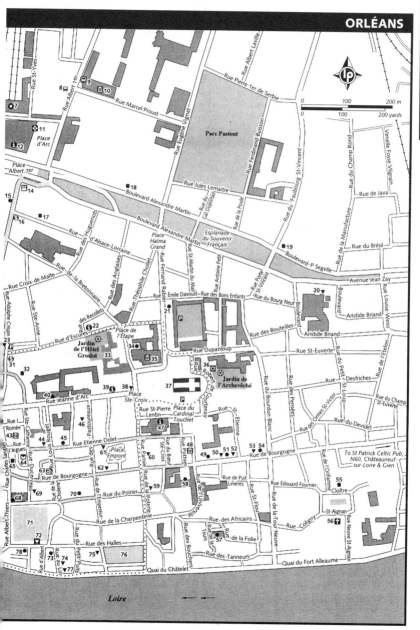

ORLÉANS

The Centre Régional d'Information Jeunesse (CRIJ; ☎ 02 38 78 91 78), 3–5 blvd de Verdun, opens 10 am to 6 pm Tuesday, Wednesday and Friday. It also opens on Saturday afternoon. It sells Wasteels/BIJ tickets and is an agent for Eurolines.

Money There are several commercial banks on place du Martroi, including Crédit Lyonnais, housed in a lovely Empire-style building (1863) at No 7. Banque de France is housed in an equally elegant hôtel particulier at 30 rue de la République.

Post The central post office, place du Général de Gaulle, opens 8 am to 7 pm on weekdays, and 8am to noon on Saturday. A smaller branch at 9 rue Ste-Catherine stays open until 6 pm on Saturday.

Email & Internet Access Monté Cristo (☎ 02 38 53 86 99), 42 rue Etienne Dolet, is a cyber club which charges 1FF per minute for Internet access. It opens 9 pm to 3 am on Wednesday and Thursday, and 8 pm to 3 am Friday to Sunday.

M@net (☎ 06 08 81 25 93, fax 02 38 62 81 40), 3 rue Louis Roguet, should have Internet hook-up in 2000. Alternatively, daytime surfers can try the Médiathèque (☎ 02 38 65 45 45), 1 place Gambetta, which has Internet access in its multimedia hall on the 2nd floor.

CRIJ (see Tourist Offices, earlier) is on-line at www.crij-centre.org and offers free Internet access between 2 and 5 pm on weekdays.

Bookshop Librairie Paes, 184 rue de Bourgogne, is a foreign-language bookshop, open 10 am to 12.30 pm and 1.30 to 7 pm Tuesday to Saturday.

Laundry Wash your socks and smocks at the laundrette at 26 rue du Poirier, Salon Lavoir at 176 rue de Bourgogne, or Lav'Club at 132 rue de Bourgogne. All three open 7 or 7.30 am to 10 pm daily. Nearer the river, Salon Lavoir, at 31 rue Notre Dame de Recouvrance, opens 7 am to 9 pm.

Medical Services The main hospital for the region, Hôpital de la Madeleine (☎ 02 38 51 44 44), is at 1 rue Porte Madeleine, south-west of place du Martroi.

Walking Tour

Place du Martroi is an obvious spot to kick off a city tour on foot. The giant **statue** of a sword-wielding Joan of Arc on horseback (1855) in its centre is an Orléans landmark. The inscription at the foot of the statue, damaged in WWII and restored in 1950, reads 'Sire sent me to save the good town of Orléans'. From here, bear east along rue d'Escures past the **Jardin de l'Hôtel Groslot** to place de l'Étape, named after a decree by Louis XII in 1500 which transformed the square into a wine market (*étape au vin*). The square is dominated by **Hôtel Groslot** and the **Musée des Beaux Arts**. A short detour north along rue Fernand Rabier allows you to peek into the rebuilt cloister of **Campo Santo** (1970). A block south sits a **synagogue**, at 14 rue Robert de Courtenay, and the magnificent Cathédrale Ste-Croix.

From place Ste-Croix, continue south along **rue Parisie** to **rue de Bourgogne** and the old university quarter. From here the River Loire is but a stone's throw away; **cycling paths** snake along its riverbanks in both directions. Cross **pont George V** for a panorama of rooftops, spires and sand banks. A downstream stroll along quai du Châtelet and quai Cypierre takes you to **Église Notre Dame de Recouvrance** (1512–19), named after the time when fishermen's wives came to thank the Virgin Mary for safely returning their husbands from sea. The valet of the future King Henri II, Guillaume Toutin, had **Hôtel Toutin** (1536–40) built on the same street at No 26, on the corner of rue de la Chèvre qui Danse (street of the goat who dances). The **Maison de Jeanne d'Arc** (see that section, later) is a couple of blocks north from here.

Hôtel Groslot

It was inside this flamboyant, Renaissance hôtel particulier on place de l'Étape that the 17-year-old king of France, François II, died in 1560. The room in which the king died, while his 19-year-old wife, Mary Stuart (Queen of Scots), and mother, Catherine de Médicis, sat at his bedside, is used as a *salle de mariage* (official marriage hall) today.

The Hôtel Groslot was built in 1550–2 for Jacques Groslot, the city bailiff and a Huguenot, whose family lived here until 1790, when the French Revolution transformed it into the town hall. Its exterior is a design of decorative gables, ornate red brickwork and stone medallions featuring the coats of arms of various noblemen and kings (including François II, whose motto was, rather inappropriately, 'I rise among eclipses'). Its interior is equally lavish and dates from 1850–54. In the marriage hall, lovers tie the knot beneath a beamed ceiling decorated with ornate, Louis XIII-style motifs.

The Hôtel Groslot opens 9 am to 7 pm on weekdays, and 5 to 9 pm on Saturday (except during weddings and ceremonies). Admission is free and there are guided tours in English. The **Jardin de l'Hôtel Groslot** (entrance on rue d'Escures) was laid out in the 19th century. The ruins of the 15th-century **Chapelle St-Jacques**, sheltered amid the magnificent floral beds, were moved here from Châtelet in 1883 and add a romantic touch.

Musée des Beaux Arts

The Musée des Beaux Arts (Museum of Fine Arts; ☎ 02 38 79 21 55), 1 rue Fernand Rabier, houses an impressive collection of European art from the 15th to the 20th centuries and is among the region's finest museums. Gaugin's *Fête Gloanec* (1888) is a 19th-century highlight. The 5th-floor modern art collection includes sculptures by Loiret-born Henri Gaudier-Brzeska and a room dedicated to the Quimper-born Jewish painter and poet Max Jacob (1876–1944), who left his native Brittany and, after a short stint in Paris, moved to St-Benoît-sur-Loire, where he lived until WWII, when he was taken to Drancy transit camp, where he died. Jacob was a great friend of Picasso – hence the portraits by Picasso exhibited here.

There are also numerous religious works of art, seized during the French Revolution and brought together in Orléans' first fine art museum in 1797–1804. Many treasures plundered from nearby chateaux – including several Mannerist paintings – are also on display. The museum opens 11 am to 6 pm Tuesday and Sunday, 10 am to 8 pm Wednesday, and 10 am to 6 pm Thursday, Friday and Saturday.

Cathédrale Ste-Croix

A church stood on place Ste-Croix as early as the 4th century, but it was not until the 17th century that the current Gothic edifice, with its ornate 114m-tall spire, was built. The original cathedral, which Bishop Robert de Courtenay commissioned in 1287, had scarcely been completed in the 16th century when the Wars of Religion broke out. Protestants occupied the cathedral and dynamited it in 1568, leaving nothing but the ruins of the 13th-century apse and some 14th-century side chapels.

Henri IV had the cathedral rebuilt in Flamboyant Gothic style from 1601. Under Louis XIII (1610–43) the choir and nave were restored. Louis XIV (1638–1715) saw to the building of the transept, while the next two Louis (1715–74) rebuilt the western facade and its towers. The raising of the spire in 1858 completed the mammoth project. In the lower nave, the series of 10 **stained-glass windows** depicting the life of Joan of Arc date from 1895. The side chapel, featuring a statue of the virgin warrior in a triumphant pose, the two leopards at her feet representing English submission to her power and authority, was unveiled in 1920 to mark her canonisation.

The cathedral opens 9.15 am to 6.45 pm. Sunday Mass, mid-May to mid-September, is celebrated in French, English, German, Italian and Spanish at 10.30 am. Tours of the 82m-tall cathedral towers leave at 3, 4 and 5 pm daily, July to September, and 3.30 and 4.30 pm on Saturday, May and June, from the southern entrance, inside the cathedral. Tickets cost 25FF (children 15FF). When entering/exiting the cathedral, beware of cavorting skateboarders on place Ste-Croix.

Old University Quarter

The old university quarter is sandwiched between the cathedral and the River Loire. All that remains of the university is the 15th-century Gothic **Salle des Thèses** (Thesis Room), on rue Pothier. Restored in 1881, the room was once used as a library and exam room. John Calvin (1509–64) was among the mass of eminent scholars who passed through its doors.

The **Préfecture de Loiret**, 181 rue de Bourgogne, at the southern end of rue Pothier, is housed in a former Benedictine monastery (1683) which was seized during the French Revolution. Its current facade dates from 1862. A few hundred metres south is the 12th-century **Collégiale St-Pierre-le-Puellier**, place du Cloître St-Pierre-le-Puellier. It is the oldest surviving church in Orléans, with a Romanesque exterior featuring an external staircase on the western facade. Its most famous parishioner was allegedly Joan of Arc's mother. The church was sold during the French Revolution and used as a salt warehouse. Today it is an exhibition centre (☎ 02 38 79 24 85).

The grandiose **Église St-Aignan**, a few blocks east, dominates Cloître St-Aignan. It was built in 1439–1509 on the site of a former church constructed in the 6th century by the people of Orléans to shelter the remains of the saintly Bishop Aignan. Since 1029, the relics have lain in the pre-Romanesque **crypt**, an underground tomb flanked by five small chapels (entrance on rue Neuve St-Aignan). Between 1798 and 1802, revolutionaries transformed St-Aignan's into the Temple de la Reconnaissance et de la Victoire (Temple of Gratitude and Victory).

The **Châtelet quarter**, on the university area's western fringe, was the commercial heart of medieval Orléans. The fortress here was built in 987 and destroyed in the 1800s; the medieval stone tower at 9 rue au Lin is all that remains of it today. Outdoor food markets continue to fill the **marketplace** at the eastern end of rue des Halles.

Orléans from medieval to modern times comes to life in the interesting **Musée Historique et Archéologique** (History and Archaeology Museum; ☎ 02 38 79 25 60), place Abbé Desnoyers. The museum is housed in the 16th-century Hôtel Cabu (1550), a mansion built for a city lawyer and once home to Diane de Poitiers, mistress of Henri II. It opens 10 am to 6 pm Tuesday to Sunday, July and August; 2 to 6 pm Tuesday to Sunday, May, June and September; and 2 to 6 pm Wednesday, Saturday and Sunday, the rest of the year. Admission costs 15FF (children 7FF).

To discover the natural history of Orléans, visit the **Musée d'Orléans** (☎ 02 38 54 61 05), next to the bus station at 6 rue Marcel Proust. It opens 2 to 6 pm daily and admission costs 20FF (students 10FF).

Maison de Jeanne d'Arc

The timber-framed Maison de Jeanne d'Arc (☎ 02 38 52 99 89), 3 place du Général de Gaulle, is a reconstruction of the 15th-century house of Jacques Boucher, treasurer to the duke of Orléans. Joan of Arc stayed here in 1429 from 29 April until 9 May. The original building – put on rails in 1909 and moved 3.5m so that the street could be widened – was destroyed during WWII. Timber beams from another house, dating from the same era, were used to build the current edifice in 1965. Inside is an exhibition dedicated to Joan of Arc. It opens 10 am to noon and 2 to 6 pm Tuesday to Sunday, April to October; and 2 to 6 pm Tuesday to Sunday, the rest of the year. Admission costs 13FF (seniors and students 6.50FF).

The **Centre Jeanne d'Arc** (☎ 02 38 79 24 92), 24 rue Jeanne d'Arc, is a documentation and research centre dedicated to the art and literature the saint's legend inspired.

Parc Floral de la Source

Visited by Voltaire in the 18th century, the vast Parc Floral de la Source, covering 35 hectares around the 17th-century **Château de la Source**, comes as a sweet-smelling delight after the bustle of Orléans city. May sees the park's unusual iris garden burst into full bloom, followed by its 400 rose species in June and July, its dahlia beds in September and indoor chrysanthemums in November. Numerous species of butterflies flutter around in a heated aviary and there's a miniature train to assist tired feet. Deer roam the forests and pink flamingos paddle in the lake. This is fed by the River Loiret, which has its humble source – completely overshadowed by the park's more colourful wonders – here. Opposite the park is the new **Université d'Orléans** (☎ 02 38 41 71 71), dating from 1962 and home to 17,000 students.

The park (☎ 02 38 49 30 00) opens 9 am to 6 pm daily, April to mid-November; and 2 to 7 pm daily, the rest of the year. From Orléans centre, take bus SY to the Centre d'Innovation stop (see Getting Around, later).

Activities

Base de Loisirs Île Charlemagne (☎ 02 38 51 92 04), 1km south of the city in St-Jean-le-Blanc, is a large recreation complex with an artificial lake, two sandy beaches and a VTT (mountain bike) circuit. You can sail and windsurf here, or hire a canoe or boat for two from the Canoë-Kayak Club (☎ 02 38 66 14 80, 02 38 51 86 84). Rental costs 30/40FF per hour for one/two people; the club also offers day and week courses, and guided trips along the River Loire for three people or more (150FF per hour per person). To get to the sports base, take bus V or RS to the end of the line (Rosette stop).

The tourist office has information on hikes and rambles organised by clubs in the region; *Orléans Poche* (see Entertainment, later) also lists them.

Organised Tours

Between May and mid-September the tourist office organises walking tours of the city on Wednesday and Saturday, departing from place d'Arc, in front of the office, at 2.30 pm. Tickets cost 35FF (children and students 17.5FF). Thematic tours include Renaissance Orléans, Romanesque and Gothic art in the city, and a Joan of Arc tour. The tourist office also arranges trips to artisans' workshops.

Special Events

The biggest event of the year is the Fête Johanniques, held around 8 May to commemorate Joan of Arc's liberation of Orléans. Celebrated religiously since 1430, one young girl is singled out to play the role of the heroine during the week-long festivities. A series of street parties, medieval-costume parades and concerts climaxes with a solemn Mass at the cathedral.

Other annual events include a Festival de Jazz at the end of June, and the Journées Cinématographiques (Cinematic Days) in November, which zooms in on Japanese films every second year. Each summer, the four-week Fête au Son des Orgues (Organ Festival) brings classical and choral concerts to the cathedral; admission to the Sunday-afternoon concerts is free.

Places to Stay

Camping The closest camp site is *Camping Municipal* (☎ 02 38 63 53 94, rue du Pont Bouchet), 7km south of Orléans in Olivet. Count on paying around 40FF for a tent, two people and car. The site opens April to mid-October.

Hostel At the time of writing, a new *auberge de jeunesse* (☎ 02 38 62 45 75) was due to open at 14 rue du Faubourg Madeleine by summer 2000.

Chambre d'Hôtes Bookings for B&B in private homes and properties in the region can be made through the *Gîtes de France* office (☎ 02 38 62 04 88, fax 02 38 62 98 37), inside the Comité Départemental du Tourisme (see Tourist Offices under Information, earlier).

Hotels The cheapest and most cheerful bet for budget travellers content to share a toilet is *Hôtel de Paris* (☎ 02 38 53 39 58, 29 rue du Faubourg Bannier), five minutes' walk from the central train station. The 13-room hotel above a busy bar-brasserie has single/double rooms with washbasin costing 130/145FF, with shower for 140/165FF and with washbasin and bath for 150/180FF. Breakfast costs 25FF and the ground-floor bar serves excellent-value lunch *formules* (main dish plus entree or dessert) costing upwards of 41FF.

Nearby, the no-star *Hôtel Le Bannier* (☎ 02 38 53 25 86, 13 rue du Faubourg Bannier) offers mediocre singles/doubles with shower costing 145/165FF. Pool tables and table football fill the ground-floor games bar.

Le Brin de Zinc (☎ 02 38 53 38 77, fax 02 38 62 81 18, 62 rue Ste-Catherine) is run by fun staff, though not the place to stay for those seeking peace. It has six doubles without/with bathroom costing 150/170FF.

Between the train station and the cathedral, friendly *Hôtel St-Martin* (☎ 02 38 62 47 47, fax 02 38 81 13 28, 52 blvd Alexandre Martin) has 22 rooms. Doubles with washbasin and bidet/shower cost 150/210FF; rooms with private bathroom go for 240FF to 310FF.

La Vieille Auberge (☎ 02 38 53 55 81, fax 02 38 77 16 63, ✆ reservation@lavieille auberge.fr, 2 rue du Faubourg St-Vincent) is a gorgeous, vine-covered 17th-century house with three delightful rooms costing 180FF to 200FF. Its restaurant serves scrumptious *menus* and has a charming garden. To guarantee a bed or table, book well ahead.

The chaotically run but endearing *Hôtel Charles Sanglier* (☎ 02 38 53 38 50, 8 rue Charles Sanglier) offers seven singles/doubles costing 200/230FF; breakfast costs 40FF.

Hôtel de l'Abeille (☎ 02 38 53 54 87, fax 02 38 62 65 84, 64 rue d'Alsace-Lorraine) has 31 stylish rooms, starting at 170FF or 190FF for a double with washbasin and bidet or washbasin, bidet and toilet. Shower- and toilet-equipped singles/doubles cost 230/260FF and breakfast is 30FF. Book ahead to snag the cheaper rooms. North of place du Martroi, two-star *Grand Hôtel* (☎ 02 38 53 19 79, fax 02 38 62 25 11, 1 rue de la Lionne) is a large, modern place above its busy, in-house Tex-Mex restaurant. Singles/doubles with all the trimmings start at 248/288FF; breakfast costs 38FF.

Two-star *Hôtel St-Aignan* (☎ 02 38 53 15 35, fax 02 38 77 02 36, 3 place Gambetta) is a towering concrete block above a car showroom. Singles/doubles with bathroom cost 265/295FF. Near the river, 62-room *Hôtel Jackotel* (☎ 02 38 54 48 48, fax 02 38 77 17 59, 18 Cloître St-Aignan) is in a quiet courtyard opposite Église St-Aignan. Singles/doubles with private bathroom cost 260/290FF and breakfast is 35FF.

Places to Eat

Restaurants Ideal for budget travellers, *Le KT (13 rue des Pastoureaux)* is run by students from a catering school on the 1st floor and dishes up 35FF *menus* and a 33FF *plat du jour* (dish of the day). The canteen opens 11.30 am to 2 pm Monday to Saturday.

Small, snug and worth popping into for a nibble is *La P'tite Porte* (☎ 02 38 62 28 00, 28 rue de la Poterne), a traditional spot tucked in the old town. Its plat du jour costs around 48FF, conjured up with fresh market produce and served on a terrace which doubles as a haven of peace. It opens Tuesday to Sunday.

The stretch of rue de Bourgogne between the préfecture and rue du Bourdon Blanc is loaded with places to eat, ranging from Chinese and Indian to Greek and Thai. Eateries housed in charming timber-framed buildings and serving game, *tarte tatin* (apple tart) and other regional dishes include *La Petite Marmite* (☎ 02 38 54 23 83), at No 178, and *Le Gargantua*, at No 134; the former is a no-smoking restaurant. A *menu du terroir* (local-dishes menu) costs 80FF to 100FF. *L'Estaminet* (☎ 02 38 54 27 57, 148 rue de Bourgogne) sticks to traditional cuisine but indulges in a more off-beat decor. It opens evenings only Tuesday to Sunday.

Rue Ste-Catherine is another hot spot: *Le Brin de Zinc* (see Hotels under Places to Stay, earlier) serves mussels, *magret de canard* (duck breast) and has 75FF, 99FF and 149FF *menus*. It houses an eccentric collection of 1920s bric-a-brac, well worth seeing. *La Daride*, at 25 rue Etienne Dolet, is a small fish restaurant with *menus* costing 110FF and 150FF. It opens on weekdays and Saturday evening.

Near the river, a more upmarket choice is *L'Epicurien* (☎ 02 38 68 01 10, 54 rue des Turcies), which sports live lobsters paddling around in a fish tank waiting to turn red. It has *menus* costing 130FF, 160FF and 190FF, and opens Tuesday to Saturday.

Nearby, *Les Antiquaires* (☎ 02 38 53 52 35, 2 rue au Lin) is one of two restaurants in the city to be starred. Acclaimed chef Philippe Bardau cooks up a mind-boggling assortment of culinary delights, with mix-and-match *menus* costing 200FF, 220FF or 300FF (including wine and coffee). Bardau opens Tuesday to Saturday, September to June. Discerning diners seeking a cheaper option could hop next door to *Auberge du Quai* (☎ 02 38 62 40 00, 6 rue au Lin). Tasty *menus* cost 70FF, 90FF, 135FF and 185FF. It opens Tuesday to Saturday, and Sunday lunchtime.

Espace Canal (☎ 02 38 62 04 30, 6 rue Ducerceau) is a unique restaurant where you can swirl, sip and swallow or spit local wines.

Cafes & Fast Food Open-air cafes line place du Martroi, overlooking the fountains. The terraces and bistro-style interiors of *La Chancellerie* (☎ 02 38 53 57 54, 95 rue Royale) and *La Martroi* (12 place du Martroi) double as popular evening dining spots.

Another sunny-day option is the pavement terrace of *Le Lutetia* (☎ 02 38 53 39 68, 2 rue Jeanne d'Arc). Pay a shocking 18FF to sip a Coca-Cola and gaze at the cathedral's lofty facade. The terrace of *Café du Théâtre* (blvd Aristide Briand) attracts a bohemian set.

Le Parisie, in the heart of the old town at 2 rue Parisie, is a quaint, green-shuttered spot with tables and chairs out front and a lunchtime 48FF formule.

Sweet and savoury crepes can be enjoyed at *Crêperie Bretonne* (☎ 02 38 62 24 62, 224 rue de Bourgogne) or at the more formal *Le Viking*, immediately opposite on the same street.

For a touch of Africa, look no further than exuberant *Le Mambassa* (☎ 02 38 24 50 22, 5 rue de l'Empereur), which specialises in speedy cuisine from the Congo.

Sandwiches and salads are the mainstay of American-inspired *Autobus Café* (☎ 02 38 54 03 93, 2 rue de la Lionne). Asian fast food is packaged into 31FF and 47FF *menus* at *Nem+Ravioli*, on place Louis XI.

Burger fiends can feast at *Packman* (3 rue de la République). Packman also has a patisserie counter offering 30FF sandwich *menus*. It opens 6 am to 10 or 11 pm.

Self-Catering Fresh fruit and veg are heaped sky high for all to prod, squeeze and buy at the outdoor *Marché de la Charpenterie*, rue des Halles, from 4 to 10.30 am on Tuesday, Thursday and Saturday. The *Intermarché* supermarket, on rue du Faubourg Bannier, opens 8.45 am to 7.30 pm Monday to Saturday, and 9 am to 12.30 pm on Sunday. Alternatively, *Carrefour*, inside Centre Commercial Place d'Arc, opens 8.30 am to 9 pm Monday to Saturday.

Entertainment

What's-on listings fill *Orléans Poche*, a free pocket-sized events magazine published monthly.

Popular drinking holes include the Irish *Shannon Pub* (open to 3 am between May and September), on place du Châtelet, *St Patrick Celtic Pub*, at 1 rue de Bourgogne, and *Amazone* (☎ 02 38 70 58 38, 105 bis rue du Faubourg Madeleine), a Creole disco within stumbling distance of the auberge de jeunesse.

Tickets for cultural events – including classical-music and rock concerts at the *Zénith* concert and congress centre (☎ 02 38 25 04 29, 1 rue du Président Schuman), choral concerts in the cathedral and events at Château de Chambord – are sold at the ticket desk inside the tourist office. It opens 9 am to 5 pm Tuesday to Saturday, and 10 am to 5 pm on Monday.

Between mid-July and mid-August, films are screened beneath the stars in parks around the city; the tourist office has details. The *UGC cinema complex* (☎ 08 36 68 68 58), inside the Centre Commercial Place d'Arc, has six screens and shows some films in their original language.

Shopping

An antiques-cum-flea market fills esplanade du Souvenir Français (the centre strip of wide blvd Alexandre Martin) from 7 am to 7 pm on Saturday.

Regional edible delicacies such as *confiture du vin* (wine jam), *poire d'Olivet* (a pear liqueur made south of Orléans, in Olivet), *cotignac d'Orléans* (a sweet quince jelly) and locally made vinegar can be picked up at Ducs de Gascogne, a luxury food shop on place du Châtelet.

Local wines are sold by the bottle or case at Cave de Marc et Sébastien, behind the covered market on the corner of rue des Hotelleries and rue des Halles. Café Jeanne d'Arc, 7 rue de la République, has sold perfumed teas and coffee beans since 1899.

Getting There & Away

Bus The bus station (☎ 02 38 53 94 75) is north-east of the central train station, at 1 rue Marcel Proust. Information and tickets are available on the 1st floor. Les Rapides du Val de Loire operates buses to numerous destinations, including Châteauneuf-sur-Loire (33FF, 35 minutes, four to six daily), Gien (70FF, 1¾ hours, one daily) and Jargeau (27FF, 45 minutes, three daily).

Tickets for Eurolines buses to various destinations in Europe (see Continental Europe under Land in the Getting There & Away chapter) are sold at CRIJ (see Tourist Offices under Information, earlier in this chapter).

Train Orléans has two train stations, the central Gare d'Orléans (☎ 02 38 79 91 00, 📧 ter@cr-centre.fr) at 1 rue St-Yves, which adjoins the Centre Commercial Place d'Arc, and Gare des Aubrais-Orléans, which is 2km north of town in Les Aubrais. Regular shuttle trains link the two stations (8 minutes). Tickets and information for services to/from either station are available at the advance reservations office on the 1st floor of Gare d'Orléans.

From Orléans, most westbound services along the Loire Valley stop at both stations, including trains to Blois (52FF, 50 minutes, 20 trains daily), St-Pierre des Corps (86FF, 50 minutes to 1¾ hours, four daily), Tours (88FF, 1¼ to 1¾ hours, four daily) and Nantes (186FF, 2½ hours, three daily).

For details of trains to Paris and the rest of France, see Other Parts of France under Land in the Getting There & Away chapter.

Car Avis has an office inside Gare d'Orléans. It opens 8 am to noon. Rent-Van & Car Ecoto (☎ 02 38 77 92 92), behind Hotel Ibis at 19 ave de Paris, offers competitive rates, starting from around 200/1000FF per day/week, with 100/1000km included.

Getting Around

Bus Tickets and timetables for SEMTAO city buses are available at the Espace Transport (☎ 02 38 71 98 38), rue de la Hallebarde, which opens 9.30 am to 12.30 pm and 2.30 to 6 pm Monday to Saturday. A Liberté ticket (20FF), valid for one day, allows unlimited travel on SEMTAO buses; bus drivers only sell tickets valid for one journey (7.80FF).

Buses are labelled with letters, not numbers. To get to La Source (20 minutes), take bus SY from the bus stop near Cinéma Artistic on blvd Alexandre Martin or from stop No 9, opposite the bus station on rue Albert 1er. For the Parc Floral get off at the Centre d'Innovation stop, at the eastern end of rue de Chartres.

Tram The first line of a new two-line tramway should be operational by September 2000. The 18km-long north–south line will link Gare des Aubrais-Orléans with Gare d'Orléans, rue de la République and place du Général de Gaulle in the centre of town, and the Parc Floral de la Source on the southern bank of the River Loire.

Bicycle There is nowhere to hire a bike in the town centre; the closest place is Kit Loisirs (☎ 02 38 63 44 34, fax 02 38 63 44 39), at 1720 rue Marcel Belot in Olivet, south of town.

ORLÉANS TO SULLY-SUR-LOIRE

The stretch of the River Loire between Orléans and Gien cuts through less trodden terrain than the stretch west of Orléans. Here, medieval chateaux are overshadowed by the valley's ecclesiastical treasures, among them France's oldest church and a beautiful Romanesque abbey sheltering St Benedict's relics. The river's northern bank is flanked by elk-rich **Forêt d'Orléans**, 38,234 hectares large and the only place in France to shelter nesting osprey. The Canal d'Orléans, which snakes across the forest's southern fringe, was dug in 1676–8 to transport wood from here to Paris. This stretch of the Loire Valley is well served by daily buses to/from Orléans. See Getting There & Away under Orléans, earlier in this chapter, for details.

Jargeau
postcode 45150 • pop 3561
On the left (southern) bank of the River Loire 20km east of Orléans, Jargeau offers several tempting culinary delights. *Andouille* is a big, fat tripe sausage, sold at Monsieur Guibet's *charcuterie* at 14 place du Martroi and glorified by the Confrèrie des Chevaliers du Goûte Andouille (Tripe Sausage Brotherhood). The Maison de Loire (☎ 02 38 59 76 90, fax 02 38 59 97 96), blvd Carnot, has details on the brotherhood's annual fêtes. Delicate constitutions can nibble on the sweet, wafer-thin biscuits known as *langues de femme* (literally 'women's tongues'). Salmon is also smoked in the village.

St-Denis de l'Hôtel, on the river's right bank, was a leper colony in medieval times.

Places to Stay & Eat By the river, *L'Isle aux Moulins* (☎ 02 38 59 70 04, fax 02 38 59 92 62) is a large camp site which rents bicycles for 20FF per hour or 50/85FF for four/eight days. Camping costs 14/10/18FF per adult/child/tent. The site opens March to mid-November.

Another budget option is the *Maison du Cordon* (☎ 02 38 59 76 60 fax 02 38 59 97 96, blvd Carnot), a *gîte d'étape* (hikers' accommodation) where beds cost 44FF for adults and 32FF for children aged six to 16. Reservation in advance is essential. *Au Bon Accueil* (☎ 02 38 59 02 19, 49 Grand Rue), in neighbouring St-Denis de l'Hôtel, offers six good-value doubles costing 120FF.

Châteauneuf-sur-Loire
To create a mini-Versailles was the grand vision of Louis Phélypeaux, secretary of state and advisor to Louis XIV. He had the 11th-century **chateau** in Châteauneuf-sur-Loire rebuilt and new stables added at the end of the 17th century. The main wing of the chateau was destroyed after the French Revolution in 1802. What remained has housed the town hall since 1926.

The main draw of the ensemble today is the stables, which shelter the fascinating **Musée de la Marine** (☎ 02 38 46 84 46, fax 02 38 46 41 01), 1 place Aristide Briand. The ground-floor exhibition shows boat construction techniques and the Loire's historical trade routes, while the 1st floor is

---

Germigny des Prés: France's Oldest Church

Germigny des Prés, 6km south-east of Châteauneuf-sur-Loire off the D60, shelters what is widely believed to be France's oldest church. A rare remaining example of Carolingian architecture, it was built in 806 as a private oratory for the powerful Théodulfe, bishop of Orléans, abbot of St-Benoît and advisor to Charlemagne. The bishop's neighbouring private villa, richly decorated with sumptuous wall murals, marble floors and mosaics, was destroyed by invading Vikings in the 9th century.

A Greek-cross-shaped floor plan forms the basis of the Église de Germigny des Prés, which was originally designed around a 10m-wide square with a symmetrical apse on each of its four sides. The western apse was demolished and replaced by a nave in the 15th century. An exquisite 9th-century mosaic – discovered in 1840 after playing children found chips of coloured glass in the church – dominates the eastern apse (the only remaining original apse). It splendidly illustrates the biblical Ark of the Covenant, accompanied by a Latin inscription from Théodulfe himself.

Germigny's architect is unknown, although the same architect is said to have designed Charlemagne's octagonal Palace Chapel at Aix-la-Chapelle (Aachen). Occasional classical-music concerts are held in the oratory; its acoustics are heart-stopping.

---

dedicated to the life of the bargemen (*mariniers*) of the River Loire. The museum opens 10 am to 6 pm Wednesday to Monday, April to October; and 4 to 6 pm Wednesday to Monday, the rest of the year. Admission costs 20FF (students 10FF).

Several **walking trails** snake through the chateau's finely manicured gardens, landscaped in traditional English style in the 19th century by botanist Huillard d'Hérou. The tourist office (☎ 02 38 58 44 79), place Aristide Briand, stocks several leaflets which map out **cycling routes** in the area.

Places to Stay & Eat The *Hostellerie du Parc* (☎ 02 38 58 42 16, fax 02 38 58 46 81, 1 Grande Rue), wedged between the chateau grounds and the village church, is a delightful wooden-shuttered place with comfortable doubles costing 280FF to 353FF. Its restaurant is worth trying, with *menus* costing 125FF and 260FF. Equally charming is Germigny des Prés' *Hôtel de la Place* (☎ 02 38 58 20 14, fax 02 38 58 21 33), on the same square as the church. Doubles with shared/private bathroom cost 160/200FF.

St-Benoît-sur-Loire
postcode 45730 • pop 1880
St-Benoît-sur-Loire, 18km south-east of Châteauneuf-sur-Loire on the D60, is famed for its 11th-century Romanesque **Basilique de St-Benoît**, which shelters the precious relics of St Benedict (480–547) in its crypt and the tomb of Philippe I (1052–1108) in its choir. The main draw, however, is the monumental porch tower, square in shape and supported by 12 stone pillars featuring heavily ornamented capitals that depict scenes from the Book of Revelations.

The basilica was built in three stages, starting with the porch tower in 1020, followed by the crypt in 1067 and the nave in 1150–1220. At the peak of its golden age, in the mid-12th century, it had 2000 manuscripts in its library and was a leading centre of monastic learning. By 1415 there were just 24 monks at the monastery; before the French Revolution of 1789 just 10 remained.

Guided tours of the basilica (☎ 02 38 35 72 43), place de l'Abbaye, are available,

from 10 to 11 am and 3 to 5 pm Tuesday to Saturday. Bewitching Gregorian masses are held in the basilica at noon Monday to Saturday, and 11 am (11.30 am in winter) on Sunday.

Opposite the basilica, *Hôtel du Labrador* (☎ 02 38 35 74 38, fax 02 38 35 72 09, 7 place de l'Abbaye) offers 46 doubles costing 175FF to 350FF. Prices reflect room size and window view.

Sully-sur-Loire
postcode 45600 • pop 5806
Château de Sully-sur-Loire, with its thickset towers and fairy-tale moats, is a notable example of a medieval fortress. Slumbering on the River Loire's left bank, it was built at the end of the 14th century to defend one of the river's few crossings, here since Gallo-Roman times. From 1602, under the ownership of Maximilien de Béthune (1556–1641), grand minister to Henri IV and the first duke of Sully, the keep was transformed into an opulent mansion with decorative beamed ceilings and ornate, sculpted fireplaces. The room where the drawbridge and *assommoir* (a hole in the floor through which boulders were dropped on top of attackers) were controlled was transformed into a treasury office, and a printing press was installed in one of the towers so that Maximilien could publish his memoirs.

Illustrious guests who passed across the chateau drawbridge include Voltaire (1696–1778), who stayed here in 1719 after being banished from Paris for his licentious prose. Remnants of the small theatre the philosopher had constructed are still visible in the upper great hall. The walls in the lower great hall are strung with a series of six monumental tapestries called *La Tenture de Psyche* (*Psyche's Tapestry*) which illustrate the romantic adventures of beautiful Psyche and her son Cupid. The chateau's other must-see is the wooden barrel-shaped roof of the great garret, dating from the 14th century. In the vast grounds, horses and horse-drawn carriages await tired feet keen to tour the park.

State-owned since 1962, Château de Sully-sur-Loire (☎ 02 38 36 36 86) opens

10 am to 6 pm daily, April to September; and 10 am to noon and 2 to 5 pm daily, February, March and October to December. Admission costs 27FF (children 17FF) and a guided tour (in French only) costs an extra 8FF. The castle hosts an annual international music festival in June.

Places to Stay & Eat The tourist office (☎ 02 38 36 23 70, fax 02 38 36 32 21), place du Général de Gaulle, makes accommodation bookings and stocks a list of chambre d'hôtes in the area.

Camping Sully-sur-Loire (☎ 02 38 36 23 93), next to the chateau on the riverbank, charges around 12/8/6FF per person/tent/car.

Hôtel de la Poste (☎ 02 38 36 26 22, fax 02 38 36 39 35, 11 rue Faubourg St-Germain) offers comfortable doubles with shower for 240FF, doubles with shower and toilet for 300FF, and 400FF family rooms. Its courtyard restaurant dishes up truly memorable cuisine: the spectacular 175FF *menu plaisir gourmand* (gourmet menu) includes a different wine with each course.

Equally tasty is the food at *La Ferme des Châtaigniers (☎ 02 38 36 51 98, chemin des Châtaigniers)*, 2.5km west of Sully off the D951. It has 120FF and 160FF *menus* and is run by a young couple who enthusiastically welcome guests to their old farmhouse. Advance reservation is vital. It's closed Sunday evening and all day on Wednesday.

GIEN TO SANCERRE
Corn fields and asparagus crops line the River Loire's southern bank between Sully-sur-Loire and the picture-postcard town of Gien, 23km south-east. **Île de Cuissy** shelters one of the Loire's largest colonies of the rare little tern (*sterne naine*) and common tern (*sterne pierregarin*). Access to the sandy island, ideal for nesting, is forbidden from 1 April to 25 July. Bridle paths, lovely for **cycling**, skirt the riverbanks here, and several mountain-bike circuits are signposted. The northern bank of the River Loire is home to the unsightly Dampierre nuclear power plant and is best avoided. From Gien,

the GR3 closely shadows the river on its course to Briare, 15km farther east.

Gien
postcode 45500 • pop 16,477
Gien is best known for its pottery (*faïence*), which has been turned here since 1821, when Thomas Hall, an Englishman, set up shop in an old convent. The distinctive *bleu de Gien* earthenware is among the pieces on display in the **Musée de la Faïencerie** (☎ 02 38 67 00 05), place de la Victoire. Factory tours are possible by appointment Monday to Thursday (except in July and August). The tourist office (☎ 02 38 67 25 28), in Centre Anne de Beaujeu on place Jean Jaurès, has details.

The red-brick **Château de Gien**, reconstructed in 1484 for Anne de Beaujeu (1460–1522), countess of Gien, houses the **Musée International de la Chasse** (International Hunting Museum; ☎ 02 38 67 69 69). Nine galleries are dedicated to expounding the history of French royalty's favourite pastime. The François Desportes gallery sports 79 works by the French painters Desportes (1661–1743) and Jean-Baptiste Oudry (1686–1755), who both worked for Louis XIV as official artists of the royal hunt.

Places to Stay Three-star *Hôtel du Rivage (☎ 02 38 37 79 00, fax 02 38 38 10 21, 1 quai de Nice)* has appealing singles/doubles costing 298/370FF. *Hôtel La Poularde (☎ 02 38 67 36 05, 13 quai de Nice)* is another family-run riverside affair, with singles/doubles starting at 260/280FF.

Château de la Bussière
The ground floor of this privately owned 17th-century chateau – dubbed '*château des pêcheurs*' (fishermen's chateau) and on an island in the middle of a lake – showcases fishing tackle, rods and every other imaginable type of fishy memorabilia. The centrepiece of Countess Henri de Chasseval's angling collection is a horribly large coelacanth – a prehistoric fish considered to be man's ancestor. The 1.2m-long fish, which weighs 50kg, was caught in 1974 off the Comoros Islands in the Indian Ocean. The

coelacanth lived at a depth of 4000m, was blind and was believed to have been extinct for 70 million years until 1938, when one of the beasts emerged.

An exhibition in the stables explains how coelacanths were caught. The block in which the stables are housed was built to store the tithes earned by the estate from its 30,000 hectares of land in the 17th century. The predominantly red-brick facade decorated with black-brick diamonds is a distinctive architectural feature of this period. Château de la Bussière's upper floors remain inhabited by the Chasseval family, who bought the chateau in the 20th century.

The gardens shelter a charming vegetable garden, restored in 1993 to its 13th-century grandeur. Vegetables grown here, along with homemade jams, wine jellies and honey, are sold at the chateau, which opens 10 am to 7 pm Wednesday to Monday, April to October. Admission costs 35FF (children 25FF) and includes the obligatory guided tour in French; a ticket valid only for the park and vegetable garden is available for 30FF. Classical-music concerts (☎ 02 38 35 93 35, fax 02 38 35 94 13) are occasionally held in the courtyard in summer. Tickets cost 100FF.

The chateau is in the village of La Bussière, 12 to 15km north of Gien. To get there from Gien, either take the D622 (a narrow country road) straight to La Bussière or follow the larger D940 and turn east onto the D43 to La Bussière.

Château de St-Brisson

Replicas of catapults and other medieval stone-fed war machines are the main attraction at this unassuming medieval chateau, built in the 12th century atop a promontory overlooking the River Loire's southern shores in St-Brisson-sur-Loire. Among the artillery displayed in the dry moat surrounding the castle is a *mangonneau*, used in the 12th and 13th centuries to fire boulders weighing up to 13kg a distance of 120m. The 15th-century *couillard* was the smallest and most efficient catapult of its day, firing three to four 20kg bullets an hour at targets up to 200m away.

The chateau interior (☎ 02 38 36 71 29) can be visited from 10 am to noon and 2 to 6 pm Thursday to Tuesday, Easter to mid-November. War-machine demonstrations take place at 3.30 and 4.30 pm on Sunday in summer. Admission costs 15FF (children 10FF).

Place to Stay & Eat In St-Brisson-sur-Loire *Auberge Chez Huguette (☎ 02 38 36 70 10)* is top of the league. Its nine rooms ('just like home') cost 180/234FF for a double/triple with shower and toilet. The auberge offers a 58FF *menu* in its brasserie-style restaurant and breakfast costs 30FF.

Pont Canal de Briare

The industrial town of Briare, some 12km south-east of Gien, is of little interest beyond the magnificent Art Nouveau canal bridge (*pont canal*) that spans the River Loire here. The iron construction – 662m long and 11m wide – was engineered in 1890–94 by the Société Eiffel and is the longest canal bridge in Europe. The Briare canal dates from 1604–42 and links the southbound Latéral canal with the Loing canal in the north. It was one of the first in a system of canals built under Henri IV in the 17th century to create a continuous waterway between the English Channel and the Mediterranean Sea.

The best view of Briare's canal bridge and its 15 impressive piles is from the southern bank of the river, at the western end of **St-Firmin-sur-Loire**. To get to Briare, on the northern bank, you have to continue 5km east to **Châtillon-sur-Loire**, where a road bridge crosses the Loire.

Between April and November boat trips across the canal bridge and along a section of the Briare canal depart from Briare's Port du Commerce (☎ 02 38 37 12 75). Cruises last 1½ hours and cost 39FF (children 26FF). Seasonal river boats and dinner cruises costing 200FF (☎ 02 38 37 16 53) depart from the Port du Plaisance, in the centre of town off rue de la Liberté.

Places to Stay & Eat In Châtillon-sur-Loire, *Camping Les Combes (☎ 02 38 31*

ORLÉANAIS & BLÉSOIS

Euroland's Centre

The centre of Euroland is 20km south-west of Briare, according to enterprising folk from Blancafort whose village was named the *centre géographique de l'Euro* (geographical centre of the euro) on 1 January 1999. A giant monument erected on the banks of the Grande Sauldre canal pays homage to Blancafort's new-found status, which has been cleverly safeguarded by the qualification 'the *first* euro centre' (the centre will, of course, shift the moment another country takes the European common currency on board).

Locals claim that Euroland's true centre does not, in fact, fall by the canal but rather in a field. Blancafort's tourist office (☎ 02 48 81 58 15, fax 02 48 81 58 16, **e** blanca fort.euro@wanadoo.fr), 3 rue du 8 Mai, doles out complicated directions.

✢ ✢ ✢ ✢ ✢ ✢ ✢ ✢ ✢ ✢ ✢ ✢ ✢ ✢ ✢

2 92), on the right bank of the River Loire (signposted immediately after crossing the bridge from Châtillon), charges around 0/8/8FF per adult/child/tent. The site opens March to October.

Briare's most pleasant place to stay is *Hôtel Le Pont Canal* (☎ 02 38 31 24 24), on the banks of the Canal de Briare, overlooking Port du Commerce. Fishy *menus* cost 110FF, 150FF and 180FF, and double rooms are excellent value at 200FF.

Sancerre

The prized Sancerre vineyards cover an area of 2350 hectares in the lower Loire Valley and are best known for their dry, fruity whites, which have commanded their own appellation since 1936 (see the 'Food & Wine of the Loire' special section).

In Sancerre itself, the best place to taste a variety of vintages is at the small auberge on Nouvelle Place, opposite the tourist office. Alphonse Mellot and Joseph Mellot are two viticultural names to look out for. Enhance the tasting experience with a Crotin de Chavignol, a type of *chèvre* (goat's-milk cheese), also produced locally and considered the perfect partner to Sancerre.

The Sancerre tourist office (☎ 02 48 54 08 21, fax 02 48 78 03 58, **e** ot.sancerre .cher@en-france.com), on Nouvelle Place, has lists of places where you can taste and buy wine. You can also find these on its Web site at www.sancerre.net. The office opens 10 am to 12.30 pm and 2.30 to 5.30 pm (6 pm on Saturday) daily, April to mid-November; and the same hours Monday to Saturday, the rest of the year. Information on wine is also available from the Bureau Interprofessionnel des Vins du Centre (☎ 02 48 78 51 07), at 9 route de Chavignol.

Places to Stay & Eat The Sancerre area offers a couple of remarkable places to stay, worth a small detour. *Château d'Ivoy* (☎ 02 48 58 85 01, **e** chateau.diovoy@wanadoo .fr), in Ivoy-le-Pré, some 30km west of Sancerre, is a fabulous 16th-century chateau with exquisitely furnished rooms costing 700FF to 1000FF, including a breakfast feast. Great garden views can be enjoyed from the bath tub of the La Fayette suite. The chateau is the former home of Dame Pichonnat, who served as treasurer, or keeper of the privy purse, to Mary Stuart and is mentioned in Alain Fournier's novel *Le grand Meaulnes*.

The Scottish Stuart clan had its summer house 8km up the road from Château d'Ivoy, in La Verrerie. *Château de la Verrerie* (☎ 02 48 81 51 60, fax 02 48 58 21 25, **e** laverrerie@wanadoo.fr) has 12 rooms costing 950FF to 1200FF. A 1.6km hiking trail encircles the lake here.

ORLÉANS TO BLOIS

There are connections with the region's literary heritage along this busy 59km stretch of the River Loire, which is followed by three roads – the A10 and parallel N152 on the right bank, and the narrower D951 on the left (southern) bank. All three can get horribly traffic clogged in July and August.

Meung-sur-Loire (pop 6000), 18km south of Orléans on the N152, was named after the medieval writer Jean de Meung (1240–1305), who added an extra 18,000 lines to Guillaume de Lorris' allegorical poem *Roman de la rose* (*Romance of the*

Rose; 1200–40). The town's chateau (☎ 02 38 44 36 47) was built as a residence for the bishops of Orléans between 1200 and 1789, and served as the headquarters for the English army at the end of the Hundred Years' War. The poet François Villon (1431–63) was imprisoned in its dungeons, which can be visited with a guide. On the riverbank, *La Mouche Abeille* (☎ *02 38 44 34 36, fax 02 38 46 52 49,* ✉ *perrody@3dnet.fr)* is a charming 18th-century mansion with singles/doubles costing 350/390FF.

There are also plenty of places to stay in neighbouring **Beaugency** (pop 7000), 5km downstream on the N152. Its tourist office (☎ 02 38 44 54 42, fax 02 38 46 45 31), 3 place du Dr Hyvernaud, has accommodation lists.

Across the river, Meung's sister village, Cléry St-André (pop 2506), is home to the **Basilique Notre Dame de Cléry**. An outstanding example of Flamboyant Gothic architecture, the basilica was built in the 15th century, destroyed during the Hundred Years' War, then rebuilt under Charles II and Louis XI (who is buried in the church).

A further 12km south-west along the D951, at **St-Laurent Nouan**, is an undelightful nuclear power plant that has chundered here since 1969; the site is poetically named 'St-Laurent des Eaux' (St Laurence of the Waters).

An absolutely fabulous place to stay in this region is the 18th-century *Château de Colliers* (☎ *02 54 87 50 75, fax 02 54 87 03 64,* ✉ *chcolliers@aol.com)*, signposted off the D951 immediately west of Muides-sur-Loire. Luxurious rooms fit for a king cost 550FF to 700FF, including breakfast.

Château de Talcy sits in the heart of Le Petit Beauce, a pancake-flat region carpeted with cereal and potato fields on the northern bank of the River Loire. It was at this 16th-century castle, built by Florentine banker Bernardo Salviati, that the Renaissance poet Pierre de Ronsard (1524–85) found the inspiration for *Les amours de Cassandre* (*The Loves of Cassandra*; 1552); Cassandre was Salviati's 15-year-old daughter, whom Ronsard wed in 1546. The chateau (☎ 02 54 81 03 01) and its 18th-century in-

---

Canoeing on the River Loire

The 10km or so stretch of the River Loire from Beaugency downstream to Muides-sur-Loire is navigable by canoe. At the Barrage de St-Laurent Nouan, at the southern foot of the nuclear power plant, canoeists have to disembark and carry their canoes round the dam. Approaching Muides-sur-Loire, you pass several sandy islands. In spring, colonies of terns nest here and consequently these islands cannot be visited between mid-April and mid-August. Grey herons are also common on these waters.

The Comité Régional du Centre de Canoë-Kayak (☎ 02 38 77 08 87) has lists of places that hire out canoes and kayaks and/or organise guided canoe trips. For practical information, as well as an interesting exhibition focusing on the Loire's flora and fauna, head to the Maison de la Loire (☎ 02 54 81 65 45, fax 02 54 81 68 07), 73 rue Nationale, St-Dyé-sur-Loire, 4km south of Muides-sur-Loire.

---

terior can be visited from 9.30 am to noon and 2 to 6 pm (4.30 pm October to March) daily, year round. Admission costs 20FF.

Le Petit Beauce's other major chateau is the wonderful 18th-century **Château de Ménars**, whose great stone walls dominate the entire length of the village. Lumbering like a great white ship 6km north-east of Blois, on the River Loire's northern bank, the chateau is owned by the frighteningly rich marquise de Pompadour and is closed to the public. Prime views of it can be enjoyed from a spot on the southern bank, signposted 'Aire de Vision de Ménars' off the D951.

Blésois

The area around Blois is graced with some of the finest chateaux in the Loire Valley, including the spectacular and stunning Chambord, the magnificently furnished Cheverny, romantic Chaumont and the modest but more personal Beauregard. North-west of Blois, the small, unassuming

Joan of Arc guards Cathédrale Ste-Croix, Orléans.

Enter the dragon, Maison de la Magie, Blois

Statue of Louis XII at ornate Château de Blois

The 'revolutionary' staircase at Château de Blois

Horses go through the motions at Chambord.

Rise above it all at Château de Cheverny.

Sully-sur-Loire, inspiration for *Sleeping Beauty*

Sturdy and feudal Château de Chaumont

Shop for *bleu de Gien* earthenware in the pretty town of Gien, defended by its red-brick chateau.

town of Vendôme is connected by high-speed TGV rail tracks to Paris (42 minutes) and serves as a transport hub for visitors travelling between Blésois and the capital.

BLOIS

postcode 41000 • pop 49,300

The medieval town of Blois (pronounced 'blwah') was once the seat of the powerful counts of Blois, from whom France's Capetian kings were descended. From the 15th to the 17th centuries, Blois was a major centre of court intrigue, and during the 16th century it served as something of a second capital of France. A number of truly dramatic events – involving some of the most important personages in French history, such as the kings Louis XII, François I and Henri III – took place inside the town's outstanding attraction, Château de Blois.

The old town, seriously damaged by German attacks in 1940, retains its steep, twisting, medieval streets. A fresh-produce market fills place de la République on Saturday, and a flea market takes over the riverbank at the foot of rue Jeanne d'Arc on the second Sunday of each month.

Orientation

Blois, on the northern bank of the River Loire, is a compact town – almost everything is within 10 minutes' walk of the train station. The old city is the area south and east of Château de Blois, which towers over place Victor Hugo. Blois' modern commercial centre is focused around pedestrianised rue du Commerce, rue Porte Chartraine and rue Denis Papin, which is connected to rue du Palais by the Escalier Denis Papin, a monumental staircase built in the 19th century.

Maps The tourist office doles out a free and accurate city map. The 20FF *Blois: La Chaussée–St-Victor* (Plan Guide Bleu & Or) includes 1:10,500 and 1:7000 maps of the city. Kümmerly+Frey covers Blois in its Blay-Foldex map series.

Information

Tourist Offices The tourist office (☎ 02 54 90 41 41, fax 02 54 90 41 49, @ blois

.tourism@wanadoo.fr), 3 ave Dr Jean Laigret, is housed in the early-16th-century Pavillon Anne de Bretagne, an outbuilding of Château de Blois. It opens 9 am (10 am on Sunday) to 7 pm daily, May to September; and 9 am to 12.30 pm and 2 to 6 pm Monday to Saturday, and 9.30 am to 12.30 pm on Sunday, the rest of the year. Staff will call around to find you a local hotel room for no charge; an actual reservation costs 12FF.

Tourist information on the Loir-et-Cher département is available at the Maison du Loir-et-Cher (☎ 02 54 90 41 41, fax 02 54 74 81 79), 5 rue de la Voûte du Château. Reservations for Gîtes de France chambre d'hôtes and information on outdoor activities and 'green tourism' in the region are handled by Service et Réservation Tourisme Vert en Loir-et-Cher (☎ 02 54 58 81 64, fax 02 54 56 04 13, @ gites41@wanadoo.fr).

Money Banque de France, 4 ave Dr Jean Laigret, opens 9 am to 12.15 pm and 1.45 to 3.30 pm on weekdays. Several commercial banks face the river along quai de la Saussaye, near place de la Résistance.

Post The post office, near place Victor Hugo on rue Gallois, also provides currency exchange. It opens 8.30 am to 7 pm on weekdays, and 8 am to noon on Saturday.

Email & Internet Access L'Étoile Tex (☎ 02 54 78 46 93, @ etoiletex.cybercafe@caramail.com), in the hotel of the same name at 7 rue du Bourg Neuf, is a busy bar with one computer. Internet access costs 1FF per minute. In addition, the post office is equipped with Cyberposte.

Laundry The laundrette at 1 rue Jeanne d'Arc opens 7 am to 9 pm. Wash'n Dry Concept, in the arcade overlooking place Louis XII, opens until 10 pm.

Medical Services The Centre Hospitalier de Blois (hospital; ☎ 02 54 55 66 33) is 2km north-east of the town centre on mail Pierre Charlot. Take bus No 1 from the train station or bus No 4 from place de la République.

BLOIS

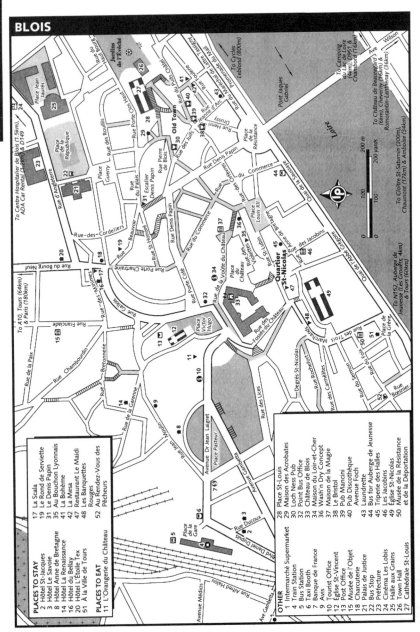

PLACES TO STAY
2   Hôtel St-Jacques
3   Hôtel Le Savoie
8   Hôtel Anne de Bretagne
14 La Renaissance
16 Hôtel du Bellay
20 Hôtel L'Étoile Tex
51 À la Ville de Tours

PLACES TO EAT
11 L'Orangerie du Château
17 La Scala
19 Le Rond de Serviette
31 Le Denis Papin
35 Au Bouchon Lyonnais
41 La Bohème
42 La Mesa
47 Restaurant Le Maïdi
48 Les Banquettes Rouges
52 Au Rendez-Vous des Pêcheurs

OTHER
1   Intermarché Supermarket
4   Train Station
5   Bus Station
6   Taxi Booth
7   Banque de France
9   Avis
10 Tourist Office
12 Église St-Vincent
13 Post Office
15 Musée de l'Objet
18 Charcuterie
21 Palais de Justice
22 Bus Stop
23 Préfecture
24 Cinéma Les Lobis
25 Halle aux Grains
26 Town Hall
27 Cathédrale St-Louis
28 Place St-Louis
29 Maison des Acrobates
30 Loch Ness Pub
32 Point Bus Office
33 Château de Blois
34 Maison du Loir-et-Cher
36 Wash'n Dry Concept
37 Maison de la Magie
38 Le Bristol
39 Pub Mancini
40 Pub Discothèque Avenue Foch
43 Laundrette
44 Bus for Auberge de Jeunesse
45 Triperie des Halles
46 Les Jacobins
49 Église St-Nicolas
50 Musée de la Résistance et de la Déportation

Château de Blois

Château de Blois (☎ 02 54 74 16 06) has a compelling and bloody history, and contains an extraordinary mixture of architectural styles. The chateau's four distinct sections are: medieval (13th century); Flamboyant Gothic (1498–1503), from the reign of Louis XII; very early Renaissance (1515–24), from the reign of François I; and Classical (17th century).

During the Middle Ages, the counts of Blois received homage and meted out justice in the huge **Salle des États Généraux** (Estates General Hall), a part of the feudal castle that somehow survived wars, re-building and – most dangerous of all – changes in style and taste. It remains the largest Gothic civil hall in France and was used as a film set by French film director Luc Besson for the trial scene in his 1999 box-office hit *Jeanne d'Arc*.

The brick and stone **Louis XII wing**, which includes the hall where entrance tickets are sold, is ornamented with porcupines, Louis XII's heraldic symbol. The facade dominating place du Château showcases an equestrian statue of Louis XII, sculpted in the 19th century by Charles Émile Seurre (1798–1858) to replace the original destroyed during the French Revolution. A **Musée des Beaux Arts** (Museum of Fine Arts), featuring 16th- to 19th-century European art, spills across the 2nd floor.

The Italianate **François I wing**, begun only 14 years after the Louis XII wing was completed, includes the famous **spiral staircase**, a magnificent structure decorated with François I's insignia, a capital 'F' and a salamander. The ground floor of this wing, the ornate exterior of which can be seen from place Victor Hugo, houses an **archaeological museum**. François I's son Henri II raised most of his 10 children, three of whom were crowned king of France, at Blois. It was here that Henri II's wife, Catherine de Médicis, died on 5 January 1589, shortly after the shock murder of the duke of Guise (see the boxed text 'Murder at Blois' on the following page). She had lived for many years on the 1st floor of this wing. Particularly noteworthy is the **Queen's Cabinet**, with 180 sculpted oak panels dating from 1530 and concealing four secret cabinets to hide jewels (or poisons, as suggested by Dumas in his novel *La Reine Margot*).

Between 1500 and 1715, seven kings and 11 queens passed through the doors of Château de Blois. In the early 18th century, servants and destitute nobles were invited to live in the chateau, the interior of which was divided into smaller rooms. It served as a barracks from 1788 to 1841, before being restored in the mid-19th century. In state hands ever since, it opens 9 am to noon and 2 to 5 pm daily, mid-October to mid-March; and 9 am to 6.30 pm (8 pm in July and August) daily, the rest of the year. Admission costs 35FF (students 25FF). Guided tours are only available in French, leaving English-speakers with no option but to fork out an additional 40FF for a written guide.

Your entry ticket also gets you into the **Cloître St-Saturnin**, a 16th-century galleried cemetery across the River Loire on rue Munier. It opens weekends only. Admission to the **Musée d'Art Religieux** (Museum of Religious Art), housed in **Les Jacobins**, a 15th- and 16th-century Dominican convent

JANE SMITH

François I (ruled 1515–47), who had a passion for building Renaissance chateaux

Murder at Blois

The most infamous episode in the history of the Château de Blois occurred during the chaotic 16th century. On 23 December 1588 at about 8 am, King Henri III summoned his rival, the ultra-powerful duke of Guise – a leader of the Catholic League (which threatened the authority of the king, himself a Catholic) – to his Salle du Conseil (Counsel Chamber). When the duke reached the Chambre du Roi (King's Chamber), he was set upon by 20 royal bodyguards, some armed with daggers, others with swords. When the violence was over, the king, who had been hiding behind a tapestry, stepped into the room to inspect the duke's perforated body. On the same day Henri had Guise's arrested brother, the cardinal of Lorraine, executed in his prison cell at Château de Blois. Overjoyed by the success of both assassinations, Henri informed his mother, Catherine de Médicis (who died a few days later), and went merrily to Mass. Henri III himself was assassinated eight months later.

❧ ❧ ❧ ❧ ❧ ❧ ❧ ❧ ❧ ❧ ❧ ❧ ❧ ❧ ❧

on rue Anne de Bretagne, is free. Admission to **Musée d'Histoire Naturelle** (Natural History Museum), also housed in Les Jacobins, costs an extra 15/5FF for adults/students (free to children aged under 12). Both museums open 2 to 6 pm Tuesday to Sunday.

Every night from early May to mid-September there's a **son et lumière** (sound and light show; ☎ 02 54 78 72 76) at 9.30, 10, 10.15 or 10.30 pm depending on the month. There is a show in English on Wednesday in May, June and September. Tickets, available 30 minutes before the show starts, cost 60FF (students 30FF). Combined same-day tickets for the show and chateau are 75FF (students 55FF).

Maison de la Magie

The Maison de la Magie (National Magic Centre; ☎ 02 54 55 26 26), also known as the Maison Robert Houdin, is across the square from the chateau at 1 place du Château. It has magic shows, interactive ex-

hibits and displays of clocks and other objects invented by the Blois-born magician Jean-Eugène Robert-Houdin (1805–71), the father of modern magic, after whom the great Houdini named himself. Beware the roaring, six-headed dragon which emerges from the house every half-hour in summer.

The Maison de la Magie opens 10.30 am to noon and 2 to 6.30 pm daily, July and August; 10 am to noon and 2 to 6 pm daily, April to June and in September; the same hours Wednesday to Sunday, October and November; and the same hours on Wednesday and at the weekend, February and March. Admission, which includes a 20-minute magic show, costs 48FF (students 42FF, children 34FF). Combination tickets (77FF) allow same-day entrance to the Maison de la Magie and chateau.

Musée de l'Objet

This contemporary-art museum, adjoining the École Municipale des Beaux Arts et des Arts Décoratifs, houses a fascinating collection of works by Man Ray, César and Christo, whose fetish for wrapping objects remains famous worldwide. The 1960s 'new realism' movement is represented by artists such as French-born Arman (1928–), known for his distinctive trash-filled plastic tablets, and Romanian-born Daniel Spoerri (1930–), who has several pieces on display. Highlights include *Eau Sale* (*Dirty Water*), *In the Spirit of Fluxus* and *Mur des Mots* (*Wall of Words*) by the Italian-born Ben (1935–). The latter comprises 300 metal plaques, each featuring a unique slogan written by Ben, screwed to one of the walls in the courtyard of the neighbouring fine arts school.

The museum (☎ 02 54 78 87 26), 6 rue Franciade, opens 1.30 to 6.30 pm Tuesday to Sunday, July and August; and 2 to 6 pm at the weekend, the rest of the year. Admission costs 15FF. Avoid it if you cannot appreciate how a fridge balanced on a chair or a mannequin wrapped in plastic can be art.

Old Town

Around the old town, the large brown explanatory signs indicating tourist sights are both informative and in English. Part of the area has been turned into a pedestrian mall, where many of the buildings have attractive white facades, red-brick chimneys and roofs of bluish slate.

Cathédrale St-Louis was rebuilt in late-Gothic style after the devastating hurricane of 1678. The crypt dates from the 10th century. The cathedral opens 7.30 am to 6 pm.

The sober **town hall**, immediately behind the cathedral, was built in the Classical style in 1700 and served as the bishops' palace. Note the **sundial**, across the courtyard at one corner of the Ecclesiastical Tribunal building; its motto reads: 'Time moves on, our work stands still, while we have the time, let us use it to do good.' A fantastic panorama of Blois and both banks of the River Loire opens out from the terrace of **Jardins de l'Évêché** (Gardens of the Bishop's Palace), behind the cathedral.

The 15th-century **Maison des Acrobates** (House of the Acrobats), 3 bis rue Pierre de Blois, across the square from the cathedral, is so-named because its timbers are decorated with characters taken from medieval farces, including acrobats and jugglers. It was one of the few medieval houses in Blois to survive the bombings of WWII; a beauty parlour fills its ground floor today. At No 13 on the same street is the equally well-preserved **Hôtel de Ville-brême**, whose half-timbered southern facade is linked to the *corps de logis* (central building) by a covered bridge.

Continuing down the hill along rue Pierre de Blois and onto rue des Juifs, you come to pretty **place Ave Maria**, from where Blois' other historic street, **rue du Puits Châtel**, runs off to the east. At No 1 on this street is a marvellous 13th-century town house, rebuilt in the 16th century and featuring a superb courtyard with superimposed galleries and staircase. The 16th-century **hôtel particulier** at No 5 bears the initials of Louis XII and Anne de Bretagne above its doorway. **Hôtel Sardini**, at No 7, dates from 1510 and sports an exceptionally well-kept, stone sculpted emblem of Louis XII on its facade. The familiar porcupine was covered up during the French Revolu-

tion to avoid destruction and was only rediscovered in its perfectly preserved state in 1975.

In the **Quartier St-Nicolas**, south of the chateau, is the interesting **Musée de la Résistance et de la Déportation,** at 1 place de la Grève. It recounts the history of the Resistance movement, subsequent deportations and eventual liberation during WWII, and opens 2.30 to 5.30 pm Tuesday to Sunday. Admission costs 15FF (students and children 5FF). Guided tours are available.

Organised Tours

From mid-May to 31 August, the Blois area's public bus company, Transports du Loir-et-Cher (TLC; ☎ 02 54 58 55 55), operates a chateau excursion from Blois to Chambord and Cheverny. There are two tours daily, departing from Blois train station at 9.10 am and 1.20 pm and arriving back in Blois at 1.10 pm and 6 pm respectively. Both buses also pick up passengers at TLC's Point Bus information office (☎ 02 54 78 15 66), at 2 place Victor Hugo, in Blois. Tours cost 65FF (students and children 50FF); admission fees to the two chateaux are not included but tour participants are eligible for reduced tariffs. Information and tour tickets are also available from the tourist office. It is possible to buy tickets on the bus, but to ensure a place get them in advance.

Places to Stay

Camping Two-star *Camping du Lac de Loire* (☎ 02 54 78 82 05), open April to mid-October, is about 4km from the centre of Blois, south of the river on route de Chambord, in Vineuil. Two people with a tent are charged 49FF. There is no bus service from town except in July and August (phone the camp site or the tourist office for details).

Hostel The *auberge de jeunesse* (☎/fax 02 54 78 27 21, 18 rue de l'Hôtel Pasquier), in Les Grouëts, is 4.5km south-west of Blois train station. It opens March to mid-November, but call before arriving – it's often full. Beds in the two large, single-sex dorm rooms cost 68FF (not including an optional breakfast). Kitchen facilities are available. Rooms are locked from 10 am to 6 pm, but it's often possible to drop off your bags during the day.

To get to the hostel, take local TUB bus No 4 (until 7 pm) from place de la République (linked to the train station by TUB bus Nos 1, 2, 3 and 6), or – if you prefer to avoid a long detour – from quai de la Saussaye, along the river. If hitching, head south-westwards along the northern quay of the River Loire, which becomes the N152. At Les Grouëts, walk along rue Basse des Grouëts to house No 32 and turn onto rue de l'Hôtel Pasquier; follow it under the tracks and then up the hill for a few hundred metres.

Hotels Near the train station your best bet is comfortable, one-star *Hôtel St-Jacques* (☎ 02 54 78 04 15, fax 02 54 78 33 05, 7 rue Ducoux), where the staff go out of their way to be friendly. Singles/doubles with washbasin and bidet cost 130/140FF, rooms with shower are 160FF and singles/doubles with shower and toilet cost 170/190FF. Rates are slightly lower out of season. The St-Jacques has bicycles to rent for 80FF per day. Across the street, family-run *Hôtel Le Savoie* (☎ 02 54 74 32 21, fax 02 54 74 29 58, 6 rue Ducoux) has neat, well-kept singles/doubles with shower, toilet and TV costing upwards of 180/200FF. Breakfast is an extra 30FF per person.

One of the cheapest places to stay is *À la Ville de Tours* (☎ 02 54 78 07 86, fax 02 54 56 87 33, 2 place de la Grève), which has seven rooms costing 150/180/250/300FF for a single/double/triple/quad. It is very close to the river.

Between the train station and the chateau, pleasant *Hôtel Anne de Bretagne* (☎ 02 54 78 05 38, fax 02 54 74 37 79, 31 ave Dr Jean Laigret) has 29 comfortable doubles starting at 200FF. Avoid the rooms in the basement.

North of the old town, 12-room *Hôtel du Bellay* (☎ 02 54 78 23 62, fax 02 54 78 52 04, 12 rue des Minimes) offers doubles costing 135FF to 160FF; hall showers are free. Double rooms with bath or shower and toilet cost 185FF (less from October to March). It also has a handful of triples/quads with shower and toilet for 240/280FF. The Bellay boasts a *complet* (full) sign in its window most days.

Try the nearby *Hôtel La Renaissance* (☎ 02 54 78 02 63, fax 02 54 74 30 95, 9 rue du Pont du Gast), which offers singles/doubles with shower and toilet costing upwards of 199/219FF. Private parking costs 30FF.

Hôtel L'Étoile Tex (☎ 02 54 78 46 93, ✉ etoiletex.cybercafe@caramail.com, 7 rue du Bourg Neuf) has nine rooms, some with private bathroom, costing 150FF to 180FF. Most are rented by students. Ask in the ground-floor bar.

Places to Eat

Restaurants There's a cluster of popular restaurants along rue Foulerie. Cosy *Les Banquettes Rouges* (☎ 02 54 78 74 92, 16 rue des Trois Marchands) serves traditional French cuisine from noon to 2 pm and 7 to 11 pm (evening only at the weekend). It has *menus* costing 89FF, 119FF and 159FF.

Crowds of people out for a splurge make for *Au Bouchon Lyonnais* (☎ 02 54 74 12 87, 25 rue des Violettes). Main dishes of traditional French and Lyon-style cuisine cost from 78FF to 128FF; *menus* are 118FF and 165FF. It opens noon to 2 pm and 7 to 10 pm Tuesday to Saturday.

Au Rendez-Vous des Pêcheurs (☎ 02 54 74 67 48, 27 rue du Foix) specialises in fish (96FF to 140FF) brought in fresh each morning from the River Loire and the sea. The beautifully handwritten menu adds a homely touch to this cottage-style restaurant off the beaten tourist track. Hours are noon to 2 pm and 7.30 to 10 pm (evening only on Monday) Monday to Saturday.

Top-notch in price and gastronomic excellence is *L'Orangerie du Château* (☎ 02 54 78 05 36, 1 ave Dr Jean Laigret), housed in the superb orange grove of the chateau which is wedged between the historic Pavillon Anne de Bretagne and Église St-Vincent. *Menus* range from 130FF to 290FF. It opens Thursday to Tuesday (closed Sunday evening).

Pasta and pizzas are dished up with style at *La Scala* (☎ 02 54 74 88 19, 8 rue des Minimes) and its summer terrace beneath trees is usually packed out. If so, try *Le Rond de Serviette* (☎ 02 54 74 48 04, 18 rue Beauvoir), which markets itself as Blois' most humorous and cheapest restaurant. Its 49FF *menu*, which includes the entree, pizza and dessert of the day, is unbeatable.

La Mesa (☎ 02 54 78 70 70, 11 rue Vauvert) is a very popular Franco-Italian joint, up the alleyway from 44 rue Foulerie. It has *menus* costing 75FF and 130FF and offers a good selection of salads. The courtyard is perfect for dining alfresco. It opens noon to 2 pm and 7 to 11 pm daily (closed Sunday out of season).

Cafes Several *cafe-brasseries* dot place de la Résistance.

Le Denis Papin, perched at the top of the Denis Papin staircase on rue du Palais, is a very simple cafe which serves sandwiches and light snacks on its charming terrace, from where the city views are wonderful.

In the old town's heart, *La Bohème* (☎ 02 54 78 68 68, 5 rue du Grenier à Sel) is a literary cafe with book shelves lining its walls and an innovative menu which includes dishes such as sweetly spiced grilled grapefruit.

Self-Catering Across the tracks from the train station, on ave Gambetta, the *Intermarché* supermarket, which has a bakery, opens 9 am to 12.30 pm and 3 to 7.15 pm Monday to Saturday.

In the old town, there's a *food market* along rue Anne de Bretagne on Tuesday, Thursday and Saturday until 1 pm. The *charcuterie* (57 rue du Bourg Neuf) has a fine selection of prepared dishes and opens Tuesday to Saturday. For tripe, you should head to the *Triperie des Halles* (5 rue Anne de Bretagne).

Entertainment

In the old town, *Pub Discothèque Avenue Foch* (☎ 02 54 90 00 00, 3 rue du Puits Châtel) opens from 10 pm daily. Several pubs overlook place Ave Maria, including

Pub Mancini, at 1 rue du Puits Châtel, and *Le Bristol*. The *Loch Ness Pub* at the intersection of rue des Juifs and rue Pierre de Blois is another watering hole.

Theatre, dance and music take to the stage inside *Halle aux Grains* (☎ 02 54 56 19 79, place de la République). Across the street is *Cinéma Les Lobis* (☎ 02 54 74 08 54, 02 54 74 08 43, 12 ave du Maréchal Maunoury).

Getting There & Away

Bus The TLC bus network is set up to transport school kids into Blois in the morning and to get them home in the afternoon. As a result, afternoon services to Blois are limited on some lines. There is reduced service during the summer school holidays and on Sunday and holidays.

TLC buses to destinations in the vicinity of Blois leave from place Victor Hugo (in front of the Point Bus office) and the bus station – little more than a patch of parking lot with schedules posted – next to the train station. To Chambord (No 2, 18.50FF, 45 minutes), there are three buses on weekdays, two on Saturday and one on Sunday during the school year. In July and August, your only bus option is TLC's tourist bus (see Organised Tours, earlier in this Blois section). Before embarking on any day trip, check all schedules thoroughly to avoid getting stranded.

Train The train station (☎ 08 36 35 35 35) is at the western end of ave Dr Jean Laigret. The information office opens 9 am to 6.30 pm Monday to Saturday (closed holidays). There are no left-luggage facilities.

There are frequent trains to/from Tours (51FF, 40 minutes, 11 to 17 daily). Nantes (159FF, two hours) can be reached via Tours or St-Pierre des Corps. About three-quarters of the trains on the line from Blois to Tours stop at Amboise (34FF, 20 minutes).

Car ADA (☎ 02 54 74 02 47) is 3km northeast of the train station at 108 ave du Maréchal Maunoury (D149). It opens 8 am to noon and 2 to 6.30 pm Monday to Saturday. Take bus No 1 from the train station or bus No 4 from place de la République to the Cornillettes stop.

Avis (☎ 02 54 74 48 15, fax 02 54 78 66 61), 6 rue Jean Moulin, opens 8 am to noon and 2 to 7 pm (6 pm on Saturday) Monday to Saturday.

Getting Around

Bus Buses within Blois, run by TUB (☎ 02 54 78 15 66), operate until 8 or 8.30 pm. There is a reduced service on Sunday and holidays. All buses, except the No 4, stop at the train station. Route maps are posted in most bus shelters. Tickets cost 6.10FF (42.50FF for a carnet of 10). For information and timetables, inquire at the Point Bus office (☎ 02 54 78 15 66), 2 place Victor Hugo, open 8 am to noon and 1.30 to 6 pm Tuesday to Friday, 9 am to noon and 1.30 to 4.30 pm on Saturday, and 1.30 to 6 pm on Monday. Its hours are shorter in July and August.

Taxi To order a taxi, contact the taxi booth (☎ 02 54 78 07 65) in front of the train station. Minibuses with space for up to eight passengers can also be hired here. A return trip to Chambord and Cheverny costs 420FF (Sunday and holidays 600FF), while to Chaumont, Amboise and Chenonceau it's 670FF (Sunday and holidays 900FF). Various combinations are possible.

Bicycle Hire two wheels from Cycles Leblond (☎ 02 54 74 30 13), 44 levée des Tuileries, which charges upwards of 30/180FF per day/week and opens 9 am to 9 pm daily. To get here, walk eastwards along promenade du Mail for approximately 800m; levée des Tuileries is the continuation of promenade du Mail.

CHAMBORD

postcode 41250 • pop 200

The pinprick village of Chambord is dominated by the largest and most spectacular chateau in the entire Loire Valley, Château de Chambord, which François I started building in 1519 as a base for hunting game in the lush Sologne forests. The forested Domaine de Chambord is larger than the whole of central Paris. Ironically, the French king, who also chose the site for its easy distance from Paris – a two-day ride by horse and carriage – stayed here for just 42 days out of his 32-year reign.

The countryside here, with its quiet country back roads, is perfect for cycling. Blois, Beauregard and Cheverny – each about 17km from Chambord – make lovely day trips. September, with its sunny days and crisp air filled with rutting animal cries, can be the most exhilarating time of the year to visit.

Château de Chambord

Built on lands belonging to the Blois counts from the 10th century and united with the Crown in 1491, the 440-room Château de Chambord was the handiwork of three kings – François I (ruled 1515–47), Henri II (ruled 1547–59) and Louis XIV (ruled 1643–1715). Its Renaissance architecture and decoration, grafted onto a feudal ground plan, may have been inspired by Leonardo da Vinci, who lived 34km southwest of here, in Amboise, at the invitation of François I, between 1516 and da Vinci's death, three years later.

François I's emblems – the royal monogram (a letter 'F') and salamanders of a particularly fierce-looking disposition – adorn many parts of the building. There is a particularly impressive display of 400 or so on the stone-sculpted, coffered ceiling on the 2nd floor of the chateau. Though forced by liquidity problems to leave his two sons unransomed in Spain and to help himself to both the wealth of his churches and his subjects' silver, the king kept 1800 construction workers and artisans busy at the chateau for 15 years. At one point, he even suggested that the River Loire be rerouted so that it would pass by Chambord. Eventually, a smaller river, the Cosson, was diverted instead.

François I died before the building was completed. Molière premiered two of his most famous plays (*Monsieur de Pourceaugnac* in 1619 and *Le bourgeois gentilhomme* in 1676) at Chambord to audiences that included Louis XIV.

The chateau's famed **Grand Staircase**, attributed by some to da Vinci, consists of two spiral staircases that wind round the same central axis but never meet (see the 'Chateaux of the Loire' special section). The rich ornamentation is in the style of the early French Renaissance. Peering into the staircase's hollow heart, it's easy to imagine mistresses and lovers chasing each other up and down the staircases.

The royal court used to assemble on the Italianate **rooftop terrace**, reached via the Grand Staircase, to watch military exercises, tournaments and the hounds and hunters returning from a day of stalking deer. As you stand on the terrace (once described as resembling an overcrowded chessboard), you are surrounded by the towers, cupolas, domes, chimneys, dormers and mosaic slate roofs that form the chateau's imposing skyline. The 56m-high Grand Staircase tower (containing the 33m-high staircase), topped with a glass lantern and a fleur de lys, is particularly impressive.

Tickets to the chateau (☎ 02 54 50 50 02) are on sale from 9.30 am to 6.30 pm daily, July and August; 9.30 am to 5.45 pm daily, April to June and September; and 9.30 am to 4.45 pm daily, October to March. Visitors already in the chateau can stay there for 45 minutes after ticket sales end. Admission costs 40FF (25FF for those aged 12 to 25 on production of a student card). A *billet jumelé* (combination ticket), covering entry to the chateau and evening show, costs 100F (a saving of 20FF). The chateau interior is blessed with excellent explanatory signs in French, English, German, Spanish and Italian, and there are quality guidebooks in half a dozen languages (39FF) on sale in the chateau. Free guided tours (1½ hours) in five languages are available, or you can rent an audio guide (20FF) from the booth at the entrance.

Domaine National de Chambord

A staggering 54 sq km of forest fans out from the chateau, which is on the western fringe of the estate (*domaine*). Since 1996 the entire estate has been protected as a historical monument. The park fell into ruin at the start of the 19th century, after Napoleon gave Chambord to Marshall Berthier as a prize for his war efforts. It was heavily reforested with Norway pines in 1860–80. Further reforestation in 1948–55 resulted in 90% of the park being forested by 1970.

Traditionally a hunting preserve, the estate is reserved solely for the use of the president of France today, a right that Jacques Chirac has chosen not to exercise. A 32km-long stone wall built in 1542–1645 – the longest such wall of its kind in France – surrounds the estate, just 12 sq km of which, on the western side of the property, is open to the public. Several **hiking and mountain bike** trails criss-cross this section and there are **aires de vision** (observation towers), where you can spot animals at dusk and dawn (see the boxed text 'Le Brame du Cerf' on the following page).

Places to Stay & Eat

On the southern bank of the River Loire at Montlivault, 4km north-west of Chambord, is an *auberge de jeunesse* (☎ 02 38 44 61 31, fax 02 38 44 14 73, levée de la Loire). At the last count, it had 28 beds costing 68FF. It opens in July and August only. The idyllic, riverside hostel is at the end of a mud track, signposted off the D951 at the Chambord junction (D84).

In Chambord itself there is one absolutely charming place to stay: *Hôtel St-Michel* (☎ 02 54 20 31 31, fax 02 54 20 36 40). Housed in Chambord's former kennels, opposite the chateau, it offers guests two unmissable experiences – stunning views of a deserted Château de Chambord at sunrise or sunset, when the coachloads have departed for the day, and tasty platters of wild boar, apple sauce and chestnut puree in its restaurant. Doubles reminiscent of a bygone era range from 290FF (shared toilet) to 450FF (private bathroom). Breakfast costs 40FF.

Gastronomic dreams are conjured up by top chef Robin Bernard – known for his game dishes – at *Le Relais de Bracieux* (☎ 02 54 46 41 22, *@ relaisbracieux .robin@wanadoo.fr*), in Bracieux, 8km south of Chambord on the D112. *Menus* of delicious local dishes cost 250FF to 580FF.

Le Brame du Cerf

Le brame du cerf (the rutting season) is a lively period, presenting visitors with a unique opportunity to view Chambord's animal antics at close range.

Wildlife observation towers (*aires de vision de la faune*) overlook the plains skirting the Forêt de Chambord's fringe and offer magnificent views of the feeding does or hinds (*biches*) and their male counterparts (*cerfs*). In a predictably territorial and masculine manner, the stag stalks the deer, rounding the females into a pack which he guards ferociously. In between defending them against other males, the stags closely surveys his females. Does are only on heat for 36 hours a year, making it vital that the stag leaps into action – in this case, into the vertical position known as *le chandelier* (literally 'candlestick') – at the prime time.

Throughout the rutting period, the unsavoury stag does not eat, but drinks and soils himself excessively. He rubs against trees, urinates and deposits stinky secretions to mark out his territory, and bells or troats to drive away threatening stags. Antler-to-antler combat between two stags is rare: they have to be of equal hierarchy within the pack to clash.

Red deer rut some time between mid-September and mid-October and are most active at dawn and dusk. The smaller and more solitary roe deer reproduces in July. The wild boar (*sanglier*), meanwhile, has a period of intense sexual activity in November and December; unlike deer, however, the chances of seeing these swine (who wallow in mires to clean themselves of parasites) are extraordinarily slim: wild boar are nocturnal.

Between mid-September and early October, the Domaine National de Chambord (☎ 02 54 50 50 00, fax 02 54 20 34 69) organises forest expeditions (150FF per person, two hours), every evening except Friday. Its 4WD forest tours between April and September (80FF per person, 1½ hours) are likewise a good opportunity to spot wildlife. During the rutting season, the domaine also runs week-long animal-photography courses (1000FF per person); one-day classes (100FF) are held from 1 April to 31 July. Advance reservations are essential for all expeditions.

❀ ❀

The restaurant opens daily in the high season (but closes Tuesday evening and all day Wednesday in the low season).

Entertainment

From mid-July to early October, Château de Chambord is ablaze at night with a bizarre and beautiful display of images, lights, music and sound. It gives a completely different perspective on the castle interior, which guests can explore with the aid of a hand-held electric lamp. Admission to *Les Métamorphoses de Chambord* costs 80FF (students 50FF, children aged under 12 free). Tickets are sold from 10.30 pm until midnight in July, from 10 to 11.30 pm in August, and from 8.30 to 9.30 or 10 pm between September and mid-October.

From May to September a *Spectacle d'Art Équestre (Equestrian Show;* ☎ 02 54 20 31 01*)* is held at the stables near the chateau. Performances begin at 11.45 am. A second show is held at 5 pm daily in July and August, and at 4 pm at the weekend in May, June and September. Tickets cost 45FF (children 30FF).

Getting There & Away

Chambord is 16km east of Blois and 20km north-east of Cheverny. To/from Blois there are TLC public buses during the school year (see Getting There & Away in the earlier Blois section) and touristy coach tours taking in Chambord and Cheverny between mid-May and 31 August (see Organised Tours in the Blois section).

In Chambord, the TLC public buses use the stop on the westbound route Charles X (D33).

Getting Around

Bicycle Two wheels are the best method of exploring the grounds of Chambord and the surrounding chateaux. Bicycles can be rented from the Echapée Belle kiosk next to Pont St-Michel. Rental charges are 25/70/120FF per hour/day/weekend; guests staying at Hôtel St-Michel get a discount. The estate authorities (☎ 02 54 87 68 76) organise four-hour cycling trips (120/160FF with/without your own bicycle) in the Forêt de Chambord. These take place once a week in July and August, and once or twice a month in September and October. Advance reservations are essential.

Horse-Drawn Carriage In summer, horse-drawn-carriage rides depart from the ticket office opposite Hôtel St-Michel. The 45-minute tour of the chateau grounds and part of the forest costs 45FF (children 30FF).

Boat From mid-May to mid-November, you can hire a rowing boat (☎ 02 54 56 00 43) from the Echapée Belle kiosk next to Pont St-Michel, to explore the canal that meanders around the chateau. A two/three/four-person boat costs 70/75/100FF per hour.

CHÂTEAU DE CHEVERNY

Château de Cheverny, privately owned by the viscounts de Sigalas since its construction in 1625–34, is the region's most magnificently furnished chateau. Sitting like a sparkling white ship amid a sea of beautifully manicured gardens, the chateau is graced with a finely proportioned neoclassical facade quite stunning to the first-time visitor. Its interior is as impeccably kept as its smooth white exterior. Two thousand hectares of forest stretch southwards beyond its 21 hectares of landscaped, lake-filled grounds, through which one can stroll freely.

Visitors are treated to room after sumptuous room fitted out with the finest of period appointments: furniture, paintings, canopied beds, chimneypieces, parquet floors, painted ceilings and walls covered with embossed Cordova leather. Among the many tapestries is the amazing *Abduction of Helen*, a 17th-century Gobelin tapestry hanging in the Salle d'Armes (Arms Room). In the richly furnished **Chambre du**

Roi (the King's Bedroom, in which no king ever slept because no king ever stayed at Cheverny), a series of six 17th-century tapestries woven in Paris carpets all four walls. Aubusson tapestries cover the Louis XIV-style chairs, while the four-poster bed has been in the chateau ever since it was built. The **Salon des Tapisseries** (Tapestry Room) is equally richly furnished. Don't miss the three-dozen panels illustrating the story of *Don Quixote* in the 1st-floor dining room.

In the grounds are an 18th-century **Orangerie**, where Leonardo da Vinci's *Mona Lisa* was hidden during WWII, and the **Salle des Trophées** (Trophy Room), a macabre chamber whose walls, pillars and ceiling are smothered with the antlers of almost 2000 stags hunted since the 1850s. Just round the corner are the **Chenils** (Kennels; see the boxed text 'La Soupe des Chiens' on the following page). Heading towards the lake, there is a **balloon pad** (☎ 02 54 79 25 05). A helium-filled balloon takes off from here between mid-March and mid-October. The 10- to 12-minute ascent and descent costs 47FF (students aged under 25 pay 43FF, children 30FF). Alternatively, you can tour part of the extensive grounds in an **electric car** or by **boat**. Departures are from the pit stop next to the balloon pad. Tours cost 30FF (students 23FF, children 17FF).

Château de Cheverny (☎ 02 54 79 96 29, @ chateau.cheverny@wanadoo.fr) opens 9.15 or 9.30 am to 6.15 pm (6.30 pm July and August) daily, April to September; and 9.15 or 9.30 am to noon and 2.15 to 5.30 pm (5 pm November to February) daily, the rest of the year. Admission costs 35FF (students 24FF, children 17FF), which includes an informative self-guide sheet in one of 12 languages. Various combination tickets are also available: chateau plus electric car tour is 65FF, chateau plus balloon flight is 84FF and chateau plus balloon plus car is 109FF.

Château de Cheverny is in Cheverny, 1km south of Cour-Cheverny. Cheverny tourist office (☎ 02 54 79 95 63), opposite the village church on rue du Chêne des Dames, opens 9 am to 7 pm daily, April to October.

ORLÉANAIS & BLÉSOIS

La Soupe des Chiens

As was the custom among the nobility of centuries past, the viscount de Sigalas – whose family has owned Cheverny since it was built – hunts with hounds. His 90 dogs, most a cross between English fox terriers and French poitevins (the white ones are pure English hounds), are quite beautiful, no matter what you think of the practice of using them to kill stags.

The dogs range in age from seven months to seven years and their paws are dipped yellow. Each has a name, meaning a fantastic feat of memory for the two dog trainers, who do, indeed, know every dog and its name. The *soupe des chiens* (feeding of the dogs) is an awe-inspiring demonstration of the control these trainers exercise over the pack.

A massive 90kg of animal parts (a sight not recommended for the faint-hearted) is brought by wheelbarrow into the cement enclosure each day and methodically arranged in a 2m-long mountain. Not until the dog master gives the word (or crack of the whip) does the pack of barking, desperate dogs dare do so much as sniff at their daily 1kg ration. The stinking offal is ripped to shreds and gobbled up in minutes. Double portions are doled out after the twice-weekly winter hunt.

The soupe des chiens takes place in the kennels (*chenils*) at 5 pm daily in summer. In January, February and between mid-September and December, the dogs are fed at 3 pm on Monday, Wednesday, Thursday and Friday only. The pack hunts every Tuesday and Saturday between September and March, departing from the majestic front entrance of the chateau if hunting in the Fôret de Cheverny.

Places to Stay & Eat

In Cour-Cheverny, *Camping Les Casseux* (☎ 02 54 79 95 63, fax 02 54 79 99 43) opens May to September and charges 13/6/9FF per adult/child/pitch. In Cheverny, 2.5km from the chateau entrance on the D102, well-run *Camping Les Saules* (☎ 02 54 79 90 01, fax 02 54 79 28 34, route de Contres) is a large site with pitches for tents (30/38FF in the low/high season plus 21FF to 30FF per adult) and caravans, as well as mobile homes and furnished canvas tents to rent. Reception opens 8.30 am to 9 pm.

Most hotel options are in Cour-Cheverny: *Hôtel des Trois Marchands* (☎ 02 54 79 96 44, fax 02 54 79 25 60, place de l'Église) and *Hôtel St-Hubert* (☎ 02 54 79 96 60, fax 02 54 79 21 17, rue Nationale) are both a 1km walk from the chateau and offer doubles costing upwards of 300FF.

The 16-room *Château du Breuil* (☎ 02 54 44 20 20, fax 02 54 44 30 40), signposted 4.5km from Château de Cheverny off the D52, is an illustrious pad with singles/doubles from a pricey 530/675FF and breakfast costing 65FF. It does not have an in-house restaurant for evening dining.

Opposite Cheverny tourist office, *Au Pichet* (☎ 02 54 79 97 23, place de l'Église) is a cosy, old-style restaurant with wine-red wooden shutters and *menus* costing 75FF to 200FF. Its adjoining cafe serves stomach-filling *rillette* (minced pork paste) sandwiches for 18FF.

In Chitenay, some 6km west of Cheverny, the *Auberge du Centre* (☎ 02 54 70 42 11, fax 02 54 70 35 03) has 25 colourfully decorated doubles costing 345FF. Dinner is served in a rose-filled patio garden. The auberge – an easy bicycle ride to/from Château de Cheverny – rents bicycles for 70FF per day and stocks reference maps marked up with various cycling itineraries.

Getting There & Away

Cheverny is 16km south-east of Blois and 20km south-west of Chambord.

The TLC bus from Blois to Villefranche-sur-Cher stops at Cheverny (14.6FF). Buses leave Blois at 6.50 am and 12.25 pm Monday to Saturday, year round. Going back to Blois, the last bus leaves Cheverny at 6.58 pm (arriving in Blois at 7.30 pm). Departure times may vary on Sunday and holidays; check with TLC (☎ 02 54 58 55 55) before setting out.

In addition, between mid-May and 31 August, TLC operates daily coach tours from Blois (see Organised Tours under Blois, earlier in this chapter).

CHAUMONT-SUR-LOIRE
Information
The village's tourist office (☎ 02 54 20 91 73, fax 02 54 20 90 34), rue du Maréchal Leclerc, stocks accommodation lists and makes bookings for a small charge (5/10FF in/outside Loir-et-Cher). It has six bicycles to rent for 10/60FF per hour/day, and sells a variety of booklets outlining cycling and hiking routes in the area. It opens 9.30 am to 7 pm daily, Easter to September.

Château de Chaumont
Seventeen kilometres south-west of Blois on the southern bank of the River Loire, Château de Chaumont is strategically set on a bluff overlooking the river and looks much more like a feudal castle than most other Blésois chateaux. The chateau's most outstanding feature is its luxurious **stables**, from where, in summer, horse-drawn carriages take visitors on a short tour of the chateau's cedar-rich grounds (30FF, 20 minutes).

In 1560 Catherine de Médicis (France's powerful queen mother) took revenge on Diane de Poitiers, the mistress of her late husband, Henri II, by forcing her to accept Chaumont in exchange for her much more favoured residence, Château de Chenonceau (see the Touraine chapter). During the years after the USA won independence, Benjamin Franklin, at the time US ambassador to France, was a frequent guest at Chaumont.

Tickets to this state-owned chateau (☎ 02 54 51 26 26) are sold from 9.30 am to 6 pm daily, mid-March to September; and 10 am to 4.30 pm daily, the rest of the year; the chateau closes 30 minutes later. Admission costs 33FF (children 21FF) and includes entry to the stables and a free self-guide brochure in the language of your choice; some rooms also have English-language explanations. Guided visits (one hour) are available in French only. The steep path leading up to the park and chateau begins at the intersection of rue du Village Neuf and rue Maréchal Leclerc (D751).

Festival International des Jardins
From mid-June to mid-October, the three-hectare park of Château de Chaumont plays host to a magnificent International Garden Festival (☎ 02 54 20 99 22, fax 02 54 20 99 24), which sees the castle grounds transformed into 25 themed gardens designed by landscape gardeners from around the world. The theme is simple and changes each year (it was the 'vegetable garden' in 1999), yet the gardens dreamed up are hugely imaginative and fantastical creations. Admission costs 48FF (children 20FF), while a billet jumelé, valid for same-day entry to the festival and chateau, costs 65FF. The park and the festival gardens are open from 9 am to dusk.

Places to Stay & Eat
In Chaumont-sur-Loire, *Camping Municipal* (☎ *02 54 20 95 22*), on the southern bank of the River Loire near the road bridge, charges 14/7/10FF per adult/child/tent. It opens May to September. The tourist office has details of other accommodation in Chaumont.

Onzain, on the northern bank of the river, offers two royal options. *Domaine des Hauts de Loire* (☎ *02 54 20 83 41, fax 02 54 20 77 32, @ hauts-loire@relaischateaux.fr*), 2km north of Onzain towards Herbault, is a gorgeous old hunting lodge transformed into a luxury hotel, complete with helipad, offering doubles from 680FF. The 18th-century, ivy-clad *Château des Tertres* (☎ *02 54 20 83 88, fax 02 54 20 89 21, @ chateau.des .tertres@wanadoo.fr, 11 rue de Meuves*) has fabulous rooms costing upwards of 400FF.

La Chancelière (☎ *02 54 20 96 95, fax 02 54 33 91 71, 1 rue de Bellevue*) is a good spot to eat in Chaumont, with *menus* costing 90FF, 120FF, 150FF and 200FF. It opens Friday to Tuesday.

Getting There & Away
By public transport, the only way to get to Chaumont-sur-Loire is by local train on the Orléans–Tours line. Get off at Onzain (eight

or more daily), from where it is a 2km walk across the river to the chateau. Single train fares to Onzain are 36/41/62FF from Blois/Tours/Orléans. By bicycle, the quiet back roads on the southern bank of the river are a tranquil option.

OTHER CHATEAUX AROUND BLOIS

Several less well-known chateaux are within easy reach of Blois, Chambord and Cheverny.

Château de Beauregard

The modest Château de Beauregard (☎ 02 54 70 36 74) is just 6km south of Blois or a pleasant 15km cycle ride through the forest from Chambord. Built in the early 16th century as a hunting lodge for François I and enlarged 100 years later, its most famous feature is its 1st-floor **Galerie des Portraits**, the walls of which feature 327 portraits of notable faces from the 14th to 17th centuries. The unusual floor is covered with 17th-century Dutch tiles. The **Cabinet des Grelots** (Chamber of Bells) is a small wood-panelled room decorated with numerous thumbnail-sized bells and with a fabulous oak ceiling. In the large grounds, the **Jardin des Portraits** (Portrait Garden) is worth a peek.

The chateau is privately owned and inhabited year round by the du Pavillon family. It opens 9.30 am to noon and 2 to 5 or 6.30 pm daily, April to September (no break in July and August); and the same hours Thursday to Tuesday, February, March and October to January. Admission costs 40FF (students and children 30FF).

Château de Villesavin

Château de Villesavin (☎ 02 54 56 42 88) sits on the southern fringe of Forêt de Chambord, 3km west of Bracieux. It was built in 1527–36 for Jean le Breton, François I's finance minister and commissioner of works at Chambord (he was also responsible for Château de Villandry, near Tours), and is in private hands today. The 16th-century marble fountain in the *cour d'honneur* (main courtyard) is so fine that

historians suspect it was actually sculpted for display at Chambord. Admission costs 30FF (students 25FF, children 20FF) and includes a guided tour of the predominantly 19th-century interior. Villesavin opens February to December.

Château de Troussay

About 3km south of Cheverny, off the D52, is the Château de Troussay (☎ 02 54 44 29 07), open 10 am to 7 pm daily, Easter to November. It was built as a rural manor house in the 15th century, and a guided tour of its small but well-furnished interior provides an interesting insight into how the lesser nobility lived at this time. A collection of agricultural tools from neighbouring farms in La Sologne (see the following section) is displayed in one of the outbuildings. Admission costs 26FF (students and children 18FF) and – unusually – picnics are allowed in the park.

Château de Fougères-sur-Bièvre

Continuing south along the D52 for 10km, you come to Château de Fougères-sur-Bièvre (☎ 02 54 20 27 18), an imposing stone fortress which has undergone a well-earned face lift in recent years and hosts interesting medieval-craft workshops (see Courses in the Facts for the Visitor chapter). Throughout the summer, concerts fill its inner courtyard.

Places to Stay

In Fougères-sur-Bièvre, the *Auberge du Château* (☎ 02 54 30 27 80, 31 rue de l'Église), opposite the chateau, is excellent value. It offers basic singles/doubles with shared bathroom costing upwards of 130/200FF, and doubles with shower costing 280FF. Simple but delicious *menus* starting at 82FF are served on the outside terrace, which overlooks the chateau and village church.

Brilliant-yellow fields of sunflowers surround the 28-room *Relais des Landes* (☎ 02 54 44 40 40, fax 02 54 44 03 89), a Best Western-chain hotel in Ouchamps, 5km north-west of Fougères-sur-Bièvre. It has a swan-filled lake, sumptuous grounds and

ORLÉANAIS & BLÉSOIS

singles/doubles costing 495/795FF. It opens April to November.

Enticing feasts are dished up with a flourish at *Le St-Vincent* (☎ *02 54 79 50 04*), in Oisly, about 10km south of Fougères-sur-Bièvre. *Menus* cost 120FF or 160FF and there's an 85FF lunchtime special. The board on the square in front of the auberge has a list of wine-makers who sell local wine.

Getting There & Away

The TLC bus from Blois to St-Aignan stops at Cellettes (8.8FF), 1km south-west of Château de Beauregard, on Wednesday, Friday and Saturday; the first Blois–Cellettes bus leaves at 12.25 pm. Unfortunately, there's no afternoon bus back except the Châteauroux–Blois line operated by Transports Boutet (☎ 02 54 34 43 95), which passes through Cellettes at around 6.15 pm Monday to Saturday, and – except during August – at about 6 pm on Sunday.

To get to Fougères-sur-Bièvre, stay on the St-Aignan bus from Blois; it stops in Fougères en route to St-Aignan.

There is no public transport to Villesavin and Troussay: you'll need your own wheels.

La Sologne

Historical Sologne, a soggy wetland of ponds and woodland, has just the one association for most French people: hunting. Its fields of maize shelter wild boar and pheasants, its thick forests – covering 240,000 hectares – are rich in deer, while schools of eels, carp and pike fill its rivers. The region's 11,000 or so lakes and ponds constitute 10% of the total pond area in France.

La Sologne covers a plateau of 490,000 hectares, wedged from north to south between the Rivers Loire and Cher. To the east is bordered by the Sancerre vineyards and to the west by the small villages of Selles-sur-Cher, Contres and Cheverny. Romorantin-Lanthenay is its largest town.

A traditional rye-growing region known as Secalonia by the Romans, La Sologne

was nothing more than a soggy, malaria-infested wasteland until the mid-19th century when, following the construction of the Paris–Vierzon train line, Napoleon III drained the water-logged plateau. As a result, vast, privately owned hunting estates subsequently mushroomed, and La Sologne was suddenly a prestigious place. Its savage landscape inspired numerous novels and films, notably Alain Fournier's classic novel *Le grand Meaulnes* and *La Règle du Jeu* (*Rules of the Game*; 1939), by French film-maker Jean Renoir.

The region's abundant hiking and cycling trails are marked on IGN's invaluable *Sologne* map (1:100,000), published as part of its Plein-Air series.

ROMORANTIN-LANTHENAY

postcode 41200 • pop 17,850

Romorantin-Lanthenay, considered the capital of La Sologne, lies 41 and 65km south of Blois and Orléans respectively, in the south-easternmost corner of La Sologne. In 1517 François I commissioned Leonardo da Vinci to construct a chateau in Romorantin for his mother, Louise de Savoie, only for the project to be abandoned and Chambord built instead. The future wife of François I, Claude de France, was born in Romorantin in 1499; *reine claude* plums (greengages) are named after her.

Several well-preserved **timber-framed houses**, evocative of this era, are clustered around the southern end of rue Georges Clémenceau – on the corner of rue de la Résistance and rue du Milieu – and south of the River Sauldre on rue Lucien Dubech and at 2 rue du Président Wilson.

Each year during the last weekend in October, Romorantin plays host to the **Journées Gastronomiques de la Sologne**, a two-day regional food festival. The tourist office has a list of dairies and farms where you can taste and buy locally made chèvre (goat's-milk cheese). Market day is Wednesday.

Orientation & Information

The tourist office (☎ 02 54 76 43 89, fax 02 54 76 96 24, ✉ romorantin-lanthenay@fnotsi.net), place de la Paix, opens 8.45 am

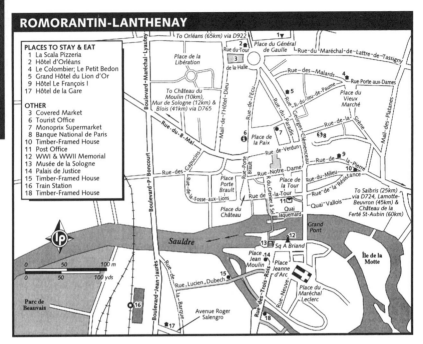

ROMORANTIN-LANTHENAY

PLACES TO STAY & EAT
1 La Scala Pizzeria
2 Hôtel d'Orléans
4 Le Colombier; Le Petit Bedon
5 Grand Hôtel du Lion d'Or
9 Hôtel Le François I
17 Hôtel de la Gare

OTHER
3 Covered Market
6 Tourist Office
7 Monoprix Supermarket
8 Banque National de Paris
10 Timber-Framed House
11 Post Office
12 WWI & WWII Memorial
13 Musée de la Sologne
14 Palais de Justice
15 Timber-Framed House
16 Train Station
18 Timber-Framed House

(10 am on Monday) to 12.15 pm and 2 to
6.30 pm Monday to Saturday, year round;
plus 10 am to noon on Sunday, July and August. Pick up its free series of brochures
which map out driving and walking tours in
the region; of particular interest is the thematic *Route des Historiques des Manoirs*
(Historical Manor House Route), available
in English.

There is a Banque National de Paris on
rue de la Sirène. The post office, on place
de la Poste, opens 8 am to noon and 1.30 to
6 pm on weekdays, and 8 am to noon on
Saturday.

Musée de la Sologne

This highly informative museum (☎ 02 54
95 33 66) is housed in a contemporary
building adjoining the 19th-century Moulin
du Chapitre, a historic mill straddling the
River Sauldre. Exhibitions on several
floors explore the flora, fauna, folkloric
traditions and sports (the most popular of

which was and is stag hunting) of La
Sologne. The museum opens 10 am to noon
and 2 to 6 pm (no break April to October)
Wednesday to Monday, year round. Admission costs 25FF (students and children
15FF).

Places to Stay & Eat

Two-star *Hôtel d'Orléans* (☎ 02 54 76 01
65, 2 place du Général de Gaulle) offers
good-value doubles with washbasin/shower
costing 160/250FF; breakfast is an extra
30FF. Reception is closed Sunday evening
and Monday out of season. Opposite the
train station, *Hôtel de la Gare* (☎ 02 54 76
20 43, 48 ave Roger Salengro) has doubles
without/with bathroom costing 110/170FF.

Le Colombier (☎ 02 54 76 12 76, fax 02
54 76 39 40, 18 place du Vieux Marché) is
a charming spot with singles/doubles/triples
with bathroom for 330/240/205FF per person. Its in-house restaurant, *Le Petit Bedon*,
is worth a visit. *Hôtel Le François I* (☎ 02

54 76 20 62, fax 02 54 96 91 64, 25 rue de la Pierre) overlooks Romorantin's most photographed timber-framed house, on the intersection of rue de la Pierre and rue du Milieu; doubles cost 220FF to 250FF. ·

Grand Hôtel du Lion d'Or (☎ 02 54 94 15 15, fax 02 54 88 24 87, ❷ liondor@ relaischateaux.fr, 69 rue Georges Clémenceau) sits on Romorantin's main shopping street. It touts four-star doubles from 650FF and is best suited to those with a corporate bank account.

La Scala (☎ 02 54 76 57 19, 12 place du Général de Gaulle) is an Italian-style pizzeria with salads costing upwards of 22FF, antipasti from 31FF and pasta from 36FF. There is a ***covered food market*** on place du Général de Gaulle and a ***Monoprix*** supermarket overlooking place de la Paix.

Getting There & Away

The train station is on place de la Gare, at the western end of ave Roger Salengro. There are six trains daily to Tours (73FF, 1¼ hours), with a change of train in Gièvres, and three trains daily to Salbris (30 minutes), from where there are trains to Orléans (1¼ hours).

SNCF also runs three buses daily to/from St-Aignan (45 minutes) to connect with trains to/from Tours (one hour).

Getting Around

The tourist office has bicycles to rent for 40/150FF per day/week, plus 300FF deposit. Advance reservations are recommended to avoid disappointment.

AROUND ROMORANTIN-LANTHENAY

This region is tough to explore without your own wheels (two or four) or a sturdy set of hiking boots.

About 10km or so west of Romorantin-Lanthenay is the 15th-century **Château du Moulin** (☎ 02 54 83 83 51), one of La Sologne's few chateaux, typically surrounded by water and tucked deep in a wood. Its well-furnished interior can be visited only as part of a guided tour (in French, 32FF), but its pretty, patterned brick ex-

terior and surrounding moat can be enjoyed independently (16FF). Only one of the original four defensive towers still stands today. The chateau opens 9 to 11.30 am and 2 to 6.30 pm daily, April to December; and the same hours at the weekend, the rest of the year.

Solognot farming traditions come to life at **La Locature de la Straize** (☎ 02 54 83 82 89), a typical 16th-century rural dwelling in which agricultural workers from nearby chateaux would stay. The little house, decked out with period furnishings, is 5km north-west of Château du Moulin. Bear north along the D20 towards Mur de Sologne, turn left at the junction for La Vionne (towards Gy en Sologne), then right at the next junction. Opening hours are 8 to 10 am and 1 to 3 pm daily, mid-March to mid-October. About 15km west of Gy en Sologne along the D143 and D63 is the smaller **Château de Chémery** (☎ 02 54 71 82 77), built in the 15th century and used as a farm from 1729. A more direct way of getting to Chémery is via the D724, N76 and D956 from Romorantin-Lanthenay, a journey of 27km.

Northern Sologne's sweetest legacy is *tarte tatin*, a legendary upside-down apple pie first cooked up by the Tatin sisters in **Lamotte Beuvron**, a small town almost equidistant from Romorantin and Orléans. It is not done to serve jam or cream with the pie, according to the Confrérie de Lichonneux de Tarte Tatin, a tongue-in-cheek brotherhood that safeguards the age-old culinary tradition of baking tarte tatin, which is widespread across France today.

Honey madeleines, still warm from the oven, can be sampled at **Château de la Ferté St-Aubin** (☎ 02 38 76 52 72), La Sologne's largest chateau, 15km north of Lamotte Beuvron. The 17th-century Renaissance edifice sports one of the largest saddleries in the region and runs cookery demonstrations in its old kitchens. The **Domaine du Ciran** (☎ 02 38 76 90 93), 5km east in Menestreau en Villette, is a nature park with botanical trails, exhibitions and other nature activities.

For details on nature-based activities in La Sologne, contact Sologne Nature

Environment (☎ 02 54 88 79 74, fax 02 54 88 95 76), 1 ave de Toulouse, Nouan-le-Fuzelier. Another handy information source is the Centre Régional de Culture Populaire en Sologne (☎ 02 54 88 71 09), at No 9 on the same street.

Places to Stay

An excellent place to stay in the heart of La Sologne is *Château de Fondjouan* (☎ *02 54 95 50 00, fax 02 54 83 91 77)*, in Mur de Sologne. The chateau's spacious estate offers accommodation to suit all budgets: a dorm bed at its *auberge de jeunesse* costs from 99FF to 165FF, including breakfast; the price depends on how many beds in a dorm are used. Hotel rooms in one of the modern outbuildings cost 170/230FF for a single/double, while rooms in the chateau are 340/400F (prices don't include breakfast). Fondjouan has a five-hectare lake, boats to hire (40/100FF per hour/day), fishing facilities (50FF per day) and bicycles to hire (50/80/160FF per day/weekend/week).

Touraine

Touraine is a quintessential pocket of the Loire Valley. Carpeted with vineyards and studded with the valley's most superb chateaux, the province is among the richest in France – culturally, historically and aesthetically. With the exception of the magnificent medieval fortresses at Chinon and Loches, Touraine's castles date from a period when defensive structures were superseded by the whimsical, decorative and fantastical – designed to pamper the soul and pander to the physical pleasures of the queen, king and his multitude of royal mistresses. Azayle-Rideau, Chenonceau, Langeais, Saché, Ussé and Villandry all comfortably fit into this category. Information on organised bus tours around Touraine's chateaux is listed under Organised Tours in the Getting Around chapter.

Tours – the capital of Touraine – is in the heart of this vine-leaf-shaped region which, since the French Revolution (1789), has formed the administrative *département* (department) of Indre-et-Loire. Tours has briefly hosted the French government twice in its history – in 1870 during the Franco-Prussian war and again in 1940, with the onset of WWII. Since then, it has become better known in France for its crisp white wines, stored in the ancient tufa cliffs that crown the Tourangeau city to the north-east. It is worth noting that accommodation is substantially cheaper in the Tourangeau capital than in its chateau-enriched surroundings.

Two of the region's major rivers – four of which cross Touraine – flow through Tours on their course to the Atlantic. The River Loire is chased by the more southern Cher, which, in turn, is shadowed by the tranquil Indre – a tamer river whose waters mirror the pearly white facade of Château d'Azayle-Rideau before joining the River Loire near a nuclear power station a few kilometres downstream. The River Vienne drains southern Touraine, the tip of the vine leaf, which, since 1996, has been protected by the Parc Naturel Régional Loire-Anjou-Touraine.

Highlights

- Tour Tours, a lively university town with a fine cathedral, museums, St Martin's relics and a noble cuisine.
- Sniff, swill, sip and spit (or swallow) the crisp white wines of the Vouvray and Montlouis vineyards on the banks of the River Loire.
- Find your dream castle amid a cluster of architectural fairy tales: Chenonceau, Villandry, Azay-le-Rideau, Saché or Ussé.
- See Leonardo da Vinci's fabulous flying machines in Amboise.
- Discover tragic, fickle and passionate love in Château de Villandry's ornamental Renaissance gardens.

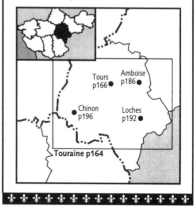

❦ ❦ ❦ ❦ ❦ ❦ ❦ ❦ ❦ ❦ ❦ ❦ ❦ ❦ ❦ ❦

Balzac, Descartes and Rabelais were born in Touraine, and the tomb of Leonardo da Vinci lies here. It was from the 15th-century court in Chinon that the future Charles VII sent a virginal warrior, Joan of Arc (Jeanne d'Arc), off to defeat the English, creating a major turning point in European history.

TOURS

postcode 37000 • pop 270,000

Lively Tours has the cosmopolitan and

bourgeois air of a miniature Paris, with wide 18th-century avenues, formal public gardens, cafe-lined boulevards and a thriving university, home to 30,000 students. There are also a number of worthwhile museums. Tours is one of the few towns in the Loire Valley with a nightlife that rocks, and the restaurants are among the region's best. The French spoken by its inhabitants is said to be the purest in all France.

With the exception of its wine, Tours' best-known product is the novelist Honoré de Balzac, a true Tourangeau, born and bred in the heart of the city in the 18th century. Food lovers should not miss the irresistible gourmet market (*marché gourmand*) which sees the finest regional food spill across place de la Résistance on the first Friday of each month.

Orientation

Thanks to the spirit of the 18th century, Tours is efficiently laid out. Its focal point is place Jean Jaurès, where the city's major thoroughfares – rue Nationale, blvd Heurteloup, ave de Grammont and blvd Béranger – meet. The train station is 300m east of place Jean Jaurès. The old city, known as Vieux Tours, is centred on place Plumereau, about 400m west of rue Nationale. The crooked streets around non-commercial rue du Petit St-Martin are loaded with artists' workshops. The northern boundary of the city is demarcated by the Rive Loire, which flows roughly parallel to the River Cher, 3km to the south. The suburbs of Joué-lès-Tours and Chambray-lès-Tours are immediately south of the Cher.

Maps Quality city maps available include IGN's *Plan de Ville de Tours et son Agglomération* (1:12,500, 29FF) and Blay-Foldex's *Tours et son Agglomération* (1:12,500, 30FF). Both include a comprehensive street index. The tourist office (see the following section) and the Maison de la Presse, at 5 rue de Bordeaux, sell maps, as does the unbeatable Géothèque *librairie du voyage* (see Bookshops under Information, next).

Information

Tourist Offices The spacious tourist office (☎ 02 47 70 37 37, fax 02 47 61 14 22, ✉ info@ligeris.com) is at 78–82 rue Bernard Palissy, across the street from the Centre International de Congrès Vinci. Local hotel reservations and bookings for organised chateaux tours are free. The tourist office has details of *son et lumière* (sound and light) shows, medieval re-enactments and other spectacular summer events performed in honour of these fabulous chateaux of Touraine. The Carte Multi-Visites (50FF), valid for a year, gets you into most of the city museums and two small chateaux. It also entitles you to a *visite guidée thématique* (guided theme tour) of the city. The tourist office opens 8.30 am to 7 pm Monday to Saturday, and 10 am to 12.30 pm and 2.30 to 5 pm on Sunday, May to October; and 9 am to 12.30 pm and 1.30 to 6 pm Monday to Saturday, and 10 am to 1 pm on Sunday, the rest of the year.

The Comité de Touraine de la Randonnée Pédestre (Touraine Ramblers Association; ☎ 02 47 70 37 35) has an information desk in the tourist office from 9 am to noon and 2 to 6 pm on Monday, Wednesday and Saturday. It organises two or three guided hikes a month and can help you map out your own hiking itinerary.

For tourist information on Indre-et-Loire, visit the Comité Départemental du Tourisme de Touraine (☎ 02 47 31 47 48, 02 47 31 42 52, fax 02 47 31 42 76, ✉ tourism .touraine@wanadoo.fr), 9 rue de Buffon. Check out the Web site at www.tourism-touraine.com.

Money Banque de France, 2 rue Chanoineau, has an exchange service through the door marked 'Bureaux', open 8.45 am to noon on weekdays. You can exchange money, cash American Express travellers cheques and wire money via Western Union at the central post office (see Post, next).

There are several banks around place Jean Jaurès, including Crédit Agricole (open Tuesday to Saturday), which has a 24-hour banknote-exchange machine, signposted 'Change 24h/24h', in the south-eastern corner of the square. On rue Nationale, Crédit Lyonnais is at No 75, and Banque National de Paris is opposite at No 86.

Post The central post office, 1 blvd Béranger, opens 8 am to 7 pm on weekdays, and 8 am to noon on Saturday. There is a branch office at 92 rue Colbert.

Email & Internet Access Tours sports a host of places with Internet hook-up, including the central post office. The Salle de Jeux Reseau PC, inside the Difintel-Micro computer shop at 4 ave de Grammont, charges 20FF per hour.

In the old town, Alli@nce Micro (☎ 02 47 05 49 50, ✉ alliance-micro@wanadoo .fr), 7ter rue de la Monnaie, off place Plumereau, charges 25FF per hour and opens 9 am to 8 pm Monday to Saturday, and 2 to 8 pm on Sunday. Web Contact (☎ 02 47 05 57 05, ✉ contact@centrale.net), 35 rue Néricault Destouches, opens 9 am to 8 pm Monday to Saturday, and its hourly rate is 20FF.

Night surfers should head to E-Café, on the 1st floor of L'Alexandra (open noon to 1 am); or to Le Cyberspace (☎ 02 47 66 29 96, ✉ cyberspace@creaweb.fr), 13 rue Lavoisier, which is an Internet pub offering Internet access for 1/20/30FF per minute/30 minutes/hour (open 2 pm to 5 am).

Cyber Micro Touraine (☎ 02 47 38 13 13, ✉ info@cmt.fr), 2 place de la Victoire, offers monthly passes only, allowing unlimited access (150FF per month).

Travel Agencies Voyages Wasteels (☎ 02 47 61 89 83), 8 place du Grand Marché, sells SNCF and Eurostar train tickets as well as plane tickets (open Monday to Saturday).

Bookshops La Boîte à Livres de l'Étranger (☎ 02 47 05 67 29), 2 rue du Commerce, offers an excellent selection of English-language fiction and nonfiction (open Monday afternoon to Saturday). An outstanding selection of maps, guides, globes

TOURAINE

TOURAINE

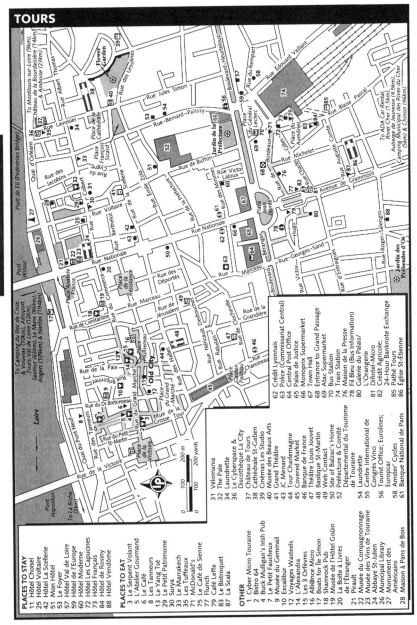

TOURS

PLACES TO STAY
11 Hôtel Choiseul
25 Hôtel Voltaire
42 Hôtel La Scellerie
51 Mon Hôtel
53 Le Foyer
57 Hôtel Val de Loire
59 Hôtel de l'Europe
60 Hôtel Moderne
72 Hôtel Les Capucines
73 Hôtel Français
84 Hôtel de Rosiny
88 Hôtel Vendôme

PLACES TO EAT
3 Le Serpent Volant
5 L'Atelier Gourmand
6 Le Café
8 Les Tanneurs
13 Le Yang Tsé
29 Le Petit Patrimoine
30 Surya
33 Le Marrakech
35 Les Tufféaux
71 McDonald's
75 Le Café de Sienne
77 Flunch
79 Café Leffe
83 Le Bistroquet
87 La Scala

OTHER
1 Cyber Micro Touraine
2 Bistro 64i
4 Buck Mulligan's Irish Pub
7 Le Petit Faucheux
9 Musée du Gemmail
10 Excalibur
12 Voyages Wasteels
14 L'Alexandra
15 Les 3 Orfèvres
16 Allî@nce Micro
18 Boats for Île Simon
20 Web Contact
19 Musée de l'Hôtel Goüin
20 La Boîte à Livres
   de l'Étranger
21 Pirault
22 Musée du Compagnonnage
23 Musée des Vins de Touraine
24 Abbaye St-Julien
26 Municipal Library
27 Monument des
   Américains
28 Maison à Pans de Bois
31 Vélomania
32 The Pale
34 Laundrette
36 Le Cyberspace &
   Discothèque La City
37 Château de Tours
38 Cathédrale St-Gatien
39 Cinémas Les Studio
40 Musée des Beaux Arts
41 Grand Théâtre
43 JC Menard
44 Tour Charlemagne
45 Covered Market
46 Banque de France
47 Théâtre Louis Jouvet
48 Basilique St-Martin
49 Web Contact
50 Site of Balzac's Home
52 Préfecture & Comité
   Départemental du Tourisme
   de Touraine
54 Laundrette
55 Centre International de
   Congrès Vinci
56 Tourist Office; Eurolines;
   Europcar Cycles
58 Amster Cycles
61 Banque National de Paris
62 Crédit Lyonnais
63 Police (Commissariat Central)
64 Central Post Office
65 Palais de Justice
66 Monoprix Supermarket
67 Town Hall
68 Entrance to Grand Passage
69 Atac Supermarket
70 Bus Station
74 Train Station
76 Maison de la Presse
78 Fil Bleu (Bus Information)
80 Galerie du Palais/
   L'Orangerie
81 Difintel-Micro
82 Crédit Agricole;
   24-Hour Banknote Exchange
85 Pathé Tours
86 Église St-Étienne

and travel accessories are sold in Géothèque (☎ 02 47 05 23 56), a travel bookshop at 6 rue Michelet.

Laundry The laundrette at 22 rue Bernard Palissy opens 7 am to 8 pm. The one at 149 rue Colbert opens till 7.45 pm.

Emergency The Police Nationale's Commissariat Central (☎ 02 47 60 70 69), 70–72 rue Marceau, opens 24 hours.

Place Plumereau

The old city, a neighbourhood of restored, half-timbered houses, is centred on place Plumereau, which has served as the area's main square since the Middle Ages. The wood and brick houses on the southern side of place Plumereau date from the 15th century.

Musée des Beaux Arts

The Musée des Beaux Arts (Fine Arts Museum; ☎ 02 47 05 68 73), housed in a 17th- and 18th-century archbishops' palace at 18 place François Sicard, has an excellent collection of paintings, furniture and objets d'art from the 14th to the 20th centuries. It is especially proud of two 15th-century altar paintings by Andrea Mantegna that were taken from Italy by Napoleon.

The museum opens 9 am to 12.45 pm and 2 to 6 pm Wednesday to Monday. Admission costs 30FF (children aged 13 to 18, seniors and students 15FF). The magnificent **cèdre du Liban** (cedar of Lebanon) tree in the courtyard was planted during Napoleon's reign (1804–15). Behind is a charming **flower garden**.

Cathédrale St-Gatien

Various parts of Tours' Gothic-style cathedral represent the 13th century (the choir), the 14th century (the transept), the 14th and 15th centuries (the nave) and the 15th and 16th centuries (the western facade). The domed tops of the two 70m-high **towers** (closed to the public) date from the Renaissance. There's a fine view of the **flying buttresses** from behind the cathedral.

Spectacular exterior aside, the interior is most renowned for its marvellous **stained-glass windows**, many of which date from the 13th to the 15th century. The most riveting are those inside the upper choir; these 15 windows were designed between 1255 and 1270 and illustrate the genealogy of Christ (with images such as the Tree of Jesse), the Passion and Resurrection. Other windows depict the lives of the apostles and saints, and one features the bishops of Tours and the canons of Loches. The 10 unique elements of each stained-glass window are explained in captions, written in five languages, inside the choir.

Volunteers at the tourist office give free guided tours on a daily basis (except Sunday); some speak English. Brochures in English are available for 1FF from a self-service table. The cathedral opens to visitors between 9 am and 7 pm (except during services); Sunday mass is celebrated in the cathedral at 10.30 am and 6.30 pm.

The Renaissance **Cloître de la Psalette** (☎ 02 47 47 05 19), dating from the 15th to 16th centuries, can also be visited (15FF, children aged under 12 free). It opens 8.30 am to 12.30 pm and 2 to 5 or 6 pm Monday to Saturday, and 2 to 5 or 6 pm on Sunday. You can get a glimpse of the cloister – including the **spiral staircase**, the extra buttresses for the northern transept and the remains of the city's **Roman walls** – through the wrought-iron fence to the right as you exit from the western facade of the cathedral.

Musée du Compagnonnage & Abbaye St-Julien

Tours' unique Musée du Compagnonnage (Guild Museum; ☎ 02 47 61 07 93), founded in 1910 at 8 rue Nationale, displays the crafts produced by the French chapter of the freemasons – skilful crafts still practised today, from stone sculpting to horseshoeing. The three associations of artisans that founded it have existed since at least the 16th century. The museum opens 9 am to noon (12.30 pm, mid-June to mid-September) and 2 to 6 pm Wednesday to Monday, year round. Admission costs 25FF (those aged 12 to 18, students and those aged over 65 15FF). If you intend to visit the neighbouring Musée des Vins de

TOURAINE

Touraine (see the following section), opt for a 30FF ticket that covers admission to both museums.

Towering across the cobbled courtyard from the museum is the Benedictine Abbaye St-Julien. The early Gothic abbey that is visible today was built between 1243 and 1259 on the site of an earlier abbey raised in 943 to shelter the relics of Sts Odon and Theodolon. The massive **porch**, 25m high, is the oldest surviving part of the church, dating from the 10th or 11th century. During the French Revolution, the abbey was sold and transformed into a stagecoach house, hence the wide opening in the wall to allow coaches in and out.

Musée des Vins de Touraine

The wine museum (☎ 02 47 61 07 93), 16 rue Nationale, occupies the vaulted, 13th-century wine cellars of Abbaye St-Julien. The museum does not give out wine samples, but it does have a roomful of displays on the significance of wine and the traditions associated with it. It opens 9 am to noon and 2 to 6 pm Wednesday to Monday. Admission costs 16FF (seniors, students and those aged 12 to 18 10FF). A ticket (30FF) which grants access to the Musée du Compagnonnage is also available (see the previous section).

Wine enthusiasts can try approaching the friendly (French-speaking only) staff at the **Maison des Vins de Touraine** (☎ 02 47 05 40 01, fax 02 47 66 57 32), tucked behind the museum at 19 square Prosper Mérimée. Access to the square is via the wrought-iron gate next to the museum entrance. Ask for the English-language booklet entitled *The Touristic Road through the Vineyards* which maps out four different driving routes through Touraine's vineyards. The Comité Interprofessionnel des Vins de Touraine et du Val de Loire also publishes explanatory leaflets in English on each of the nine Touraine appellations (see Wine in the Food & Wine of the Loire special section).

Musée du Gemmail

This museum (☎ 02 47 61 01 19), at 7 rue du Mûrier, specialises in *gemmail*, an artis-

tic medium that consists of superimposed pieces of coloured glass embedded in a colourless enamel and lit from behind. Gemmail was conceived in 1935, perfected in 1950 and popular in the 50s and 60s. The museum opens 10 am to noon and 2 to 6.30 pm Tuesday to Sunday, Easter to October. Admission costs 30FF (students 20FF, children 10FF).

Musée de l'Hôtel Goüin

This archaeological museum (☎ 02 47 66 22 32), 25 rue du Commerce, is housed in Hôtel Goüin, a splendid Renaissance residence built around 1510 for a wealthy merchant. Its Italian-style facade (all that was left after the conflagration of June 1940) is worth seeing, even if the eclectic collection of prehistoric, Gallo-Roman, medieval, Renaissance and 18th-century artefacts don't interest you. The museum opens 10 am to 7 pm daily, July and August; and 10 am to 12.30 pm and 2 to 6.30 pm daily, March to June and September and October. Admission costs 21FF (seniors 16FF, children 12FF).

Basilique St-Martin

Fans of late-19th-century ecclesiastical architecture should not miss this extravagant, pseudo-Byzantine church on rue Descartes, erected between 1886 and 1924. The crypt of the ornate basilica shelters the **tombeau de St-Martin** (St Martin's tomb). A soldier in the Roman army, St Martin converted to Christianity after meeting a beggar in Amiens (Picardy) who inspired him to slash his cloak in half with his sword and give half to the beggar. In 372 he became bishop of Tours. Following his death in Candes St-Martin (previously called Candes) in 397, Tourangeaux followers stole his corpse and rowed it down the River Loire back to Tours.

The first basilica was built on this site in 471. During the Wars of Religion it was badly damaged and its treasures plundered, including all the relics of St Martin, except a fragment of his arm bone and part of his skull. During the French Revolution the Basilique St-Martin was transformed into horse stables. **Tour Charlemagne**, one of the few remains of a 12th-century basilica that was torn down to make way for rue des Halles in 1802, is across the street from the northern end of the basilica.

The basilica usually opens 8 am to 7 pm daily; in winter it sometimes closes from noon to 2 pm. Throughout the month of November the remaining fragment of St Martin's skull is displayed above the high altar.

Château de Tours

The unimpressive buildings of Château de Tours, 25 quai d'Orléans, across the street from Pont de Fil, house an **Aquarium Tropical** (☎ 02 47 64 29 52). Admission costs 33FF (seniors and students 30FF, children aged under 12 18FF). It opens 9.30 am to noon and 2 to 6 pm (9.30 am to 7 pm in July and August) Monday to Saturday, and 2 to 6 pm on Sunday, April to mid-November; and 1 to 6 pm daily, the rest of the year.

Historial de Touraine (☎ 02 47 61 02 95), a wax museum in the same building, features 31 tableaux and 165 different characters. It opens 9 am to noon and 2 to 6 pm (6.30 pm with no lunchbreak, July and August) daily, April to October; and 2 to 5.30 pm daily, the rest of the year. Admission costs 35FF (students 24FF, children 20FF). The 3rd floor of the chateau houses changing art exhibitions (free admission).

Other Things to See

There is a beautiful example of a **maison à pans de bois** – timber-framed architecture with terracotta-tile inlays – at 7 place Foire de Roi (off rue Colbert); and a number of interesting Romanesque, Gothic, Renaissance and neoclassical houses along **rue Briçonnet** (at Nos 16, 21, 25, 29 and 31).

Rue Nationale, the main shopping street, which links place Jean Jaurès with the River Loire, was laid out in 1763. Balzac was born at No 45 (next to the present-day CGR Rex Cinema), although his original family home, along with the rest of the street, was destroyed during WWII. The River Loire is spanned by 18th-century **Pont Wilson** (1765–79), rebuilt after it collapsed in 1978 and aflutter with flags today. The best view of its underside is from aboard the traditional

wooden sailing boat which departs in summer from 11 am to 1 pm and 4 to 8.30 pm, Thursday to Monday, from the **embarcadère** (landing stage) on the quai 25m west of the bridge. The boat sails between the quai and **Île Simon**, a green isle in the middle of the River Loire, ideal for strolling and a picnic. A round trip costs 5FF. If there's no boatman in sight, ring the bell or wave wildly.

Some 500m upstream is the pedestrian **Pont de Fil** (1847). The 19th-century suspension bridge replaced a fortified stone bridge that was built in 1035 to link Château de Tours on the southern bank with the road to Paris on the northern bank. The last of its weary, flood-damaged arches was washed away in 1784.

Away from the city bustle the **Jardin des Prébendes d'Oè**, at the southern end of rue Nationale and its continuation, ave de Grammont, is a beautiful green park with an island, swans and plenty of cedar, sequoia and plane trees. During the Ancien Regime (Old Order), which is generally considered to apply to Louis XIV's reign between 1643 and 1715, it was a market garden whose revenue (*prébende*) went to the Provost of Oè.

River Trips

In summer, short river cruises depart from Rochecorbon, on the northern bank of the River Loire on the N152, 4km east of the city centre. Boats operated by Ligérienne de Navigation (☎ 02 47 52 68 88, @ georges .marchand@wanadoo.fr) depart at 3, 4, 5 and 6 pm daily in July and August. There's a boat at 4 pm on Wednesday, Sunday (also at 5 pm on Sunday) and daily during school holidays, April to June, September and October. The company has a Web site at www .chateau-croisiere.com. Trips cost 50FF (children aged under 12 35FF). There's also a family ticket (two adults and two children aged under 12) for 150FF. To get here from the centre of Tours, take Fil Bleu bus No 60 or 61 from the bus stop on place Anatol France to the Observatoire stop.

Language Courses

For details of the many language schools, see Courses in the Facts for the Visitor chapter.

euro currency converter 10FF = €1.52

TOURAINE

Organised Tours

Mid-April to mid-September, the tourist office runs two-hour walking tours (30FF) of the city, usually leaving at 10 am, at the weekend only, April to June and September, and daily, July and August. Narration is in French and, if requested, in English. From June to September there are thematic guided tours, also on foot, usually on Saturday and Sunday afternoons but also sometimes during the week. Themes include Balzac in Tours, Renaissance Tours, Antique Tours, Historic Gardens and an innovative Summer for Six- to 12-Year-Olds children's tour. For further details contact the tourist office.

For details about visiting chateaux by bus or minibus, see Organised Tours in the Getting Around chapter.

Special Events

Tours hosts a big street fair during the first weekend in May and a Foire à l'Ail et au Basilic (Garlic and Basil Fair) at the end of July. At the end of June, there's Les Fêtes Musicales en Touraine, a classical-music festival, while jazz concerts abound during Jazz en Touraine (☎ 02 47 50 72 70), a 10-day jazz festival in mid-September. October's Sonates d'Automne (Autumn Sonatas) is a festival for lovers of chamber music.

Places to Stay

Camping The closest camp site is three-star *Camping Municipal des Rives du Cher* (☎ 02 47 27 27 60, 63 rue de Rochpinard, St-Avertin), 5km south of Tours. It opens April to mid-October and charges around 14/14/8/8FF per tent/adult/child/car. To get there from place Jean Jaurès, take bus No 5 to the St-Avertin bus terminal, then follow the signs. About 10km north-east of Tours in Vouvray (see Around Tours later in this chapter), pool-equipped *Camping du Bec de Cisse* (☎ 02 47 52 68 81) is across the N152 and 200m down the hill from the tourist office. Open from mid-May to September, it charges 26FF for tent and car, plus 16/9/5FF per adult/child/animal.

Hostels About 500m north of the train station, *Le Foyer* (☎ 02 47 60 51 51, fax 02 47 20 75 20, 🖳 fjt.tours@wanadoo.fr, 16 rue Bernard Palissy) is a dormitory for workers of both sexes aged 16 to 25. In summer, if it has space, it accepts travellers of all ages. A single/double room costs 100/160FF and breakfast costs an additional 9FF; guests can also dine in its cheap, self-service canteen. Reception opens 9 am to 6 pm on weekdays, and 8.30 to 11 am on Saturday.

Tours' *auberge de jeunesse* (☎ 02 47 25 14 45) is 5km south of the train station (and 2km south of the River Cher) at ave d'Arsonval in Parc de Grandmont. A place in a four- or six-bed room costs 48FF; breakfast costs 19FF. Until 8.30 or 8.45 pm, you can take bus No 1 or 6 from place Jean Jaurès; between 9.20 pm and about midnight, take Bleu de Nuit line N1 (southbound). Advance reservations are essential given that the hostel gets full fast.

Chambre d'Hôtes Bookings for Gîtes de France B&B accommodation in and around Tours can be made through Accueil Rural en Touraine (☎ 02 47 27 56 10, fax 02 46 48 13 39), at 38 rue Augustin Fresnel in Chambray-lès-Tours.

Hotels – Train Station Area One-star *Hôtel Val de Loire* (☎ 02 47 05 37 86, 33 blvd Heurteloup) looks almost as it might have done when it was a turn-of-the-century bourgeois home, with hardwood floors, high ceilings and some of the gas lighting still in place. Basic singles/doubles with washbasin and bidet cost 100/150FF (130/180FF with shower, 200/250FF with bath and toilet). Hall showers/breakfast cost 15/25FF.

Mon Hôtel (☎ 02 47 05 67 53, 40 rue de la Préfecture), 500m north of the train station, can provide one-star singles/doubles for 100/115FF (170/200FF with shower and toilet). Showers cost 15FF. Another cheapie is the unremarkable *Hôtel de Rosiny* (☎ 02 47 05 23 54, fax 02 47 05 12 45, 12–19 rue Blaise Pascal), which offers singles/doubles starting at 110/160FF. Breakfast costs 28FF and it claims to offer discounted rates for stays of a week or more. One-star *Hôtel Les Capucines* (☎ 02 47 05 20 41, 6 rue Blaise

Pascal) has grim singles/doubles with basin and bidet for 100/140FF (130/160FF· with shower or bath; 150/180FF with toilet too).

Hôtel Français (☎ *02 47 05 59 12, 11 rue de Nantes)* provides an astonishingly cold welcome and is only worth frequenting for those who really need to penny-pinch: singles/doubles/triples/quads with washbasin and bidet are cheap at 120/140/150/170FF (140/160/170/180FF with shower or 155/190/220/250FF with shower and toilet). A hall shower/breakfast costs 10/28FF. Reception opens Monday to Sunday morning.

An excellent choice, a little away from the station but worth the hike, is cheerful **Hôtel Vendôme** (☎ *02 47 64 33 54, @ hotel vendome.tours@wanadoo.fr, 24 rue Roger Salengro)*, run by an exceptionally friendly couple. Simple but decent singles/doubles start at 140/160FF (150/185FF with shower and toilet). Warm, family-run **Hôtel Moderne** (☎ *02 47 05 32 81, fax 02 47 05 71 50, 1–3 rue Victor Laloux)* offers comfortable doubles with basin/shower/shower and toilet and high ceilings from 188/230/255FF. Breakfast costs 36FF.

To the right as you exit the train station, two-star **Hôtel de l'Europe** (☎ *02 47 05 42 07, fax 02 47 20 13 89, 12 place du Général Leclerc)* has high ceilings and strip-carpeted hallways that give it an early-20th-century ambience. The rooms, equipped with old-fashioned furnishings, cost upwards of 230/280FF for a single/double with shower and toilet. An extra bed/breakfast costs 40/32FF.

Hotels – Near the River A solid bet not far from the River Loire is **Hôtel Voltaire** (☎ *02 47 05 77 51, 13 rue Voltaire)*, which has basic but pleasant singles/doubles costing 120/135FF (150/175FF with shower). Shower- and toilet-equipped rooms for one/two/three/four people cost 170/195/230/250FF. All rooms have a small terrace, breakfast costs 25FF and garage parking is 30FF.

Hôtel La Scellerie (☎ *02 47 05 38 84, fax 02 47 05 38 99, 22 rue de la Scellerie)* is graced with two stars and sits in the heart of Tours' 'designer shop land'. It has good-value singles/doubles with basin and bidet

costing 165/180FF (220/245FF with shower and toilet). Breakfast and use of a private garage cost an extra 39FF each.

Two-star **Hôtel Choisel** (☎ *02 47 20 85 76, fax 02 47 05 74 87, 12 rue de la Rôtisserie)* sits snug in the heart of the old city on a pedestrian street. It has 17 rooms, starting at 180/210FF for a single/double with shower, toilet and TV – all charmingly maintained by the friendly Italian owner. Breakfast costs 29FF.

Places to Eat

In the old city, place Plumereau and nearby rue du Grand Marché and rue de la Rôtisserie are loaded with restaurants, cafes, creperies and boulangeries – most of which have lovely street terraces to watch the world go by. There's another cluster of cafes and restaurants along semi-pedestrianised rue Colbert.

Restaurants A small but sweet option that won't break the bank is **Le Petit Patrimoine** (☎ *02 47 66 05 81, 58 rue Colbert)*. Tempting 50FF and 70FF lunchtime *menus* (set menus) are served amid sun-flooded stone walls and a wood-beamed ceiling; don't miss the cheeseboard crammed with regional *chèvres* (goat's cheeses).

L'Atelier Gourmand (☎ *02 47 38 59 87, 37 rue des Cerisiers)*, in the heart of the artisans' quarter, boasts the city's most atmospheric (and romantic) courtyard terrace, and has a *plat du jour* (dish of the day; 49FF) on weekday lunchtimes, and a 100FF *menu*.

Near the train station, simple but attractive **Le Bistroquet** (☎ *02 47 05 12 76, 17 rue Blaise Pascal)* has *menus* of solid French food costing 44FF, 51FF and 62FF, but its speciality is paella.

Les Tuffeaux (☎ *02 47 47 19 89, 19–21 rue Lavoisier)* specialises in innovative *cuisine gastronomique* (gourmet food) made with fresh local products. *Menus* cost 110FF to 200FF (open Monday evening to Saturday evening). Next door at No 15, there's no wondering what **Le Temple des Moules** (☎ *02 47 66 60 83)* specialises in. Mussels soaked in a choice of 15 different sauces cost 56FF to 78FF per 1kg portion

euro currency converter 10FF = €1.52

TOURAINE

TOURAINE

(open Tuesday evening to Saturday evening except Thursday lunchtime).

Le Marrakech (☎ *02 47 66 64 65, 111 rue Colbert)* dishes up tasty Moroccan couscous and *tajines* (stews) for 65FF to 95FF a plateful (open Wednesday to Monday). For those who like it hot hot hot, spicy *Surya* (☎ *02 47 64 34 04, 65 rue Colbert)* serves a wholesome selection of North Indian dishes including curries, tandoori items and all sorts of rice biryani (closed Monday lunchtime). Its lunch/dinner *menu* runs for 59/85FF. *Rio Loco*, inside the Galerie du Palais/L'Orangerie shopping mall off ave de Grammont, is a cactus-clad, Tex-Mex joint. Count on paying around 60FF to 80FF per person, not including alcohol.

La Scala (☎ *02 47 20 81 91, 32 ave de Grammont)* serves the most authentic, thin-crust pizzas in town, cooked over a wood-fuelled fire. Pizzas cost from 35FF to 69FF and there's a lunchtime plat du jour for 48FF and a lunchtime *menu* for 69FF.

Cafes & Fast Food A highlight in the old city is *Le Serpent Volant (54 rue du Grand Marché)*, which, with its local clientele and simple decor, is the quintessential French cafe. A contemporary favourite, less imaginatively named but rather more funky, is *Le Café (39 rue du Dr Bretonneau)*.

Place Jean Jaurès and nearby sections of ave de Grammont sport countless eateries. *Café Leffe* (☎ *02 47 61 48 54, 15 place Jean Jaurès)*, named after a Belgian beer called Abbaye de Leffe, has brasserie meals, and *moules marinières* (mussels cooked with white wine and onions) and french fries for 49FF.

A lovely cafe, handily placed near the stations, is Italian-style *Le Café de Sienne*, a bar and *spaghettéria* whose wicker chairs spill out onto sun-drenched place du Aumônes. Expect to pay between 40FF and 140FF.

Hole-in-the-wall *Le Yang Tsé* (☎ *02 47 61 47 59, 83 bis rue du Commerce)* doles out Chinese main courses costing 30FF to 35FF, including rice (open Monday evening to Sunday evening, March to November).

Budget travellers can try sweet-talking their way into *Les Tanneurs*, the university resto-cum-cafe near the main university building on rue des Tanneurs. To dine you need a student ticket. There are some good *sandwich stalls* selling well-filled baguettes and pastries inside the Grand Passage shopping mall at 18 rue de Bordeaux.

Self-Catering Tours' large *covered market* is 500m west of rue Nationale on place Gaston Pailhou (opens 7 pm). East of rue Nationale, food shops abound along rue Colbert. A *marché gourmand* (gourmet market) fills place de la Résistance on the first Friday of the month from 4 to 10 pm.

In front of the train station, *Atac (5 place du Général Leclerc)* supermarket opens 8.30 am to 8 pm Monday to Saturday, and 9.30 am to 12.30 pm on Sunday. At 17 bis place Jean Jaurès (inside the Galerie du Palais/L'Orangerie shopping mall), *Champion* supermarket has a mouth-watering selection of prepared salads. Bakery-equipped *Monoprix (77 rue Nationale)* opens 7 am to 7.30 pm Monday to Saturday.

Entertainment
Pubs, Bars & Clubs In the old city, cafe nightlife is centred on place Plumereau. Nearby, *Les 3 Orfèvres* (☎ *02 47 64 02 73, 6 rue des Orfèvres)* has live music (rhythm and blues, blues, rock, soul, jazz and so on) from 11pm Tuesday or Wednesday to Saturday. Other old-city hot spots, ideal for those wanting to discover Tours' student scene, include tiny rue de la Longue Echelle and the southern strip of adjoining rue du Dr Bretonneau. *Buck Mulligan's Irish Pub (39 rue du Grand Marché)* has several beers on tap.

Live jazz venues favoured by students include *Le Petit Faucheux* (☎ *02 47 38 67 62, 23 rue des Cerisiers)*, an alternative cafe-theatre in the old city, and the brilliant *Bistro 64* (☎ *02 47 38 47 40, 64 rue du Grand Marché)*, which plays latin, blues and *musique Française* in a 16th-century interior (open Tuesday to Sunday).

L'Alexandra, on rue du Commerce, and *Shamrock Pub*, at 12 rue de Constantine (open 6 pm to 2 am), are two mainstream pubs. *The Pale (18 place Foire de Roi)* is another Irish-inspired bar. Among its many activities, it screens sports matches on its TV.

Central *Discothèque La City* (☎ 02 47 66 29 96, 13 rue Lavoisier) rocks from 11 pm to 5 am (open Thursday to Saturday). In the old city, *Excalibur* is opposite 36 rue Briçonnet.

Opera, Theatre & Music Opera and classical-music buffs should head for the majestic *Grand Théâtre* (☎ 02 47 60 20 20, rue de la Scellerie); the box office opens 10 am to 5.30 pm Monday to Saturday, and 10 am to 12.30 pm and 1.30 to 5.30 pm on Saturday. Contemporary plays and sketches take to the stage at *Théâtre Louis Jouvet* (☎ 02 47 64 50 50), 12 rue Léonard de Vinci.

The *Centre International de Congrès Vinci* (☎ 02 47 70 70 70, 26 blvd Béranger) is a popular venue for rock concerts. Tickets and programmes are available at the Vinci Spectacles ticket office (entrance on rue Bernard Palissy).

Cinemas Films in their original language (with subtitles in French) are screened at *Cinémas Les Studio* (☎ 02 47 64 42 61 for a recorded message, 08 36 68 20 15, 2 rue des Ursulines) and also at the eight-screen *Pathé Tours* (☎ 08 36 68 22 88, 4 place François), which is 50m from the train station.

Shopping

Stuffed prunes are a sweet speciality of Tours. Buy some at JC Menard (☎ 02 47 05 66 75), 6 rue de la Scellerie, or Pirault, at 31 rue Nationale, which has served as a *maison des pruneaux farcis* (stuffed-prune shop) since 1807; the latter also mints *la livre Tournaise* (the Tourangeau pound) from chocolate.

The strip of rue de la Scellerie east of the Grand Théâtre is lined with quality art and antique shops. An antique market is held on rue de Bordeaux on the first and third Friday of the month and on place de la Victoire every Wednesday and Saturday.

Mainstream chain stores fill Galerie Nationale, an indoor shopping mall at 72 rue Nationale.

Getting There & Away

Many chateaux can be reached from Tours by train or SNCF bus. These include Amboise, Azay-le-Rideau, Blois, Chenonceau, Chinon, Langeais, Saumur and, somewhat less conveniently, Villandry (to Savonnières). See the respective entries for details.

Air Aéroport de Tours-Val de Loire (☎ 02 47 49 37 00, fax 02 47 42 59 45, ✆ admin@ tours-aeroport.com) is 12km north of the city centre. See Air in the Getting There & Away chapter for flight details.

Bus The bus station (☎ 02 47 05 30 49) is opposite the train station on place du Général Leclerc. The information desk (☎ 02 47 05 30 49) opens 7.30 am to noon and 2 to 6.30 pm Monday to Saturday. Tickets are sold on board. From here, buses operated by Touraine Fil Vert (☎ 02 47 47 17 18) link Tours with numerous destinations all over the département of Indre-et-Loire, including Amboise (13FF, 45 minutes, 10 daily); Descartes (20FF, one hour, six daily); Château-Renault (13FF, one hour, two daily) via Rochecorbon (6.60FF, 15 minutes) and Vouvray (6.60FF, 20 minutes); and Richelieu (20FF, two hours, three daily) via Ste-Maure de Touraine (13FF, 55 minutes, five daily). Services are severely reduced on Sunday and public holidays; some do not operate at all. Fil Bleu (see Bus under Getting Around later in this Tours section) operates many more buses between Tours and Rochecorbon/Vouvray. SNCF buses run from the bus station to Loches (50 minutes).

In summer, you can make an all-day circuit by public bus to Chenonceaux and Amboise by taking CAT (Compagnies des Autocars de Touraine) bus No 10 for the hour-long ride to Chenonceaux (13FF) at around 10 am; catching the bus from Chenonceaux to Amboise (6.60FF, 35 minutes) at around noon (during July and August, there's another bus in the afternoon); then returning to Tours by bus (at around 5 or 6 pm; 13FF) or by train (see Getting There & Away under Amboise, later in this chapter). Buses arrive/depart from Tours bus station in front of Tours train station.

TOURAINE

Eurolines' ticket office (☎ 02 47 66 45 56), 76 rue Bernard Palissy, opens 9 am to noon and 1.30 to 6.30 pm Tuesday to Friday, 2 to 6 pm on Monday, and 9 am to noon and 1.30 to 5.30 pm on Saturday. See Continental Europe or The UK under Land in the Getting There & Away chapter for route information.

Train The train station (☎ 08 36 35 35 35), off blvd Heurteloup, overlooks place du Général Leclerc. The information office opens 8.30 am to 6.30 pm Monday to Saturday, except on public holidays. Tours is linked to St-Pierre des Corps – Tours' TGV train station – by shuttle trains. Information about trains to/from Paris is under Other Parts of France under Land in the Getting There & Away chapter.

Local trains run between Tours and Orléans at least hourly (88FF, 1¼ hours). Stops on this route include St-Pierre des Corps (eight minutes), Montlouis-sur-Loire (12 minutes), Amboise (28FF, 20 minutes) and Blois (51FF, 35 minutes). There are TGV and non-TGV services to Nantes (152FF, 1½ to two hours, four to eight daily) and five TGVs daily between St-Pierre des Corps and Vendôme (100FF, 15 minutes).

Southbound, there are two trains daily to/from Loches (44FF, 45 minutes), and from St-Pierre des Corps there are eight trains daily to/from Poitiers (116FF, 40 minutes). Westbound destinations include Saumur (56FF, 40 minutes, eight daily), and northbound there are four trains daily to/from Le Mans (103FF, one hour).

Car ADA Car Rental (☎ 02 47 64 94 94) is south of the centre at 49 blvd Thiers, 250m west of the huge Hôtel Altéa at place Thiers (the intersection of ave de Grammont and blvd Thiers). Take bus No 3 or 6 from the train station or bus No 1, 2, 3, 5 or 9 (southbound) from place Jean Jaurès to the Thiers stop. Europcar (☎ 02 47 64 47 76), 76 blvd Bernard Palissy, opens 8 am to noon and 2 to 6.30 pm (6 pm on Saturday) Monday to Saturday. Rent-Van & Car Ecoto (☎ 02 47 66 75 00), 8 rue Tribut, is a smaller company which offers competitive rates (from 200/500FF per day/weekend including 100/800km).

Getting Around
To/From the Airport Fil Bleu bus No 60 links place Anatole France in the centre of Tours with the Rostand bus stop, a two-minute walk from Aéroport Tours-Val de Loire. A single ticket costs 6.50FF and journey time is about 30 minutes.

Bus The bus network serving Tours and its suburbs is called Fil Bleu. Almost all the lines stop around the edge of place Jean Jaurès. Fil Bleu No 60 links place Jean Jaurès with Rochecorbon, and No 61 with Vouvray. Two Bleu de Nuit lines – N1 and N2 – operate every 55 minutes from about 9.30 pm until just after midnight. Tickets, which cost 6.50FF if bought singly, are valid for one hour after being time-stamped. A carnet of five/10 tickets costs 32/60FF and there's a 27FF one-day travel pass.

Fil Bleu has an information office (☎ 02 47 66 70 70) at 5 bis rue de la Dolve, 50m west of place Jean Jaurès. It opens 7.30 am to 7 pm on weekdays, and 9 am to 5.30 pm on Saturday.

Bicycle Amster' Cycles (☎ 02 47 61 22 23, fax 02 47 61 28 48), 5 rue du Rempart, rents road and mountain bikes for 80/125/330/450FF for 24 hours/two days/one week/two weeks. Tandems cost 160/260FF for one/two days. The friendly staff provide cyclists with a puncture-repair kit and map. Amster' Cycles opens 9 am to 7 pm Monday to Saturday, and 9 am to 12.30 pm and 5 to 7 pm on Sunday, May to September.

Vélomania (☎ 02 47 05 10 11, fax 02 47 05 79 77), 109 rue Colbert, charges 85/125/295/430FF per day/two days/one week/two weeks; it also has tandems. It opens 10 am to 1.30 pm and 3.30 to 7.30 pm Tuesday to Sunday (no lunchbreak on Saturday), and 3.30 to 7.30 pm on Monday.

AROUND TOURS
The industrial suburb of La Riche, 3km west of Tours, is crowned with two historic jewels, the 15th-century **Château de Plessis**, where Louis XI came to play (and die), and the elegant ruins of **Prieuré de St-Cosme**, an 11th-century priory where the Renaissance

poet Pierre de Ronsard sought inspiration (and a burial place). The chateau can no longer be visited but Prieuré de St-Cosme opens 9 am to 7 pm daily, June to mid-September; and 9.30 am to 12.30 pm and 2 to 5 pm daily, the rest of the year. Admission costs 24FF (students 17FF, those aged seven to 18 13FF).

Rochecorbon offers an exceptional (and exceptionally expensive) place to stay and eat, *Les Hautes Roches*, the Loire Valley's only cave hotel (see the boxed text 'Cave Dwellings'). In the Tourangeau suburb of St-Cyril-sur-Loire, also on the northern bank, fine French cuisine is created in the kitchen of top chef Jean Bardet, whose *hotel and restaurant* (☎ 02 47 41 41 11, fax 02 47 51 68 72, 57 rue Groison) lures two culinary stars and many a star. Once a week he opens his kitchen doors to other cooks keen to learn a trick or two (see Cookery under Courses in the Facts for the Visitor chapter).

Vouvray & Montlouis-sur-Loire

Vouvray (pop 2900), planted 10km upstream from Tours on the northern bank of the River Loire, is famed for its distinctive white wines, which are fruity in aroma and adopt tastes of honey when mature. Surrounded by 2000 hectares of vineyards, Vouvray – granted its own AOC (*appellation d'origine contrôlée*; certificate of quality) in 1936 – produces 100,000 hectolitres of wine a year, both still and sparkling. It celebrates a Foire aux Vins (Wine Fair) in Febuary and August.

On the opposite side of the river, wedged between the Rivers Loire and Cher, are the Montlouis vineyards, which cover 350 hectares. Like Vouvray, its white wines are made purely from the chenin grape variety, known locally as Pineau de la Loire, which thrives on this area's chalky, tufaceous subsoils and limestone top soils. See also the Food & Wine of the Loire special section.

Neither village is overly attractive, but both are home to countless *caves* (wine

TOURAINE

Cave Dwellings

Troglomania hits tourists head-on in Rochecorbon, a northern suburb of Tours riddled with troglodyte dwellings – Swiss-cheese-like caves hollowed in the chalky bluffs which dominate the riverbanks. In 1713 the marquise de Doisonville lived at the **Manoir des Basses-Rivières** (☎ 02 47 52 80 99), an 18th-century manor house partly hewn out of Rochecorbon's white tufa rock which can be visited 2 to 7 pm daily, July and August, and 2 to 7 pm at the weekend, April to June and September. Next on the agenda is an abandoned tufa quarry (rock from here was used to build many of the region's chateaux), sculpted inside with 34 wall murals to create **Les Caves Rupestres** (☎ 02 47 52 57 58) on rue Vaufoynard. It can be visited from 10.30 am to 7 pm daily, July and August, and 2 to 6 pm daily, April to June and September and October; the 35FF admission includes a glass of wine.

True vintages can be sampled in neighbouring Vouvray at the **Musée de la Vigne et du Viticulture** (☎ 02 47 52 60 77), a cave wine museum on the Château Moncontour estate which explains the entire wine production process; guided visits depart at 10 am and 3.30 pm daily (admission costs 20FF). Wines from the chateau's vineyards can be tasted and bought. See Bus under Getting Around in the Tours section for information on how to get to Rochecorbon and Vouvray.

Tastebuds can likewise be titillated 10km north in Valmer at **Château de Valmer** (☎ 02 47 52 93 12), a working chateau known for its Renaissance gardens, its 16th-century troglodyte chapel and its sparkling and still Vouvray whites. The 80-hectare park (35FF) opens 2 to 7 pm Tuesday to Sunday, July and August; and 2 to 7 pm at the weekend, May, June and September.

At the end of a hard day cave-seeing, **Les Hautes Roches** (☎ 02 47 52 81 30, fax 02 47 52 81 30, ✉ hautes-roches@wanadoo.fr, 86 quai de la Loire, Rochecorbon) offers the ultimate in cave culture. Dug by monks from Marmoutier as a safe haven during the Wars of Religion, these caves form a four-star hotel today. Doubles cost 520FF to 1080FF; bath tubs are of the enamel (rather than rock) variety.

euro currency converter 10FF = €1.52

cellars) where you can taste and buy AOC Vouvray and AOC Montlouis wines.

Information In Vouvray, there's a tourist office (☎ 02 47 52 68 73, fax 02 47 52 67 76) on the corner of route du Vignoble (N152) and ave Brulé (D46). It opens 9 am to 6 pm Monday to Saturday, and 9 am to 1 pm on Sunday, April to September; and 9 am to 1 pm Tuesday to Saturday, the rest of the year. The tourist office has bicycles to rent (70/300FF per day/week, plus 2500FF deposit) and stocks a handy brochure outlining 6km and 14km walking trails around Vouvray. The Maison du Vouvray (☎ 02 47 52 72 51), opposite the tourist office at 24 ave Brulé, is as good a place as any to kick off a wine-tasting spree. It opens 9.15 am to 12.30 pm (12.15 pm in winter) and 1.30 to 7 pm (6.45 pm in winter) Thursday to Tuesday.

In Montlouis-sur-Loire, the tourist office (☎ 02 47 45 00 16, fax 02 47 45 10 87), place de la Mairie, and the Maison de la Loire (☎ 02 47 50 97 52), 60 quai Albert Baillet, both stock information. The latter has flora and fauna exhibitions and opens 2 to 6 pm (admission costs 20FF).

Getting There & Away Fil Bleu's bus No 61 links Tours' place Jean Jaurès with Vouvray (6.5FF, 20 minutes, approximately every 40 minutes). Montlouis-sur-Loire, on the southern bank, is served by bus line C2 (13FF, 40 to 50 minutes, eight daily), which is operated by Fil Vert.

CHENONCEAUX
postcode 371501 • pop 300
The unstartling village of Chenonceaux – 34km east of Tours, 10km south-east of Amboise and 40km south-west of Blois – has one startling sight: Château de Chenonceau.

Orientation & Information
Chenonceaux village (spelt with an 'x') is neatly arranged either side of rue du Dr Bretonneau (D40), on the opposite side of the train tracks from the chateau. The chateau entrance is flagged by a caterpillar of coaches lined up in its car park, which is immediately in front of the train station, a 300m walk away.

The tourist office (☎ 02 47 23 94 45), 1 rue du Dr Bretonneau, opens 10 am to 1 pm and 2 to 7 pm Monday to Saturday, and 2 to 7 pm on Sunday.

Château de Chenonceau
With its stylised (rather than defensive) moat, drawbridge, towers and turrets, 16th-century Château de Chenonceau is everything a fairytale castle should be – from the outside. Its interior – crammed with period furniture, tourists, paintings, tourists, tapestries and tourists – is only of moderate interest.

However, Chenonceau's vast park, landscaped gardens and forests, covering an area of 70 hectares either side of the River Cher, afford stunning views of the chateau exterior and ensure sufficient space and calm for one to soak up the castle's unique heritage. Alongside the famed gardens of Diane de Poitiers and Catherine de Médicis, there's a quaint **16th-century farm** to explore; an **atelier des fleurs** (flower workshop) where you can buy Chenonceau-grown rose bushes, dried floral arrangements and other green-fingered things; a **cave** where you can sample and buy wine produced on the estate; a **moat** and river where you can row, row, row your boat in summer (20FF per hour); and a peaceful **orangeaie** (orange grove) where you can dine on a green lawn away from the madding crowds.

Château de Chenonceau was built by the passions of five remarkable women (see the boxed text 'Girl Power'). Diane de Poitiers, mistress of Henri II, planted the garden to the left (east) as you approach the chateau, first along an avenue of plane trees then down a gravel path lined with ornamental orange trees. After the death of Henri II in 1559, she was forced to give up her beloved Chenonceau by the vengeful Catherine de Médicis, Henri II's widow, who then applied her own formidable energies to the chateau and, among other works, laid out the garden to the right (west) as you approach the castle.

In the 18th century, Madame Dupin, the chateau's owner at the time, brought Jean

Smashing pumpkins at Château de Villandry

Lose yourself in the cobbled streets of Chinon.

Catherine de Medicis' gallery at Chenonceau

Stylish and calm Château d'Azay-le-Rideau

Ancient Amboise and a modern mobile by Calder

NICOLA WILLIAMS

The twin towers of Cathédrale St-Gatien, Tours

NICOLA WILLIAMS

Atlantes props up the majestic town hall, Tours.

DIANA MAYFIELD

'La vie en rose' in picturesque Loches

DIANA MAYFIELD

See da Vinci's flying machines in Le Clos Lucé.

DIANA MAYFIELD

The virgin warrior shows off her blade in Chinon

Girl Power

Nowhere is the power of the Renaissance woman more obvious than at Château de Chenonceau, an architectural and horticultural feat that arose purely from the efforts of five strong-willed women.

As royal mistress to Henri II, the beautiful and brilliant Diane de Poitiers (1499–1566) was showered with fabulous gifts by the king of France, who made her a duchess and – on the death of her cuckold husband in 1547 – gave her Château de Chenonceau. Thus, the riverside chateau was transformed into a palace fit for a king. A bridge was built across the River Cher and 12,000m sq of low-lying land were raised to create a royal garden; its decorative beds were planted with a manicured feast of white mulberry and banana trees, melons, artichokes, strawberries and violets. Today a merry band of 12 gardeners ensures that its vast lawn is cut 70 times a year and its beds potted out with 32,000 plants twice yearly.

Ironically, Diane de Poitiers failed to see her ambitious five-year landscaping project completed. In 1559 Henri II died, prompting his

JANE SMITH

Ambitious Diane de Poitiers, royal mistress and gardener extraordinaire

royal mistress to cede the chateau to her arch-rival, the queen: Catherine de Médicis (1519–89). Henri's widow had a ball at Chenonceau. Parties galore were thrown, most famously in 1577, when male guests came dressed as women and female guests as men, while many – beneath the glittering rocks and priceless gems – were half-naked. Catherine's secret weapon to further her ambitions was a group of beautiful, scantily clad women dubbed the Escadron (Flying Squad), who enlivened festivities at the chateau by jumping out from behind bushes and seducing her opponents. The Médicis era saw a gallery built atop Diane's bridge and a second ornamental garden laid out.

Louise de Lorraine (1553–1601) cast a grey cloud over Chenonceau. Her husband, Henri III, was assassinated the same year she inherited the chateau from Catherine de Médicis, prompting the bereaved queen to drape its interior in black while donning nothing but white – the royal colour of mourning – herself. With the death of 'la dame blanche' (the white lady), Château de Chenonceau passed into the hands of Louise's niece, Françoise de Lorraine, and thus out of royal hands.

The flamboyant Louise Dupin (1706–99), daughter of an actress, was the fourth femme fatale to leave her indelible mark on Château de Chenonceau. Her literary salons drew a crowd of elite figures who would rush through the Renaissance castle's exquisite grounds in an artistic frenzy, frantically jotting down the wildly romantic and elevated ideas its floral beds incited. Jean Jacques Rousseau's play Sylvie's Path was inspired by a riverside path that ran along the Cher here. Madame Dupin died at Chenonceau at the ripe old age of 93.

Under Marguerite Pelouze from 1864, a rigorous renovation project aimed at restoring Château de Chenonceau's 16th-century form was embarked upon. In 1888 Pelouze was declared bankrupt, paving the way for the first male proprietor – industrialist and chocolatier Henri Menier – to adopt Château de Chenonceau as his queen.

TOURAINE

Jacques Rousseau to Chenonceau as a tutor for her son. During the French Revolution, the affection with which the peasantry regarded Madame Dupin saved the chateau from the violent fate of many of its neighbours. Her monumental stone tomb, which sits aloft four lion paws, lies in the forested grounds of the chateau. It can be accessed via the unique 60m-long **gallery** which crosses the River Cher. This five-arched gallery was the creation of Catherine de Médicis and was used as a hospital during WWI. Between 1940 and 1942, the demarcation line between Vichy-ruled France and the German-occupied zone ran down the middle of the Cher: the castle itself was under direct German occupation, but the gallery's southern entrance was in the area controlled by Marshal Pétain. For many people trying to escape to the Vichy zone, this room served as a crossing point. Temporary art exhibitions are hosted here.

Other highlights include Catherine's lovely little **library** on the ground floor, with a coffered ceiling dating from 1525; the portrait of **Les Trois Grâces** (*The Three Graces*) by Van Loo which hangs next to the Renaissance chimney in François I's bedroom; and the **bedroom** where Louise de Lorraine (see the boxed text 'Girl Power') lived out her final days after the assassination of her husband, Henri III, in 1589. Macabre illustrations of bones, skulls, shovels and teardrops adorn the dark walls. The chateau's lively history is illustrated by 15 tableaux in the **Musée de Cires** (Wax Museum), housed in one of the outbuildings.

Chenonceau (☎ 02 47 23 90 07, ✉ chateau .de.chenonceau@wanadoo.fr) opens 9 am until some time between 4.30 pm (mid-November to January) and 7 pm (mid-March to mid-September) daily, year round. Admission to the chateau and its grounds costs 50FF (students and those aged seven to 18 40FF) and includes a self-guide brochure in a choice of 11 languages. Admission to the wax museum costs an additional 10FF. Bored or chateau-sick children can run wild in the **Jardin d'Enfants**, a stone garden equipped with swings, a slide and see-saw.

Places to Stay & Eat

A 50m walk from Chenonceaux train station, on the chateau side of the train tracks and signposted from the station, is *Camping La Fontaine des Prés*. It opens from Easter to September and charges 12/8FF per adult/child, plus 8/10FF per tent/tent and car.

Chenonceaux village boasts several oases of comfort and charm, dotted the length of rue du Dr Bretonneau. The cheapest is *Hostel du Roy* (☎ *02 47 23 90 17, fax 02 47 23 89 91)* at No 9. Singles/doubles with washbasin and bidet cost 130/150FF, and doubles/triples with shower and toilet are 220/260FF. Opposite at No 10 is three-star *Relais de Chenonceau* (☎ *02 47 23 98 11)*, which offers 24 rooms starting at 190/400/480/530FF for two/three/four/five people.

La Renaudière (☎ *02 47 23 90 04, fax 02 47 23 90 51)*, at No 24, is in the former home of Pierre-Fidèle Bretonneau (1778–1862), after whom the street is named. The stately residence has variously named rooms, ranging from Louis XI (210/250FF for one/two people) to François 1 (380/420FF). The hotel has a pool, gym, sauna and copious grounds for guests to explore. At No 7 is *La Roseraie* (☎ *02 47 23 90 09, fax 02 47 23 91 59)*, an ivy-clad inn with 16 rooms (280 to 480FF), a floral park, pool and succulent terrace restaurant. Book well in advance for both these hotels.

Luxurious pads fill the regal but snooty *Hôtel du Bon Laboureur et du Château* (☎ *02 47 23 90 02, fax 02 47 23 82 01, 6 rue du Dr Bretonneau)*. Rooms cost 320FF to 700FF and it has mountain bikes to rent (only to guests).

Getting There & Away

From Tours, there are plenty of bus tours to the chateau; see Organised Tours in the Getting Around chapter for details.

Chenonceaux train station is bang in front of the chateau, making train the easiest way of getting here from Tours. Between Tours and Chenonceaux there are two or three trains daily (32FF, 30 minutes). Less appealing are the handful of local trains serving the Tours–Vierzon line which stop at Chisseaux (33FF, 24 minutes, six daily), 2km east of Chenonceaux.

Year round, CAT bus No 10 leaves Tours for Chenonceaux (13FF one way, one hour) at 10 am; a bus back to Tours departs at 4.45 pm. Get off at the 'Chenonceaux – Le Château' stop, outside the tourist office on rue du Dr Bretonneau. There are no Sunday buses.

AZAY-LE-RIDEAU
postcode 371190 • pop 3050

The fate of the old Gallo-Roman settlement of Azay-le-Rideau has been inextricably linked to that of its chateau, ever since the first defensive edifice was raised here in the Middle Ages.

The bloodiest incident in Azay's history – a subject of invariable fascination for modern-day visitors – occurred in 1418 when the crown prince (later Charles VII) was insulted by a Burgundian guard during a visit to Azay's fortified castle. Enraged, the future king had the town burned to the ground and executed some 350 soldiers and officers. Rather horribly, the small town thus became known as Azay-le-Brûlé (*brûlé* means 'burned') for a brief period.

Azay-le-Rideau is 26km south-west of Tours on the banks of the River Indre, and served as a vital river crossing between Tours and Chinon in medieval times. With the exception of a few fragments of Église St-Symphorien, the present-day town and chateau date from the mid-16th century.

Orientation & Information

Azay-le-Rideau, on the northern bank of the River Indre, is 7km west of Saché. The quiet riverside roads running either side of the river (D84 and D17) are a delight to walk or cycle along.

The train station in Azay is on ave de la Gare (D57) at the far western end of the village; the village centre and chateau are a good 2km stroll eastwards along ave de la Gare and its continuation, ave Adélaïde Riché. Azay-le-Rideau tourist office (☎ 02 47 45 44 40, fax 02 47 45 31 46, ✉ otsi.azay .le.rideau@wanadoo.fr), place de l'Europe, has information and accommodation lists

for Azay and Saché (see Château de Saché, later in this Azay-le-Rideau section). The office opens 9 am to 1 pm and 2 to 7 pm daily, March to October; and 2 to 6 pm Tuesday to Saturday, the rest of the year.

Château d'Azay-le-Rideau

This chateau (1518–23), built on an island in the River Indre and surrounded by a quiet pool and park, is harmonious and elegant. The best time to visit is on a sunny day when the reflection of its pearly white facade – adorned with stylised fortifications and turrets intended both as decoration and to indicate the rank of the owners – shimmers like a mirage in the surrounding lily-pricked waters. Inside, the seven rooms open to the public are, beyond a few 16th-century Flemish tapestries, disappointing.

The present chateau was begun by Giles Berthelot, one of François I's less-than-selfless financiers, exactly a century after Charles VII's burning escapade. When the prospect of being audited and hanged drew near, Berthelot fled abroad and never completed the structure. The finishing touches weren't put on until the 19th century. It remains the only state-owned chateau in Touraine today.

The chateau (☎ 02 47 45 42 04) opens 9.30 am to 6 pm daily, April to June and September; 9 am to 7 pm daily, July and August; and 9.30 am to 12.30 pm and 2 to 5.30 pm daily, October to March. Admission costs 35FF (those aged 18 to 25 23FF, those aged under 18 free). You can either walk around on your own, guided by the sketchy and confusing brochure, with the aid of an audiocassette which you can hire, or join a 1½-hour tour in French at no extra cost.

Between mid-May and mid-September, the chateau hosts *Les Imaginaires (The Make-Believe)* a **son et lumière** show starting at 10.30 pm between May and July, 10 pm in August, and 9.30 pm in September. There is no stage and guests are free to wander around the illuminated chateau and grounds. Admission costs 60FF (those aged 12 to 25 35FF). If you intend to visit the chateau during the day, buy a combination ticket covering chateau and show for 80FF (those aged 18 to 25 50FF, those aged 12 to 18 35FF). In both cases, children aged under 12 are free.

Château de Saché

The most famous guest at Château de Saché, 7km east of Azay-le-Rideau in Saché, was Honoré de Balzac, who stayed here several times between 1829 and 1837 when a close friend of his owned it (see the boxed text 'Balzac in Touraine'). The study where Balzac worked in the 16th-century chateau is furnished exactly as it was when he was there.

The chateau (☎ 02 47 26 86 50) opens 9.30 am to noon and 2 to 6 pm daily, February to November (to 5 pm in low season and no lunchbreak in July and August). Admission costs 23FF. Combination tickets to other attractions are available.

More recently, Saché village served as home to American sculptor Alexander Calder (1898–1976); one of his mobiles decorates place de la Saché.

Places to Stay & Eat

In Azay-le-Rideau, *Camping Le Sabot* (☎ 02 47 45 42 74, fax 02 47 45 49 11) opens from Easter to October and charges 49/53FF for a tent pitch, car and one or two people in the low/high season; reception opens 8 am to 9 pm.

Bar Les Sports, at 5 rue Carnot, has rooms to let above the bar costing 100FF. A mere 50m walk from Château d'Azay-le-Rideau, on a quiet pedestrian street, is busy *Hôtel de Biencourt (☎ 02 47 45 20 75, fax 02 47 45 91 73, 7 rue de Balzac).* It offers doubles with shower costing 210FF, or 270FF with shower and toilet. Triples/quads with private

Balzac in Touraine

Allusions to Touraine in Balzac's works are abundant. Château de Moncontour in Vouvray is said to have been the inspiration for the fictional Château de Vonne in *Le lys dans la vallée (The Lily in the Valley*; 1835), while Balzac's homeland is the backdrop for tales such as *La femme de trente ans (The 30-Year-Old Woman), Les deux amis (The Two Friends)* and *Le curé de Tours (The Priest of Tours),* all written in the 1830s. Saumur serves as the setting for *Eugénie Gradet (1833)* and is described by Balzac as a country town whose far-from-revolutionary-minded inhabitants spend 10 hours out of 12 spying on, and gossiping about, each other.

Château de Saché was home to Jeanne de Margonne, the reputed lover of Balzac's mother, a Parisian who was married off at the age of 19 to Balzac's father, a 51-year-old Tourangeau who changed his name from Balssa to Balzac then added a 'de'. An impoverished and eccentric Balzac retreated often to Saché, where he had his own study, writing part of *Le père Goriot (Old Goriot*; 1834) and much of *Le lys dans la vallée* here.

The authoritarian rule of the Oratorian college in Vendôme, where the realist novelist was schooled between 1807 and 1814, is evoked in Balzac's semi-autobiographical *Louis Lambert.* After leaving the school, Balzac went on to work as a law clerk then a writer in Paris, producing several unsuccessful novels under pseudonyms such as Lord R'Hoone. A failed attempt as a printer prompted him to retrieve his quill and write his first published work, *Les Chouans (1829),* under his own name. It was set in Brittany during the 1789 Revolution, and Chouans was the name given to royalist rebels. *La comédie humaine (Human Comedy)* followed, a collection of 91 books featuring more than 2000 fictional characters.

Balzac's works – a realist portrayal of French society in the late 18th and early 19th centuries – were banned in Italy in 1841 by the Catholic Church on religious grounds, in Russia in 1850, and *Les contes drolatiques (Droll Stories)* was banned in Canada in 1914. This work was also banned by customs in New York, USA, in 1914 on the grounds that it was tantamount to mailing obscene literature. This was followed in 1953 by Franco's purge of Balzac works in Spain. All bans have since been lifted.

bathroom cost 380/370FF. *L'Aigle d'Or* (☎ 02 47 45 24 58, 10 ave Adélaïde Riché) has an inspiring, flower-filled garden in which it serves 105/155FF lunchtime/evening *menus*.

In Saché, one-star *Auberge du XII Siècle* (☎ 02 47 26 88 77), opposite the chateau, is *the* place to eat. Rustic in decor and rich in culinary delights, this 17th-century inn makes an ideal pit stop. *Menus* dreamed up by Bourland (an acclaimed chef) start at 150FF.

About 22km upstream on the outskirts of Montbazon is *Château d'Artigny* (☎ 02 47 34 30 30, fax 02 47 34 30 39, *✆* artigny@wanadoo.fr), a multi-starred hotel in an 18th-century chateau built for the perfumer Coty. Between October and March it hosts musical evenings on Saturday (concert and cocktail costs 180FF) and it offers weekend breaks. Doubles start at 670/890FF in the low/high season. The chateau rents bicycles on which to roam its 25-hectare estate.

Getting There & Away

Château d'Azay-le-Rideau features on most tour itineraries from Tours; see Organised Tours in the Getting Around chapter. Azay-le-Rideau is on SNCF's Tours–Chinon train line (four or five daily Monday to Saturday, one on Sunday). From Tours, the 30-minute trip (50 minutes by SNCF bus) costs 27FF; the station is 2.5km from the chateau. The last train/bus to Tours leaves Azay at 6.35 pm (8 pm on Sunday).

CHÂTEAU DE VILLANDRY

Château de Villandry is famed for its formal Renaissance-style gardens, laid out on three levels. The last of the Loire chateaux to be built during the Renaissance, it was the creation of François I's finance minister, Jean le Breton, who studied the art of the Italian Renaissance garden while serving as ambassador to Italy. Le Breton also oversaw the construction of Chambord for François I.

Designed to create the impression of being an extension of the chateau interior, **Jardin d'Ornement** (Ornamental Garden) comprises intricate, geometrically pruned hedges and flowerbeds loaded with romantic symbolism so abstract that you can happily tour the entire garden without comprehending its true meaning (even with the aid of the free English-language brochure and map available at the entrance). 'Tender', 'tragic', 'passionate' and 'fickle' love are all there to find amid the manicured hedges, yew trees and rose bushes of this middle-tier garden.

Above the Jardin d'Ornement, on the top tier, is the Classical **Jardin d'Eau** (Water Garden), designed around a swan-filled lake shaped like a Louis XV mirror. The lowest tier, between the chateau and the nearby village church, is filled with neatly arranged rows of cabbages, pumpkins and vegetables of various colours that are used to form nine squares. The resultant **Potager** (Kitchen Garden) is a cross between the vegetable plots in which medieval monks grew their food and the formal gardens so beloved in 16th-century France. Between the Potager and the church there's a medieval **Jardin des Simples** (Herb Garden or Garden of the Common People) filled with herbs and medicinal plants. Children can run riot in the **Jardins des Enfants** (Children's Playground) or get lost in the **Labyrinthe de Charmille**, a box-hedge maze.

Villandry's gardens were actually destroyed in the 19th century to make way for an English-style park. It was not until 1906, after Spanish-born Nobel Prize winner Joachim Carvallo bought the chateau, that the original Renaissance landscaping was restored.

The chateau itself was completed in 1536. The classical outbuildings and the sparsely furnished interior date from the 18th century, when the chateau was passed into the hands of the marquis de Castellane from Provence. The hallways adorned with mediocre paintings can easily be skipped, though the 13th-century Moorish **mosque ceiling**, which was brought from Spain, is of moderate interest. The view from the tower – from which the intricate gardens can be seen in their entirety, as can the Rivers Loire and Cher – is only slightly better than the magnificent one that can be

TOURAINE

had for no extra cost from the terraced hill east of the chateau.

Villandry's gardens open 9 am to dusk (last tickets sold at 7 or 7.30 pm in summer). The chateau (☎ 02 47 50 02 09) itself – which, unlike the gardens, opens only from mid-February to mid-November – can be visited from 9 or 9.30 am to some time between 5 and 6.30 pm daily. Admission to the gardens costs 33FF (those aged eight to 18 and students 22FF), and a combination ticket for the gardens and chateau costs 45FF (those aged eight to 18 and students 32FF). Guided tours of the chateau interior (one hour 10 minutes) are in French only.

Several festivals are held here, such as Nuits des Mille Feux (Nights of a Thousand Fires) in July, Festival de Musique Baroque in August, and Journées du Potager (Days of the Kitchen Garden) in September (see the boxed text 'Feasts & Festivals' in the Facts for the Visitor chapter for details).

Getting There & Away

Château de Villandry is in Villandry, 17km south-west of Tours and 31km north-east of Chinon. By road, the shortest route from Tours is on the D7, but cyclists will find less traffic on the D88 (which runs along the southern bank of the River Loire) and the D288 (which links the D88 with Savonnières). If heading south-westwards from Villandry towards Langeais, the best bike route is the D16, which has no verges but has light traffic.

Villandry is included on most tour circuits; see Organised Tours in the Getting Around chapter for details. By public transport the only way between Tours and Villandry is by train to Savonnières (17FF, 10 minutes, two or three daily), about 4km east of Villandry. The first train from Tours is at 12.28 pm (at noon on Sunday and public holidays); the last train back to Tours is at 1.39 pm (5.30 pm on Saturday). It may be possible to take your bicycle with you.

LANGEAIS

postcode 37130 • pop 4000

Flowery Langeais, 10km north of Azay-le-Rideau and 24km south-west of Tours on the northern bank of the River Loire, is filled by the formidable Château de Langeais, a must for anyone into tapestries.

Information

The tourist office (☎ 02 47 96 58 22, fax 02 47 96 83 41), near the chateau on place du 14 Juillet, has information on wine cellars and walks. It opens 9.15 am to 12.45 pm and 2.30 to 6 pm (7 pm, late June to mid-September) Monday to Saturday, and 10 am to 12.30 pm on Sunday (also Sunday afternoon, July and August), Easter to mid-October; and 3 to 6 pm Monday to Saturday, the rest of the year.

Château de Langeais

Built in the late 1460s to cut the most likely invasion route from Brittany, Château de Langeais presents two faces to the world. From the town you see a 15th-century fortified castle – a prime example of medieval military architecture, with its nearly windowless, machicolated ramparts rising forbiddingly from the drawbridge. The sections facing the courtyard, however, are fitted with the large windows, dormers and decorative stonework characteristic of later chateaux designed for more refined living. The ruined **Donjon de Foulques Nerra** (Black Falcon Keep) across the garden from the courtyard dates from around 944 and is the oldest such structure in France.

Of the Loire chateaux, Langeais has the most interesting interior after that of Cheverny. The unmodernised configuration of the rooms and the **period furnishings** (chests, beds, stools, tables and chairs) give you a pretty good idea of what the place looked like during the 15th and 16th centuries. The walls are decorated with fine but somewhat faded Flemish and Aubusson **tapestries**, many of which are in the *millefleurs* (thousand flowers) style; the carpeted walls of the **Salon des Fleurs** illustrate beautifully this particular technique. In the chapel, there's an ornately carved, 13th-century reliquary featuring the wise and foolish virgins from the biblical parable of the 10 virgins.

The most memorable moment in the chateau's history was the marriage of Charles

VIII to Duchess Anne de Bretagne, which took place in the now aptly named **Salle de Marriage** on 6 December 1491. Wax figures in period costume re-enact this event, which brought about the final union of France and Brittany and ironically put an end to the chateau's strategic importance. The 15-year-old bride – who pledged to marry any subsequent king of France on Charles VIII's death (he died seven years later) – wore gold embroidered brocade lined with 160 sable furs as part of her bridal outfit.

Château de Langeais (☎ 02 47 96 72 60), owned by the Institut de France since 1904, opens 9 am to 6.30 pm (9 pm, mid-July to August) daily, April to September; 9 am to 12.30 pm and 2 to 6.30 pm, October; and 9 am to noon and 2 to 5 pm daily, the rest of the year. Admission costs 40FF (those aged over 60, students and children 35FF). Free guided tours are in French, but there are explanatory signs in English and other languages.

Places to Stay & Eat

The tourist office has a comprehensive list of places to stay and eat. Highlights include the fabulous *Château de Cinq Mars* (☎ 02 47 96 40 49, fax 02 47 96 36 60, **✉** chateau-cinq-mars@wanadoo.fr), 5km to the west of Langeais in Cinq Mars-la-Pile. The 15th-century chateau offers three doubles costing 440FF, including breakfast. Equally appealing is *Le Vieux Château* (☎ 02 47 24 95 13, fax 02 47 24 68 67), in Hommes, 15km north of Langeais. The medieval castle has doubles/suites costing 495/550FF, including breakfast.

Getting There & Away

Langeais train station (☎ 02 47 96 82 19), 400m from the chateau, is on the Tours–Savonnières–Saumur line. The trip from Tours (27FF, three to six daily) takes 15 to 25 minutes. The last train back to Tours is at 6.37 pm (5.30 pm on Saturday, 7.15 or 8.20 pm on Sunday and public holidays). Tickets cost 14FF to Savonnières (4km from Villandry) and 39FF to Saumur (25 minutes).

SMALLER CHATEAUX

The riverbanks around Tours are dotted with small privately owned chateaux, many of which can be easily combined in a day trip with one of their grander counterparts.

Château de Luynes

Château de Luynes (☎ 02 47 55 67 55) was built on the site of a former Roman citadel, 3km east of Langeais and 7km west of Tours on the northern bank of the River Loire. Despite being heavily restored in the 16th and 17th centuries, the stone fortress has maintained its medieval feudal shape, complete with thickset cylindrical towers. The best view of the chateau is from the other side of the river. Still inhabited, its richly furnished interior can be visited as part of a guided tour (in English and French); tours leave on the hour between 10 am and 5 pm daily, April to September. The tour costs 45FF (students 25FF, those aged seven to 15 20FF).

Château de Champchevrier

Depending on the day, animal lovers will adore or detest Château de Champchevrier (☎ 02 47 24 93 93), 17km north-east of Langeais and 1km north of Cléré-les-Pins. It is one of the few chateaux to still have kennels full of barking hounds, which, twice a week, hunt deer in the forest. The 70 dogs are fed a meal of poultry giblets (supplied by local slaughterhouses) once a day. On Tuesday and Thursday, visitors have the pleasure of watching during the **soupe des chiens** (dog-feeding time) at 5.30 pm. Various dead animals are displayed in the hunting gallery, including the stuffed head of one of the last wolves to be hunted in the region in 1870. When Louis XIII came to stay in 1619, he allegedly traded in his fine silk mattress for a Turkish carpet in the hay loft.

Château de Champchevrier opens 11 am to 6 pm daily, July to September; and 11 am to 6 pm at the weekend, May and June. Its interior can only be visited on a guided tour (40FF, 45 minutes) but visitors are free to wander in the grounds (25FF).

euro currency converter 10FF = €1.52

Château de Planchoury

Downstream, past Langeais, is the unstartling Château de Planchoury, 3.5km west of Langeais. Among the 50 or so models on display in the chateau's **Musée Cadillac** (☎ 02 47 96 81 52) is the 1933 V16 town car that belonged to Marlene Dietrich. The cadillac museum is in a building adjoining the chateau and opens 10 am to 6 pm daily, April to September. Admission costs 39FF (children 22FF).

Château d'Ussé

This turreted cake on the northern edge of the Forêt de Chinon has been owned by the marquis de Blacas since the 19th century. Less formal and more 'lived in' than most Loire chateaux, Château d'Ussé is a treasure to explore. While staying here in the 17th century, writer Charles Perrault was inspired to write the fairy tale *La belle au bois dormant* (*Sleeping Beauty*).

Architecturally, Ussé is split into three: the 15th-century wing where guided tours of the interior start, the Renaissance gallery which was later transformed into living quarters, and the pavilion built in 1690. Interior highlights include the unusual 17th-century trompe l'oeil ceiling of imitated marble in the **Salles des Gardes** (Guardroom); the **Cuisine** (Kitchen), where visitors can peer down a tunnel that provided the former inhabitants with a secret escape route to the Forêt de Chinon; the **Chambre du Roi**, lavishly prepared for the king of France should he drop by; and the **Grande Galerie**, the walls of which are hung with 18th-century Flemish tapestries.

A climb to the top of the **Tour de la Belle au Bois Dormant** (Sleeping Beauty's Tower) for a panorama of the Loire and Indre Valleys completes the tour. Note the sculpted stone medallions above the doorway to the **chapel** (1528), hidden behind the Lebanese cedar tree (1808) in the grounds.

Château d'Ussé (☎ 02 47 95 54 05) opens 9 am to noon and 2 to 5.30 or 6.45 pm (no break in July and August) daily, year round. Admission costs 59FF (those aged eight to 16 19FF).

Château de la Bourdaisière

This fanciful chateau has a history of passion, intrigue and tomato cultivation. The dry moats are all that remain of the original 14th-century structure. The present-day chateau dates from the 16th century, when François I, a frequent visitor, destroyed the medieval fortress and had it rebuilt in an Italianate Renaissance style. Having done this, he gave Château de la Bourdaisière to his favourite mistress, Marie Gaudin (he allegedly had 27 in all). Gaudin's great grandchild, Gabrielle d'Estrées, born at La Bourdaisière, became the legendary mistress of Henri IV. She died while pregnant with her fourth blue-blooded child; the famous School of Fontainebleau nipplepinching portrait of the mistress and her sister (displayed in the Louvre in Paris) features Estrées a few months before her death.

In the 18th century Château de la Bourdaisière fell into the hands of Louis XV's prime minister, the duke of Choiseul, who already owned Château de Chanteloup (see Pagode de Chanteloup under Around Amboise later in this chapter). Preferring the latter, the duke used boulders from La Bourdaisière to extend Chanteloup.

A retirement home until the mid-1960s, the chateau is a *chambre d'hôte* (B&B; see Places to Stay & Eat, next) and the private residence of the Broglie family, who, among other things, have restored the original 19th-century **potager** (vegetable garden). It is famed for the 450 tomato varieties cultivated here, many of which are pickled and on display in one of the stables. Tomato jam and liqueur are sold at the chateau, which celebrates an annual Festival de la Tomate in July and August.

The chateau opens 10 am to noon and 2 to 6 or 7 pm daily, April to October (no lunchbreak, June to September). Admission costs 32FF (students 27FF) and includes a guided tour in French (ask for an information sheet in English). Admission to the grounds and potager costs 25FF.

Places to Stay & Eat

At the foot of Luynes on the N152, *Camping Les Granges* (☎ 02 47 55 60 85) opens mid-May to mid-September and charges 65FF per night for two or three people with tent and car. It also has self-catering bungalows to rent for 200/250FF per night in low/high season. Another option is *Camping Municipal de Savonnières* (☎ 02 47 50 15 71, *route du Bray, Savonnières*). It opens Easter to October and charges 30/50/83FF for one/two/four people, including tent and car.

Four kilometres north-west of Luynes is *Domaine de Beauvois* (☎ 02 47 55 50 11, fax 02 47 55 59 62, @ *beauvois@wanadoo.fr*), a 140-hectare estate with a 15th-century manor house and doubles costing upwards of 590/790FF in the low/high season. The estate has a pool, tennis court, helicopter pad, plenty of forest, a huge lake and hiking trails – ask for the free *Promenades* (*Walks*) brochure at reception. Guests can borrow a bicycle to explore the extensive grounds; the restaurant prepares picnic hampers (80FF).

Château de la Bourdaisière (☎ 02 47 45 16 31, fax 02 47 45 09 11, @ *labourd@club-internet.fr*), 10km east of Tours near Montlouis-sur-Loire, has 14 rooms fit for a king costing between 650FF and 1100FF, including breakfast. Some cheaper rooms are housed in the adjoining pavilion.

Getting There & Away

See Organised Tours in the Getting Around chapter for details of tours around these chateaux. Château de la Bourdaisière is easily accessible by public bus or bicycle from Tours.

AMBOISE

postcode 37400 • pop 11,000

The picturesque town of Amboise, nestling under its fortified chateau on the southern bank of the River Loire, reached its peak during the decades around 1500, when the luxury-loving Charles VIII enlarged it and François I held raucous parties here. These days, the town makes the most of its association with Leonardo da Vinci, who lived his last years here under the patronage of François I.

Amboise is protected from the River Loire by a dike, whose flower-covered heights are a fine place for a riverside promenade. Some of the best views of town are from Pont Général Leclerc; alternatively, stroll along the narrow footpath which meanders along the riverbank on Île d'Or.

Tours, 23km downstream, and Blois, 34km upstream, are easy day trips from here. Amboise is also a good base for visiting the Loire's grandiose chateaux east of Tours (see the Orléanais & Blésois chapter).

Orientation

Amboise train station is across the river from the centre of town. It is about 800m from the station (follow the signs to 'Centre Ville') to the chateau. Le Clos Lucé, once home to Leonardo da Vinci, is 500m south-east of the chateau entrance along rue Victor Hugo. En route you pass several troglodyte dwellings.

Place Michel Debré – effectively an extension of rue Victor Hugo and sometimes called place du Château – stretches westwards from the northern end of rue de la Tour to the pedestrian rue Nationale, Amboise's main commercial and most touristy street.

Maps The tourist office doles out free plans of the city. Maps of all sorts are sold at the well-stocked Maison de la Presse, 24 rue Nationale.

Information

Tourist Offices The tourist office, Accueil d'Amboise (☎ 02 47 57 09 28, fax 02 47 57 14 35, @ tourisme.amboise@wanadoo.fr), in a pavilion opposite 7 quai du Général de Gaulle, has a free English-language map and brochure for walking around Amboise. Local hotel reservations cost 5FF per phone call. Ask here for hiking and cycling maps of the Amboise area, including the strenuous 65km *Circuit des Trois Châteaux: Amboise, Chenonceau et Chaumont*. The office opens 9 am to 12.30 pm and 2 to 6.30 pm Monday to Saturday, November to Easter; plus 10 am to noon on Sunday, the rest of the year. Information is also available on the office's Web site at www.amboise-valdeloire.com.

TOURAINE

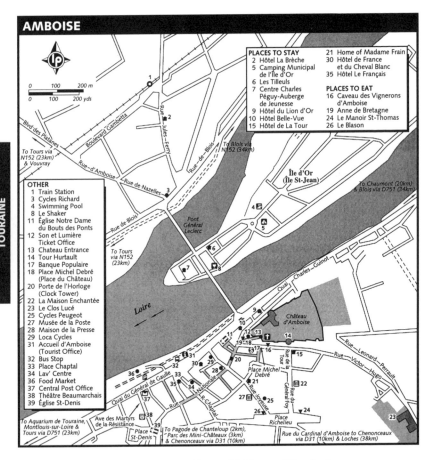

AMBOISE

PLACES TO STAY
2 Hôtel La Brèche
5 Camping Municipal de l'Île d'Or
6 Les Tilleuls
7 Centre Charles Péguy-Auberge de Jeunesse
9 Hôtel du Lion d'Or
10 Hôtel Belle-Vue
15 Hôtel de La Tour
21 Home of Madame Frain
30 Hôtel de France et du Cheval Blanc
35 Hôtel Le Français

PLACES TO EAT
16 Caveau des Vignerons d'Amboise
19 Anne de Bretagne
24 Le Manoir St-Thomas
26 Le Blason

OTHER
1 Train Station
3 Cycles Richard
4 Swimming Pool
8 Le Shaker
11 Église Notre Dame du Bouts des Ponts
12 Son et Lumière Ticket Office
13 Chateau Entrance
14 Tour Hurtault
17 Banque Populaire
18 Place Michel Debré (Place du Château)
20 Porte de l'Horloge (Clock Tower)
22 La Maison Enchantée
23 Le Clos Lucé
25 Cycles Peugeot
27 Musée de la Poste
28 Maison de la Presse
29 Loca Cycles
31 Accueil d'Amboise (Tourist Office)
32 Bus Stop
33 Place Chaptal
34 Lav' Centre
36 Food Market
37 Central Post Office
38 Théâtre Beaumarchais
39 Église St-Denis

Île d'Or (Île St-Jean)

Loire

Money

There are several banks on rue Nationale. Opposite the chateau entrance, Banque Populaire, 14 place Michel Debré, opens 8.30 am (9.30 am on Monday) to 12.30 pm and 2 to 5.30 pm on weekdays.

Post

The central post office, 20 quai du Général de Gaulle, opens 8.30 am to noon and 1.30 to 6 pm on weekdays, and 8.30 am to noon on Saturday. There is a branch office at the train station.

Laundry

Lav' Centre, 9 allée du Sergent Turpin, opens 7 am to 9 pm (last wash 8 pm).

Château d'Amboise

The rocky outcrop topped by Château d'Amboise has been fortified since Roman times. Charles VIII (ruled 1483–98), who was born and brought up here, began work to enlarge the chateau in 1492 after a visit to Italy, where he was deeply impressed by that country's artistic creativity and luxurious lifestyle. He died only six years later after hitting his head on a low lintel while on his way to a tennis game in the moat, leaving behind him the widowed 22-year-old Anne de Bretagne (obliged by contract to marry the new king of France, Louis XII).

François I (ruled 1515–47) also grew up here – as did his sister, the reform-minded Renaissance author Marguerite d'Angoulême, also known as Marguerite de Navarre. François I lived in the chateau during the first few years of his reign, a lively period marked by balls, masquerade parties, tournaments and festivities of all sorts. During the reign of Henri II (1547–59), the chateau was five times larger than what remains of it today, and visitors expecting a regal and opulent interior will be disappointed.

Only a few of the 15th- and 16th-century structures have survived. These include the Flamboyant Gothic **Chapelle St-Hubert** (Leonardo da Vinci's remains are thought to be in the tomb in the northern transept) and, inside the main building, the **Salle des États** (Estates Hall), where a group of Protestant conspirators were tried before being hanged from the balcony in 1560. From 1848 to 1852, Abdelkader, the military and political leader of the Algerian resistance to French colonialism, was imprisoned here. The **ramparts** afford a fine panorama of the town and Loire Valley.

The only way to exit the chateau is via the souvenir shop: the side door signposted 'Sortie' (Exit) leads to **Tour Hurtault** (1495), the interior of which consists of a circular ramp decorated with sculpted faces. The entrance to the chateau (☎ 02 47 57 00 98) is at the end of rampe du Château. The chateau opens 9 am to 6.30 pm (8 pm, July and August) daily, April to October; and 9 am to noon and 2 to 5 or 5.30 pm daily, the rest of the year. Admission costs 40FF (students 33FF, children 21FF).

On summer nights, a splendid pageant of 450 costumed actors, fireworks, lights and music fills Château d'Amboise's courtyard. The 1½-hour son et lumière show entitled *A la Cour du Roy François* (*At King François' Court*) is held on Wednesday and Saturday evenings between mid-June and 30 August. Tickets costing 75FF or 100FF should be reserved in advance from Animation Renaissance Amboise (Son et Lumière Ticket Office; ☎ 02 47 57 14 47, fax 02 47 57 70 38), 7 rampe du Château. The office opens 9 am to 12.30 pm and 1.30 to 6 pm (5 pm on Friday) on weekdays.

Le Clos Lucé

The *Mona Lisa*'s painter, Leonardo da Vinci, came to Amboise in 1516. Until his death three years later at the age of 67, da Vinci lived and worked in Le Clos Lucé, a brick manor house 500m up rue Victor Hugo from the chateau at 2 rue du Clos Lucé.

The building is filled with restored rooms and scale models of some 40 of da Vinci's fascinating inventions (see the boxed text 'Fabulous Flying Machines' on the following page). With its lovely garden, watch tower reminiscent of the manor's former fortified state, dovecote and canned Renaissance music, it is infinitely more evocative of the age than the far-too-sober chateau.

Le Clos Lucé (☎ 02 47 57 62 88) opens 9 am to 7 pm (8 pm, July and August) daily, March to December; and 9 am to 6 pm (10 am to 5 pm in January) daily, the rest of the year. Admission costs 39FF (students 32FF, children 20FF). A free brochure, in various languages, is doled out as you twirl through the turnstile at the foot of the watch tower.

Rue Victor Hugo – the road that leads to Le Clos Lucé – passes several **troglodytic dwellings**, caves in the limestone hillside in which people still live (with all mod cons, including satellite dish). Abodes worth a peek include those at Nos 31, 59, 81 and 83; or those at the end of the alley between Nos 27 and 29, or next to No 65.

Other Museums

In the heart of old Amboise, **La Maison Enchantée** (Enchanted House; ☎ 02 47 23 24 50), 7 rue du Général Foy, is a privately run museum which displays 300 *automates* (automaton dolls), cleverly and comically arranged in 25 contrasting miniature scenes. Particularly appealing to children, it opens 10 am to noon and 2 to 6 pm daily, April to June; 10 am to 7 pm daily, July and August; 10 am to noon and 2 to 6 pm Tuesday to Sunday, September, October and January to March; and 2 to 5 pm Tuesday to Sunday, November and December. Admission costs 30FF (children 22FF).

TOURAINE

Fabulous Flying Machines

Leonardo da Vinci (1452–1519) was an extraordinary architect, engineer and inventor as well as a painter. His technical drawings anticipated advanced principles that were only realised four centuries later. The machine gun, armoured tank, parachute, hydraulic turbine and a self-propelled vehicle were all conceived by the artist, who dedicated much of his life to his scientific discoveries.

The visionary in da Vinci aspired to achieve a feat considered impossible in the age in which he lived: flight. He observed and sketched birds in flight and, through his technical study of a bat and its wings, invented his own fabulous flying machine – using an interconnected system of ropes, pulleys and pedals to set his human wings in motion. Other drawings illustrate his discovery of vertical elevation by horizontally revolving blades, an idea subsequently used to build the first helicopter. His ludicrous idea of throwing oneself off a cliff edge, attached to a canvas tent measuring 21ft both in height and diagonally, came to fruition with the creation of the parachute centuries later.

Da Vinci painted little during the three years he lived in Amboise, where he died. His remains are assumed to be in the tomb in the northern transept in Chapelle St-Hubert at Château d'Amboise.

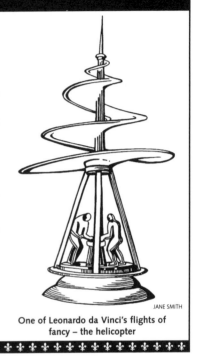

JANE SMITH

One of Leonardo da Vinci's flights of fancy – the helicopter

Nearby is the **Musée de la Poste** (Postal Museum; ☎ 02 47 56 00 11), 6 rue Joyeuse, which houses an interesting collection of stagecoach and ship models, mail carriers' uniforms and lithographs. The building – the Hôtel Joyeuse, designed by Italian architects in the 16th century – is worth a peek, even if you don't fancy its contents. The museum opens 9.30 or 10 am to noon and 2 to 5.30 pm (6.30 pm, April to September) Tuesday to Sunday, year round. Admission costs 20FF (students and children 10FF).

Wine-Tasting

The innovative Caveau des Vignerons d'Amboise (☎/fax 02 47 57 23 69), tucked inside the chateau walls opposite 42 place Michel Debré, is a *cave* run by an enterprising bunch of local wine growers. Here you can taste – for free – six different whites, three reds and two rosés, as well as two types of Touraine Crémant de Loire (a sparkling drink likened to champagne). To ensure the most untickled of tastebuds are titillated, the friendly wine growers also offer different local foods to taste – such as foie gras, *magret de canard* (duck breast), *rillettes* and *rillons* (pork-paste dishes) and *gelée de vins de Touraine* (wine jelly). They also offer delicious 40FF *assiettes* (plates) comprising lunchtime portions of local gastronomic delights, including five types of goat's cheese. The caveau opens 10 am to 7 pm daily, Easter to October.

Special Events

Amboise hosts a two-day Marché Renaissance (Renaissance Market) on the first weekend in July. It sees vendors running around in period costumes and cabarets performed. The town holds its annual Foires aux Vins (Wine Fairs) over Easter weekend and on 15 August. Summer-long, there's the son et lumière show at Château d'Amboise (for details see Château d'Amboise earlier in this Amboise section).

Places to Stay

Camping The 420-pitch *Camping Municipal de l'Île d'Or* (☎ 02 47 57 23 37, 02 47 23 47 23), on Île d'Or (the island in the middle of the River Loire, also known as Île St-Jean), opens from April to September. It costs 24FF for a tent and car, plus 13/7.30/5FF per adult/child aged under 12/dog. Admission to the neighbouring swimming pool costs 12.50FF. Other facilities include mini-golf, a mountain-bike circuit and tennis courts. Amboise Canoe Club (☎ 02 47 23 26 52) is next door.

Hostel Also on Île d'Or is *Centre Charles Péguy-Auberge de Jeunesse* (☎ 02 47 57 06 36, fax 02 47 23 15 80). Beds cost 52FF and breakfast is another 15FF. Reception generally opens 3 to 9 pm on weekdays, and 6 to 8 pm at the weekend; if you arrive when it's closed, try screeching into the intercom.

Chambre d'Hôtes The tourist office has a complete list of private homes offering B&B in Amboise and the surrounding area. Highlights in the city centre include the *home of Madame Frain* (☎ 02 47 30 46 51, 14 quai des Marais), in a quaint timber-framed house; and *Les Tilleuls* (☎ 02 47 57 00 54, 24 rue de l'Entrepont), on Île d'Or. Both charge around 250FF for a double, including breakfast.

Out of town, *Château du Pintray* (☎ 02 47 23 22 84, fax 02 47 57 64 27) in Lussault-sur-Loire, 5km west of Amboise on the D283, is a wine-producing estate which has five double rooms (550FF, including breakfast) in its 16th-century chateau. Pintray grapes have been turned into delicate white wines (AOC Montlouis) since 1837; you can taste and buy the estate's wines.

Hotels Heading south towards the river from the train station, you pass charming

Hôtel La Brèche (☎ 02 47 57 00 79, 26 rue Jules Ferry). Doubles with washbasin/shower/shower and toilet cost 170/220/270FF – extraordinary value given its leafy setting and tree-shaded terrace garden where guests can breakfast on warm days (35FF).

Older *Hôtel de France et du Cheval Blanc* (☎ 02 47 57 02 44, fax 02 47 57 69 54, 6–7 quai du Général de Gaulle) is always packed thanks to its cheap rooms. Doubles start at 155FF (255FF with shower, TV and toilet). There is no hall shower, breakfast costs 35FF and it costs 35/10FF to park your car/bicycle in the garage. Hôtel de France opens from mid-March to mid-November.

Hôtel de la Tour (☎ 02 47 57 25 04, 32 rue Victor Hugo), above a bar in the heart of Amboise, offers eight singles/doubles/triples with washbasin and bidet costing 120/175/230FF; showers are free. Reception (at the bar) opens 7.15 am to 8 pm Friday to Wednesday, except during July and August, when it opens daily; the hotel closes for two weeks in March and three weeks in September.

Two-star *Hôtel Le Français* (☎ 02 47 57 11 38, fax 02 47 57 71 42, 6 rue Voltaire) has 14 comfortable, sound-proofed doubles with shower and toilet costing upwards of 230FF (250FF with a river view). It also has a couple of shower-equipped rooms without toilet for 190FF. Breakfast costs 30FF and dogs can stay for 20FF per night.

Opposite the southern end of Pont Général Leclerc is three-star *Hôtel Belle-Vue* (☎ 02 47 57 02 26, fax 02 47 30 51 23, 12 quai Charles Guinot). Singles/doubles/triples cost 270/300/360FF (open from mid-March to October). A couple of doors away, the similarly priced *Hôtel du Lion d'Or* (☎ 02 47 57 00 23, fax 02 47 23 22 49, 17 quai Charles Guinot) sits snug beneath the chateau walls.

Places to Eat

Restaurants The southern side of place Michel Debré is lined with some of Amboise's best spots for a light, lunchtime snack. Foodies seeking a taste of Touraine

TOURAINE

should look no further than the lunchtime assiettes served with a flourish (and a free glass of wine) at *Caveau des Vignerons d'Amboise* (see Wine-Tasting earlier in this Amboise section). *Anne de Bretagne (☎ 02 47 57 05 46, 1 rampe du Château)* is another good bet. The restaurant serves a *menu*/plat du jour for 54/40FF, and tourists love the alcohol-soaked crepes.

Le Blason (☎ 02 47 23 22 41, 11 place Richelieu), also a hotel, offers good-value *menus* from 165FF, accompanied by a snug setting in an ageing, timber-framed town house.

Four-star *Le Manoir St-Thomas (☎ 02 47 57 22 52, 1 mail St-Thomas)* is housed in a sumptuous mansion overlooking place Richelieu. It has 175FF, 265FF and 295FF *menus* and features delights such as *rillons aux poireaux et pruneaux farcis de foie gras* (leek rillons and plums stuffed with duck liver paté) on its a la carte menu. Book in advance and come armed with a credit card (preferably not your own).

Self-Catering Rue Nationale is lined with *sandwich shops*, *fast-food outlets*, *boulangeries* and *creperies*. An open-air *food market* spills across quai du Général de Gaulle on Friday and Sunday mornings.

Entertainment
Le Shaker (☎ 02 47 23 24 26, quai François Tissard) is a busy cocktail, drinks and ice-cream bar, favoured for its fabulous views of the chateau from its waterside terrace (open 6 pm to 2 or 3 am).

In summer, classical-music and organ concerts are held in *Église St-Denis* on place St-Denis. The tourist office has programme and ticket (60FF) details. *Théâtre Beaumarchais (☎ 02 47 57 13 69, ave des Martyrs de la Résistance)* is the only venue for theatre performances and cinema screenings.

Getting There & Away
Bus Buses to and from Amboise stop at the bus shelter next to the tourist office, a far more convenient place to begin a visit than the train station on the other side of the river, even though buses are slower.

CAT's line No 10 links Amboise with Tours' bus terminal (13FF one way, 30 to 50 minutes); it runs eight times daily Monday to Saturday, and six times daily during the summer school holidays. Bus No 10 also runs to Chenonceaux for Château de Chenonceau.

Train Amboise train station (☎ 02 47 23 18 23), on blvd Gambetta, is across the River Loire from the centre of town. About three-quarters of the trains on the Blois–Tours line (11 to 17 daily) stop here. Fares are 34FF to Blois (20 minutes) and 28FF to Tours (20 minutes).

See Other Parts of France under Land in the Getting There & Away chapter for details of trains to/from Paris.

Getting Around
Bicycle Cycles Richard (☎ 02 47 57 01 79), 2 rue de Nazelles, rents, sells and repairs all species of two-wheel vehicles. Hiring a bicycle or mountain bike costs 80FF per day. The shop opens 9 am to noon and 2.30 to 9 pm Monday to Saturday.

South of the river, Cycles Peugeot (☎ 02 47 57 00 17), 5 rue Joyeuse, has bikes to rent for 50/80/200FF per half-day/day/week. A 600FF deposit is required on weekly rentals. Peugeot opens 9 am to noon and 2 to 7 pm Tuesday to Saturday, and 9 am to noon on Sunday.

Nearby, Loca Cycles (☎ 02 47 57 00 28), 2 bis rue Jean-Jacques Rousseau, has mountain bikes costing 70/90/450FF per half-day/day/week. The shop opens 9 am to 12.30 pm and 2 to 7 pm.

AROUND AMBOISE
Delights within spitting distance of Amboise include a Chinese-style pagoda, white Egyptian donkeys and a host of shrunken chateaux at the Parc des Mini-Châteaux.

Pagode de Chanteloup
This seven-storey Chinese-style pagoda, 44m high, is one of the more pleasing follies left over from the 18th century. It is all that remains of a chateau that was torn down in 1823.

Built between 1775 and 1778, the pagoda combines Louis XVI French architectural fashions with elements from China, a country of great fascination at the time. At the top (a 152-step climb), visitors are rewarded with an impressive view of the Loire Valley. Also visible are the overgrown outlines of the once-splendid pools, the gardens, and seven forest paths radiating out from the pagoda, which was once the centrepiece of the 18th-century estate and chateau. Château de Chanteloup (1711) was purchased in 1761 by Louis XV's prime minister, the duke of Choiseul, who retired to the estate following his disgrace and exile from court in 1770. His pagoda was modelled on the pagoda that Augusta, princess of Wales (1719–72), had built in Kew Gardens in London in 1761. The estate passed through several hands until 1823, when its bankrupt owner was forced to sell the chateau, literally stone by stone, for quick cash. Its former splendour is apparent in the floor plans displayed in the **museum**, housed in a small outbuilding at the head of the path leading to the pagoda.

All told, this eccentric pagoda is a delightful **picnic** venue. Hampers bursting with regional treats are sold at the entrance (50FF). You can hire a **boat** to row your sweetheart around the lake (40FF per hour) and there is a good collection of **old-fashioned games** to play (free to use and fascinating for young and old alike). Senior visitors might prefer a game of **croquet** on the lawns.

The Pagode de Chanteloup is 2.5km south of Amboise; from the centre head south on rue Bretonneau (Bléré direction) and follow the plentiful signs to 'La Pagode'.

The Pagode de Chanteloup (☎ 02 47 57 20 97) opens 10 am to 6 pm daily, May; 10 am to 7 pm daily, June and September; 9.30 am to 8 pm daily, July and August; and 10 am to noon and 2 to 5 or 5.30 pm daily, March, April and October to mid-November. Admission costs 35FF (students 30FF, children 25FF). Each year during the Fête des Œufs (Festival of Eggs) on Easter Monday, Easter egg treasure hunts are held around the pagoda.

Parc des Mini-Châteaux & Aquarium de Touraine

The exteriors of Chambord, Chenonceau and other Loire chateaux can be ogled in miniature form at the tacky **Parc des Mini-Châteaux**, 3km south of Amboise. The wooden maquettes spread across two hectares are illuminated in summer. Admission costs 59FF (children 39FF). A **Parc le Fou de l'Âne** – home to donkeys of all sizes, colours and species – is on the same site. Admission costs 45FF (children 30FF).

Further afield is the interesting Aquarium de Touraine, which markets itself as Europe's largest inland aquarium. Some 10,000 freshwater, tropical and coral-reef fish swim around in four million litres of water. River fish typical to the Loire dart above your head in the discovery tunnel. The in-house sharks are fed on Tuesday and Saturday and the crocodiles on Wednesday, both at 3 pm. Admission to the aquarium costs 59FF (children 39FF).

The Parc des Mini-Châteaux is at the intersection of the D31 and southbound D81; from Amboise, bear south along route de Chenonceaux. The Aquarium de Touraine is mid-way between Amboise and Montlouis-sur-Loire off the D751.

All three theme parks (☎ 08 36 68 69 37) open 9 or 10 am until 5, 6 or 7 pm daily, April to mid-November. The Parc des Mini-Châteaux and Aquarium de Touraine open until 10.30 pm on Saturday in July and August (last admission 8.30 pm). If you intend to visit two/three of the above sites, buy a combination ticket for 96/139FF (children 58/98FF).

Public buses between Amboise and Tours serve the Pagode de Chanteloup and Parc des Mini-Châteaux; get off at the Pagode stop for the former (6.50FF from Amboise) and the Mini-Chateaux stop (12FF from Amboise) for the latter. See Bus under Getting There & Away under Amboise and Tours for more details.

LOCHES

postcode 37600 • pop 6550

Medieval Loches, with its cobbled streets and imposing castle keep perched on a rocky

TOURAINE

spur, could be a film set. The 11th-century keep was built by Foulques Nerra (Falcon the Black; ruled 987–1040), and the town's feudal chateau saw a victorious Joan of Arc persuade the dauphin to march to Reims in June 1429 to be crowned. The royal court that Charles VII subsequently established at Loches was notorious for its wild parties and decadent banquets, thrown primarily to woo the scandalously wicked yet stunningly beautiful Agnès Sorel (1422–50), a legendary royal mistress who died aged 28. Her tomb lies in Loches.

The town's golden age ended in 1461 with the ascension to the throne of Louis XI, who turned the keep into a state prison (which remained in use until 1926). Charles VIII (ruled 1483–98) and Louis XII (ruled 1498–1515) extended the royal dwelling here, but never again were the seductive heydays of sexy Sorel – immortalised on canvas by the famous painter Fouquet with one breast exposed – to be repeated.

Orientation & Information

The citadel sits south of the old town, on the western bank of the River Indre. The train and bus stations are across Pont Pierre Senard on the eastern bank of the river.

The tourist office (☎ 02 47 91 82 82, fax 02 47 91 61 50, ✉ loches.en.touraine@wandaoo.fr), place de la Marne, is wedged between Pont Pierre Senard and rue de la République, the main commercial street. It opens 9.30 am to 7 pm Monday to Saturday, and 9.30 am to 1 pm and 2 to 7 pm on Sunday. The office's Web site is at www.lochesentouraine.com. There is a Banque National de Paris at 30 rue Picois, and the post office on rue Descartes has Cyberposte.

Citadel

The 11th-century **Porte Royale** was the only entrance to the citadel, which is also known as the Cité Médiévale. The gate is flanked by two 13th-century towers and was served by a portcullis and drawbridge. It is the only

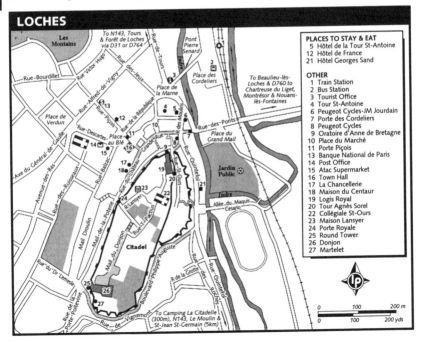

LOCHES

PLACES TO STAY & EAT
5 Hôtel de la Tour St-Antoine
12 Hôtel de France
21 Hôtel Georges Sand

OTHER
1 Train Station
2 Bus Station
3 Tourist Office
4 Tour St-Antoine
6 Peugeot Cycles-JM Jourdain
7 Porte des Cordeliers
8 Peugeot Cycles
9 Oratoire d'Anne de Bretagne
10 Place du Marché
11 Porte Piçois
13 Banque National de Paris
14 Post Office
15 Atac Supermarket
16 Town Hall
17 La Chancellerie
18 Maison du Centaur
19 Logis Royal
20 Tour Agnès Sorel
22 Collégiale St-Ours
23 Maison Lansyer
24 Porte Royale
25 Round Tower
26 Donjon
27 Martelet

opening in the 2km of sturdy wall encircling the medieval city.

Around the **donjon** (castle keep; 1010–35), at the southernmost point of the rocky promontory, the defensive wall is 2.3m thick and 37m high. The donjon is the oldest structure within the citadel and was the handiwork of Foulques Nerra (ruled 987–1040). The **Round Tower** and **Martelet**, notorious for the torture of their inhabitants, were built under Louis XI as prisons. Infamous guests include Duke Ludovico Sforza of Milan, captured by Louis XII in 1500 and held here from 1504 to 1508, and Cardinal La Balhue, who slumbered here for 11 years, tortured in the **Cage Louis XI** for some of the time. The cage weighed 2.5 tonnes; a replica of the original found in the Round Tower during the French Revolution is displayed.

The northern end of the citadel contains the **Logis Royal** (Royal Residence), an attractive ensemble consisting of the **Tour Agnès Sorel**, the Flamboyant Gothic **Oratoire d'Anne de Bretagne** and the main dwelling rooms of the Logis Royal linking the two. The 15th-century funerary urn of 'La Belle Agnès' is in the northern wing of the logis, built for Charles VIII and Anne de Bretagne in the 16th century. The triptych (1485) to the north of the tomb originates from Fouquet's School of Tours (see Painting under Arts in the Facts about the Loire chapter). In summer, a **son et lumière** (☎ 02 47 59 01 76) is held in the citadel at 10 pm on Friday and Saturday. Medieval banquets are occasionally held in the logis (260FF per person). The terrace offers a fine panorama of Loches tumbling down the hillside towards the Indre Valley.

The Logis Royal opens 9 am to 7 pm daily, July to September; and 9 am to noon and 2 to 5 or 6 pm daily, the rest of the year. Admission costs 23FF (children 13FF) and a combination ticket for the chateau and donjon costs 31FF.

The neighbouring 12th-century **Collégiale St-Ours** is a fine example of Romanesque architecture. **Maison Lansyer** (☎ 02 47 59 05 45), the former home of landscape painter Emmanuel Lansyer (1851–93), on rue Lansyer, houses a small museum dedicated to the artist, who studied under Gustave Courbet (1819–77).

Architectural gems just outside the citadel walls include the 16th-century **Maison du Centaur**, 10 rue du Château, which has an ornate carved motif of Hercules aiming a poisoned arrow at Nessos on its eastern gable; and the lovely mansion called **La Chancellerie** (1551) next door at No 8.

Places to Stay & Eat

At **Camping La Citadelle** (☎ 02 47 59 05 91, *@ camping@lacitadelle.com, ave Aristide Briand*), open between mid-March and mid-November, it costs 72FF for a tent pitch, car, two adults and a child; each additional adult/child costs 16/8FF. It also has mobile homes and caravans to rent. To get to the site from the town centre, head south along rue Quintefol (N143) for 300m.

Hôtel de la Tour St-Antoine (☎ 02 47 59 01 06, fax 02 47 59 13 80, 2 rue des Moulins) has basic doubles with washbasin costing 150FF, with shower for 180FF, and shower- and toilet-equipped doubles costing 230FF. Nearby **Hôtel de France** (☎ 02 47 59 00 32, fax 02 47 59 28 66, 6 rue Piçois) has a courtyard restaurant, private parking and rooms for two from 295FF.

Three-star *Hôtel Georges Sand* (☎ 02 47 59 39 74, fax 02 47 91 55 75, 37 rue Quintefol) has an idyllic terrace restaurant overhanging the River Indre and is the top place in town to stay; doubles with citadel/river view start at 260/400FF and breakfast costs 38FF.

Out of town in St-Jean St-Germain, 5km south on the N143, is *Le Moulin* (☎ 02 47 94 70 12), an 18th-century water mill on the banks of the River Indre which has been transformed by its British proprietors into a charming chambre d'hôte. It has six doubles with bathroom costing 350FF (breakfast included). Four-course evening meals (conjured up by a professional chef) cost an extra 150FF and include aperitif, wine and coffee.

A succulent fruit, vegetable, sausage and cheese *market* spills across place du Marché and along rue St-Antoine on Wednesday morning. *Atac* supermarket is next to the post office.

TOURAINE

Getting There & Away

Loches is on the Tours–Châteauroux train line. The tiny train and bus stations are across Pont Pierre Senard on place des Cordeliers. To/from Tours there are two trains daily (44FF, 45 minutes) and three or four SNCF buses (44FF, 50 minutes).

Getting Around

Peugeot Cycles-JM Jourdain (☎ 02 47 59 02 15), 7 rue des Moulins, rents road/mountain bikes for 50/80FF per day or 300/500FF per week. It has a repair outlet (which also rents bikes) farther south on the same street. Both open 8.30 am to noon and 1.30 to 7 pm Tuesday to Saturday.

VALLÉE DE L'INDROIS

Cross the River Indre at Loches and two roads (D31 and D764) take you through scenic landscape into the heart of the **Forêt de Loches**, a thick forest wedged between the River Indre to the west and the Vallée de l'Indrois to the east. This area is delightful cycling territory and offers several easy day trips from Loches.

The small and unremarkable church of **Nouans-lès-Fontaines**, at the far eastern edge of the valley on the D760, showcases this area's most fabulous treasure. Its altarpiece is an original painting on wood by Jean Fouquet (1420–81) entitled *La Pietà* (*Pity*) and discovered hidden behind the altar by the church cleaner in 1931. It features a scene from the Passion and is one of the few medieval panel paintings to survive in France. Restoration work in 1980 confirmed it was the work of the French court painter, who probably completed the panel around 1455. Slot 10FF in the box to the right of the altar to illuminate the painting and listen to a recorded explanation in English, French or German.

Apple orchards and wheat fields line the westbound D760 from Nouans to **Montrésor**, one of France's most beautiful villages, with a lovely Gothic **Collégiale** (1520–41) with Renaissance ornamentation. The beautiful village is crowned by a 16th-century chateau, handsomely restored from 1849 by Polish emigré Count Xavier Branicki. *Le*

Moulin de Montrésor (☎ 02 47 92 68 20, fax 02 47 92 74 61), signposted off the D10 towards Genillé, is a four-room chambre d'hôte, housed in a superbly renovated water mill. Doubles start at 280FF.

From here the D760 twists west away from the valley and into Forêt de Loches. On the forest fringe, 6km west of Montrésor, is the half-ruined **Chartreuse du Liget**, an abandoned Carthusian monastery built under Henri II between 1176 and 1189 to expiate the murder of Thomas à Becket. The last monk fled during the 1789 Revolution, following which the estate was sold off, literally stone by stone. The ruins of the chapel, the western wall of the choir and a handful of cells are all that remain of the original 12th-century edifice. Another abandoned chapel from this epoch stands alone at **St-Jean du Liget**, 2km farther west in the forest; ask staff at Chartreuse du Liget for the key. The monastical complex is now privately owned. One of the outbuildings at Chartreuse du Liget is a self-catering *gîte rural* which sleeps 16 and can be rented through Gîtes de France (see Chambre d'Hôtes under Places to Stay in the Tours section earlier in this chapter).

Back in Montrésor, the picturesque D10 snakes west along the valley – past an artificial lake at **Chemillé-sur-Indrois** where you can swim, surf board and camp – to **Genillé**, 8km to the north-west, home to a handful of cold, dank, unappealing and abandoned **cave dwellings**. From here, the D764 cuts north to **Château de Montpoupon**, a roadside chateau which houses a **Musée de Veneur** (Hunting Museum; ☎ 02 47 94 21 15); the stables and saddlery are quite interesting. Westwards, the pretty D10 continues along the valley to Azay-sur-Indre, the confluence of the Rivers Indrois and Indre, from where the **Indre Valley** strikes north. The **Parc des Labyrinthes** (☎ 02 47 42 63 62; open July to September), 3km north of Azay in **Reignac-sur-Indre**, is worth a pit stop for motorists with bored children. The giant open-air mazes, cut from corn across vast fields, are guaranteed to thrill.

CHINON

postcode 37500 ● pop 8627

Chinon's massive, 400m-long fortress
looms over the town's medieval quarter.
The uneven, cobblestone streets are lined
with ancient houses, some built of decaying
tufa stone, others half-timbered and brick.
The contrast between the triangular, black
slate roofs and the whitish-tan tufa gives the
town its distinctive appearance.

It was in Chinon, 47km south-west of
Tours and 30km east of the Anjou town of
Saumur, that a usurped dauphin took refuge
prior to Joan of Arc persuading him to raise
an army for her to defeat the English at
Orléans.

The Chinon area is noted for its noble
vineyards on the Vienne riverbanks and the
nuclear power station north of town on
the southern bank of the River Loire. The
Tourangeaux chateaux of Villandry, Azay-
le-Rideau, Langeais and Ussé make easy
day trips from Chinon if you have your own
wheels (two or four).

Orientation

Rue Haute St-Maurice, the main street in
the medieval quarter, becomes rue Voltaire
as you move east. The train station is about
1km south-east of place du Général de
Gaulle, the commercial hub also known as
place de l'Hôtel de Ville.

Information

Tourist Office The tourist office (☎ 02 47
93 17 85, fax 02 47 93 93 05), place de
Hofheïm, arranges guided city tours between June and September, departing from
outside the office at 10 am and 3.30 pm on
Tuesday, Thursday, Saturday and Sunday.
The office opens 9 am to 6.30 or 7 pm Monday to Saturday, in winter; plus 10 am to
12.30 pm on Sunday, in summer.

Money There are several banks along quai
Jeanne d'Arc, including Crédit Mutuel next
to the post office. Caisse d'Epargne, on the
corner of rue Buffon and place Jeanne
d'Arc, opens 8.45 am to 12.30 pm and 2
to 7.15 pm (4 pm on Saturday) Monday to
Saturday.

Post The post office, quai Jeanne d'Arc,
opens 8 am to noon and 1.30 to 5.45 pm on
weekdays, and 8 am to noon on Saturday.

Email & Internet Access L'Astrol@be
(☎ 02 47 98 01 00), 26 rue Rabelais, opens
9.30 am to noon and 2 to 7 pm Tuesday to
Saturday. On-line access starts at 1/25/45FF
for one minute/30 minutes/one hour.

Laundry Salon Laverie, 40 quai Charles
VII, opens 7 am to 9 pm.

Château de Chinon

Perched atop a rocky spur high above the
River Vienne, this huge, mostly ruined
medieval fortress was built to protect the
Vallée de la Vienne. It consists of three
fortresses, spread across three hectares and
separated by waterless moats. Little remains of **Fort St-Georges**, named after England's patron saint and built in the 12th
century to protect the chateau's vulnerable
eastern flank and block access to the royal
residence. At the western tip, **Fort du
Coudray** was built under the direction of
King Philippe-Auguste (best known for de-
feating the English in 1205) and is one of
the better-preserved keeps in France today.
It has several cylindrical and polygonal
dungeons from the 12th and 13th centuries.
Secret underground passages, 35m deep, ra-
diate outwards. From the ramparts there are
great views in all directions. The chateau is
illuminated at night during the summer
months.

After crossing the moat (once spanned
by a drawbridge) you pass under the **Tour
de l'Horloge** (Clock Tower) to enter
Château Milieu. The four rooms inside the
tower are dedicated to Joan of Arc, who
picked out the dauphin from among a crowd
of courtiers in 1429 in the castle's **Salle du
Trône** (Throne Room). Other parts of the
almost undecorated **Logis Royaux** (Royal
Residences), dating from the 12th to 15th
centuries, are in better condition.

Château de Chinon (☎ 02 47 93 13 45)
opens 9 am to 6 pm (7 pm in July and August and 5 pm in October) daily, mid-March
to October; and 9 am to noon and 2 to 5 pm

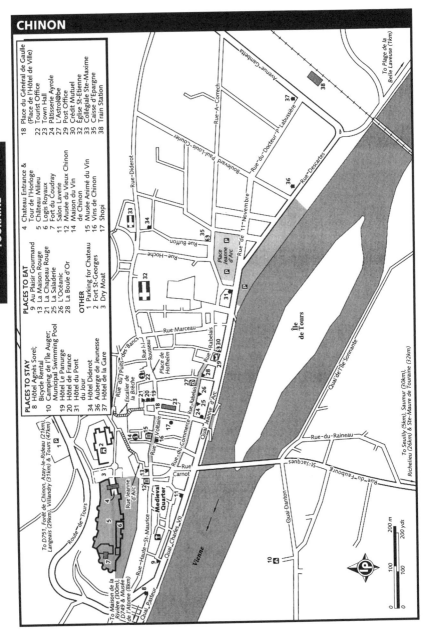

CHINON

PLACES TO STAY
8   Hôtel Agnès Sorel;
    Bicycle Rental
10 Camping de l'Île Auger;
    Municipal Swimming Pool
19 Hôtel Le Panurge
20 Hôtel de France
31 Hôtel du Pont
    du Jour
34 Hôtel Diderot
36 Auberge de Jeunesse
37 Hôtel de la Gare

PLACES TO EAT
9   Au Plaisir Gourmand
13 La Maison Rouge
21 La Chapeau Rouge
25 La Saladerie
26 L'Océanic
28 La Boule d'Or

OTHER
1   Parking for Chateau
2   Fort St-Georges
3   Dry Moat
4   Chateau Entrance &
    Tour de l'Horloge
5   Chateau Milieu
6   Logis Royaux
7   Fort du Coudray
11 Salon Laverie
12 Musée du Vieux Chinon
14 Maison du Vin
    de Chinon
15 Musée Animé du Vin
16 Vins de Chinon
17 Shopi
18 Place du Général de Gaulle
    (Place de l'Hôtel de Ville)
22 Tourist Office
23 Town Hall
24 Pâtisserie Ayrole
27 L'Astrol@be
29 Post Office
30 Crédit Mutuel
32 Église St-Etienne
33 Collégiale Ste-Maxime
35 Caisse d'Epargne
38 Train Station

daily, the rest of the year. Admission costs 28FF (seniors 19FF, children 16FF).

To get to the chateau from town, walk up the hill to rue du Puits des Bancs and turn left. By car, route de Tours (the continuation of the D751 from Tours) takes you to the back of the chateau, where parking is available.

Musée Animé du Vin
The kitsch Musée Animé du Vin (Animated Wine Museum; ☎ 02 47 93 25 63), 12 rue Voltaire, has life-sized mechanical figures that demonstrate how wine and wine barrels are made, accompanied by piped commentary in English. It opens 10.30 am to 12.30 pm and 2 to 7 pm, April to September. The 25FF admission fee (children 21FF) includes a sample of local wine and *confiture de vin* (sweet wine jelly).

Genuine vinophiles seeking hardcore information should try the **Maison du Vin de Chinon**, a block west on impasse des Caves Peintres. The local Syndicat des Vins de Chinon (☎ 02 47 93 30 44) is based here, as is the Confrérie des Bons Entonneurs Rabelaisiens (see Chinon under Wine in the Food & Wine of the Loire special section), a brotherhood which owns the allegedly marvellous painted caves at the end of impasse des Caves Peintres (closed to the public). The Maison du Vin opens 9 am to noon and 2 to 6 pm on weekdays. Taste and buy wine here, or at the Vins de Chinon wine shop at 13 rue Voltaire, or direct from one of the 210 *viticulteurs* (wine growers) who work the Chinon vineyards stretching from Beaumont-en-Véron east to Crouzilles and south to Ligré.

Musée du Vieux Chinon
The Musée du Vieux Chinon (Museum of Old Chinon; ☎ 02 47 93 18 12) is housed in a lovely stone building at 44 rue Haute St-Maurice. In October 1428 the future Charles VII held the assembly of his *États generaux* (Estates general) here. A hotchpotch of items relating to the history of Chinon are displayed here today.

Next door at No 45 is **La Maison Rouge** (The Red House), the best example of medieval, half-timbered architecture in town. Believed to have been built around 1400, it

stood next to the Hostellerie du Grand Carroi, where Joan of Arc stayed in 1429 while waiting to meet the dauphin. Several more half-timbered houses and *hôtels particuliers* (mansions) can be found along rue Haute St-Maurice, which was Chinon's main street in the medieval era.

Maison de la Rivière
Strategically placed overlooking the River Vienne, Chinon's Maison de la Rivière (House of the River; ☎ 02 47 93 21 34), 12 quai Pasteur, explores the history of the Loire's maritime trade. Numerous fishing vessels, including traditional wooden *galiotes* (flat-bottomed boats), are displayed. The museum opens 10 am to noon and 2 to 5 pm Tuesday to Friday, and 3 to 6 pm at the weekend, April to June and September; 10.30 am to 12.30 pm and 2 to 6.30 pm Tuesday to Sunday, July and August; and 2 to 5 pm Tuesday to Sunday, the rest of the year.

Musée de l'Atome
This museum of the atom (☎ 02 47 98 77 77) is housed in France's first commercial reactor, erected between 1957 and 1963 on the Loire's southern bank, 8km north-west of Chinon in Avoine. The station has two decommissioned units and four active, pressurised water reactors rated at 900 megawatts.

To arrange a free visit (1½ hours) call the station a few days ahead (a day ahead in July and August); bring along some form of ID. On weekdays from May to September there are four tours daily; tours are less frequent the rest of the year. The working reactors can only be visited on weekdays. The tourist office (☎/fax 02 47 58 45 40), opposite the main entrance to the plant on the D749, can help arrange visits; it opens 10 am to 7 pm Monday to Saturday, and 2 to 7 pm on Sunday, April to September.

Special Events
On the first weekend in August, musicians, dancers and locals dress up in period costume for the Marché Rabelais, where all manner of crafts and local products go on sale. Events are held throughout the town but centre on the medieval quarter. Two

euro currency converter 10FF = €1.52

weeks later, on the third weekend of August, wines and traditional regional food products are sold at the Marché à l'Ancienne, a re-creation of a 19th-century farmers' market. This is also held all over town though pre-dominantly in the medieval quarter.

Places to Stay

Camping Riverside *Camping de l'Île Auger* (☎ 02 47 93 08 35), open April to October, is on the southern side of the River Vienne. Fees are 11FF per tent/car/adult.

Hostel The friendly *auberge de jeunesse* (☎ 02 47 93 10 48, fax 02 47 98 44 98, 60 rue Descartes) also functions as a Foyer des Jeunes Travailleurs (a young working people's hostel). A bed in the basic, institu-tional dormitories costs 51FF. You can re-serve a place and leave your bags all day long, but check-in is only on weekdays be-tween 6 and 10 pm; curfew is 10 pm. Guests can use the laundry facilities, the large kitchen and the TV room.

Hotels Bang smack in the centre of town, overlooking a cafe-filled leafy square, is *Hôtel Le Panurge* (☎ 02 47 93 09 84, 45 place du Général de Gaulle). Doubles cost 135FF (160/185FF with shower/shower and toilet).

Hôtel du Pont du Jour (☎ 02 47 93 07 20, place Jeanne d'Arc) is above a simple bar-cum-cafe. Doubles with washbasin/ shower/shower and toilet are good value at 120/150/170FF. The hotel also has apart-ments and a gîte rural to let on a weekly or monthly basis. There are several other, more expensive, hotels on place Jeanne d'Arc.

Across the street from the train station, two-star *Hôtel de la Gare* (☎ 02 47 93 00 86, fax 02 47 93 36 38, 14 ave Gambetta), also called Gar' Hôtel, has large but plain doubles/quads with shower and toilet cost-ing 280/340FF.

In the hub of things, three-star *Hôtel de France* (☎ 02 47 93 33 91, fax 02 47 98 37 03, 47–49 place du Général de Gaulle) of-fers doubles costing upwards of 340FF, and breakfast costs a steep 45FF. Reception opens Monday morning to noon on Sunday

(from Monday afternoon during October, November and March). The hotel opens from March to November.

Small but sweet *Hôtel Agnès Sorel* (☎ 02 47 93 04 37, fax 02 47 93 06 37, ✉ catherine .rogereck@wanadoo.fr, 4 quai Pasteur) is in a charming, riverside spot and run by a friendly family. It has six rooms, costing 220/300FF without/with private shower and toilet; it rents bicycles too.

Equally charming and also away from the madding crowds is *Hôtel Diderot* (☎ 02 47 93 18 87, fax 02 47 93 37 10, 4 rue Buffon). Singles/doubles in this select spot with a flower-clad courtyard start at 250/300FF.

Places to Eat

All summer long, tree-shaded place du Général de Gaulle is transformed into one huge *outdoor cafe*. Among the many eater-ies along rue Rabelais is *La Saladerie* (☎ 02 47 93 99 93), at No 5, which has meal-sized salads (about 45FF), meat dishes (50FF to 63FF) and, except in summer, *chaud patats* (baked-potato dishes) and *gratins* (dishes made with cheese), both 40FF to 50FF. It opens Tuesday to Sunday.

L'Océanic (☎ 02 47 93 44 55), at No 13, specialises in seafood, with *menus* swim-ming in at 110FF and 160FF. Similarly priced is *La Boule d'Or* (☎ 02 47 98 40 88), at No 21, which has a 99FF and 148FF *menu du terroir* (regional menu). *Terrine de la mer aux pistaches* (fish terrine with pis-tachio nuts) is a speciality. Both places open daily in season and Tuesday to Saturday out of season.

On place du Général de Gaulle *Le Chap-eau Rouge*, named after the red caps worn by the king's royal messengers, is worth try-ing for its central location, quaint setting and cosy atmosphere. Dining here won't break the bank. Not to be confused with Le Chap-eau Rouge is *La Maison Rouge* (☎ 02 47 98 43 65, 38 rue Voltaire), at the foot of the steep cobbled street leading to the chateau (this should also not be confused with the Maison Rouge next to Musée du Vieux Chi-non). It serves *assiettes Rabelaisiennes* of local specialities (69FF, 79FF or 98FF) and 50cl *pichets* (jugs) of Chinon wine (43FF).

Chinon's top spot to dine is three-star *Au Plaisir Gourmand* (☎ 02 47 93 20 48, *quai Charles VII*), where divine delights are conjured up by Jean Claude Rigollet, one of the region's most celebrated chefs. *Menus* cost from 175FF to 360FF.

Self-Catering A handy supermarket is *Shopi* (*22 place du Général de Gaulle*). The sweet-toothed should bite into *Pâtisserie Ayrole* (*5 rue de l'Hôtel de Ville*); try its *langues de femme* (literally 'women's tongues').

At the northern end of place du Général de Gaulle, there's an *outdoor market* until 1 pm on Thursday, Saturday and Sunday mornings. Place Jeanne d'Arc plays host to a *food market* on Thursday morning.

Getting There & Away
Chinon train station (☎ 02 47 93 11 04), about 1km east of the medieval quarter, is linked by a tertiary line with Tours (48FF, 50 minutes). There are eight trains or SNCF buses daily on weekdays, five on Saturday, and two on Sunday and holidays. Stops en route include Azay-le-Rideau (21FF), making it possible to visit Chinon and Azay in a day from Tours (departing from Tours by SNCF bus at 7.50 am, from Chinon by train at 1.17 pm, and from Azay by train or bus at 5.52 or 6 pm respectively).

Getting Around
The best bicycle rental outlet (☎ 02 47 93 04 37) is at 4 quai Pasteur, inside Hôtel Agnès Sorel. Rental costs 90/150FF per day/weekend; children's bikes are slightly cheaper.

VALLÉE DE LA VIENNE
Rabelais' home, Richelieu's ruined palace, and the village church where Joan of Arc's sacred sword was sent from heaven are all within striking distance of medieval Chinon and the Vallée de la Vienne in which it sits. **Forêt de Chinon** to the north-east is crisscrossed by cycling tracks, hiking trails and the D751, which slices straight through the wooded area to Azay-le-Rideau (see Azay-le-Rideau earlier in this chapter).

Since 1996, the northern section of the Vallée de la Vienne has been protected by

the **Parc Naturel Régional Loire-Anjou-Touraine**, a 260,000-hectare park embracing southern Touraine and much of neighbouring Anjou to the west. Vast undulating plains of wheat fields and walnut-tree orchards cover the land south of the River Vienne.

Pays de la Rabelais
'Drink well, drink always' was the well-known philosophy of the 15th-century comic novelist François Rabelais (1494–1533), born in the heart of Chinon wine-making country in **Seuilly**, 5km south of Chinon. The son of a Chinon lawyer, Rabelais spent the first 15 years of his childhood at **La Devinière**, his family country house, which is open as a museum today. He studied at the **Abbaye de Seuilly**, home to the headquarters of the Parc Naturel Régional Loire-Anjou-Touraine (☎ 02 47 97 21 00, fax 02 47 97 21 09) today. Several surrounding villages – such as the picturesque village of **Lerné**, carved out of white tufa stone 3km west – inspired many of Rabelais' works.

Richelieu
Nineteen kilometres south of the River Vienne is this quaint market town. Dubbed the *cité du cardinal* (city of the cardinal), it only flourished in the 17th century thanks to Cardinal Richelieu, who had a **chateau** built here between 1631 and 1634. Sold off after the Revolution, the chateau was demolished for its stones in 1805, leaving nothing but the wine cellar and orangery intact. The park, which can be visited, is now owned by the Sorbonne University in Paris. A rose garden has been planted where the chateau once stood but water still fills the original moats.

From Richelieu, a **train à vapeur** (steam train) puffs its way 16km north along the banks of the River Veude to **Ligré**. The 1930s locomotive stops at **Champigny-sur-Veude** on the way. The train (☎ 02 47 58 12 98) makes one trip daily at weekends only, mid-July to mid-August (see Train in the Getting Around chapter for details).

Ste-Maure de Touraine
This cheesy town of 4000 inhabitants marks the valley's easternmost point, prior to the

euro currency converter 10FF = €1.52

TOURAINE

river's rapid southwards descent. Its highlight is **Les Halles**, a grandiose covered market dating from 1672; a food market is held here every Friday morning. Don't miss the cheese stalls, laden with a cylindrical-shaped goat's cheese – called Ste-Maure de Touraine – which has been produced in the town under its own AOC since 1971.

The tourist office (☎ 02 47 65 66 20), place du Château, has a list of places where you can taste and buy goat's cheese. Alternatively, head straight to **Fromage de Chèvre Fermier** (☎ 02 47 65 65 03), a goat farm where you can learn about the cheese-making process. The farm, 2km north of Ste-Maure and signposted off the N10, is home to 150 goats and charges 19FF a cheese.

Six kilometres farther north is **Ste-Catherine de Ferbois**, where a memorial plaque in the Gothic **Église Ste-Catherine** (1480) pays homage to '*Jeanne la pucelle*' (Joan the virgin, aka Joan of Arc), who defeated the English thanks to her sword, engraved with five holy crosses and found behind the altar in Église Ste-Catherine. In 1429 Joan celebrated mass three times in the original church, which was destroyed by fire in 1440. Her statue dominates the village square, overlooked by a small museum and tourist office, open Monday, Tuesday and Thursday to Saturday afternoon, June to September.

Descartes

Southern Touraine's other famous child is the world-famous French philosopher René Descartes (1596–1650), the son of a rich bourgeois family from the unmomentous town of La Haye, 10km east of the Vallée de la Vienne proper on the banks of the River Creuse. La Haye was renamed Descartes in 1967.

The **Musée Descartes** (☎ 02 47 59 79 19), inside the house at 29 rue Descartes where Descartes was born, illustrates the life of the philosopher, who studied at a Jesuit school in La Flèche before moving to Holland, where he remained for 20 years (1629–49). Descartes was one of the first philosophers to write in French rather than Latin, thereby making his writings more accessible (see Science & Philosophy in the Facts about the Loire chapter for more information).

The house museum opens 2 to 6 pm Wednesday to Monday, mid-January to mid-November. Admission costs 25FF.

The **Musée Départemental de Préhistoire** (Departmental Museum of Prehistory; ☎ 02 47 94 90 20), inside the 12th- to 16th-century Château du Grand-Pressigny 8km south of Descartes, is worth the small detour if you are in this neck of the woods. The museum opens 9.30 am to 6 pm daily, July and August; and 9.30 am to 12.30 and 2.30 to 5.30 pm (6 pm, mid-March to June) daily, the rest of the year. Admission costs 24FF (those aged seven to 18 13FF).

Getting There & Away

The valley is practically impossible to explore by public transport.

Anjou

The Loire Valley's sprinkling of Renaissance chateaux peters out in Anjou, where chalky-white tufa cliffs line the riverbanks instead. Ancient stone quarries and dwellings hewn into the rock conceal an astonishing underworld of wine cellars, mushroom farms and monumental art sculptures. Above ground, black slate roofs pepper the vine-rich land. Outstanding architectural gems in Anjou's crown include the cathedral and Abbaye de St-Serge in Angers (two beautiful examples of Angevin vaulting) and the Romanesque Abbaye de Fontevraud.

Anjou is in the administrative *département* (department) of Maine-et-Loire. It is bordered to the west by an area that was part of Brittany until the 1960s (and is now in Loire-Atlantique) and to the east by Touraine, a region that belonged to Grand (Greater) Anjou under the Angevin dynasty of fearsome Falcon counts. By the time the 21-year-old Angevin Henri Plantagenêt II was crowned king of England in 1154, the Anjou counts controlled a vast territory embracing Poitou, Toulouse, Gascony, Périgord and Limousin, as well as Anjou, Maine and Touraine.

The capital of Maine-et-Loire – named after two of the many rivers that cross it – is Angers, home to the world-famous medieval *L'Apocalypse* tapestry. Saumur, the second-largest town, 50km downstream, enjoys an awesome reputation as the centre of equestrian sport in France and is home to the prestigious Cadre Noir. Europe's highest concentration of troglodyte caves dots the Loire riverbanks north and south of Saumur.

In the south-west of Anjou is Les Mauges, a barren floodland across which the blood of the Vendée War spilled in 1793–6.

Angers & Around

ANGERS
postcode 49000 • pop 141,500
Ancient Angers is rich in treasures. Its crown jewel – showcased inside the city's

Highlights

- Gaze in awe at the world's largest medieval tapestry at Château d'Angers; recoil in horror from its contemporary counterpart in the Musée Jean Lurçat in Angers.

- Wander around Château de Serrant, a Renaissance gem crammed with priceless arts and furnishings.

- Watch the elite Cadre Noir perform its equestrian tricks at Saumur's prestigious École Nationale d'Équitation.

- Learn how cavemen lived in troglodyte valley – you too can eat, sleep and drink here.

- Delve into the fascinating history of the Romanesque Abbaye de Fontevraud.

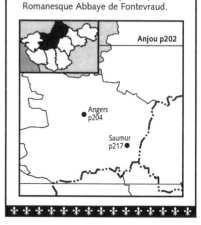

Anjou p202

Angers p204

Saumur p217

ANJOU

mighty chateau – is a medieval tapestry which depicts the Apocalypse and is the oldest of its size in the world. The biblical drama is also beautifully reflected in stained glass inside the city's majestic cathedral. The wealth of half-timbered town houses and luxurious *hôtels particuliers* (mansions) that stud the town's streets evoke the glittering courts of the Falcon counts and Plantagenêt dynasty.

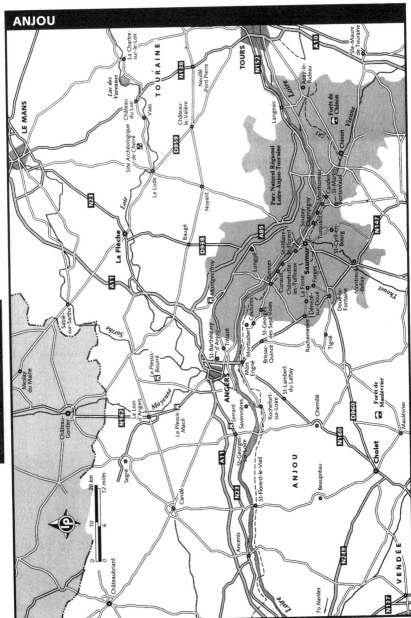

The Angevin capital is nestled either side of the River Maine, a short stretch of water that links the Rivers Sarthe and Mayenne downstream with the River Loire 10km upstream. Well situated in the centre of the Maine-et-Loire département, Angers serves as a convenient base for exploring the slate mines of 'black' Anjou and the chalky tufa troglodytes of 'white' Anjou.

History
Angers enjoyed power from an early age. First settled by the Andes Celtic tribe, as the Gallo-Roman city of Juliomagus it later became the capital of Civitas Andecavorum (the Roman administrative region), in around AD 1. In the 3rd century a wall was built to protect the city from invasions by the Franks, who came from the Rhine area, and Christianity was adopted. Vikings sacked the city in 854 and again in 872 when, after a long siege, Charles the Bald delivered the city and took control of it. His death in 877 marked the end of the Carolingian dynasty and prompted a battle for power, eventually won by the House of Anjou under Foulques le Roux (Falcon the Red) in 898.

Angers flourished during the rule of the Anjou count Foulques Nerra (987–1040), although the subsequent territorial expansion under the Plantagenêts in the 12th century saw the ducal court shift from Angers to Chinon under Henri II and to Saumur under Louis I d'Anjou. However, Angers ultimately remained the cosmopolitan capital of the region, Louis I commissioning a monumental tapestry for Château d'Angers in 1375. The university he established flourished under his grandson René (1409–80), luring some 5000 students, and in 1476 the Loire's first printing press opened in Angers. The Wars of Religion (1562–98) took their toll on the city, with hundreds of Protestants being slaughtered during the Saint Bartholomew's Day massacres on 23–24 August 1572. More blood was spilled in 1793–6 during the Vendée War, when Republicans and pro-royalist Vendéens clashed in Angers.

Angers embraced a new industrial era with the arrival of the Paris–Nantes railway in 1849. Much of the city was bombed during WWII. The town then briefly served as the seat of the exiled Polish government in 1940 and as the regional headquarters of the Gestapo in 1942.

Orientation
Angers is pleasantly walkable. The River Maine cuts through the city from north to south. The historic heart of the city is on the left (eastern) bank of the river, nicely squared off by blvd Ayrault and its continuation, blvd Carnot, to the north; blvd du Maréchal Foch to the east; and blvd du Roi René to the south. Château d'Angers sits in the far south-western corner of this square, overlooking place du Président Kennedy at the western end of blvd du Roi René.

The train station is an 800m walk south of place du Président Kennedy. The bus station is about 800m north of the chateau, overlooking the river on place de la Poissonnerie (quai Bazin).

South-west of the city, the River Maine flows into Lac de Maine, which, in summer, is a popular venue for canoeing, kayaking and other water sports.

Maps The free city map doled out by the tourist office is of poor quality – no doubt the reason why the office also sells Kümmerly+Frey's *Angers et sa Banlieue* (Blay-Foldex, 28FF). The best selection of maps is stocked by the Maison de la Presse, at 6 rue Chaperonnière.

Information
Tourist Offices Angers tourist office (☎ 02 41 23 51 11, fax 02 41 24 01 20, ✉ angers.tourisme@ville-angers.fr) is inside the Maison Départmentale du Tourisme at 11 place du Président Kennedy. It sells tickets for cultural events and arranges guided city tours (see Organised Tours later in this Angers section). It also makes hotel reservations (free for hotels in Angers, 15/25FF in Maine-et-Loire/other départements). The office opens 9 am to 7 pm Monday to Saturday, and 10 am to 1 pm and 2 to 6 pm on Sunday, early May to September; and 9 am (11 am on Monday) to 6 pm

ANJOU

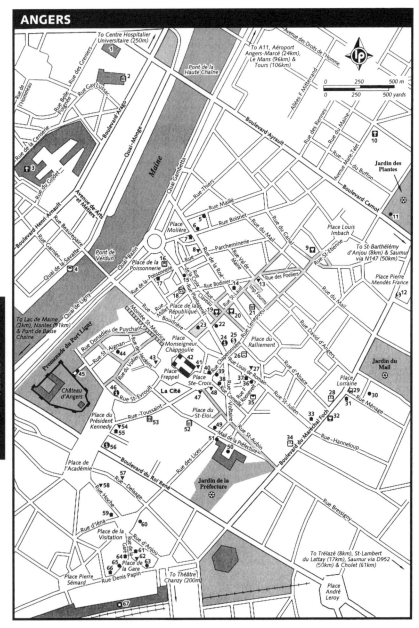

ANGERS

PLACES TO STAY
- 7 Hôtel des Négociants
- 14 Hôtel du Centre
- 17 Hôtel Ibis
- 31 Hôtel d'Anjou
- 33 Bleu Marine
- 37 Hôtel Continental
- 55 Hôtel Marguerite d'Anjou
- 59 Hôtel Royal
- 61 Hôtel Coupe d'Or
- 64 Hôtel l'Univers
- 66 Hôtel de France

PLACES TO EAT
- 8 Le Péché Gourmand
- 13 Le Grandgousier
- 27 L'Entr'acte
- 41 La Treille
- 43 La Ferme
- 47 La Gourmandaise
- 48 Pub Le Kent
- 54 Le Duc d'Anjou
- 57 La Rose d'Or
- 58 Le Lucullus
- 62 Le Relais

OTHER
- 1 Centre Régional d'Art Textile
- 2 Musée Jean Lurçat et de la Tapisserie Contemporaine
- 3 Abbaye Ronceray
- 4 Boat Trips
- 5 Sport Eco
- 6 SPAD
- 9 Le Twist
- 10 Abbaye St-Serge
- 11 Centre de Congrès
- 12 Banque de France
- 15 Laverie Les Halles
- 16 Bus Station
- 18 Copy Boutique
- 19 Le Sunset
- 20 Le Louisiane
- 21 Musée Pincé
- 22 Traiteur aux Rillauds d'Or
- 23 Covered Market
- 24 Hôtel des Vins
- 25 BNP Bank; SNCF Train Tickets
- 26 Grand Théâtre d'Angers
- 28 Gaumont Colisée
- 29 Bus Stop
- 30 Espace Lorraine
- 32 Café-Concert Le Coursive
- 34 Gaumont Variétés
- 35 Post Office
- 36 Une Deux
- 38 Lavomatique
- 39 Maison de la Presse
- 40 Maison d'Adam
- 42 Entrance to Cathédrale St-Maurice
- 44 Logis du Croissant; Maison de l'Étain
- 45 Entrance to Château d'Angers
- 46 Maison du Vin de l'Anjou
- 49 Tour St-Aubin
- 50 Préfecture
- 51 Ducs de Gascogne
- 52 Musée des Beaux Arts
- 53 Galerie David d'Angers; Cloître Toussaint
- 56 Tourist Office; Gîtes de France; Logis de France
- 60 Laverie du Cygne; L'Îlot Courses
- 63 Budget; Hertz
- 65 Europcar
- 67 Train Station

Monday to Saturday, and 10 am to 1 pm on Sunday, the rest of the year. Check out the Web site at www.ville-angers.fr.

The Comité Départemental du Tourisme de l'Anjou (☎ 02 41 23 51 51, fax 02 41 88 36 77, ❷ anjou.cdt@wanadoo.fr) is in the same building. There are clean public toilets in the basement. Gîtes de France and Logis de France have an office on the 2nd floor and take bookings for accommodation in Maine-et-Loire; see Places to Stay later in this Angers section.

Money Banque de France, overlooking place Pierre Mendès France, has a currency exchange desk open from 9 am to noon on weekdays.

Post The post office, 1 rue Franklin Roosevelt, opens 8 am to 7 pm on weekdays, and 8 am to noon on Saturday.

Email & Internet Access There is a Cyberposte station inside the post office.

Alternatively, try Copy Boutique (☎ 02 41 88 96 26, ❷ copyboutique@wanadoo.fr), 48 rue Plantagenêt, which charges 20FF per 30 minutes for on-line access and opens 9 am to 7.30 pm on weekdays, and 9 am to 12.30 pm and 2 to 7.30 pm on Saturday.

Laundry Lavomatique, 3 rue Corneille, opens 7 am to 9.30 pm. Laverie Les Halles, 15 rue Plantagenêt, opens 8 am to 9 pm. Laverie du Cygne, place de la Visitation, is closest to the train station hotels.

Château d'Angers

The 17 dark-grey, grizzly towers of Château d'Angers, built on a rocky promontory on the left bank of the Maine, are a forbidding sight. The unassailable, 30m-tall towers – chiselled in 1232 from black schist and embedded with decorative chains of chalky white tufa – made Angers the best-defended fortress in Louis IX's kingdom.

The 13th-century fortress remains one of the finest examples of feudal architecture in

euro currency converter 10FF = €1.52

ANJOU

the Loire. It stands on the site of an 11th-century stone castle built by Foulques Nerra (987–1040) and could be entered through two gates, each defended by a double portcullis.

The contrasting **Logis Royal** (Royal Residence), **Chapelle** (Chapel) and landscaped gardens that languish gracefully inside the great lumbering walls date from the 14th and 15th centuries and were built to host the court of the Anjou dukes. The northern wing of the Logis Royal, raised under Louis II d'Anjou, was added in 1435–53 by his son René, who had the **Gallerie du Roi René** built. Today's gallery is a replica of the original, which was destroyed during WWII.

Most people visit Château d'Angers to see *L'Apocalypse* (*The Apocalypse*), a series of 68 scenes measuring 103m in all in length and forming the oldest tapestry of this size in the world. Commissioned by Louis I d'Anjou in 1375, the remarkably well-preserved hangings illustrate the last book of the Bible according to St John and have been on display in a purpose-built bunker inside the fortress since 1996.

Château d'Angers (☎ 02 41 87 43 47), 2 promenade du Bout du Monde, opens 9.30 am to 7 pm (last admission 6.15 pm) daily, mid-May to mid-September; and 10 am to 6 pm (5 pm from November to mid-March) daily, the rest of the year. Admission costs 35FF (children 25FF). The Logis Royal, Logis au Gouverneur (Governor's Residence) and Porte des Champs (Gate to the Fields) can only be visited as part of a guided tour (in French only). Free explanatory brochures are available in English.

Quartier de la Cité

The historic heart of Angers, known as La Cité, spills out to the north and east of Château d'Angers. Its centrepiece is the magnificent **Cathédrale St-Maurice**, built in the 12th and 13th centuries and famed for its striking Norman porch (1170) and nave (1150–1250), which contains outstanding examples of Angevin vaulting. The three convex vaults form a perfect square (of 16.39 sq metre) and pre-empted the emerging Gothic style when built in 1149 under Henri II.

Equally noteworthy is the cathedral's exceptional collection of stained-glass windows, which date from the 12th to the 16th centuries. The apocalypse is depicted in the stunning north and south rose windows in the transepts. An English-language leaflet about the windows is sold for 5FF at the front of the cathedral. From place Monseigneur Chappoulie, the square in front of the cathedral, there is a splendid view of the River Maine, which can be reached from the cathedral by the **monumental staircase** along montée St-Maurice.

There are several **hôtels particuliers** on the quiet, pedestrian streets which link the cathedral with the chateau, including **Hôtel de la Haute-Mule** at 13–15 rue St-Evroult; the arcaded, 16th-century **Hôtel de Cunault** at 18 rue Donadieu de Puycharic; and the **Logis du Croissant** (1448), on parallel rue St-Aignan, which houses a Maison de l'Étain (Pewter House) filled with pewterware for tourists to ogle and buy.

Place Ste-Croix behind the cathedral holds Angers' most photographed edifice. The half-timbered **Maison d'Adam** was built around 1500 as a bourgeois town house. Its ornate facade is studded with wooden sculptures of cheeky medieval characters and the tree of life decorates the corner beam. Inside, locally produced handicrafts are sold in the Maison des Artisans (☎ 02 41 88 06 27).

Four blocks north of place Ste-Croix, at 32 bis rue Lenepveu, is another hôtel particulier (1523–35), built for 16th-century city mayor Jean de Pincé. Its floor plan is traditionally Gothic in shape, but its facade has decorative flourishes typical to early Renaissance architecture. Inside, **Musée Pincé** (☎ 02 41 88 94 27) exhibits a mix of Greek, Roman and Egyptian antiquities and Oriental arts and opens 9 am to 6.30 pm. Admission costs 10FF.

Some remains of the **medieval ramparts** that protected Angers until the French Revolution still stand on rue Toussaint, which runs south-west from place Ste-Croix. Bear left (east) along rue du St-Eloi to get to the **Musée des Beaux Arts** (Fine Arts Museum; ☎ 02 41 88 64 65), 10 rue du Musée. The museum will remain closed until 2002, when renovation work costing an estimated 162 million FF is due to be completed.

Temporary art exhibitions are housed in the 52m-tall **Tour St-Aubin**, the imposing tower of an 11th-century abbey dominating the eastern side of place du St-Eloi.

Galerie David d'Angers

At the southern end of rue Toussaint is the breathtaking David d'Angers Gallery (☎ 02 41 87 21 03). This art gallery showcases the monumental sculptures of Angevin sculptor David d'Angers (1788–1856) and is housed inside the 11th-century Abbaye Toussaint (All Saints' Abbey). Founded in 1040, the abbey was abandoned during the Revolution and fell into ruins until 1980–94, when French architect Pierre Prunet renovated the abbey and transformed it into a masterpiece of contemporary architecture. Natural light floods in through a glass roof supported by steel beams and the resultant play of sun and shadow on d'Angers' sculptures is stunning.

The Galerie David d'Angers opens 9 am to 6.30 pm Tuesday to Sunday, mid-June to mid-September; and 10 am to noon and 2 to 6 pm Tuesday to Sunday, the rest of the year. Admission costs 10FF (students and children 5FF).

Abbaye St-Serge

The 7th-century Abbaye St-Serge, 2km north of La Cité, served as a Benedictine monastery until 1802. Its choir, dating from 1220–5, remains among Anjou's finest examples of the *style Angevin*, with its elegant Angevin vaults. The contrasting nave was built in the 15th century to replace its Romanesque counterpart, which was destroyed during the Hundred Years' War. A stained-glass window in the chapel depicts the saintly relics of Brieuc, which were sheltered in the abbey between 851 and 1793.

The abbey, off rue Talet, is a block west of the **Jardin des Plantes**, a lovely green strolling space, and the modern **Centre de Congrès** (Congress Centre).

Musée Jean Lurçat et de la Tapisserie Contemporaine

These unique museums dedicated to Jean Lurçat and contemporary tapestry are across the river at 6 blvd Arago. They are housed in a former hospital, built in 1175–80 under Henri II. The hospital closed in 1865.

Since 1968 the vast wards – 60m long and divided into three Gothic vaulted naves – have served as an exhibition hall for a series of 10 contemporary monumental tapestries entitled *Le Chant du Monde* (*The Song of the World*). Woven in 1959–66 in Aubusson, the tapestries are the creation of French-born artist Jean Lurçat (1892–1966), who adopted tapestry as an artistic medium after viewing *L'Apocalypse* in Château d'Angers for the first time in 1937. The 10 hangings tell the horror story of human destruction and are disturbing. A grisly green skeleton depicts *Homme d'Hiroshima* (*Hiroshima Man*). From the far end of the ward, a door leads to the peaceful, birdsong-filled cloister, a welcome relief after Lurçat's draining tale.

The Musée de la Tapisserie Contemporaine is in the modern annexe adjoining the hospital. Innovative temporary art exhibitions fill the ground floor, and further Lurçat works – paintings, ceramics and more tapestries – are displayed on the 1st floor.

Museum Passes

The **Passeport Musées d'Angers** (Angers Museum Passport) costs 25FF, is valid for one year, and includes one entrance to the Galerie David d'Angers, Musée Jean Lurçat et de la Tapisserie Contemporaine, Musée Pincé, Musée d'Histoire Naturelle and Musée des Beaux Arts (when it opens in 2002). Buy your passport at the tourist office or at any of the museums involved in the scheme.

If you intend visiting Château d'Angers, invest in a **billet jumelé**. This costs 50FF, is valid for one year and allows a single entrance to the chateau as well as to the Galerie David d'Angers, Musée Jean Lurçat et de la Tapisserie Contemporaine and the Musée des Beaux Arts. It is available at the tourist office.

ANJOU

Admission to the Musée Jean Lurçat (☎ 02 41 24 18 45) and Musée de la Tapisserie Contemporaine (☎ 02 41 24 18 48) costs 20FF (those aged under 18 free). Both museums open 9 am to 6.30 pm daily, mid-June to mid-September; and 10 am to noon and 2 to 6 pm Tuesday to Sunday, the rest of the year.

Abbaye Ronceray

Farther south along the right bank is the 11th-century, Romanesque Abbaye Ronceray. This Benedictine abbey was founded in 1028 by the wife of Foulques Nerra and was the city's only sanctuary for women until 1790, when it was abandoned.

Eastbound rue Beaurepaire links the abbey with **pont de Verdun**. The bridge offers unsurpassable views of Château d'Angers, the cathedral and the old town ensemble.

Wine-Tasting

The **Maison du Vin de l'Anjou** (☎ 02 41 88 81 13, fax 02 41 86 71 84), across from the chateau at 5 bis place du Président Kennedy, is the perfect spot to sample Anjou and Saumur wines. Different grape varieties, such as cabernet sauvignon, cabernet franc, chardonnay, chenin blanc and so on, are pickled in jars and displayed here. The Maison du Vin opens 9 am to 1 pm and 3 to 6.30 pm Tuesday to Sunday (closed Sunday, October to March).

Regional wine information is available at the **Hôtel des Vins** (☎ 02 41 87 62 57, fax 02 41 86 71 84) at 73 rue Plantagenêt. The mansion houses, among other things, the Conseil Interprofessionnel des Vins d'Anjou et de Saumur on the 3rd floor, which opens 8 am to 12.30 pm and 2 to 5.30 pm on weekdays. Enter the building via door No 5.

The tourist office stocks a list of places offering *dégustation* (tasting). It also sells *Route Touristique des Vignobles Val de Loire: Découvertes en Terroir Anjou-Saumur* (Éditions Ouest-France, 50FF), a book listing 145 *vignerons* (wine growers) who can help you taste and buy Anjou's noblest treasure.

Activities

Six- to 13km-long **canoeing** trips (50FF to 110FF), 40km **cycling** excursions (60FF) and two-hour **horse-riding** trips along the banks of the River Maine (180FF) can be booked through the tourist office. The Canoë-Kayak Club de Lac de Maine (☎ 02 41 72 07 04), at the Parc de Loisirs du Lac de Maine, offers canoeing lessons, courses and trips. In August the tourist office organises **painting and photography** excursions (50FF to 100FF) to pretty nature spots.

There are **boat trips** along the River Maine from mid-June to mid-September on Saturday and Sunday, departing from the landing stage on quai de la Savatte at 4.30 pm. Trips last two hours and cost 47FF (children 28FF). From mid-July to the end of August, there are additional trips on Thursday and Friday.

A visit to Anjou is not complete without trying your hand at **boule de fort**, the Angevin adaptation of regular French *boules* or *pétanque*. For details of clubs, see Activities in the Facts for the Visitor chapter.

Courses

Fascinating tapestry workshops are held at Angers' Centre Régional d'Art Textile, where new tapestries are woven and old ones restored in a series of independent workshops. See Tapestry & Medieval Arts under Courses in the Facts for the Visitor chapter for details.

Organised Tours

The tourist office organises numerous tours, detailed in the free brochure *Les Rendez-Vous d'Angers Tourisme*. Taxi tours to sights outside Angers for up to four people, with an English-speaking commentary, are also operated by the tourist office. There's a choice of five circuits, starting at 113FF per person for a 2½-hour chateau tour. The three-hour Vignobles d'Anjou tour of Angers' surrounding vineyards is interesting but pricey (upwards of 197FF per person).

Special Events

Angers L'Été in July and August brings concerts of all musical genres and epochs to

Power station, Doué-la-Fontaine

Typical local carving, Saumur

Be careful cycling home after tasting the local wines in Saumur.

Europe's largest concentration of cave dwellings is hewn from tufa cliffs near Saumur.

Romanesque Abbaye de Fontevraud (1106–17)

Showing off a *courbette* at Saumur's Cadre Noir

Grand-Moûtier cloisters, Abbaye de Fontevraud

Neolithic Dolmen de la Madeleine, near Gennes

Half-timbered Maison d'Adam, Angers

town; open-air concerts (50FF) are held every Tuesday and Thursday at 9 pm in the Cloître Toussaint on rue Toussaint (Théâtre Chanzy in case of rain). Between April and October, the chateau hosts a handful of concerts; the tourist office has details. Jazz is performed in various venues during August's Les Heures Musicales du Haut Anjou.

In early September, films are screened at Château d'Angers during the three-day Nuits du Cinéma; tickets cost 35FF. La Semaine du Goût in mid-October is a week-long gastronomic festival which focuses very much on consuming Anjou wines and liqueurs.

Places to Stay

Gîtes de France (☎ 02 41 23 51 23, fax 02 41 23 51 26, @ anjou.cdt@wanadoo.com), place du Président Kennedy, has its office and reservation service on the 2nd floor of the tourist office building. Information and reservations for gîtes, chambre d'hôtes and so on throughout Maine-et-Loire are available here. The office opens 9.30 am to 1 pm and 2 to 5.30 pm on weekdays.

Camping The *Camping du Lac de Maine* (☎ 02 41 73 05 03, fax 02 41 73 02 20, ave du Lac de Maine) is some 2.5km south-west of the city, overlooking Lac de Maine. The 162-pitch site opens mid-March to mid-October and charges 80FF per day for a tent pitch, car and two people, plus 8/12.50FF for each additional person aged under/over seven. To get here from the city centre, take Cotra bus No 16 from outside the train station, bus station or place Ralliement to the Perussaie stop on rue de la Chambre aux Deniers, a 500m walk from the lake shore.

Hostel The *auberge de jeunesse* (☎ 02 41 22 32 10, fax 02 41 22 32 11, 49 ave du Lac de Maine) is housed inside the Centre d'Accueil du Lac de Maine. The riverside hostel has doubles (with two beds) costing 170FF, including breakfast. To get here from the centre of Angers, follow the same instructions as for Camping, above.

Hotels The *Hôtel Marguerite d'Anjou* (☎ 02 41 88 11 61, fax 02 41 87 37 62, 13

place du Président Kennedy) is well positioned within a stone's throw of the chateau. Its eight rooms, equipped with TV, telephone and bathroom, start at 180/220/260FF for one/two/three people. The adjoining bar-brasserie doubles as reception.

Close to Angers' busy nightlife is *Hôtel du Centre* (☎ 02 41 87 45 07, 12 rue St-Laud), above a busy pub of the same name. It has 15 rooms starting at 110/130FF for a single/double.

Among the many hotels near the train station, nine-room *Hôtel Coupe d'Or* (☎ 02 41 88 45 02, fax 02 41 86 01 58, 5 rue de la Gare) is among the best value. Singles/doubles with shared bathroom cost 120/135FF, and rooms with private facilities start at 150/175FF.

Near the bus station, *Hôtel des Négociants* (☎ 02 41 88 24 08, 2 rue de la Roë), overlooking place Molière, is a cheapie. Shower-equipped doubles cost 155FF and triples/quads with two large beds cost 185/220FF.

Bang smack in the heart of Angers' shopping district is the unspectacular but convenient *Hôtel Continental* (☎ 02 41 86 94 94, fax 02 41 86 96 60, 12–14 rue Louis de Romain). Singles/doubles with shower and toilet cost upwards of 195/220FF, and breakfast is 34FF. Buzz on the intercom to contact reception.

Opposite the bus station, 95-room *Hôtel Ibis* (☎ 02 41 86 15 15, fax 02 41 87 10 41, rue de la Poissonnerie) is part of a chain and is a safe bet. Singles/doubles cost 305/340FF.

Near the train station, two-star *Hôtel Royal* (☎ 02 41 88 30 25, fax 02 41 81 05 75, 8 bis place de la Visitation) is a bright and cheerful spot with smart singles/doubles with all mod cons starting at 188/230FF. Equally pleasant is *Hôtel l'Univers* (☎ 02 41 88 41 62, fax 02 41 20 95 19, 16 rue de la Gare). Shower- and toilet-equipped doubles cost 250FF and it has quads with shower (toilet in the corridor) for 330FF. Rooms for one or two with basin and bidet cost 150FF.

Three-star *Hôtel de France* (☎ 02 41 88 49 42, fax 02 41 86 76 70, 8 place de la

ANJOU

Gare) is an upmarket pad opposite the train station. Its 55 rooms cost 395FF to 565FF.

Closer to parkland is atmospheric **Bleu Marine** (☎ *02 41 87 37 20, fax 02 41 87 49 54, 18 blvd du Maréchal Foch)*, an elegant establishment with singles/doubles costing upwards of 390/450FF. Three-star **Hotel d'Anjou** (☎ *02 41 88 24 82, fax 02 41 87 22 21, 1 blvd du Maréchal Foch)* is part of the Best Western hotel chain and is rated for its upmarket restaurant, called La Salamande. Doubles cost 580FF to 780FF, breakfast is 60FF and private parking costs 48FF.

Places to Eat

Restaurants On the pavement directly opposite Maison d'Adam, **La Treille** (☎ *02 41 88 45 51, 12 rue Montault)* has a couple of tables and chairs and offers a good-value lunchtime *menu express* (quick set menu) costing 55FF. The terrace filling place Ste-Croix is equally popular at lunchtime; it's run by **Pub Le Kent** (☎ *02 41 87 88 55, 7 place Ste-Croix)*.

Those who prefer a cathedral view should munch at **La Ferme** (☎ *02 41 87 09 90, place Freppel)*. It specialises in poultry dishes and has a terrace (closed Sunday and Wednesday).

Tasty grilled meats are cooked on a wood fire at **Le Grandgousier** (☎ *02 41 87 87 47, 7 rue St-Laud)*. Crottin de Chavignol (a type of goat's cheese) served with a raspberry coulis is among its regional specialities. Seafood is the dish of the day at **Le Péché Gourmand** (☎ *02 41 81 04 76, 48 rue Parcheminerie)*, which has a good-value 68FF *menu*, served until 9 pm on weekday evenings.

In Angers' commercial heart, behind the Grand Théâtre d'Angers, is **L'Entr'acte** (☎ *02 41 87 71 82, 9 rue Louis de Romain)*. It is a traditional *bouchon* (a bistro typical to Lyon), serving hearty delights such as *boudin blanc* (white-meat sausage) and *andouillette* (tripe sausage) in a rich and fabulous setting. *Menus* cost 98FF or 155FF (closed Saturday lunchtime and all day Sunday).

Between the train station and the chateau, **Le Lucullus** (☎ *02 41 87 00 44, 5 rue*

Hoche) is a select spot with a medieval cellar hidden beneath its ultra-modern facade. *Menus* featuring local gastronomic delights start at 85/119FF for lunch/dinner; there's also a 60FF children's *menu*.

Closer still to the train station is recommended **Le Relais** (☎ *02 41 88 42 51, 9 rue de la Gare)*, run by a friendly, apron-clad patron who takes great pride in the excellent cuisine his chef cooks up; *menus* start at 98FF.

La Rose d'Or (☎ *02 41 88 38 38, 21 rue Delâge)* features lots of local specialities on its 110FF and 180FF handwritten *menus*, and has an extensive wine list crammed with Saumur, Bourgueil and other regional vintages. It's closed Sunday and Monday.

Cafes On the corner of place Ste-Croix and rue St-Aubin, **La Gourmandaise** sells top-rate sandwiches, filled baguettes and other satisfying lunchtime bites; count on a long queue. Close to the chateau, **Le Duc d'Anjou** (55 rue Toussaint) is the spot for an early-morning coffee and croissant while waiting for the chateau to open.

Self-Catering Near the train station, **L'Îlot Courses**, place de la Visitation, is a small grocery store, open 8 am to 9 pm Monday to Saturday, and 9 am to 1 pm on Sunday.

Stock up on meaty treats, including *rillons* (fat-fried pork cubes) and *rillauds* (variation on rillons), two regional specialities, at the **Traiteur aux Rillauds d'Or** (☎ *02 41 88 03 13, 59 rue St-Laud)*. Delicacies to suit all budgets and tastes are packaged with finesse at **Ducs de Gascogne**, on the corner of rue des Lices and mail de la Préfecture.

Entertainment

Pubs, Bars & Clubs There is a cluster of pubs and bars at the southern end of rue St-Laud, including busy **Le Sunset** at No 44 and American-inspired **Le Louisiane** on the corner of rue des Deux Haies. Irish bars dot the pedestrian section of nearby rue des Poeliers. **Le Twist** (8 rue St-Etienne) is a fun, 50s-style American-beer bar where you can slam tequila shots too.

ANJOU

Café-Concert Le Coursive (☎ 02 41 25 13 87, 7 bis blvd du Maréchal Foch) is a jazzy bar which hosts live bands several times a week from 9.30 pm. The club opens 5 pm to 2 am Monday to Saturday.

Opera, Theatre & Music The *Grand Théâtre d'Angers*, on place du Ralliement, was built in 1871 and is home to the Angers Opera (☎ 02 41 25 32 22); tickets cost 70FF to 195FF and are sold in advance at the box office (☎ 02 41 24 16 40), open 11 am to 7 pm Tuesday to Saturday. In season (October to May), the theatre hosts Mardis Musicaux (☎ 02 41 88 64 96), which sees a musical concert fill the theatre most Tuesdays. Baroque music concerts are hosted by Anacréon (☎ 02 41 44 33 80), in the *Chapelle des Ursules*.

Cinemas Weekly cinema listings are included in *Angers Poche*, a fortnightly entertainment guide, distributed free at the tourist office. Cinemas showing mainstream films in their original language include *Gaumont Colisée* (☎ 08 36 68 75 55, 8 blvd du Maréchal Foch), *Gaumont Variétés* (☎ 08 36 68 75 55, 34 blvd du Maréchal Foch) and *400 Coups* (☎ 08 36 68 00 72, 12 rue Claveau).

Getting There & Away
Air Aéroport Angers-Marcé (☎ 02 41 33 50 20, 02 41 33 50 16) is 24km north-east of Angers in Marcé, off the A11 (exit No 12, signposted 'Seiches-sur-le Loir'). See Air in the Getting There & Away chapter for more on domestic flights.

Bus Eurolines buses depart from quai H at Angers bus station, place de la Poissonnerie, for Amsterdam (410FF, 15 hours, one weekly), Brussels (310FF, 12 hours, one weekly) and London (460FF, 13½ hours, one weekly).

Regional buses are operated by Anjou Bus (☎ 02 41 88 59 25); its information and ticket office at the bus station is open from 6.30 am to 7.15 pm. Destinations served include Brissac-Quincé (25 minutes, six daily), Cholet (No 12, 1½ hours, eight to 10

daily), Doué-la-Fontaine (55 minutes, six daily), La Flèche (No 14, one hour, three or four daily), Le Lion d'Angers (No 1, 40 minutes, seven daily), Montreuil-Bellay (1¼ hours, six daily), St-Georges-sur-Loire (No 18 or 18B, 40 minutes, about five daily), Saumur via Coutures and St-Georges des Sept Voies (No 5, 1½ hours, four daily) and Saumur via the right bank of the River Loire (No 11, 1¼ hours, five or six daily).

Train Angers SNCF train station (Angers St-Laud on most timetables) is on place de la Gare. In town, advance tickets can be bought from the SNCF ticket machine in the BNP bank at 2 rue St-Pierre.

The city is well served by trains. There is at least one train every hour between Angers and Tours (83/103FF for a non-TGV/TGV, 50 minutes to 1½ hours) between 7 am and 11.45 pm, stopping en route at Saumur (42FF, 20 minutes) and St-Pierre des Corps (83/103FF for a non-TGV/TGV, 55 minutes). Change trains in Tours or St-Pierre des Corps to get to/from Poitiers or Blois, Orléans and other eastern Loire destinations.

Westbound along the Loire Valley, there are at least half-hourly trains to/from Nantes (71/81FF, 40 minutes/one hour by TGV/non-TGV), from where there are connecting southbound train services to La Rochelle, Bordeaux and Toulouse. Between Angers and Cholet there are 13 trains daily (55FF, 50 minutes). Northbound destinations include Le Mans (77/87FF, 40 minutes/1¼ hours by TGV/non-TGV, 10 or more daily).

For details of trains to/from Paris, see Other Parts of France under Land in the Getting There & Away chapter.

Getting Around
Bus Local buses are operated by Cotra, which has its terminus on place Lorraine, east of the centre. Tickets and passes are sold inside Espace Lorraine (☎ 02 41 33 64 64), open 7.45 am to 6.30 pm on weekdays, and 8.45 am to 12.15 pm and 1.30 to 5.30 pm on Saturday. A ticket valid for a single journey costs 6.50FF, a carnet of five/10 costs 28/53FF, and a one-day travel pass allowing

umlimited travel on Cotra buses is available for 18FF.

Car Europcar (☎ 02 41 87 87 10) has an office in front of the train station on place de la Gare. Budget (☎ 02 41 88 23 16), 16 rue Denis Papin, is opposite the station, as is Hertz (☎ 02 41 88 15 16), next door.

Bicycle & Rollerblades Sport ECO (☎ 02 41 87 07 77), 45 rue Maillé, has bicycles and rollers to rent. Bikes cost 70/130/295FF per day/weekend/week, and rollerblades cost 70/130/295FF. The shop opens 10 am to noon and 2 to 7 pm Tuesday to Saturday.

Une Deux, a kite and boarding shop in the Galerie Palace shopping mall, corner of rue Louis de Romain and rue Franklin Roosevelt, has rollerblades to hire. SPAD, 53 rue Broisnet, sells and repairs bicycles. Both shops open Tuesday to Saturday.

AROUND ANGERS

An eclectic assortment of museums and chateaux – the Loire's westernmost – sprinkle the Angevin suburbs. South of the city, the River Maine joins with the River Loire for the final leg of the grand journey to the Atlantic. The riverbanks immediately west of this confluence have been planted with vineyards since the 11th century and remain the source of some of the valley's most noble wines – Savennières, Coteaux du Layon and so on.

North of Angers, the Rivers Mayenne and Sarthe slice across the plateau. About 15km downstream along the Sarthe, the masculine Loir – not to be confused with the feminine Loire – carves eastwards through the pretty Vallée du Loir.

The sterile plateau of Les Mauges occupies the area south of Angers.

Château de Serrant

Château de Serrant is a good example of Renaissance architecture and has an unusually well-furnished interior. Fifteen kilometres west of Angers on the N23, it is the westernmost of the Loire chateaux. Its library houses over 12,000 books and is one of the largest private libraries in France.

The sturdy tower basements and secret passageways which allowed guards to move around the chateau are all that remains of the original medieval fortress, built to defend the Loire crossing at Chalonnes, 7km south. Work started on the Renaissance edifice in 1539, using plans drawn up by Jean Delespine, the same architect who designed Angers' Hôtel Pincé. The main wing was furnished and two more wings built by Guillaume de Bautru, chateau owner from 1636. In the 18th century the chapel was raised and the estate sold to the Walsh family, shipowners of Irish descent who fled to Nantes from Ireland during William and Mary's Glorious Revolution of 1688. A painting in the library depicts Antoine Walsh disembarking in Scotland with Bonnie Prince Charlie in 1745; Walsh had previously given the Stuart prince two ships. Valentine Walsh married into the Trémoïlle family in 1830, in whose hands the chateau remains today.

Among the particularly outstanding furnishings is a priceless **cabinet d'ébène** (ebony cabinet) carved by the Dutch cabinet maker Pierre Gole in the 17th century. Its intricate interior and exterior carvings conceal 33 secret drawers and the piece is just one of four known to exist in the world (the others are in Windsor Castle, Château de Fontainebleau and the Rijksmuseum in Amsterdam). Displayed in the **grand salon** (drawing room), the cabinet sits beneath a magnificent carved wooden ceiling, designed by architect Lucien Magne (1849–1916) in 1890 to disguise the badly damaged original ceiling. The ceilings of carved white tufa in the rooms inside the tower are equally unique. The **chambre** (bedroom) on the tower's first floor remains furnished exactly as it was when Napoleon came to stay (but left two hours later) in 1808.

Designer Georges Jacob's mahogany table with lion paws in the **salle à manger** (dining room) is still used by Prince de Ligne la Trémoïlle and his family, who dine here during the four months of the year they spend at the chateau. A hand-operated lift was installed in Château de Serrant in 1900, followed by electricity in 1905 and running water in 1920 (the bath water still flows into the moat today).

Between April and mid-November, the chateau (☎ 02 41 39 13 01) can only be visited with a guided tour in French; explanation sheets in English are available. Admission costs 45FF (those aged under 18 25FF). Tours depart at 20 minutes past the hour from 10.20 am to 5.20 pm, with extra tours at 10 minutes to the hour in July and August. No tours run between 11.20 and 2.20 pm in summer while the family has lunch.

Wine-Tasting

Serrant is kissed to the south by one of the Loire's most celebrated white wine appellations, AOC **Coteaux du Layon**, whose vineyards cover a prized 1700-hectare pocket of land around the River Layon (south of the Loire). Made exclusively from the chenin grape, Coteaux du Layon are sweet full-bodied wines, golden in colour and honeyed in aroma. They are best served alone as an aperitif, or with a smattering of *foie gras*. Its highly famed *crus* (great wines), Quarts de Chaume, are sweeter dessert wines (1995 and 1996 being top vintages). The **Domaine des Baumard** in Rochefort-sur-Loire produces some of the best; count on paying 220FF for a bottle of Baumard's 1996 Quarts de Chaume.

On the opposite side (north) of the River Loire are 76 hectares of AOC Savennières vines, neatly arranged in strict rows around **Savennières** village. Wines produced here are refreshingly dry or semi-dry and age well. La Roche aux Moines and Coulée de Serrant are its much sought-after Savennières *crus*; the Clos de la Coulée de Serrant domaine produces both.

The Musée de la Vigne et du Vin d'Anjou is the best place to learn more about these wines. The museum is in **St-Lambert du Lattay**, 20km from Angers via the cut-throat N160 or a little farther via the picturesque D751, which winds from Mûrs Erigné west along the Loire riverbank to the dramatic **Corniche d'Angevine**, carved in the cliff face west of Rochefort-sur-Loire.

A delightful place to stay (and eat), particularly for wine lovers, is the *Prieuré de l'Epinay* (☎/fax 02 41 39 14 44, 📧 bgaultier@compuserve.com) in St-Georges-sur-Loire, 1km south-west of Château de Serrant down a country lane off the N23. The upmarket chambre d'hôte is run by a friendly wine connoisseur and his wife; he knows every vigneron in the vicinity and will happily take guests on wine-tasting and buying tours of the surrounding Layon and Savennières wine cellars. Spacious double suites in a restored outbuilding of the 13th-century priory cost 400FF, including breakfast. Evening meals cost 140FF, including an excellent selection of wines. The priory has a swimming pool and bicycles to explore the area. It opens Easter to September.

Musée Cointreau

White Dream, Golden Lady and Between the Sheets are among the numerous cocktail creations concocted with Cointreau, an orange-flavoured liqueur which has been distilled from bitter orange peel near Angers since 1849. The factory (☎ 02 41 31 50 50), today on blvd des Bretonnières in the Angevin suburb of St-Barthélémy d'Anjou, 8km east of Anjou via the D61, can be visited on a 1½-hour guided tour, departing daily at 10.30 am and 2.30 and 4.30 pm. Tours cost 35FF (those aged under 18 17FF) and end with a quick taste of the sweet but strong, 40% alc/vol liqueur. The distinctive square-shaped bottles are sold in the adjoining shop.

Château de Pignerolle

This neoclassical, 18th-century chateau, also in St-Barthélémy d'Anjou, is a replica of Le Petit Trianon at Versailles, near Paris. It was designed by the Angevin architect Bardoul de la Bigottière and served as the seat of the exiled Polish government for a few months in June 1940. It was subsequently used as a communication centre for the Nazi admiral Dönitz and his submarines. After the Liberation, it was used as an American base under the command of General Patton.

Today the chateau houses the **Musée Européen de la Communication** (☎ 02 41

93 38 38), which showcases the history of communication through a vast collection of exhibits, scientific gadgets and reconstructions. It opens 10 am to 12.30 pm and 2.30 to 6 pm daily, in summer; and the same hours at the weekend and during school holidays, in winter. Year round, you can call ahead to arrange a visit. Admission costs 45FF (those aged under 18 and students 25FF).

Musée de l'Ardoise

Slate has been mined at Trélazé since the 12th century, and the history of slate mining is explored in the Musée de l'Ardoise (Slate Museum; ☎ 02 41 69 04 71). Housed near an old open-cast mine, the museum tells the tale of a miner's life and covers the geology of slate and its different uses over the centuries. Guided tours end with a slate-cutting demonstration. The museum, signposted 'Centre Culturel Musée de l'Ardoise', is 7km east of Angers on chemin de la Marqichère, off rue Ludovic Ménard. It opens 2 to 6 pm daily; demonstrations start at 3 pm.

Château de Montgeoffroy

About 23km east of Trélazé, off the N147, is Château de Montgeoffroy, yet another privately owned castle. Two round towers are all that remains of the original 16th-century edifice; the rest is a mid-18th century creation exhibiting the same neoclassical traits as Château de Pignerolle.

Montgeoffroy was designed by the Parisian architect Nicolas Barré in 1772 for Érasme de Contades, commander of the German army during the Seven Years' War and governor of Alsace for 25 years. Remarkably, its late-18th-century interior remains almost intact, down to the 260 copper pots hanging in the kitchen. The stables on the estate hold a fine collection of saddles.

The chateau (☎ 02 41 80 60 02), 2km north of Mazé on the D74, can be visited by guided tour only from 9.30 am to noon and 2.30 to 6.30 pm (no break from mid-June to mid-September) daily, April to mid-November. Admission costs 55FF (students 35FF, children aged under 12 30FF).

Château de Brissac

Heading south from Angers towards Saumur via the D748 and its continuation, the D761, you pass Château de Brissac, a highly ornate, chocolate-box folly which has been home to the dukes of Brissac since 1502. Comprising seven storeys, it is the highest chateau in France and sits royally amid grounds studded with cedar trees and stretching across 800 hectares.

Inside, flamboyant furnishings and heavy ornamentation coat the 203 rooms of this fairy-tale castle. The exquisite 16th-century tapestries in the **Chambre des Chasses** (Hunting Room) are said to have belonged to King Louis Philippe (1830–66). The opulent 200-seat theatre (1883) on the 2nd floor was the whimsical creation of the vicomtesse de Trèdene, a soprano with a passion for the arts. It is lit with Venetian crystal chandeliers.

Château de Brissac (☎ 02 41 91 22 21) can only be visited with a guided tour. Tours, which take in the theatre and the estate's sumptuous *caves* (wine cellars), depart at 10 and 11 am and 2.15, 3.15, 4.15 and 5.15 pm Wednesday to Monday, April to June and in September; and from 10 am to 5.45 pm daily, July and August. Admission costs 45FF (students and children 35FF).

Brissac-Quincé is connected with Angers (25 minutes) by Anjou Bus Nos 9 and 9B, both of which plough the Angers–Montreuil-Bellay–Doué-la-Fontaine route about six times daily (less frequently during school holidays). The bus stop in Brissac is opposite the tiny tourist office (☎ 02 41 91 21 50) on place de la République, from where steps lead down the hill to the chateau on place Basse du Tertre.

Vallée de la Mayenne

The calm and tranquil River Mayenne, which peacefully meanders from Angers to Laval, 60km north in neighbouring Brittany, is one of the few river stretches in the Loire Valley that is navigable. Canalised in the 19th century, it sports 39 locks and can be explored afloat. Few villages line the Mayenne's steep riverbanks.

Château du Plessis-Macé About 15km north of Angers, the chateau was built in the 15th century for Louis XI's chamberlain. Its exterior is adorned with an unusual suspended gallery and there is some well-preserved Gothic panelling in the chapel. The chateau (☎ 02 41 32 67 93), 3km off the N162 on the D103, can be visited by guided tour (29FF) 10.30 am to 6.30 pm daily, July and August; 10 am to noon and 2 to 6.30 pm Wednesday to Monday, June and September; and 1.30 to 5.30 pm Wednesday to Monday, March to May and October and November.

Château du Plessis-Bourré Another 15th-century chateau graces the Vallée de la Mayennne, 18km north-east of Plessis-Macé. Seemingly a medieval fortress, safeguarded by a moat and double drawbridge, the four defensive corner towers and 2m-thick walls of Château du Plessis-Bourré (1468–73) shelter a Renaissance-inspired interior, reflecting the transition between architectural trends. Most of its interior furnishings date from 1911, when the family of the current proprietors acquired the chateau. Of particular interest is the carved wooden ceiling in the **salle des gardes**. The 24 painted ceiling panels date from the 15th century and feature allegorical and alchemy motifs. A wolf who only eats virgins (thus its thin state) and a young girl peeing into a hat to make gold out of urine are among the unsavoury images. The ceiling was covered up during the French Revolution, which is how it survived.

Visits to the chateau (☎ 02 41 32 06 01) are by guided tour only. It opens 10 am to 6 pm daily, July and August; 10 am to noon and 2 to 6 pm Friday to Tuesday, and 2 to 6 pm on Thursday, May, June and September; and 2 to 6 pm Thursday to Tuesday, March, April, October and November. Admission costs 45FF (students 40FF, children 30FF).

Le Lion d'Angers About 6km north of Plessis-Macé and 9km west of Plessis-Bourré is Le Lion d'Angers, home to the **Haras National d'Isle Briand** (Isle Briand National Stud Farm; ☎ 02 41 18 05 05), dat-

ing from 1797 and home to 55 horses of varying breeds today. Its stallions leave the stud in February, spend the spring performing their siring function, then return to the fold in July.

Horse races have been held on the Isle Briand estate since 1874. It plays host to some 15 race meetings a year, the highlight being **Le Mondial du Lion**, an international three-day event. See Equestrian Sport under Spectator Sports in the Facts for the Visitor chapter for details.

Guided visits of the Haras National d'Isle Briand are possible between Easter and mid-September. Daily tours depart at 11 am and 3 and 4.15 pm and cost 35FF (children 15FF, families 85FF). From the car park, follow the 'Accueil' signs, a 15-minute walk across the 19-hectare estate.

Vallée du Loir

The lengthy River Loir runs for 350km from its source near Chartres, south of Paris, to its confluence with the Sarthe, 20km or so north of Angers.

La Flèche This is the main town of Maine Angevine, a historic region in northern Anjou that became part of Maine in 1790. Several factories spot its suburbs and an impressive national military academy (1808) dominates its centre.

The tourist office in La Flèche (☎ 02 43 94 02 53, fax 02 43 94 02 53), blvd de Montréal, stocks accommodation lists and tourist information on the surrounding Pays Flèchois, and has details on guided visits to the military school, housed in a Jesuit college founded by Henri IV in 1606. Within the academic ensemble, **Église St-Louis** (1607–37) has buried within it the heart-shaped urns containing the ashes of the hearts of Henri IV and his queen, Marie de Médicis. Blvd de Montréal is named after the New World city that Jérôme le Royer de la Dauversière and his companions from La Flèche founded in 1642.

Château du Lude The chateau (☎ 02 48 94 60 09) graces the southern river bank, 20km east of La Flèche in **Le Lude**. Standing on the site of an 11th-century fortress, the current edifice is a patchwork of architectural styles spanning the 13th to the 18th centuries. Its interior dates from the 19th century, the notable exception being the frescoes (1560–85) by Italian painter Giovanni da Udine in the south-western tower.

In Le Lude, *Hôtel Ste-Anne (☎ 02 43 94 69 04, fax 02 43 94 41 98, 14 rue Boule d'Or)* offers cheap singles/doubles costing upwards of 130/220FF. On-line tourist information on the town is available at www.loir-valley.com.

East of Le Lude Gallo-Roman remains dating from the 1st and 2nd centuries speckle the **Site Archéologique de Cherré**, 7km east of Le Lude off the D305. In Vaas, the **Moulin à Blé de Rotrou** is a century-old flour mill, still functioning and open to visitors 2.30 to 5.30 pm daily, 15 July to 15 August; and the same hours on Sunday and during school holidays, April to 15 July and 15 August to October. Water-sports enthusiasts should head to **Lac des Varennes**, a lake and sports base 5km east of Château du Loir along the picturesque D61, and 20km or so from the departmental border with Touraine.

Les Mauges

Les Mauges embraces the south-western corner of Anjou, from the River Loire in the north to the départements of Vendée and Deux-Sèvres in the south and west, and as far east as Doué-la-Fontaine.

Unlike neighbouring Saumurois to the east, which has rich, wine-yielding soils and a strong medieval heritage, Les Mauges is a sterile plateau with acid earth which its inhabitants struggle to farm. The plain is bare of forest or woodland and is easily flooded, despite the *bocage* landscape – a grid of hedges and trees – that farmers have planted in a bid to quell the waters.

Staunchly Catholic and unsympathetic to the Revolution, the region played a key role in the bloody Vendée War (1793–6), which spilled into Anjou from neighbouring Vendée, ruining the towns and villages of Les Mauges. The 12th-century **Église Notre Dame** in Chemillé, 29km south of Angers, and the 18th-century priory in St-Florent-le-Vieil, on the southern bank of the Loire, 40km north of Cholet, are among the scant few historic buildings that survived. The tomb of Vendéen leader Bonchamps, who allegedly pardoned 5000 captured Republicans before dying himself in 1793, rests inside the **Abbaye St-Florent-le-Vieil**. The tomb was carved by the Angevin sculptor David d'Angers in 1825 and illustrates the 'heroic' tale.

Some of the goriest battles between the Republican *Bleus* (Blues) and pro-Royalist, Catholic *Blancs* (Whites) took place in **Cholet**, the modern-day capital of Les Mauges, 60km south of Angers. The city is better known for its handkerchief production today. East of the city, a chapel – a haunting memorial to 1200 Vendéen women and children massacred by the Bleus on 25 March 1794 – lies in the **Forêt de Maulévrier**, the only forest in Les Mauges. The chapel is about 10km north of Maulévrier along the D196.

Saumur & Troglodyte Valley

Europe's highest concentration of cave dwellings slumbers underground north and south of Saumur. The caves provided a refuge for 75% of the populations of Angers and Saumur during the French Revolution. Those that pierce the southern bank of the River Loire are hewn from white tufa cliffs, the distinctive feature of this left-bank stretch. Those inland, around Doué-la-Fontaine, are dug out of shelly falun. Today, these subterranean caverns are used to store wine, grow mushrooms, tap apples and bake *fouaces*, a type of pita bread typical to this troglodyte valley.

SAUMUR
postcode 49400 • pop 30,100
Small-town Saumur's notability rides on the renown of its École Nationale d'Équitation, stabled on the western outskirts in

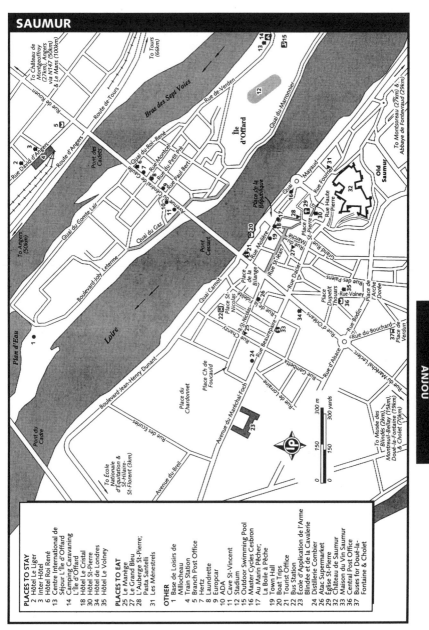

SAUMUR

PLACES TO STAY
2 Hôtel Le Liger
3 Inter Hôtel
6 Hôtel Roi René
13 Centre International de Séjour L'Île d'Offard
14 Camping Caravaning L'Île d'Offard
18 Hôtel Le Cristal
30 Hôtel St-Pierre
34 Hôtel de Londres
35 Hôtel Le Volney

PLACES TO EAT
25 Le Manège
27 Le Grand Bleu
28 L'Auberge St-Pierre; Pasta Santelli
31 Les Ménestrels

OTHER
1 Base de Loisirs de Millocheau
4 Train Station
5 Branch Post Office
7 Hertz
8 Laundrette
9 ADA
10 Europcar
11 Cave St-Vincent
12 Stadium
15 Outdoor Swimming Pool
16 Master Cycles Cesbron
17 Au Marin Pêcher; La Boîte à Pêche
19 Town Hall
20 Boat Trips
21 Tourist Office
22 Bus Station
23 Ecole d'Application de l'Arme Blindée et de la Cavalerie
24 Distillerie Combier
26 Atac Supermarket
29 Eglise St-Pierre
32 Château de Saumur
33 Maison du Vin Saumur
36 Central Post Office
37 Buses for Doué-la-Fontaine & Cholet

St-Hilaire-St-Florent. This, coupled with a military school that has been stationed in the town centre since 1599, makes Saumur a fascinating place to visit.

Old Saumur, the historic heart sprawled at the foot of the town's 13th-century chateau, is enriched with elegant yet sober hôtels particuliers. These private mansions date from the late 16th and 17th centuries, when wealthy wine merchants, followed by professors from the Protestant Academy (1599), settled in Saumur. This golden age lasted until the revocation of the Edict of Nantes in 1684, which smashed the Protestant stronghold and saw the city's population fall.

Today, personnel from the cavalry school – easily identifiable by their khaki-coloured uniforms and matching berets – buzz about town on bicycles, creating a pleasing, old-fashioned atmosphere.

Orientation

The chateau, old town, shops and most hotels are clustered on the southern (left) bank of the River Loire.

Pont Cessart links the 'mainland' with ave du Général de Gaulle, the main street that crosses Île d'Offard, an islet in the middle of the Loire. Pont des Cadets is the continuation of ave du Général de Gaulle and links Île d'Offard with the northern (right) bank.

Information

The tourist office (☎ 02 41 40 20 60, fax 02 41 40 20 69, ✉ off.tourisme.saumur@ interliger.fr), place de la Bilange, opens 9.15 am to 7 pm Monday to Saturday, and 10.30 am to 12.30 pm and 3.30 to 6.30 pm on Sunday. Have a look at the Web site at www.saumur-tourisme.com.

The central post office, housed in a sumptuous building on place Dupetit Thouars, opens 8 am to 6.30 pm on weekdays, and 8 am to noon on Saturday. It is equipped with Cyberposte. There's a branch office close to the train station, at 3 rue David d'Angers.

The laundrette at 74 ave du Général de Gaulle opens 7 am to 9 pm daily.

Château de Saumur

Construction work started on the imposing structure of Château de Saumur under Louis IX in 1246, although the riverside perch had been used by both the counts of Blois and the Plantagenêt kings as residence and dungeon from the 10th century. Under Louis I d'Anjou, pre-Renaissance turrets and ornamentation were added, transforming the defensive fortress into a pleasure palace. Its 15th-century interior dates from the reign of René, the last and most popular of the Anjou dukes, while its fortifying walls and bastions were built during Saumur's golden age as Protestant stronghold in the 16th century. With the arrival of the First Empire, the chateau was used as a prison, then as a military arsenal from 1815.

Today it houses two museums. The **Musée du Cheval** (Horse Museum) is in the former ducal living quarters, which languish beneath an impressive hull-shaped vaulted ceiling. The museum recounts the history of horse riding from antiquity to the 20th century, although there is practically nothing on Saumur's own illustrious equestrian history. Several Flanders tapestries and 18th-century ceramics are the focus of the **Musée d'Arts Décoratifs** (Decorative Arts Museum). The dungeons can also be visited. Restoration work on the southern wing and western tower should be complete by the end of 2000.

In July and August, the castle (☎ 02 41 40 24 40) is illuminated and open to visitors on Wednesday and Saturday from 8.30 pm. Daytime opening hours are 9.30 am to 6 pm daily, June to September; and 9.30 am to noon and 2 to 5.30 pm Wednesday to Monday (also open on Tuesday, April and May), the rest of the year. Admission costs 38FF (students, and children aged seven to 18 27FF). Family tickets costing 110FF are available for groups of two adults and two children or more.

Île d'Offard, on the opposite side of the river, offers the best views of the chateau and old town ensemble.

École Nationale d'Équitation

Saumur's star attraction is its École Nationale d'Équitation (National Equestrian

School), which has been based in the Saumurois quarter of St-Hilaire-St-Florent, 3km west of the centre, since 1972. The school trains instructors and riders at competition level, prepares teams for the Olympic Games, and is home to the elite Cadre Noir (see the boxed text below).

Guided tours provide visitors with an idea of the overwhelming size of the prestigious school, which accepts no more than 200 students per year, each of whom hopes to leave the school 10 months later as a qualified equestrian instructor. Facilities include Europe's largest indoor riding arena, 15 outdoor arenas, 50km of sand gallops and 400 horses cared for by 70 grooms and fed and

watered four times a day by overhead pipes that automatically drop feed and water into each horse box. Horse droppings are removed via an underground conveyor belt that dumps the 10 tonnes of daily waste onto a manure mountain (subsequently recycled by the surrounding mushroom farms).

The school dates from 1599, when a riding academy was established in Saumur's Protestant Academy. Following the reorganisation of the French cavalry under Louis XV in 1763, the Corps des Carabiniers (Mounted Corps) was stationed in Saumur and a cavalry school opened. Closed by the Revolution but revived by Louis XVIII in 1814, the École Royale de Cavalerie (Royal

Cadre Noir

Three moves set the Cadre Noir apart from its equestrian counterparts in Vienna: the *croupade*, which requires the horse to stretch its hind legs 45° into the air while its front legs stay on the ground; the *courbette*, which sees its front legs raised and tucked firmly into its body; and the demanding *cabriole*, which elevates the horse into the air in a powerful four-legged leap.

These acrobatic feats, far from being seen as crude or cruel, are considered the height of grace, elegance and classicism. They are only achieved after 5½ years of rigorous training, which starts when a horse is three years old. Daily training sessions last 1½ hours, following which the horse is untacked, washed down and dried (in a solarium), then boxed for the remaining 22 hours of the day. These horses – Anglo-Arabs, Arabs, Selles Français or thoroughbreds – retire between the ages of 13 and 22.

JANE SMITH

A Cadre Noir horse kicks up its heels and performs the famous *croupade*.

The Cadre Noir rider competes on a national or international level in dressage, three-day eventing or show jumping, and is a qualified riding instructor. The lone female in today's otherwise exclusively male Cadre Noir – traditionally made up of 24 members – is the third woman to have been awarded this status; the first woman was accepted in 1984. Members today can be civilians.

A black cap and jacket, gold spurs and three golden wings on the rider's whip are the distinctive trademarks of this elite band. Stirrup-less saddles are identical to those used in medieval jousting tournaments. Horse manes are plaited and decorated with three white ribbons, and the horse's two back feet are not shod (to prevent injuring a rider during the execution of a school movement).

Cavalry School) gave its first public performance of *haute école* (literally 'high school') equestrian tricks in 1828 during a *carrousel* (tournament) in honour of 'the duchess of Berry.

By 1943 the officers at the École Royale were no longer learning military tactics on horseback but, rather, in armoured tanks. Thus the school was renamed **École d'Application de l'Arme Blindée et de la Cavalerie** (School of Armoured Divisions and Cavalry). The military school is still based in the centre of Saumur today, at the western end of ave du Maréchal Foch.

Tours of the École Nationale d'Équitation (☎ 02 41 53 50 60, ✉ enecadrenoir@ symphonie-fai.fr) depart at 9.30 am Tuesday to Saturday, and between 2 and 4 pm on weekdays, April to September. Morning tours (35FF, 1½ hours) include 30 minutes watching the Cadre Noir train (except in August or when the Cadre Noir is on tour). Afternoon tours (25FF) last one hour. Tours are in English if there is an Anglophone majority.

Musée du Champignon

The Musée du Champignon (Mushroom Museum; ☎ 02 41 50 31 55), hidden in a cave in St-Hilaire-St-Florent, is dedicated to Saumur's thriving button mushroom (*champignon de Paris*) industry, which occupies 800km of caves in the Saumurois region, employs 3000 people and accounts for 65% of national production (182,000 tonnes annually). The museum – which takes visitors through a series of caves filled with different types of mushroom beds – is run by France Champignon, the country's largest button mushroom producer. It opens 10 am to 7 pm daily, mid-February to mid-November. Admission costs 38FF (students 30FF, children 20FF).

Musée des Blindés

The Musée des Blindés (Museum of Armoured Tanks; ☎ 02 41 53 06 99), 2km south of the centre at 1043 rue de Fontevraud, claims to house the largest collection of tanks in the world and is popular with young boys and ageing war veterans. The giant-sized bunker is split into several halls; the contemporary Leclerc tank (1990) is the centrepiece of the Salle de France, while a chilling collection of vehicles once hidden well behind the Iron Curtain fill another hall. Some 100 of the 700-odd armoured vehicles on display are in working order.

The museum opens 9.30 am to 6.30 pm daily, July to September; and 10 am to 5 pm daily, the rest of the year. Admission costs 25FF (children 15FF).

Distillerie Combier

Orange peel has been distilled at the Combier Distillery (☎ 02 41 40 23 00) since 1834, when Triple Sec, the alcoholic drink for which Combier is best known, was first made. The distillery opened its doors in 1832 and boasts a mind-boggling range of sweet alcoholic liqueurs today, including *crème banane*, *crème menthe* and *liquer de poire*. While its renowned Triple Sec notches up 40% alc/vol, most other Combier liqueurs hover around 25% alc/vol.

Those keen to know how to concoct their own Jolie Blonde (Pretty Blonde) cocktail can visit the distillery at 48 rue Beaurepaire as part of a guided tour, 10 am to noon and 2 to 6 pm Wednesday to Monday, May to October. Admission costs 20FF (students and those aged 12 to 18 12FF).

Wine-Tasting

The Saumur vineyards yield a healthy crop of white, red and sparkling wines which are all labelled with their own AOCs. Coteaux de Saumur is an elegant dry white, Cabernet de Saumur a dry rosé, while Saumur-Champigny – the best-known Saumur wine – is a light red, best drunk young.

The Syndicat Viticole des Côtes de Saumur is housed in the **Maison du Vin Saumur** (☎ 02 41 51 16 40, fax 02 41 51 16 14), 25 rue Beaurepaire. It stocks an abundance of information on Saumur wines, has a list of wine growers you can visit to taste and buy their vintages, and offers free tasting (*dégustation*) sessions. The Maison du Vin opens 9 am to 12.30 pm and 2 to 6.30 pm Monday to Saturday (Tuesday to Saturday, October to May), year round.

Sparkling Saumur gets its bubbles from a second fermentation in the bottle, following which it is laid to rest for nine months in tufa *caves*. To get a taste of it, head 3km west to St-Hilaire-St-Florent, home to the region's leading **sparkling wine houses**, including Gratien & Meyer, Ackerman-Laurance and Buvet-Ladubay.

The latter was founded in 1851, and the fabulous Art Deco theatre built by Etienne Buvet to entertain himself and his clients can be visited; part of the building on rue de l'Abbaye houses a **Centre d'Art Contemporain** which hosts modern-art exhibitions. There's also a **Musée du Masque** (Mask Museum; ☎ 02 41 50 75 26) on site, and you can visit the **Buvet wine cellars** (☎ 02 41 83 83 83). The cellars and the two museums open 8.30 am (10 am at the weekend) to noon and 2 to 6 pm daily. Admission costs 5FF (children 2.50FF).

Activities

Boat trips along the River Loire, operated by Batellerie de Loire (☎ 02 41 50 23 26), depart twice daily, Tuesday to Sunday, from the landing stage (*embarcadère*) opposite the town hall. Trips costs 34FF (students and children 22FF) and run from mid-June to mid-September.

On place de la République, Au Marin Pêcher, at No 3, and La Boile à Pêche, at No 7, are two well-equipped **fishing** shops; the former sells fishing licences (35FF per day).

You can **canoe** and **sail** down the Loire from the Base de Loisirs de Millochea (☎ 02 41 51 17 65 for sailing, 02 41 50 62 72 for canoeing), at the western end of Île d'Offard on the shore of the *plan d'eau* (artificial lake). The sports base organises half- and whole-day canoeing and sailing trips (see Canoeing & Kayaking under Activities in the Facts for the Visitor chapter for details).

Local cycling club Les Cyclotouristes Saumurois (☎ 02 41 50 24 50, 02 41 51 31 28), based in the Maison des Cyclistes at 585 rue Lamartine, organises **cycling and hiking** trips.

In St-Hilaire-St-Florent, the Centre Équestre Saumur-Petit Souper (☎ 02 41 50

29 90), almost opposite the entrance to the École Nationale d'Équitation on ave de l'École Nationale d'Équitation, is a riding school offering **horse-riding** sessions for 125/520FF per hour/five hours.

Special Events

Equestrian events are the mainstay of Saumur's cultural calendar (see Spectator Sports later in this Saumur section), the biggest event of the year being the annual **Carrousel**. Armoured tanks roll through the streets and mounted military personnel perform a whole host of historical pageants and spectacles. The five-day festival is held in mid-July.

May sees the townsfolk get tipsy on the **Fête de la Vigne et du Vin**, their annual wine festival.

Places to Stay

Camping The *Camping Caravaning L'Île d'Offard* (☎ 02 41 40 30 00, fax 02 41 67 37 81, rue de Verden) is a huge site with a spectacular range of facilities to entertain kids, including table tennis, crazy golf, a pétanque court, tennis courts and an outdoor swimming pool (open in summer only). The site also has mountain bikes to hire (70FF per day). It costs 37/46FF to pitch a tent in the low/high season, plus 22.50/26FF per adult and 11.50/13.50FF per child. The site opens mid-January to mid-December.

Hostels The *Centre International de Séjour L'Île d'Offard* (☎ 02 41 40 30 00, fax 02 41 67 37 81) adjoins the camp site and has the same telephone and fax numbers. Open from mid-January to mid-December, the centre has beds in two- or four-bed rooms with shower for 106FF per person. A bed in an eight-bed room with shared shower costs 82.50FF. Rates, which drop by 20FF from the third consecutive night, include sheets and breakfast. Additional meals/picnics are available for 47.50/38FF.

In St-Hilaire-St-Florent, *Village Hotelier* (☎ 01 42 50 94 41, fax 02 41 50 55 32, ✉ villehot@club-internet.fr, ave de l'École

ANJOU

Nationale d'Équitation) has furnished chalets to rent, costing 220/290FF for one/two people. It opens year round.

Hotels The cheapest hotels are clustered opposite the train station. *Hôtel Le Liger* (☎ 02 41 67 40 04), on the corner of rue David d'Angers and rue Choudieu, offers bargain doubles with washbasin for 130FF (170FF with shower, 230FF with shower and toilet).

Marginally more upmarket is *Inter Hôtel* (☎ 02 41 67 31 01), a couple of doors down on the same street, where singles/doubles/triples with shower and TV cost 210/240/260FF.

Heading across pont des Cadets to Île d'Offard, *Hôtel Roi René* (☎ 02 41 67 45 30, fax 02 41 67 74 59, 94 ave du Général de Gaulle) is a grand spot, perched on the riverbank and offering splendid views of the River Loire and its sand banks from its 280FF doubles. Parking costs 30FF.

On the 'mainland', *Hôtel Le Cristal* (☎ 02 41 51 09 54, fax 02 41 51 12 14, 10–12 place de la République) offers two-star doubles starting at 200FF. It has six bicycles to hire too (from 80/450FF per day/week). On busy rue d'Orléans, *Hôtel de Londres* (☎ 02 41 51 23 98, fax 02 41 51 12 63), at No 48, has double-glazed singles/doubles/triples costing upwards of 180/220/310FF, and private parking for 25FF. Tucked away from the action in a quiet street is *Hôtel Le Volney* (☎ 02 41 51 25 41, fax 02 41 38 11 04, 1 rue Volney). Rooms cost 160FF (washbasin), 170FF (washbasin and toilet) or 220FF (shower and toilet).

Three-star *Hôtel St-Pierre* (☎ 02 41 50 33 00, fax 02 41 50 38 68, 8 rue Haute Pierre), tucked alongside Église St-Pierre in the heart of Old Saumur, has upmarket doubles costing 310FF to 730FF.

Places to Eat

A lovely selection of cafes, creperies and other places to eat surrounds pretty place St-Pierre in Old Saumur. Regional cuisine is well served at *L'Auberge St-Pierre* (☎ 02 41 51 26 25), housed in a medieval half-timbered house at No 6. *Menus* are good value at 55FF, 78FF and 98FF, and the atmosphere on the terrace is unbeatable. It's closed Sunday and Monday.

Next door at No 8 is Italian *Pasta Santelli* (☎ 02 41 50 71 20), a little pasta bar run by a charming husband-and-wife team who dish up delicious mix-and-match pastas and sauces.

At the foot of the chateau, just off quai Mayaud, is the popular but pricey *Les Ménestrels* (☎ 02 41 67 71 10, 11 rue Raspail), whose tempting treats include langoustine and basil ravioli topped with a creamy lobster sauce, and roast pigeon served with an unusual fig compote. Its *menu saveur* (local-specialities set menu) costs 165FF; advance reservations are recommended.

Le Manège (☎ 02 41 83 92 22) is a refined spot on the corner of rue Chanzy de Monsieur and rue St-Nicolas, with tempting 70FF to 250FF *menus*. Seafood is the speciality of *Le Grand Bleu* (☎ 02 41 67 41 83, 6 rue du Marché).

In the chateau grounds is the pricey but sought-after *Délices du Château*, where diners can splash out on 185FF and 200FF *menus* (lunchtime 130FF), said to reflect chef Pierre Millon's love of nature.

Self-caterers can choose from an excellent selection of regional wines at *Cave St-Vincent*, 15 ave du Général de Gaulle. The *Atac Supermarket*, on the corner of rue de la Fidelité and rue St-Nicolas, opens 8.30 am to 7.30 pm Monday to Saturday, and 9 am to noon on Sunday.

Spectator Sports

Equestrian events are hosted in the arena on place du Chardonnet, opposite the military school, or out of town in one of the arenas at the École Nationale d'Équitation in St-Hilaire-St-Florent. See Equestrian Sport under Spectator Sports in the Facts for the Visitor chapter for details.

Getting There & Away

Bus From Saumur bus station, place St-Nicolas, there is a daily bus service to/from Angers (1¼ to 1½ hours); Anjou Bus No 5 follows the left-bank route via St-Georges des Sept Voies and Coutures, while bus No 11 takes the right-bank route. Both lines make the return journey four to six times daily (except on Sunday and during school holidays, when services are drastically reduced).

Anjou Bus also operates daily services to/from Doué-la-Fontaine (No 23, 30 minutes, eight to 10 daily) and Cholet (No 23, 1½ hours, two to four daily). Many of these buses depart from the bus stop on place de Verdun. Buses to/from Fontevraud (No 16, 25 minutes, three daily) use Saumur bus station.

Northbound, SNCF operates a handful of daily buses to Le Mans (103FF, two hours) from the train station.

Train Saumur sits on the train line between Tours (56FF, 30 to 50 minutes) and Angers (42FF, 30 minutes), with regular trains – at least hourly – in both directions.

Getting Around
Bicycles can be hired from Master Cycles Cesbron (☎ 02 41 67 69 32), 57 quai Mayaud, open 9 am to noon and 2 to 7 pm (6 pm on Saturday) Monday to Saturday. Day/weekend/fortnight rates are 80/370/500FF.

Camping Caravaning L'Île d'Offard has bicycles to hire (see Places to Stay, earlier).

ANGERS TO SAUMUR
This 50km stretch is the cultural corner of troglodyte valley. Subterranean art galleries sit underground, while a Roman amphitheatre and a beautiful Romanesque church – one of the Loire valley's finest – grace the land above ground. From Angers, the D751 twists its way inland through artichoke crops and fruit orchards to Gennes, from where it snakes along the riverbanks. For information on buses between Angers and Saumur, see the Getting There & Away sections under those cities. For places to stay, see the end of this section.

Coutures
This small hamlet, tucked amid vineyards around the domain of the privately owned Château de Montsabert (1374–80), is home to the **Manoir de la Caillère** (☎/fax 02 41 57 97 97, ✉ richard.rak1@libertysurf.fr), a private art gallery which showcases the works of contemporary artist Richard Rak in a cave. Rak's works start at 6000FF a piece. The gallery, signposted north at the western end of the village, opens 10 am to 8 pm Tuesday to Sunday in summer. Coutures celebrates its annual **Foire aux Artichauts** (Artichoke Fair) in mid-September and is 20km east of Angers on the inland D751.

Hélice Terrestre de l'Orbière
A startling piece of monumental art – intended to stimulate all the senses – is the centrepiece of this screw-shaped subterranean gallery, 2.5km east of Coutures in **St-George des Sept Voies**. The underground sculpture – shaped like a helicoid, or spiral – was the creation of Jacques Warminski (1946–96). It took several years to complete and involved removing 1000 tonnes of rock. The resultant *Hélice* is a labyrinth of twists and turns, duplicated in reverse above ground. The figure of eight, carved in rock and pitch dark, is particularly disorientating to wander round on foot. These caves remained inhabited until WWI.

The site opens 11 am to 8 pm daily, May to September; and 2 to 6 pm daily, the rest of the year. Admission costs 25FF.

Gennes
Riverside Gennes (population 2000), 30km upstream from Angers and 15km downstream from Saumur, has one sight to see: a magnificent **Gallo-Roman amphitheatre**, built to stage sporting contests, chariot races and the bloody spectacles so beloved by the Roman public. Up to 5000 spectators at a time gathered here to watch wild animals pitted against other animals or gladiators (usually slaves or criminals). The fight only ended when one of them was either killed or surrendered (in the latter case his throat was usually then slit).

The amphitheatre opens from 10 am to 12.30 pm and 3 to 6.30 pm daily, July and August; and the same hours on Sunday,

April to June and in September. In summer, several *Animations Gallo-Romaines* are staged (without blood); the Maison du Tourisme (☎ 02 41 51 55 05), square de l'Europe, has details.

From the Gothic bell tower of Gennes' **Église Romane St-Eusèbe**, in the centre of the village, there are good panoramic views of this stretch of the Loire Valley.

South of the village on the D70 is the **Moulin de Sarré** (☎ 02 41 51 81 32), a working water mill that has milled flour since 1908. Guided visits of the mill (20/14FF for adults/children) depart at 3 and 5 pm, May to September. The *auberge* here serves 90FF and 115FF *menus*, but is only open by appointment.

Just south of Gennes, and visible from the southbound D69 towards Doué-la-Fontaine, is the Dolmen de la Madeleine. The stone burial chamber is believed to date from the Neolithic period (about 4000 to 2400 BC) and is among the region's oldest monuments.

Cunault

About 2km east of Gennes is Cunault, an unassuming riverside hamlet which is blessed with one of the region's most exquisite examples of Romanesque architecture. An abbey was founded here as early as 847 by Benedictine monks from Île de Noirmoutier, but it was not until the 11th century that the monastery's **Église de Cunault** was raised. A beautiful sculpture of the Virgin Mary surrounded by triumphant angels is at the entrance to the church. The relics of Saint Maxenceul, a follower of St Martin (who converted the area to Christianity in the 5th century) rest in an unusual 13th-century wooden trunk, painted and sculpted with figures depicting the 12 apostles.

Each Sunday at 5 pm in July and August, a compelling classical-music concert fills this peaceful sanctuary during **Les Heures Musicales de Cunault**. Some concerts are hosted in the Église de Trèves, in neighbouring Trèves. Tickets (85FF) and programme details are available from Angers and Saumur tourist offices.

Places to Stay

Camping Européen de Montsabert (☎/fax 02 41 57 91 63), in Coutures on the D751, has tent pitches and mobile homes to rent. It charges 80/95FF in the low/high season for a tent, car and two people. Mobile homes for four start at 200/1400FF per night/week. Facilities include a pool, tennis courts and 10 hectares of parkland to play in.

In Chênehutte-les-Tuffeaux, 6.5km downstream from Saumur, *Camping Beauregard* (☎ 02 41 38 08 57, fax 02 41 38 08 58) overlooks the River Loire. It charges 11/10FF per tent/person. Both sites are open from May to September.

In Gennes, *Hôtel Le Lion d'Or* (☎ 02 41 38 05 63, 33 rue de la République) offers six cheap doubles costing upwards of 110FF. Nearby *Aux Naulets d'Anjou* (☎ 02 41 51 81 88, fax 02 41 38 00 78, 18 rue Croix de Mission) is a solid mid-range choice, with singles/doubles costing 220/280FF.

Top of the range is the exclusive *Hostellerie du Prieuré* (☎ 02 41 67 90 14, fax 02 41 67 92 24, ✆ prieure@wanadoo.fr), a former 12th- to 16th-century priory on a 25-hectare estate in Chênehutte-les-Tuffeaux. Its 25 rooms with period furnishings start at 600/750FF in the low/high season. *Soirées musicales* (musical evenings) are hosted here (180FF including cocktail).

DOUÉ-LA-FONTAINE
postcode 49700 • pop 7200

On the surface, Doué-la-Fontaine is plain dull. But dig a bit deeper and a unique subterranean world – a zoo, 'cathedrals', dwellings and coffin manufacturers – lurks beneath its streets in cold, dank caves.

The chalky plateau on which Doué-la-Fontaine sits, 19km south-west of Saumur, is riddled with troglodyte dwellings. Most date from the 14th century, when lime quarries were dug beneath the falunian land to extract shell-marl, rich in carbonate of lime. From the burned marl, hydrated lime was extracted as a fertiliser or to tan hides. Falun boulders were also extracted and used as building material.

Troglodyte culture fired the imagination of a host of writers and artists, including Touraine-born François Rabelais (1494–1533), who set part of his five-volume comic epic *Gargantua et Pantagruel* in **Les Arènes**, a quarried crater used as an amphitheatre in the 15th century. The crater subsequently served as a prison and ammunition dump, and now hosts Doué-la-Fontaine's **Journées de la Rose** (Days of the Rose) flower festival in mid-July. For details, contact the tourist office (☎ 02 41 59 20 49, fax 02 41 59 93 85, ✉ tourisme@ ville-douelafontaine.fr) at 30 place du Champ de Foire, on the main square.

Tigné, 12km west of Doué-la-Fontaine on the D84, is worth a pit stop for fans of the fabulous, big-nosed French actor Gérard Depardieu, who owns Château de Tigné (closed to the public) and produces light red wines from his 50 hectares of vineyards.

The town's troglodytic sights are 2 to 3km out of the centre and impossible to reach without your own wheels.

Les Perrières
A visit to the 18th-century quarry site at Les Perrières, in Doué, sheds new light on the region's cave phenomenon. Its series of vast subterranean chambers, known as *cathédrales* (cathedrals), demonstrates how the falun rock was extracted from the 18th century on. Keen to safeguard the use of their land, local people dug just a small opening on the surface, beneath which they hollowed out giant-sized conical chambers up to 20m deep.

Embracing a total surface area of almost five hectares, 10% of the site at Les Perrières can be visited. Stone extraction ground to a halt in 1930. Mushrooms were grown here in the 1980s. Today, part of the site shelters a gîte (see Places to Stay & Eat later in this section).

Les Perrières opens 10 am to 6 pm Tuesday to Sunday, mid-June to mid-September. Admission costs 18FF (children 10FF).

Cave aux Sarcophages
Stone coffins were extracted from falun between the 6th and 9th centuries at the Cave aux Sarcophages, a chilling site uncovered and excavated by archaeologists in 1989–96. In total, around 35,000 stone coffins are believed to have been produced at the Merovingian mine.

The cave (☎ 02 41 59 24 95), 1 rue Croix Mordret, can be visited 10 am to noon and 2 to 7 pm daily, April to October. A dual ticket covering entry to the Cave aux Sarcophages and La Fosse (see Villages Troglodytiques later in this section) costs 30FF (children aged six to 14 24FF).

Zoo de Doué
This privately owned zoo – lavishly landscaped with bamboo and lush foliage, and with canned bird-song music – is best known for its underground setting. Giraffes live in old falun pits and cranky crocodiles languish in water pools inside clammy caves.

The zoo (☎ 02 41 59 18 58), off route de Cholet (D960), opens 9 am to 7 pm (7.30 pm, July and August); daily, April to September; and 10 am to 6 or 6.30 pm daily, October to mid-November and February to March. The vultures are fed at 3.30 pm daily, followed by the penguins at 4.30 pm. Admission costs 65FF (children 35FF).

Villages Troglodytiques
Six kilometres north of Doué-la-Fontaine on the D761, 'troglo' culture throws up two underground farms, 20 rooms and a subterranean chapel in the troglodytic village of **Rochemenier**, built around an open-cast quarry in the 17th and 18th centuries and abandoned in the early 20th century. Wine presses and machines to crush walnuts are exhibited, as are bread ovens and oil lamps (fuelled with hemp-seed oil and less smoky than pine-resin candles).

A modern dwelling demonstrates how these centuries-old caves can still be lived in today; the temperature inside a cave dwelling averages 12°C year round, thus it requires less heating than a contemporary home above ground. The site (☎ 02 41 59 18 15, ✉ troglody@club-internet.fr) opens 9.30 am to 7 pm daily, year round. Admission costs 24FF (children 13FF).

ANJOU

Pagan art uncovered by marauding children in 1950 and the source of speculation ever since can be viewed in the **Cave aux Sculptures** (☎ 02 41 59 15 40), 3km east of Rochemenier in Dénezé-sur-Doué. Heading 4km east of here is **La Fosse**, an authentic 17th-century hamlet that was inhabited until the mid-1990s. The subterranean site is cared for by one of its former inhabitants, who has spent a lifetime living in caves. Spread across 1.3 hectares, there are several homes to visit and a farmstead, complete with chickens, turkeys, a pet weasel and a family of rabbits who reside in the former vegetable store. La Fosse (☎ 02 41 52 27 60) opens 9.30 am to 7 pm daily. Admission costs 25FF (children 15FF). Combination tickets covering entry to the Cave aux Sarcophages are available.

Places to Stay & Eat

In Doué-la-Fontaine, *Le Dagobert* (☎ 02 41 83 25 25, fax 02 41 59 76 51, 14 place du Champ de Foire) offers simple doubles with washbasin costing 120FF. Doubles with shower cost 135FF and doubles/triples with shower, toilet and TV go for 180/250FF.

At Les Perrières, you can sleep in a cave at *Centre des Perrières* (☎ 02 41 59 71 29), an underground gîte that has 55 beds to let. Ring for details.

The place to dine is Doué's *Le Caveau* (☎ 02 41 59 98 28, fax 02 41 59 85 79, 4 bis place du Champ de Foire), one of two cave restaurants in the region. The highly atmospheric cave, which gets packed out, serves a 110FF *menu* featuring an aperitif, stuffed *galipettes* (a type of mushroom grown locally), *fouaces* (pitta bread) with various fillings including *rillettes*, goat's cheese salad, a dessert, coffee and as much red Anjou wine as you can drink. Le Caveau opens daily, mid-April to mid-September; and weekends only, the rest of the year. Book in advance. In Rochemenier, *Les Caves de la Genevraie* (☎ 02 41 59 34 22) offers a similar style of dining, touting an almost identical *menu* (110FF excluding coffee). The cellar restaurant opens Thursday and Sunday lunchtime, Friday evening and all day Saturday. Smoking is forbidden.

Getting There & Away

Doué-la-Fontaine is served by frequent buses to/from Angers (55 minutes, about six daily), Montreuil-Bellay (20 minutes, about six daily) and Saumur (30 minutes, eight to 10 daily). For more information call the Anjou Bus office in Angers (☎ 02 41 88 59 25). In Doué, buses use the stop on place du Champ de Foire.

SAUMUR TO TOURAINE

Caves serve as wine cellars along this short stretch of the River Loire, from Saumur 27km east to Montsoreau and its pretty little sister, Candes St-Martin, across the departmental border in neighbouring Touraine. The D947 snakes along the southern riverbank, backed by impressive limestone cliffs. The Saumur-Champigny vineyards fan out south in a neat square. Of all the Saumurois appellations, fruity, red Saumur-Champigny is the most respected. Its 1000 hectares of vines, which have had their own AOC label since 1957, yield 60,000 hectolitres a year. Its fields of cabernet franc and sauvignon grapes are delineated by the River Loire in the north, the Anjou-Touraine border in the east, the N147 to the south, and the River Thouet to the west.

Wine, Apples & Mushrooms

Saumur-Champigny reds – light and fruity when drunk young and a bit spicy when aged – can be sampled at **Les Grandes Caves** (☎ 02 41 38 24 78), cave cellars in Souzay-Champigny. Another large cellar at which to taste and buy is in St-Cyril-en-Bourg, 6km inland. The **Caves des Vignerons de Saumur** is a cooperative of 260 wine growers who produce one-third of Saumur wine.

Pommes tapées (literally 'tapped apples') are the bizarre speciality of a cave in Val Hulin, 3km east of Souzay-Champigny. Pommes tapées are a 19th-century gastronomic delight that remained popular until WWI. Apples are slowly dried out in a wood-stoked oven for several days, squashed in their skins to form flat circles, and later rehydrated with spicy mulled wine at the **Musée de la Pomme Tapée** (☎ 02 41

51 48 30). Tours end with a chance to have a taste.

Turquant, 2km west of Montsoreau, oozes wine growers offering wine to taste and buy. Mid-way between Turquant and Montsoreau on the D947 is **La Grand Vignerolle** (☎ 02 41 38 16 44), a feudal 16th-century troglodytic manor house complete with dovecote, chapel and underground wine cellars.

Mushrooms are the mainstay of the **Cave à Champignons** (☎ 02 41 51 70 30) in Le Saut aux Loups, on Montsoreau's western fringe. Mushrooms cultivated on beds here are sold and turned into tasty treats in *Les Galipettes*, the adjoining restaurant, open from March to November.

Montsoreau & Candes St-Martin

The medieval frontier that set Montsoreau (population 560) in Anjou apart from Candes St-Martin (population 240) in Touraine is scarcely discernible today, as is the modern departmental boundary that draws a line between these twin villages. The two villages, certified as being among France's '*plus beaux*' (most beautiful), are a harmonious blend of mellow-hued rooftops snug on the confluence of the Rivers Loire and Vienne.

Until 1820, when the D947 was built, the River Loire licked the walls of the **Château de Montsoreau** and the castle thereby commanded hefty river tolls from passing traffic. The *corps de logis* (main chateau building) is all that survives of the original edifice, built in 1440–55 for Charles VII's counsellor, Jean des Chambres, whose great-grandson led the Saint Bartholomew's Day massacres in Anjou. The Renaissance staircase tower dates from 1520. The chateau opens 10 am to noon and 2 to 6 or 6.30 pm (no break in July and August) daily, April to November. Admission costs 32FF. Concerts are held here at 9 pm on Saturday or Sunday during the **Saison Musicale au Château de Montsoreau** in July and August; tickets (70FF) are sold here or at Angers tourist office.

St Martin died in **Candes St-Martin** (previously just called Candes) in 397, prompting his followers to build a church

in his honour. Today, it is the richly decorated facade of the 12th- to 13th-century **collégiale** (collegiate church), on place de l'Église, that dominates the village. Its vaulted porch rests on a central pillar, sheltering a main door adorned with sculpted figurines, statues and medallions. The church's western facade was fortified in the 15th century. From place de l'Église, a cobbled path heads uphill to a **belvedère** on rue du Panorama, from where a breathtaking panorama of the Loire and Vienne Valleys unfolds. By car, follow the signs reading 'Panorama voitures'.

Places to Stay & Eat The *Camping L'Isle Verte* (☎ 02 41 51 76 60, quai de la Loire), next to the tourist office in Montsoreau, charges 60FF for a tent, car and two people; additional adults/children cost 19/9FF. Reception opens 8 am to noon and 2 to 8 pm.

In Montsoreau, *Hôtel Le Bussy* (☎ 02 41 38 11 11, fax 02 41 38 11 10, 4 rue Jeanne d'Arc) offers comfortable doubles costing upwards of 288FF, and has a good restaurant worth trying called *Diane de Méridor* (☎ 02 41 51 70 18) on the riverfront.

Auberge de la Route d'Or (☎ 02 41 95 81 10, 2 place de l'Église), in Candes St-Martin, has a roaring fire in winter, a terrace in summer and delicious 85FF (lunch), 120FF and 150FF *menus* year round (closed Tuesday and Wednesday from September to June).

ABBAYE DE FONTEVRAUD

The breathtaking, Romanesque Abbaye de Fontevraud (1106–17) forms the largest monastic ensemble in France. From its inception in 1101 to its forced closure by the French Revolution in 1793, the Benedictine-inspired Fontevrist order was unique in that its nuns and monks were governed by a woman: the abbess even fell outside the jurisdiction of the bishop in the diocese and was answerable only to the pope. Only the nuns in the mixed order at Fontevraud could elect the abbess.

At the peak of the order's power in the 12th century, Grand-Moûtier – one of four priories within the abbey – sheltered 600

ANJOU

nuns (virginity being the prerequisite for women to enter this particular priory). Ste-Marie Madeleine's was filled with repentant prostitutes, married women and unwanted female relatives of the nobility; lepers lived in the priory of St-Lazare; and Fontevraud's 50-odd monks were relegated to St-Jean de l'Habit.

The abbey, afforded royal protection under Henri Plantagenêt II (ruled 1154–89), became a royal necropolis upon Henri's death in 1189. The ornate, polychrome royal effigies of Henri II, his wife Eleanor d'Aquitaine (who lived at Fontevraud from 1194 until her death in 1204) and son, Richard the Lionheart (Cœur de Lion), remain a centrepiece of Fontevraud's abbey church today. The royal tombs, originally in the church crypt, were destroyed during the Revolution.

In 1804 the pillaged abbey was turned into a prison which, by the 1850s, housed over 2000 inmates. These inmates were used as slave labour in the cloth factories that were subsequently installed in the former abbey buildings. The prison – among France's largest and harshest – closed in 1963, although the last prisoners did not leave until 1985. Many assisted with the renovation and restoration of the complex.

The Abbaye de Fontevraud (☎ 02 41 51 71 41) opens 9 am to 7 pm daily, June to mid-September; and 9.30 am to 12.30 pm and 2 to 5.30, 6 or 6.30 pm daily, the rest of the year. Admission costs 32FF (those aged 12 to 25 21FF). There are free guided tours (one hour) in English between June and mid-September. Tickets for the evening show at 9.30 pm in August cost 85FF (those aged 12 to 25 50FF); see the boxed text 'Son et Lumière' in the Facts for the Visitor chapter for details. Various concerts, workshops and exhibitions are held in the on-site Centre Culturel de l'Ouest (☎ 02 41 51 73 52).

Places to Stay & Eat

The former priory of St-Lazare today houses the *Prieuré St-Lazare* (☎ 02 41 51 73 16, fax 02 41 51 75 50, ✆abbayefontevraud.prieure@wanadoo.fr), a 52-room

hotel with comfortable and modern singles/doubles costing upwards of 310/440FF. Breakfast costs 55FF and guests pay just 10FF to visit the adjoining abbey. Half-board costs 490/750FF for one/two people.

Getting There & Away

Abbaye de Fontevraud is some 4km south of Montsoreau or Candes St-Martin, off the D947. There are three buses daily (No 16, 25 minutes) between Saumur and Fontevraud village, from where the abbey is five minutes' walk.

VALLÉE DU THOUET

A tributary of the River Loire, the River Thouet follows a southbound course from Saumur, along the western fringe of the Champigny vineyards, to the fortified medieval village of Montreuil-Bellay. From here it heads into Poitou.

Château de Montreuil-Bellay

The moat around Château de Montreuil-Bellay, 5km south of Saumur, has remained dry ever since 1145, when the castle was besieged by the Plantagenêts, who filled in the trenches surrounding the keep. The ramparts and 13 towers visible today date from the 13th century. Two drawbridges have to be crossed to access the heart of the complex; the first drawbridge leads to the 13th-century **barbican**; the second to the **Château Neuf** (New Chateau), dating from 1485–1505 and still inhabited by the Grand-maison family, which has owned the estate for almost two centuries.

Guided tours include a fascinating visit to the **cuisine** (kitchen), built as a separate block in 1450. The collection of copper pots here is almost as impressive as the kitchen's single vault ceiling, central fireplace and gigantic sink cut from a single stone. In the depths of the *caves* (wine cellars), the tale is told of how Baron Georges de Grand-maison (1865–1943) founded the Confrérie des Sacavins in 1904, a wine brotherhood whose members could be sworn in only after consuming a large volume of the chateau vintage and then successfully walking backwards up the spiral stairs from the cellar without touching the walls. The vaulted cellars served as a prison for women during the Revolution; many died of typhoid and were buried in the graveyard of the **Église Notre Dame** (1472–84). WWI saw the cellars used as a hospital.

The chateau (☎ 02 41 52 33 06) opens 10 am to noon and 2 to 5.30 pm Wednesday to Monday, April to November. Admission costs 45FF (students 30FF, children 20FF) and includes a free guided tour.

Getting There & Away Montreuil-Bellay is served by six buses daily to/from Angers (1¼ hours) and Doué-la-Fontaine (20 minutes). Services are drastically reduced or nonexistent on Sunday and during school holidays.

ANJOU

Loire-Atlantique & Vendée

This is Pays de la Loire's coastal quarter. Here the longest river in France, the Loire, ends its magnificent 1020km journey, rushing past the land of kings and castles towards the Atlantic coast and its terrain of sand dunes and salt pans.

On the last leg of its voyage, the River Loire cuts through Nantes, a university town 56km from the sea and kissed by vineyards from which France's famed muscadet wines originate. Historically part of Brittany, Nantes is the regional capital of Pays de la Loire, much to the disgust of many Nantais, who dream of the day when the city's Breton status will be restored. Since 1985 some smaller towns in the northern half of this region have sported bilingual, Breton-French, street signs. Graffiti shouting 'BZH' – short for *Breizh* (Breton for Brittany) – remains a common sight on walls, lamp posts and billboards.

The great but gruesome tidal mouth of the River Loire – 60km long and 3km wide – is embraced by an oil refinery at Donges, and St-Nazaire, an industrial port on the estuary's northern bank. La Baule, a glitzy beach resort, and the protected Brière wetlands are to the north and west. Several smaller coastal resorts, such as Le Croisic and Piriac-sur-Mer, and the Atlantic islands of Noirmoutier and Yeu, which lie to the south, are still counting the environmental cost of the oil slick that washed across the sandy beaches in December 1999. Most years, oysters, mussels and eels are abundant here in season.

Much of the region south of the River Loire is embraced by Vendée, a vulnerable area of marshland and swamp that was ripped to shreds by the Vendée War (1793–6).

NANTES
postcode 44000 • pop 493,000

Nantes, France's seventh-largest city, is the most important commercial and industrial centre in west-central France. A lively place with a mild Atlantic climate and an un-

St-Nazaire p244

Nantes pp232–3

Loire-Atlantique & Vendée p231

believable number of cafes and restaurants, it also has fine museums, carefully tended parks and gardens, an ultra-modern tram system, a university of 33,000 students and (of course) a chateau.

The Edict of Nantes, a landmark royal charter guaranteeing civil rights and freedom of conscience and worship to France's Protestants, was signed here by Henri IV in 1598. During the Reign of Terror (September 1793 to July 1794), the guillotine was deemed too slow by the local representative of the Committee of Public Safety. Instead,

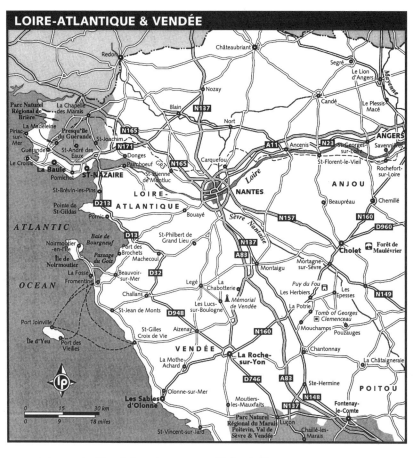

LOIRE-ATLANTIQUE & VENDÉE

suspected counter-Revolutionaries were stripped, tied together in pairs and loaded onto barges that were then sunk in the middle of the River Loire.

Outside the pleasantly pedestrian old city, Nantes has its fair share of 1960s concrete creations, most notably the 29-storey Tour de Bretagne (Brittany Tower), which towers between place de Bretagne and cours des 50 Otages. The eyesore houses a Centre de Communication de l'Ouest (Communication Centre of the West) and serves as an uneasy (and ugly) reminder of the city's true Breton roots.

Orientation

Nantes sits snug on the northern bank of the River Loire, just 56km east of the Atlantic. The centre's two main arteries, both served by tram lines, are the north–south, partly pedestrianised cours des 50 Otages (named in memory of 48 people taken hostage and shot by the Germans on 22 October 1941), and an east–west boulevard that connects the train station (east) with quai de la Fosse (west). They intersect near the Gare Centrale bus/tram hub, east of place du Commerce (also known as place Sarajevo).

Nantes' commercial centre runs from Gare

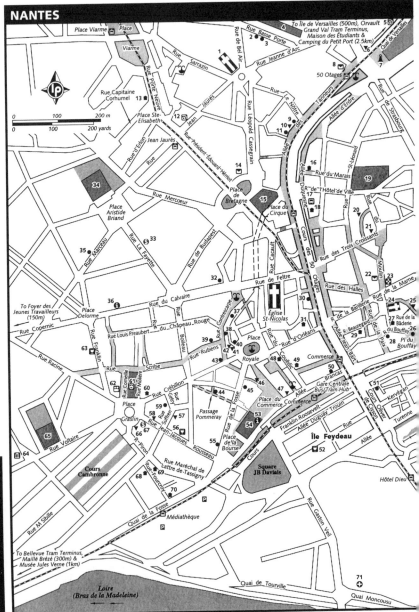

NANTES

Place Viarme / Place Viarme

To Île de Versailles (500m), Orvault
Grand Val Tram Terminus,
Maison des Étudiants &
Camping du Petit Port (2.5km)

To Foyer des
Jeunes Travailleurs
(150m)

To Bellevue Tram Terminus,
Maillé Brézé (300m) &
Musée Jules Verne (1km)

Loire
(Bras de la Madeleine)

Île Feydeau

Square
JB Daviais

Hôtel Dieu

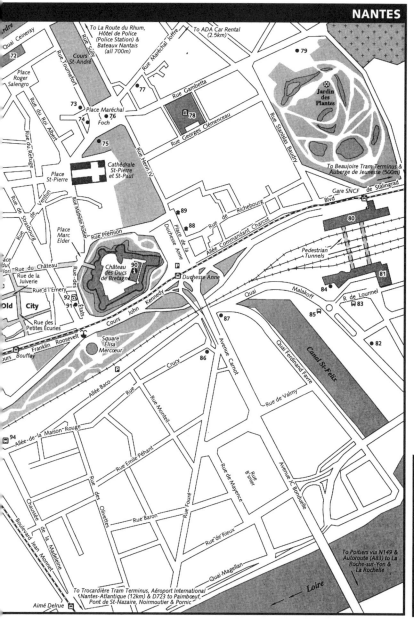

NANTES

Quai Ceineray

To La Route du Rhum,
Hôtel de Police
(Police Station) &
Bateaux Nantais
(all 700m)

To ADA Car Rental
(2.5km)

79

Place
Roger
Salengro

Cours
St-André

Rue Maréchal Joffre

Rue Gambetta

77

Jardin
des
Plantes

73

Place Maréchal
Foch

76

74

78

Rue Georges Clémenceau

Rue Stanislas Baudry

75

Rue du Roi Albert

Rue du Refuge

Rue Henri IV

Cathédrale
St-Pierre
et St-Paul

To Beaujoire Tram Terminus &
Auberge de Jeunesse (500m)

Place
St-Pierre

Rue de Verdun

Rue Strasbourg

Gare SNCF de Stalingrad

Blvd

89

Rue de Richebourg

Place
Marc
Elder

Rue Prémion

88

80

Rue Mathelin Rodier

Place de la Duchesse Anne

Allée Commandant Charcot

Pedestrian
Tunnels

Rue du Château

Château
des Ducs
de Bretagne

90

81

Rue de la
Juiverie

P

84

R. de Lourmel

Rue d'l'Emery

Duchesse Anne

Quai

Malakoff

83

Old   City

92

States

91

85

Cours John Kennedy

Rue des
Petites Écuries

87

82

Franklin Roosevelt

Square
Elisa
Mercœur

Canal St-Félix

ours Bouffay

P

86

Crucy

Avenue Carnot

Quai Ferdinand Favre

Allée Baco

Rue Monteil

Rue de Valmy

Rue Émile Péhant

Rue
B'smer

Avenue C Bonduelle

94

Allée-de-la-Maison-Rouge

Rue des Olivettes

Rue Fouré

Rue de Mayence

Rue Baron

Chaussée de la Madeleine

Rue de Rieux

To Poitiers via N149 &
Autoroute (A83) to La
Roche-sur-Yon &
La Rochelle

Boulevard Jean Monnet

Quai Magellan

Loire

To Trocardière Tram Terminus, Aéroport International
Nantes-Atlantique (12km) & D723 to Paimbœuf,
Pont de St-Nazaire, Noirmoutier & Pornic

Aimé Delrue

euro currency converter 10FF = €1.52

NANTES

PLACES TO STAY
13 Résidence Porte Neuve
16 Hôtel d'Orléans
18 Hôtel du Tourisme
27 Hôtel St-Daniel
29 Hôtel Renova
31 Hôtel St-Patrick
48 Jules Verne
49 Grand Hotel Mercure Central
60 Hôtel de France
68 Hôtel Fourcroy
69 Hôtel de l'Océan
70 Hôtel de la Bourse
88 Hôtel Duchesse Anne
89 Hôtel du Château

PLACES TO EAT
6 L'Océanide
10 Brasserie Le Carnivore;
   L'Arbre de Vie
20 Le Bouchon
21 D'Après Nature
25 Aux Vieux Quimper
41 Le Petit Flore
42 Le Mont Liban
46 McDonald's
47 La Mie Câline
57 Aux Petits Oignons
58 Le Bouche à Oreille
66 La Cigale

OTHER
1 Église St-Similien
2 Pannonica Jazz Café
3 Salle Paul-Fort
4 Marché de Talensac

5 Cyber House Café Internet
7 Monument des 50 Otages
8 Branch Post Office
9 Laundrette
11 Rent-a-Car Système
12 Cyber Nova
14 Central Post Office
15 Tour de Bretagne
17 Northbound Bus Station
19 Town Hall
22 Branch Post Office
23 Galeries Lafayette
24 Église Ste-Croix
26 Covered Market
28 Laverie du Bouffay
30 Librairie Durance
32 Monoprix
33 Banque de France
34 Palais de Justice
35 Le Fief de Vigne
36 Centre Régional Information
   Jeunesse
37 La Compagnie Nantaise des
   Antilles
38 Fromage Centrale
39 Poissonnerie Paon
40 Air France
43 British-American Institute
44 Maison de la Culture de
   Loire-Atlantique
45 Georges Gautier
50 Espace Transport (TAN)
51 Laundrette
52 Le Petit Marais
53 Tourist Office
54 Palais de la Bourse; FNAC

55 SNCF Boutique
56 Au Coup d'Canon
59 Pierre qui Roule
61 Théâtre Graslin
62 Cinéma Katorza
63 Paddy Dooley's
64 Musée Dobrée
65 Musée d'Histoire Naturelle
67 Change Graslin
71 CHR de Nantes
   (Hospital)
72 Préfecture
73 Hôtel d'Aux
74 Hôtel Montaudion
75 Porte St-Pierre
76 Colonne Louis XVI
77 Noctambule Alimentation
78 Musée des Beaux Arts
79 Hothouses
80 Train Station
   (Northern Entrance)
81 Train Station
   (Southern Entrance)
82 Apache
83 SNCF Bus Stop
84 Budget; Europcar; Hertz
85 Buses for Airport
86 Ancienne Usine LU
   Warehouse
87 Ancienne Usine LU
90 Sunday Tourist Office Desk
91 Espace Randonnée
92 Joystick Spirit
93 Géothèque
94 Southbound Bus Station;
   Eurolines

Centrale north-east to rue de la Marne, and north-west to rue du Calvaire; it includes place Royale, which is linked to place des 50 Otages by rue d'Orléans. The old city is to the east, between cours des 50 Otages and Château des Ducs de Bretagne.

The pedestrian alleys that run along the sides of the major thoroughfares are called *allées*.

Maps Géothèque (☎ 02 40 47 40 68), at 10 place du Pilori, is a top-notch travel bookshop (*librairie du voyage*) which sells an unbeatable selection of maps and guides.

Information

Tourist Offices The tourist office (☎ 02 40 20 60 00, fax 02 40 89 11 99) is inside the Palais de la Bourse (also home to FNAC) on place du Commerce. It opens 10 am to 7 pm Monday to Saturday. This is a good place to pick up bus, tram and city maps. The tourist office operates an information desk in the chateau on Sunday only; hours are 10 am to noon and 2 to 6 pm (no lunch-break in July and August).

The Centre Régional Information Jeunesse (CRIJ; ☎ 02 51 72 94 50), 28 rue du Calvaire, opens 2 to 6.30 pm Monday and Saturday, and 10 am to 6.30 pm Tuesday and Friday. The Maison des Étudiants (House of Students; ☎ 02 40 37 55 10, fax 02 40 4 37 13, ✉ m.d.e@wanadoo.fr), 3 route de la Jonelière, opens 9.30 am to 6 pm on weekdays and acts as an information centre and meeting point for students.

The Comité Départemental du Tourisme (☎ 02 51 72 95 30), 2 allée Baco, handles tourist information on the Loire-Atlantique *département* (department). Gîtes de France (☎ 02 51 72 95 65, fax 02 40 35 17 05) also has its office here. The Comité Régional du Tourisme des Pays de la Loire (☎ 02 40 48 24 20, fax 02 40 08 07 10, ✉ crt.promo@ wanadoo.fr), covering regional information, is at 2 rue de la Loire.

Money Banque de France, 14 rue La Fayette, exchanges money from 8.45 am to 12.30 pm on weekdays. There are several commercial banks farther along the street.

Change Graslin, an exchange bureau at 17 rue Jean-Jacques Rousseau, opens 9 am to noon and 2 to 6 pm (4.45 pm on Saturday) Monday to Saturday.

Post The central post office, place de Bretagne, opens 8 am to 7 pm on weekdays, and 8 am to noon on Saturday; its services include a Musée de la Poste (Postal Museum), of more interest to kids than philatelists. Currency exchange is also available. There is a smaller, branch office opposite the 50 Otages tram stop on allée des Tanneurs, and another in the city centre at 5 rue du Moulin.

Email & Internet Access Both branch post offices are equipped with a Cyberposte station.

Cyber House Café Internet (☎ 02 40 12 11 84), 8 quai de Versailles, opens 1 pm to 2 am on weekdays, and 3 pm to 2 am on Saturday. Cyber Nova (☎ 02 40 12 07 07), 14 rue Jean Jaurès, opens 10 am to 10 pm and charges 40FF per hour for on-line access. A 10-hour card costs 360FF. Opposite the entrance to the chateau on rue des États, Joystick Spirit charges 10/40FF per 10/30 minutes.

Bookshops Librairie Durance (☎ 02 40 48 68 79), 4 allée d'Orléans, cours des 50 Otages, has a fair selection of English-language novels and guides in its basement

and opens 9.30 am to 7 pm Tuesday to Saturday, and 2 to 7 pm on Monday.

Cultural Centre The British-American Institute (☎ 02 40 89 78 16, ✉ british .institute@wanadoo.fr) is at 3 rue Contrescarpe, on the corner of rue Crébillon.

Laundry The laundrettes at 8 allée des Tanneurs (along cours des 50 Otages) and 3 allée Duguay Trouin (along cours Franklin Roosevelt) open 7 am to 8.30 pm. The full-service Laverie du Bouffay, at 3 rue du Bouffay, opens 8.45 am to 7 pm Monday to Saturday.

Medical Services The 24-hour Service d'Urgences (Emergency Room; ☎ 02 40 08 38 95) of the vast CHR de Nantes is on quai Moncousu.

Emergency The Police Nationale's police station (☎ 02 40 37 21 21, tram stop Motte Rouge) at place Waldeck Rousseau (1km north-east of the Monument des 50 Otages) is staffed 24 hours per day; enter via the **entrée du public**.

Château des Ducs de Bretagne

The impressive Château des Ducs de Bretagne (Chateau of the Dukes of Brittany), 4 place Marc Elder, is surrounded by a dry moat. Work started on the lumbering edifice under François II, duke of Brittany (1435–88), in 1466, and was continued by his daughter Anne de Bretagne (1477–1514) following her marriage to Charles VIII, king of France, in Langeais in 1491. After the Edict of Nantes, it served as a barracks and a prison.

From the outside, the chateau appears to be a standard medieval castle, with high walls and crenellated towers, yet the parts facing the inner courtyard are wholly Renaissance in style. Entry to the courtyard is free, as is walking along part of the ramparts or in the landscaped moat. Admission to the **Musée du Château** (☎ 02 40 41 56 56, ✉ musee.chateau@mairie-nantes.fr) costs 20FF (students and children aged seven to 18 10FF). The museum holds temporary

LOIRE-ATLANTIQUE &

Nantes & the Slave Trade

In the 18th century, Nantes was France's most important slave-trading centre. In what was known euphemistically as 'the triangular trade', local merchants sent ships carrying manufactured goods – guns, gunpowder, knives, trinkets – to West Africa. The goods were bartered for slaves, who were transported in horrific conditions to the West Indies. The slaves who survived were then sold to plantation owners in exchange for an assortment of tropical products. Finally, the ships, laden with sugar, tobacco, coffee, cotton, cocoa, indigo and the like, sailed back to Nantes, where such commodities brought huge profits and made possible the construction of the splendid public buildings and luxurious mansions that still grace the city.

All along the River Loire, factories making sweets, chocolates and preserves sprang up to take advantage of the ready availability of West Indian sugar. Nearby ironsmiths worked overtime to produce the leg irons, handcuffs and spiked collars required to outfit the slave ships.

Slavery was abolished in French colonies in 1794, re-established by Napoleon in 1802 and suppressed after 1827. It continued clandestinely until 1848, when it was finally outlawed.

exhibitions and is housed in the **Harnachement**, built in the 18th century as an armoury for the barracks. It opens 10 am to noon and 2 to 6 pm Wednesday to Monday (no lunchbreak in July and August).

Extensive renovations which started in 1994 will be complete in 2008. The 122 million FF project will see a history museum open in the **Grand Logis** in 2001, plus numerous other attractions between 2003 and 2008.

Cathédrale St-Pierre et St-Paul

This Flamboyant Gothic cathedral dominating place St-Pierre was built over a period of four and a half centuries. The western facade and the towers are from the latter half of the 15th century, the nave is from the 16th century, and the transept and choir were begun in the mid-17th century. The interior is pristine because it was completely restored after a fire in 1972.

The **tomb of François II** (ruled 1458–88), duke of Brittany, and his second wife, Marguerite de Foix, in the southern transept is considered a masterpiece of Renaissance art. Commissioned by François II's daughter Anne de Bretagne, the ensemble was carved in Italian marble between 1502 and 1507 by Tourangeau sculptor Michel Colombe. The statue facing the nave, which represents Prudence, has a female body and face on one side and a bearded male face on the other. Although part of the original tomb was destroyed during the 1789 Revolution, the city architect hid fragments of the sculpted masterpiece until 1817, when what was left of it was returned to the cathedral. The tomb is lit by natural light which streams in through the largest **stained-glass window** in France, a modern creation glowing 25m high and 5.3m in width.

The cathedral opens 8.45 am to nightfall or 7 pm, whichever comes first. Sunday mass is celebrated at 9 am (10 am in summer) and 6 pm.

The true size of the cathedral is best appreciated from **place Maréchal Foch**, a monumental square north of the cathedral. Lovely 18th-century **hôtels particuliers** (mansions) surround the square, the centre of which is pierced with the phallic **Colonne Louis XVI** (1790).

Jardin des Plantes

Nantes' Jardin des Plantes, across blvd de Stalingrad from the train station, is one of France's most exquisite botanic gardens. Founded in the early 19th century, it has lawns like putting greens, beautiful flower beds, duck ponds, fountains and even a few California redwoods (sequoias). There are **hothouses** and a **children's playground** at the northern end.

Île Feydeau

The channels of the River Loire that once surrounded Île Feydeau (the neighbourhood where Jules Verne was born, south of Gare Centrale) were filled in after WWII, but the

Voyages Extraordinaires

JANE SMITH

Footloose and fanciful Jules Verne, father of science fiction

Jules Verne (1828–1905) is considered the father of science fiction. He was born in Nantes of sea-faring parents, and his fabulous tales evoking *voyages extraordinaires* (extraordinary journeys) took him (and his readers) to unexplored realms around the world. As a child he ran off to sea to become a cabin boy, only to be dragged home by an authoritarian father who pushed his son through his baccalauréat in Nantes and into a law degree (which Verne quit) in Paris.

The Verne family had a holiday home in Nantes after moving to Paris in 1848. Today it houses the **Musée Jules Verne** (☎ 02 40 69 72 52), about 2km south-west of Nantes tourist office at 3 rue de l'Hermitage. Documents, models, posters and first-edition books connected in some way with Jules Verne evoke the novelist's progressive vision, expounded in such works as *De la terre à la lune* (*From the Earth to the Moon*), one of a handful of titles published in the 1860s. The house museum opens 10 am to noon and 2 to 5 pm Monday and Wednesday to Saturday, and 2 to 5 pm on Sunday (except public holidays). Admission costs 8FF (children 4FF).

Verne travelled throughout his life, buying a series of yachts (*St-Michel II* and *St-Michel III*) in 1876 and 1877 to sail around Europe. *Le tour du monde en 80 jours* (*Around the World in 80 Days*) was published in 1873.

---

area's 18th-century mansions, built by rich merchants from the ill-gotten profits of the slave trade, are still standing. Some of them are adorned with stone carvings of the heads of African slaves.

Passage Pommeraye, a delightful shopping arcade opened in 1843, and hardly changed since, is two blocks north-west of Île Feydeau. Its ornate interior shelters exclusive art galleries and designer shoe shops, and is a must for window and serious shoppers alike.

Museums

The renowned **Musée des Beaux Arts** (Fine Arts Museum; ☎ 02 40 41 65 65), 10 rue Georges Clémenceau, constructed in the 1890s, mainly displays paintings, including three works by Georges de la Tour. It opens 10 am (11 am on Sunday) to 6 pm (9 pm on Friday) Wednesday to Monday, except on holidays. Some of the exhibits are closed from 11.45 am to 2 pm. Admission costs 20FF (students 10FF, those aged under 18 free) except from 6 to 9 pm on Friday evening and on the first Sunday of each month, when admission is free; after 4.30 pm daily, admission costs 10FF.

The old-fashioned but excellent **Musée d'Histoire Naturelle** (Natural History Museum; ☎ 02 40 99 26 20, ✉ museum .sciences@mairie-nantes.fr), 12 rue Voltaire, founded in 1799, features a **vivarium** with live pythons, crocodiles and a green iguana. It opens 10 am to noon and 2 to 6 pm Tuesday to Saturday, and 2 to 6 pm on Sunday. Admission costs 20FF (those aged over 65 and students 10FF, those aged under 18

LOIRE-ATLANTIQUE & VENDÉE

euro currency converter 10FF = €1.52

free), except on the first Sunday of the month, when admission is free. The most interesting way to get to the museum from cours des 50 Otages is to walk via **place Royale** (1790) and **place Graslin**, on the northern side of which stands **Théâtre Graslin** (1788).

Musée Dobrée (☎ 02 40 71 03 50), 18 rue Voltaire, part of which is housed in the Manoir de la Touche, a 15th-century bishops' palace, has exhibits of classical antiquities, medieval artefacts, Renaissance furniture and items relating to the French Revolution. Its highlight, however, is the **heart of Anne de Bretagne**, encased in ivory and gold. The reliquary originally rested in a Carmelite church in Nantes, following the death of the 37-year-old queen in 1514. The museum opens 10 am to noon and 1.30 to 5.30 pm Tuesday to Sunday. Admission costs 20FF (those aged over 65, students aged under 25 and those aged 10 to 18 10FF).

The 132.6m-long and 12.7m-wide French navy destroyer *Maillé Brézé* (☎ 02 40 69 56 82), in service from 1957 to 1988, is moored on quai de la Fosse, about 1km west of the main tourist office. It can be visited 2 to 6 pm daily, June to September; and 2 to 5 pm on Wednesday, weekends and holidays, the rest of the year. The excellent (and obligatory) guided tour – in English in summer – costs 30/45FF for the one-hour/1½-hour version (children aged under 12 15/25FF); the longer tour includes a visit to the engine room. Written information in English is available.

Boat Trips & Riverside Promenades

The **Promenade de l'Erdre** is a network of riverside paths which follow both banks of the River Erdre from the Monument des 50 Otages north for about 7km. The **Île de Versailles**, an island 500m north of the monument, is home to a Japanese garden and, at its northern end, a children's playground.

Bateaux Nantais (☎ 02 40 14 51 14, tram stop Motte Rouge), quai de la Motte Rouge, 1km north-east of the Monument des 50 Otages near the Hôtel de Police, runs **boat excursions** along the River Erdre. Trips de-

part at 3 and 5 pm daily (1¾ hours) between June and August, and on Saturday at 9 pm (2¼ hours) year round. Day/evening trips cost 55/75FF (children aged under 12 25FF). In April, May and September to November there are excursions at the weekend and possibly on Wednesday. Bateaux Nantais also arranges 2½-hour, sightseeing lunchtime (250FF) and dinner (285FF) cruises.

Walking

Espace Randonnée (☎ 02 40 20 15 10), 2 rue de Strasbourg, houses two nonprofit hiking organisations: Escapades sells topoguides and maps and can provide tips for ramblers, while the Fédération Française de la Randonnée Pédestre (FFRP; ☎ 02 51 88 95 40) organises hikes in the surrounding area. The office opens noon to 6 pm on weekdays, and 2 to 6 pm on Saturday; the FFRP desk is staffed between 1 and 5 pm.

Places to Stay

Nantes is a gold mine of excellent cheap hotels. Most have plenty of rooms in July and August; during the rest of the year, they can be full at the weekend.

Camping Open year round, *Camping du Petit Port* (☎ 02 40 74 47 94) is about 3km due north of the train station, at 21 blvd du Petit Port. A tent/tent and car costs 26/37FF plus 18/12FF per adult/child. To get there, take tram No 2 northbound to the Morrhonnière stop.

Hostels Travellers are welcome year round at *Résidence Porte Neuve* (☎ 02 40 20 63 63, fax 02 40 20 63 79, 1 place Ste-Elisabeth), a dormitory for young people run by a nonprofit organisation. Beds cost 80/95FF in a triple/single room, including breakfast. Advance reservations by telephone or fax are compulsory.

The *auberge de jeunesse* (☎/fax 02 40 29 29 20, 2 place de la Manu) is 600m east of the train station's northern entrance. It charges 48FF for a dorm bed; breakfast costs an additional 19FF. Kitchen facilities are available. Reception opens 8 am to noon and 5 to 11 pm.

Le Petit Beurre

France's best-known butter biscuit – the *petit beurre*, with its just-asking-to-be-nibbled tooth-combed edge – originates in Nantes. It is the timeless creation of the LU biscuit factory, born out of a cake shop run by Monsieur Lefèvre and Mademoiselle Utile (hence the name) at 5 rue Boileau.

In 1889, three tonnes of biscuits were produced daily at the **Ancienne Usine LU** (old LU factory), which opened its doors in 1850 on allée Baco. In 1886 the first petit beurre was baked, and by 1897 LU was cooking up 15 tonnes of 200 different cookie types (requiring 25,000 eggs) per day.

The fancy octagonal **tower** (1905–9) with its ornate dome and sculpted angel which still stands on the corner of allée Baco and ave Carnot is a beautiful example of early-20th-century eclecticism. Its twin, which stood on the opposite side of ave Carnot, was destroyed during WWII. In 1922 a warehouse, topped with two squat biscuit-box-shaped towers, was built on the corner of rue Crucy; the original, giant-sized petit beurre on its facade ensures it remains distinguishable today.

One the eve of WWI, LU employed 1200 factory workers, a workforce that peaked at 2000 in 1950. Since 1986, when the BSN group took control of LU (manufactured under the General Biscuits name today), the petit beurre has been baked in La Haie-Fouassière, south of Nantes.

Hotels There are several two- and three-star hotels in the charmless area across from the train station's northern entrance. Reception at the hotels listed below generally opens 7 am to 9 or 10 pm Monday to Saturday, and more limited hours on Sunday.

Between the chateau and the train station, little *Hôtel du Château* (☎ 02 40 74 17 16, fax 02 40 14 01 15, 5 place de la Duchesse Anne) is in a peaceful location; singles/doubles with bidet and washbasin cost 135/155FF, and singles/doubles with shower are 155/185FF (180/200FF with toilet).

In the old city, 22-room *Hôtel Renova* (☎ 02 40 47 57 03, fax 02 51 82 06 39, 11 rue Beauregard) has been run by the same family since 1966. Doubles start at 130FF (160FF with shower, 180FF with shower and toilet). There are no hall showers.

Nearby *Hôtel St-Daniel* (☎ 02 40 47 41 25, fax 02 51 72 03 99, 4 rue du Bouffay) offers fairly spacious doubles costing 150FF with shower and 170FF with shower and toilet.

Close to the Médiathèque tram stop, one-star *Hôtel de la Bourse* (☎ 02 40 69 51 55, fax 02 40 71 73 89, 19 quai de la Fosse) is among the best deals in town. It has tidy doubles starting at 105FF (120FF with shower, 146FF with shower and toilet). Hall showers cost 18FF.

Up the block, the excellent-value 19-room *Hôtel Fourcroy* (☎ 02 40 44 68 00, 11 rue Fourcroy), run by the same family since 1978, has pleasant and exceptionally well-kept doubles with upholstered doors costing 137FF with shower and 157FF with shower and toilet. There is free parking in the courtyard.

A block east is slightly more upmarket *Hôtel de l'Océan* (☎ 02 40 69 73 51, 11 rue Maréchal de Lattre de Tassigny), home to straightforward doubles costing 159FF, or ones with shower and toilet costing 169FF.

Founded by an Irish couple many years ago, 24-room *Hôtel St-Patrick* (☎ 02 40 48 48 80, 7 rue St-Nicolas) offers simple, modern doubles costing upwards of 135FF (145FF with shower, 165FF with shower and toilet). Reception is on the third floor (no lift). Hall showers are free. Buzz on the intercom to enter.

Friendly *Hôtel d'Orléans* (☎ 02 40 47 69 32, 12 rue du Marais) offers plain doubles costing upwards of 130FF (160FF with shower). Rooms with shower and toilet cost 185FF. Hall showers are free. Equally in the heart of things, opposite the Tour de Bretagne on cours des 50 Otages, is *Hôtel du Tourisme* (☎ 02 40 47 90 26, fax 02 40 35 57 25, 5 allée Duquesne). Doubles with washbasin clock in at 140FF, rooms with

LOIRE-ATLANTIQUE & VENDÉE

shower and TV are 165FF, and doubles with shower, toilet and TV cost 185FF.

Close to the chateau, charming *Hôtel Duchesse Anne* (☎ 02 51 86 78 78, fax 02 40 74 60 20, 3–4 place de la Duchesse Anne) has lovely doubles starting at 290FF; private parking costs 30FF.

In the heart of the shopping centre, stunning *Hôtel de France* (☎ 02 40 73 57 91, fax 02 40 69 75 75, 24 rue Crébillon) is a venerable three-star place occupying an 18th-century mansion. Bath-equipped doubles, which boast high ceilings and are designed in different period styles such as Regence or Louis XVI, start at 350FF. Rooms priced at 580FF are royally huge.

Modern options include *Grand Hotel Mercure Central* (☎ 02 51 82 10 00, fax 02 51 82 10 10, 4 rue du Couëdic) and Best Western's *Jules Verne* (☎ 02 40 35 74 50, fax 02 40 20 09 35, 3 rue du Couëdic) opposite. Both offer three-star doubles costing 420FF.

Places to Eat

Restaurants Off place Royale, *Le Petit Flore* (☎ 02 40 48 24 88, 1 rue des Vieilles Douves) is a must for anyone into healthy living. Delicious quiches, sweet and savoury *tartines* (tarts or crispy toasts with a variety of toppings), salads and an 80FF brunch star on the menu of this charming, lunchtime spot. Count on a short wait for a table. Next door, *Le Mont Liban* (☎ 02 40 89 18 31, 3 rue des Vieilles Douves) is an authentic Lebanese spot that gets equally packed by noon, thanks to its astonishingly good-value 46FF and 58FF lunchtime *menus*. Its cuisine is delicate, lightly perfumed and likewise worth the wait.

A grander choice is nearby *La Cigale* (☎ 02 51 84 94 94, 4 place Graslin), the interior of which is classified as a historic monument. It is stunningly decorated with 1890s tilework and painted ceilings that mix Baroque with Art Nouveau. Breakfast (50FF) is served daily from 7.30 to 11 or 11.30 am, lunch from 11.45 am to 2.30 pm, and dinner from 6.45 pm to 12.30 am; many dishes are available all afternoon. The *menus* vary from 75FF (lunch) to 150FF

(dinner) and it serves numerous seafood platters (195FF) and oysters for 99F per dozen.

Hearty regional fodder is dished up at *Aux Petits Oignons* (☎ 02 40 71 84 84, 2 rue Suffren), a delightful place to try *tripaux* (tripe), *cuisses de grenouilles* (frogs legs), *andouillette de troyes* (a big fat offal sausage) or pan-fried *rognons. de veaux* (calf kidneys). *Menus* cost 67FF (until 9 pm) and 106FF.

Andouillette (tripe sausage) is a typical dish at *Le Bouche à Oreille* (☎ 02 40 73 00 25, 14 rue Jean-Jacques Rousseau), a traditional Lyonnais *bouchon* (bistro-style restaurant) which serves food until midnight and offers a 69FF lunchtime *menu*. Do not miss the delicious *saucisse de morteau* (a meaty sausage from the Jura region in eastern France) or *quenelles* (poached pike dumplings), swilled down with a bottle of St-Nicolas de Bourgueil (98FF) from the Loire Valley.

Another memorable choice is *Le Bouchon* (☎ 02 40 20 08 44, 7 rue Bossuet), which has the most gorgeous flower-filled summer garden in which to dine in the entire city. Its *carpaccio thon frais* (fresh tuna carpaccio) melts in your mouth. *Menus* cost 138FF to 210FF and it opens Monday to Saturday.

L'Océanide (☎ 02 40 20 32 28, 2 rue Paul Bellamy) is *the* place for seafood. Most diners opt for a *plateau de fruits de mer* (seafood platter), despite the lobsters and langoustines swimming around in tanks on display waiting to be eaten. Platters range from 109FF to 530FF and there is an excellent 200FF *menu cuisine Nantaise* featuring local dishes such as pike-perch in *beurre blanc* (white butter sauce).

Brasseries & Cafes There are several *brasseries* and *cafes* with inexpensive steak and chips both on and around place du Commerce, their saving grace being their sunny pavement terraces. The pedestrian streets in the old city – two blocks west of the chateau around rue de la Juiverie, rue des Petites Écuries and rue de la Bâclerie – are riddled with cheap places to snack,

Cycling along the Atlantic coast necessitates frequent pit stops for splashing or lying around.

Fishing for everyone's dinner at St-Brévin-les-Pins

Sailing along at Les Sables d'Olonne

Deck chairs are in short supply along this coast.

At Futuroscope, see space-age architecture...

...be dazzled by 3D movies at Le Solido...

...get disorientated at Tapis Magique...

...and marvel at the world's largest wall of images.

Study the intricate stonework and colourful stained glass of Église Notre Dame la Grande, Poitiers.

sitting down or standing up. Pizza, tapas, couscous, crepes and Asian cuisines are among the choice offerings.

The aptly named *Brasserie Le Carnivore* (☎ 02 40 47 87 00, 7 allée des Tanneurs) is a huge, Louisiana/Old West-style place which serves all sorts of meats, including bison (130FF), ostrich (110FF) and kangaroo (89FF), as well as smoked salmon and paella. The *menus* cost 57FF (lunch), 88FF and 138FF.

L'Arbre de Vie (☎ 02 40 08 06 10, 8 allée des Tanneurs) offers a vegetarian, organic alternative to Le Carnivore. The lunch *menus* cost 64FF, 74FF and 84FF (open Monday to Saturday).

Healthy cuisine is also produced at the small and quaint *D'Après Nature* (☎ 02 40 20 33 86, 4 rue des Trois Croissants), a brunch-cum-lunch place with a soulful, bohemian air.

Some of Nantes' best savoury and sweet crepes (10FF to 44FF) are on offer at *Aux Vieux Quimper* (☎ 02 40 35 63 99, 10 rue de la Bâclerie). For freshly filled baguettes, stuffed so full they are tied with string, follow the crowd to *La Mie Câline* at the western end of allée Brancas.

Self-Catering A small *covered market* fills place du Bouffay and the huge *Marché de Talensac* spills along rue Talensac until about 1 pm (open Tuesday to Sunday). Pedestrian rue Contrescarpe has some lovely little food shops: buy cheese at the traditional *Fromage Centrale* (☎ 02 40 12 02 70, 8 rue Contrescarpe), housed in an old building with a ceramic-tiled facade, and fresh coffee beans at *La Compagnie Nantaise des Antilles* at No 12. Round the corner is a fabulous fishmonger, *Poissonnerie Paon* (8 rue Rubens). Chocolates to make your mouth water are exquisitely displayed in a historic interior at the old-fashioned chocolatier *Georges Gautier* (9 rue de la Fosse).

Monoprix supermarket at 2 rue du Calvaire opens 9 am to 9 pm Monday to Saturday. Choice wines are sold at *Le Fief de Vigne* (☎ 02 40 47 58 75, 16 rue Marceau). Just north off place Maréchal Foch is *Noc-* *tambule Alimentation* (89 rue Maréchal Joffre), a night shop open 5.30 pm to 2 am Tuesday to Sunday, and 9 pm to 2 am on Monday.

Entertainment

The weekly listings *Nantes Poche* is sold (3FF) at tobacconists and has details of films, live music and so on, as does the freebie *Pulsomatic*, published weekly. The tourist office publishes the free monthly *Le Mois Nantais*, a comprehensive sports and culture listing.

Tickets for cultural events are sold at the tourist office or across the hall in the same building at the FNAC ticket counter (☎ 02 51 72 47 23), open 10 am to 8 pm Monday to Saturday. Theatre tickets and programmes are available at the Maison de la Culture de Loire-Atlantique (☎ 02 51 88 25 25, fax 02 40 47 92 04), 10 Passage Pommeraye; the culture centre opens 11 am to 7 pm.

Bars & Clubs One of the few remaining traditional *bar à vins* (wine bars) is *Au Coup d'Canon* (rue Jean-Jacques Rousseau). You can choose from a huge selection of wines in an authentic, rustic setting.

Pannonica Jazz Café (☎ 02 40 48 74 74, 9 rue Basse Porte) is a jazzy spot which hosts live performances, most Thursday and Friday evenings (except in July and August) from 8.30 or 9 pm. Admission costs 30FF to 80FF, depending on who's playing. Tickets for concerts at Pannonica Jazz Café are sold at *Salle Paul-Fort* (☎ 02 51 72 10 10, ✉ la.bouche.dair@infonie.fr), a rock-concert venue next door to Pannonica. The ticket office opens 10 am to 1 pm and 3 to 6 pm Tuesday to Friday, and 10 am to 1 pm on Saturday.

Up the hill from Théâtre Graslin, there are plenty of mainstream pubs along rue Scribe. *Paddy Dooley's* (☎ 02 40 48 29 00, 9 rue Franklin) is a spacious Irish-owned pub which hosts live music two to four times a month.

Le Petit Marais (☎ 02 40 20 15 25, 15 rue Kervégan) is a friendly, mainly gay bar, open 5 pm to 2 am. Several other bars, not necessarily gay, line this street.

Opera, Theatre & Classical Music The *Théâtre Graslin (☎ 02 40 41 90 60, 1 rue Molière)* is also home to *Opéra de Nantes (☎ 02 40 69 77 18, 02 40 41 90 63, ✪ opera@mairie-nantes.fr)*. Opera tickets cost 60FF to 286FF depending on seating. Plays and concerts take to the stage here.

Getting There & Away

Air The Aéroport International Nantes-Atlantique (☎ 02 40 84 80 00, fax 02 40 84 82 11, ✪ aerop-nte@calva.net) is about 12km south-west of the centre of town. For details of international and domestic arrivals and departures, see Air in the Getting There & Away chapter. In town, Air France has an office at 6 place Royale (open Monday to Saturday).

Bus The southbound bus station (☎ 02 40 47 62 70, 08 25 08 71 56), across from 13 allée de la Maison Rouge, is used by CTA buses serving areas of Loire-Atlantique that are south of the River Loire, including the seaside towns of Pornic (60FF, 1¼ hours, three daily) and St-Brévin-les-Pins (60FF, 1½ hours, one or two daily). The information office opens 6.45 to 10.30 am and 3.45 to 6.30 pm on weekdays, and 10 am to 1.45 pm on Saturday. The northbound bus station (☎ 02 40 20 46 99), 1 allée Duquesne (on cours des 50 Otages), run by Cariane Atlantique, handles buses to destinations north of the River Loire.

SNCF buses to Pornic (53FF, 50 minutes, three daily), Poitiers (141FF, 3½ hours, one daily), Cholet (55FF, 55 minutes, five daily), Noirmoutier-en-l'Île (90FF, 1¾ hours, three or four daily) and Les Sables d'Olonne (89FF, 3¾ hours, three daily) all arrive and depart at the bus stop across the street from the southern entrance to the train station. For tickets and schedules, ask in the train station.

Eurolines (☎ 02 51 72 02 03), inside the southbound bus station, opens 10 am to noon and 1.30 to 6 pm on weekdays, and 9 am to 12.30 pm on Saturday. For information on international routings see Continental Europe or The UK under Land in the Getting There & Away chapter.

Train The train station (☎ 08 36 35 35 35) has two entrances: Accès Nord (northern entrance) at 27 blvd de Stalingrad, across the street from the Jardin des Plantes; and Accès Sud (southern entrance), across the tracks on rue de Lourmel. The information offices open 9 am to 7 pm Monday to Saturday, except on holidays. Left-luggage lockers, accessible between 6 am and 11 pm, are in the northern part of the station.

Tickets and information are also available at the SNCF Boutique, 12 place de la Bourse. It opens 9 am to 7 pm Tuesday to Saturday, and noon to 7 pm on Monday. There is also an SNCF ticketing desk, open 8.30 am to 7 pm on weekdays, inside TAN's Espace Transport at 2 allée Brancas.

Destinations well served by trains include TGV and non-TGV services to Tours (152FF, 1½ to two hours, four to eight daily), stopping at most Loire Valley destinations en route; St-Gilles Croix de Vie (71FF, 2½ hours); Les Sables d'Olonne (89FF, 1½ hours); Le Croisic (74FF/94FF for regional/TGV trains, one to 1¼ hours); and St-Nazaire (56FF, 40 minutes).

For information on trains to/from Paris and other parts of the country, see Other Parts of France under Land in the Getting There & Away chapter.

Car Budget, Europcar and Hertz each have an office outside the train station's southern entrance. Apache (☎ 02 51 25 26 27), nearby at 45 quai Malakoff, rents cars from 170FF per day, including 100km and a deductible/excess of 3500FF (open weekdays and on Saturday morning). Another cheapie, Rent-a-Car Système (☎ 08 36 69 46 95) has its office in town on allée des Tanneurs.

Getting Around

To/From the Airport The TAN-Air public bus links the airport with the Gare Centrale bus/tram hub and the southern entrance of the train station. One-way tickets are sold individually (38FF) or in *carnets* (books) of four (100FF); they must be time-stamped on boarding the bus. Journey time is 20 minutes; bus times correspond with flight arrivals/departures.

Bus & Tram Nantes' urban mass transit system is run by TAN (☎ 08 01 44 44 44). The city's modern tram system (an earlier tram network was phased out in 1958) has two lines that intersect at the Gare Centrale (Commerce), the city centre's main bus/tram transfer point. By September 2000, line No 1 will extend a further 5.3km westwards, and a third new line (5.8km long) will connect central place de Bretagne with place Viarme (where the pro-Royalist Vendéen leader Charette was publicly executed in 1796). Nantes' tramway – 27km long in 1999 – is the longest in France.

Most bus lines run until 8 or 9 pm. From 9.15 pm to 12.15 am, TAN runs an hourly night service, which includes the two tram lines and seven bus lines; all pass by Gare Centrale.

Bus/tram tickets, sold individually (8FF) by bus (but not tram) drivers and in carnets of five/ten (32/59FF), are valid for one hour after being time-stamped for travel in any direction. A *ticket 24 heures* (24-hour ticket) costs 21FF and a seven-day pass costs 68FF. Travelling without a ticket warrants a 190FF on-the-spot fine; tickets that aren't time-stamped command a fine of 125FF.

TAN's information and ticket office, called Espace Transport, at 2 allée Brancas (across the street from the Gare Centrale hub) opens 7.15 am to 7 pm Monday to Saturday.

Bicycle & Rollerblades Bicycles are not allowed on TAN buses, but you can travel on the tram with your bicycle before 7.15 am and after 6.30 pm, Monday to Saturday, and all day Sunday.

Pierre qui Roule (☎ 02 40 69 51 01), 1 rue Gretry, has bicycles and rollers to hire. The daily rate for a mountain/road bike is 65/45FF and rollers cost 80/65FF per day for adults/children. Weekend rates start at 80/120/150FF for road bikes/mountain bikes/skates. Opening hours are 9.30 am to 12.30 pm and 2 to 7.30 pm.

ST-NAZAIRE
postcode 44600 • pop 64,800
Strategically placed at the mouth of the Loire estuary, 61km downstream from Nantes, the lumbering port town of St-Nazaire was completely rebuilt in the 1960s following its destruction by German forces in WWII. The result is a grey, concrete city which has little to lure visitors not into New Age industrial sights. During WWII, St-Nazaire was the last pocket of Europe to be liberated.

The city's harbour is France's fourth largest. An estimated 25 million tonnes of freight passes through it annually. St-Nazaire's Atlantic shipyards are among the country's largest, and its aeronautics industry employs some 4200 people to manufacture and assemble Airbus parts. Elf's primary oil refinery in France is 10km east, in Donges, on the estuary's northern bank.

Orientation & Information
Ave de la République forms a north–south axis between the train station on place Pierre Sémard and blvd du Président Wilson, the coastal road overlooking plage du Petit Traict. The port, with its giant basins and shipyards, lies to the east of, and parallel to, ave de la République.

The tourist office (☎ 02 40 22 40 65, fax 02 40 22 19 80), place François Blancho, opens 9.45 am to noon and 2 to 6 pm on weekdays. It arranges organised tours (65FF) to the shipyards, the Aérothèque, where Airbus parts are constructed and the city's aeronautical industry is explored, and a subterranean tour of the French submarine *Espadon*.

The post office, at 11 ave de la République, has a Cyberposte work station. Surfers can also access the Net at the US-style Pheonix Cybercafé, 58 rue Albert de Mun. Opening hours at the Hallwash laundrette, 101 ave de la République, are 9 am to 8 pm. City and regional maps and guides are sold at the Papeterie Alfa 2000, 90 rue Albert de Mun.

Things to See & Do
St-Nazaire has two sights: the metallic 3.3km-long **pont de St-Nazaire** (1975) which crosses the River Loire, and its port. At the port, local history is well explained in the **Ecomusée** (☎ 02 40 22 35 33) and nearby **Sous Marin** *Espadon*, a submarine

LOIRE-ATLANTIQUE & VENDÉE

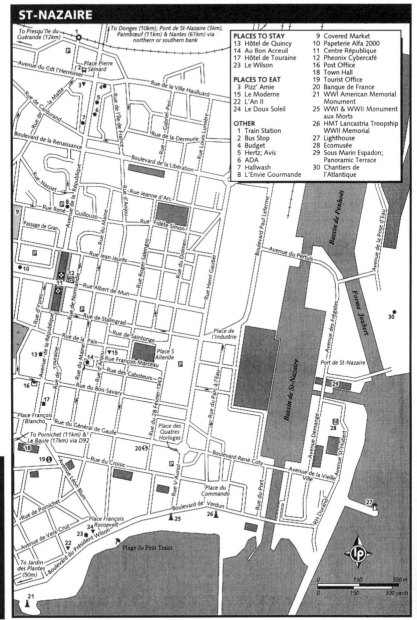

ST-NAZAIRE

To Presqu'île du Guérande (12km)

To Donges (10km), Pont de St-Nazaire (3km), Paimbœuf (11km) & Nantes (61km) via northern or southern bank

Place Pierre Sémard

Avenue du Cdt l'Herminier

Rue de la Ville Haulluard

Rue de la Matte

Rue de Cardurand

Rue de l'Île de France

Rue Gabriel-Petit

Boulevard de la Renaissance

Rue de la Dermurie

Rue Louis Lumière

Rue Nasriet

Boulevard de la Libération

Rue de la République

Rue Jeanne d'Arc

Passage de Gran

Rue René Guillouzou

Avenue de la Maine

Rue d'Anjou

Rue Fidèle-Simon

Rue Jean-Jaurès

Rue Roger-Salengro

Rue du Dolmen

Rue Albert de Mun

Rue de Normandie

Boulevard Paul Leferme

Bassin de Penhoët

Avenue de la Prise d'Eau

Avenue du Pertuis

Rue Henri Gautier

Rue d'Ypres

Rue de Stalingrad

Forme Joubert

Rue de la République

Rue de la Paix

Rue de Saintonge

Place de l'Industrie

Avenue des Frégates

Place S Allende

Rue François-Marceau

Rue du Maine

Rue d'Anjou

Rue des Caboteurs

Rue de Touraine

Rue du Bois Savary

Rue du 28 Février-1943

Bassin de St-Nazaire

Port de St-Nazaire

Place François Blancho

Rue du Général de Gaulle

Rue du Parc à l'Eau

Avenue Demange

Avenue St-Hubert

To Pornichet (11km) & La Baule (17km) via D92

Place des Quatres Horloges

Boulevard René Coty

Avenue Léon Blum

Rue du Croisic

Rue du Port

Avenue de la Vieille Ville

Rue V-Auriol

Place du Commando

RH Durand

Rue de Pornichet

Boulevard de Verdun

Place François Roosevelt

Boulevard du Président Wilson

Plage du Petit Traict

Avenue de Vera-Cruz

To Jardin des Plantes (50m)

PLACES TO STAY
13 Hôtel de Quincy
14 Au Bon Acceuil
17 Hôtel de Touraine
23 Le Wilson

PLACES TO EAT
3 Pizz' Amie
15 Le Moderne
22 L'An II
24 Le Doux Soleil

OTHER
1 Train Station
2 Bus Stop
4 Budget
5 Hertz; Avis
6 ADA
7 Hallwash
8 L'Envie Gourmande
9 Covered Market
10 Papeterie Alfa 2000
11 Centre République
12 Pheonix Cybercafé
16 Post Office
18 Town Hall
19 Tourist Office
20 Banque de France
21 WWI American Memorial Monument
25 WWI & WWII Monument aux Morts
26 HMT Lancastria Troopship WWII Memorial
27 Lighthouse
28 Ecomusée
29 Sous Marin Espadon; Panoramic Terrace
30 Chantiers de l'Atlantique

0   150   300 m
0   150   300 yards

moored beneath a fortified lock which can be toured. Both open 10 am to 6 pm and admission costs 45FF (children aged four to 12 25FF). By mid-2000 **Escal' Atlantic** will open at the port, providing visitors with a glimpse into life aboard one of the many ocean liners built here to cross the Atlantic in the 1930s.

The port and bridge are best viewed from Port de Mindin on the estuary's southern side. In summer, ugly views of Donges can be enjoyed afloat *La Pimpante 2*. Estuary boat trips (☎ 02 40 31 64 55) depart from **Paimbœuf**, 11km east of St-Nazaire on the southern bank.

In July and August, a **son et lumière** (sound and light show; free) is held in the port from 10 pm to midnight.

Places to Stay

At *Hôtel de Touraine* (☎ 02 40 22 47 56, fax 02 40 22 55 05, 4 ave de la République), a block north of what has to be the ugliest town hall in France, guests can have breakfast in a pretty garden in summer. Basic doubles with washbasin cost 120FF, with bidet and TV 135FF, and with shower and TV 160FF.

Nearby *Hôtel de Quincy* (☎ 02 40 66 70 82, fax 02 40 22 04 30), at No 15 on the same street, has two-star doubles with shower costing 180FF (200FF with toilet).

Sea views are part of the deal at *Le Wilson* (☎/fax 02 40 70 21 20, 36 blvd du Président Wilson), an attractive house sheltering 10 furnished self-catering studios costing 130FF to 250FF. *Au Bon Accueil* (☎ 02 40 22 07 05, fax 02 40 19 01 58, 39 rue François Marceau) is the top place to stay in town; singles/doubles go for 350/410FF.

Places to Eat

Close to the Atlantic, *L'An II* (☎ 02 40 00 95 33, 2 rue Villebois Mareuil) specialises in seafood and is among the better places to eat. Its stuffed oysters are delicious. Nearby, *Le Doux Soleil* (☎ 02 40 70 30 20, 31 blvd du Président Wilson) serves a good selection of savoury *galettes* (savoury buckwheat crepes; upwards of 38FF) and sweet crepes (10FF to 25FF).

Good pizzas are dished up at *Pizz' Amie* (☎ 02 51 76 08 08), opposite the train station on ave du Commandent l'Herminier. *Le Moderne* (☎ 02 40 22 55 88, 46 rue d'Anjou) is a small, exclusive place popular with corporate diners. *Menus* cost 85FF to 230FF.

Regional wines are sold at upmarket *L'Envie Gourmande* (85 ave de la République), a refined food shop which offers wine-tasting sessions on most Saturday mornings.

Flowers, clothes and an abundance of fresh and fishy produce fill the *covered market (place du Commerce)* between 6 am and 3 pm on Tuesday, Friday and Saturday.

Getting There & Away

Bus The surrounding Presqu'île du Guérande is well served by STRAN (☎ 02 40 00 75 75) buses. There are daily services between St-Nazaire and Pornichet (Nos 82 and 83, 18FF, 35 minutes, at least hourly), Le Croisic (No 81, 36FF, one hour, about eight daily), La Baule (No 81, 27FF, 30 minutes, about eight daily) and Guérande (No 80, 27FF, 35 minutes, five or six daily). Bus timetables are distributed in the information and ticket office at the SNCF train station. Buses arrive and depart from the bus stop in front of the train station. A one-day travel pass allowing unlimited travel on the Presqu'île du Guérande is available for 25FF.

Train From St-Nazaire, trains chug along the coast to Le Croisic (30FF, 30 minutes, eight to 10 daily), stopping en route at Pornichet, La Baule, Le Pouliguen and Batz-sur-Mer; not all trains stop at La Baule and Batz-sur-Mer.

Eastbound, there are trains every 30 minutes to/from Nantes (56FF, 40 minutes), from where there are trains to most Loire Valley destinations.

Car Hertz and Avis are next door to each other at 126 ave de la République, and ADA (☎ 02 40 22 25 25) is at No 122 on the same street. Budget (☎ 02 51 76 02 48) is opposite the train station.

PRESQU'ÎLE DU GUÉRANDE

A curious landscape of salt pans (*marais salants*) and sandy beaches makes up the Guérande peninsula, a ball of land jutting into the Atlantic Ocean to the north of St-Nazaire. In summer a sea of poppy-red *salicornes* (an aquatic plant, pickled and eaten) carpets many of the salt-pan bottoms, while bathers flock to the beach at La Baule to dip their toes into its sparkling blue waters.

Cliffs and dunes sweep west towards Le Croisic, an old fishing settlement marooned on Pointe du Croisic, the peninsula's south-westernmost point. At the time of writing, the beaches here were recovering from the oil slick that washed ashore from an oil tanker in December 1999, devastating the sandy coastline (see the boxed text 'Oil Spill' in the Facts about the Loire chapter). Inland is fortified Guérande, a medieval village walled in by 14th-century ramparts, where most of the peninsula's salt workers (*paludiers*) live. East of here sprawls the Parc Naturel Régional de Brière, created in 1970 to protect the unique wetland.

La Baule

postcode 44500 • pop 15,000

It was the *belle époque* (literally 'beautiful age') that bequeathed the region La Baule, one of the Atlantic coast's most glamorous resorts, in 1879. It is best known for its long and wide golden beach, which is sheltered to the north by pine forests, which were planted in 1840 to stabilise shifting sand dunes that buried the village of Escoublac in 1527. Luxury hotels, a casino, surf shops, restaurant terraces and plenty of benches litter the smooth promenade that hugs the beach.

The tourist office (☎ 02 40 24 34 44, fax 02 40 11 08 10) is next to the bus station on place de la Victoire. Walk south along ave du Maréchal Foch to get to the beach. You can hire a bicycle for 45FF per day from Location Chaillou (☎ 02 40 60 07 06), across the square at 3 place de la Victoire; and rollerblades from Pierre qui Roule (☎ 02 40 60 40 41) on the prom at 16 blvd Hennecart.

Places to Stay The *Hôtel Hermitage* (☎ 02 40 11 46 46, fax 02 40 11 46 45, *ℓ* hermitage@lucienbarriere.com, 5 esplanade Lucien Barrière) and *Hôtel Royal-Thalasso* (☎ 02 40 11 48 48, fax 02 40 11 48 45, *ℓ* royalthalsso@lucienbarriere.com, 6 ave Pierre Loti) sit on the beach front and are La Baule's most prestigious pads. Rooms without/with sea view start at around 900/1300FF. The latter adjoins the Centre de Thalassothérapie (☎ 02 40 11 99 97), where seawater therapy rejuvenates the tired and weary.

Getting There & Away La Baule is 17km west of St-Nazaire and linked to it by train (21FF, 15 minutes) and bus No 81 (27FF, 30 minutes, about eight daily). The bus station can be phoned on ☎ 02 40 11 53 00.

Le Croisic

postcode 44490 • pop 4400

Oysters and shell fish form the backbone of Le Croisic, 10km west of La Baule. A 19th-century **auction room**, where fish was auctioned from 1878, sits elegantly on the portside, while inland the fishing village's streets are speckled with historic **half-timbered houses**; lovely examples are on place de l'Église, place du Pilori and rue St-Christophe. The beaches around Le Croisic, not to mention its bird life, were among the worst hit by the *Erika* oil slick in late 1999 (see the boxed text 'Oil Spill' in the Facts about the Loire chapter).

The tourist office (☎ 02 40 23 00 70, fax 02 40 62 96 60) is almost opposite the train station on place du 18 Juin 1940; exit the station and bear right along rue du Traict. You can exchange money at Banque Populaire, 19 rue du Traict, and there's an ATM inside the post office on place Dinan. Pascal Bihoré (☎ 02 40 62 92 81), 34 rue du Traict, rents bicycles.

The eastern end of the port is dominated by **Mont Lénigo**, a hillock that served as a ballast depot until 1761, when it was planted with trees. A path leads to its tip, from where there are good views of the **Rade du Croisic**, the 850m-long jetty and lighthouse (1872). The fully automated fish auction house used today is also here, as is an **embarcadère** (landing stage; opposite Hôtel l'Estacade on quai du Lénigo) from where boat trips and sea-fishing excursions (☎ 02 40 62 94 93) depart in summer. Follow the signs east along quai du Lénigo to get to the **aquarium** on ave de St-Goustan.

Places to Stay & Eat Le Croisic is crammed with cheap, charming places to stay. *Hôtel-Bar Le Paris (☎ 02 40 23 15 19, 66 rue du Traict)*, opposite the train station, offers doubles costing upwards of 155F. *Le Fin Gourmet (☎ 02 40 23 00 38, fax 02 40 62 96 27, 1 place du Pilori)*, in the historic heart, has singles/doubles costing upwards of 170/210FF. The quays alongside the port are lined with *brasseries* where you can taste oysters (in season), eat bowlfuls of *bouillabaisse breton* (a local fish soup-cum-stew), sample crepes made from black Breton flour, or indulge in the local speciality, *bar au sel de guérande* (sea bass in Guérande salt).

Getting There & Away Le Croisic is at the end of the train line from St-Nazaire (30FF, 30 minutes, eight to 10 daily); the last stretch of the line from Batz-sur-Mer cuts straight through salt pans and is particularly picturesque. Some TGV trains run between Nantes and Le Croisic (74FF/94FF for regional/TGV, one to 1¼ hours).

Parc Naturel Régional de Brière
postcode 44720 • pop 70,000

The Parc Naturel Régional de Brière embraces an area of 40,000 hectares in the centre of the Presqu'île du Guérande. At the core of this curious wetland is the **Grande Brière**, a 7000-hectare marsh comprising reed beds, prairie and dozens of water pools (*étangs*). Since 1471 it has been owned by the local inhabitants, who, over the centuries, have learned how to farm this harsh marshland. The GR3 and GR39 hiking trails thread their way through here.

The park is criss-crossed by 120km of canals which every so often splay out into abandoned peat-digging sites, since filled with water to form small lakes. Peat was traditionally cut in July, when water levels

were at their lowest, then left to dry in bricks until winter, when it would be burned as fuel. Over the centuries, many of the natural prairies have been over-run by reeds. These reed beds are rich in wildlife and cover some 50% of the park; another 46% is carpeted with wet grassland.

The park headquarters are housed in the **Maison du Parc** (☎ 02 40 91 68 68, fax 02 40 91 60 58, ✉ info@parc-naturel-briere .fr), 177 Île de Fédrun, in **St-Joachim**, 12km north of St-Nazaire. Useful information is given on its Web site at www.parc-naturel-briere.fr. In the same village, the **Musée de la Mariée** (Museum of the Bride), at No 130, illustrates the Brièron tradition of making bridal head-dresses from orange blossoms.

Flora and fauna typical to the swamps are explained in the **Maison de l'Éclusier** (Lock Keeper's House; ☎ 02 40 91 17 80), 1km south of St-Joachim in **Rosé**. Next to the museum, a botanical trail leads across reed beds and grassland through the **Parc Animalier** (Animal Park). On the western side of the park, **Ker Anas Parc Ornithologique** (☎ 02 40 01 27 48), in St-André des Eaux, is a bird farm with over a hundred different duck species. There's a **Ferme aux Biches** where deer are reared in La Madeleine, north of Guérande. Traditional Brièron cottages, complete with thatched roofs, can be visited in **Kerhinet**, 2km farther north of La Madeleine off the D51.

Information on *gîtes* (houses to rent) and **boat trips** in the park is available from the Maison du Tourisme de Brière (☎ 02 40 66 85 01) in La Chapelle des Marais, in the north of the park. The village also houses a **clog-making museum**. In Guérande, the efficient **tourist office** (☎ 02 40 24 96 71), in the Tour St-Michel, is an invaluable source of information. IGN's blue-jacketed map *Parc Naturel Régional de Brière* (Top 25 1022 ET) is vital for anyone intent on exploring the park in any depth.

Guérande is linked by bus with St-Nazaire (see Getting There & Away under St-Nazaire earlier in this chapter), but you need your own transport (or boatman) to explore the rest of the park.

LOIRE-ATLANTIQUE & VENDÉE

VENDÉE

Sitting snug at the foot of Loire-Atlantique, Vendée is not considered part of the Loire Valley proper. However, its proximity to the land of kings and castles makes it an easy getaway for those seeking a gulp of sea and swamp air.

The Coast

South of the River Loire and its estuary, Loire-Atlantique moves south, past a rash of small seaside resorts such as **St-Brévin-les-Pins** and **Pornic**, to meet Vendée, its next-door neighbour. Good views of this stretch of coastline can be enjoyed from **Pointe de St-Gildas**, a small headland studded with ruined WWII bunkers used by the Germans between 1940 and 1945.

The leading seaside resort along this section of the Atlantic coast is **Les Sables d'Olonne** (population 15,830), a built-up concrete spot with a promenade called Le Remblai (literally 'the embankment') running the 3km length of its golden-sand beach. The tourist office (☎ 02 51 96 85 70, fax 02 51 96 85 71), on the beach front at 1 promenade Joffre, has information on cheap accommodation and the abundance of water sports and outdoor activities on offer. Alternatively, check out its Web site at www.ot-lessablesdolonne.fr.

The house where the uncompromising French prime minister Georges Clemenceau (1841–1929) retired, aged 78, after signing the Treaty of Versailles in 1919 and thus officially ending WWI, is 20km farther south along the coast in St-Vincent-sur-Jard. Much of the furniture inside the seaside **Maison de Georges Clemenceau** (☎ 02 51 33 40 32) remains as it was when he died. The house museum, overlooking a cove which buzzes with sexy bionic surfers, can be visited by guided tour (open Wednesday to Monday, October to March). Admission costs 25FF. Clemenceau was buried in the tiny hamlet of La Potrie in eastern Vendée (see Inland later in this chapter).

East of here, the swampy Marais Poitevin squelches across the southern tip of Vendée into neighbouring Poitou (for details, see that section in the Poitou chapter).

The Islands

The Vendéen Île de Noirmoutier and Île d'Yeu lie approximately 20 and 35km respectively off the western coast; the former is attached to the mainland by a bridge and the more interesting **Passage du Gois**, a causeway that you can cross by foot or by car at low tide. Islanders call mainland Vendée 'Le Continent'.

Both spots are alluring, invigorating and sprinkled with heady pine forests and sandy golden beaches. Cycling tracks thread their way across each. Information on sailing, surfing and bird-watching opportunities on the islands is listed under Activities in the Facts for the Visitor chapter.

Île de Noirmoutier This is the largest and most developed of the two islands. It is 20km long but no more than 1km wide. The only town, **Noirmoutier-en-l'Île** (population 4840), is on the eastern side of the island. The western coast is flooded by silver salt pans, farmed by 40 or so salt workers. Noirmoutier is better known, however, for its oyster beds and potato crops; don't miss *pain à la pomme de terre* (potato bread).

Things to see in Noirmoutier-en-l'Île include a **sea aquarium** (☎ 02 51 39 08 11), the **Musée de la Construction Navale** housed in an old salt store on rue de l'Écluse, and the historical and ethnographical **Musée du Château** (☎ 02 51 39 10 42), which dominates place d'Armes, the central square where several Vendéen Royalist generals were shot on 7 January 1794 during the Vendée War.

Other island sights include the **Musée de Chèvrerie** (☎ 02 51 39 16 19), route de l'Herbaudière, where goats are raised and their milk turned into cheese; and the **Maison du Sel** (House of Salt; ☎ 02 51 39 08 30) at Noirmoutier Port, where salt production is explained. It is also possible to visit the **salt pans**; Noirmoutier tourist office (☎ 02 51 39 80 71, fax 02 51 39 53 16), route du Pont (D38), at the first roundabout after crossing Passage du Gois, has details. It has lists of the island's many camp sites and hotels, as does its Web site at www.ile-noirmoutier.com.

La Route de l'Huître

The Route de l'Huître (Oyster Route) is the tasty idea of enterprising oyster farmers who offer oyster tastings to travellers seeking a taste of the sea.

The Baie de Bourgneuf, where the oyster beds of 132 farmers lie, falls within France's third-largest oyster-producing region. Its average annual yield of 500 tonnes originates from thumbnail-sized larvae which are bred farther along the coast in oyster-rich La Rochelle, then brought to the bay. Here, across 114 hectares, breeding continues for another 2½ to three years at sea, after which the oysters are harvested from their beds and 'ripened' in salt-water pools. It is this final stage that transforms the anonymous oyster into a Huître Vendée-Atlantique, worthy of its own AOC (*appellation d'origine contrôlée*; certificate of quality).

Heading south along the coast from Pornic, the first port of call on the Route de l'Huître is **Lyorne** (☎ 02 51 74 61 33), where oysters, mussels (*moules*) and other shell fish (*coquillages*) are produced. Tours and tasting are possible from 10 am to noon and 4 to 7 pm Monday to Saturday. Nearby in **Port des Brochets** is the farm of Monsieur Léon Longepée (☎ 02 51 68 66 58), a local authority on oyster farming who gives guests a glass of wine to swill down their half-dozen oysters. He knows other farmers who offer tastings; it costs 30FF per person (children aged under 12 are free).

In early 2000 the fate of the region's oyster-farming industry hung in the balance following the sinking of the *Erika* oil tanker (see the boxed text 'Oil Spill' in the Facts about the Loire chapter). The *préfet* (prefect) of Loire-Atlantique banned the sale of all Baie de Bourgneuf oysters on 7 January 2000 after spilled oil was discovered in its oyster beds. At the time of going to press, tests were being conducted to see what effect the oil could have on surviving oysters.

Île d'Yeu This little granite island, 10km long and 4km wide, is less built up and boasts a wilder and less sophisticated terrain than its big sister. Touring the island is best on two wheels and there are plenty of **bicycle rental** places the length of pretty **Port Joinville**, the main port. Most hotels, restaurants, shops and the tourist office (☎ 02 51 58 32 58, fax 02 51 58 40 48) are clustered here. Sandy beaches fan out along the sunny eastern coast, north and south of the port.

The skyline of Port Joinville is dominated by the sturdy defensive **citadelle** (1856–8) where the head of the pro-German Vichy government, Maréchal Henri Philippe Pétain (1856–1951), was imprisoned from 1945; the house at Port Joinville where his wife lived while he was in prison is a **Musée Historial** dedicated to island history today. The French marshal, tried for treason after WWII and sentenced to death (subsequently commuted to life imprisonment), died in prison aged 96 and was buried in the island's **Cimetière St-Sauveur** off the D22. His grave faces the opposite direction from all the other graves.

On the savagely rocky southern coast of the island stands the **Vieux Château** (Old Chateau), dating from the 14th century; it can be visited in July, August and September as part of a guided tour. For breathtaking panoramic views, scale the 198 steps inside the **Grand Phare** (1950), a lighthouse on the island's northernmost point (open 9.30 to 11.45 am and 1 to 5 pm in July and August; ☎ 02 51 58 30 61 to arrange a time, the rest of the year).

Inland

Heading inland, tourist information on the Vendée département is available from the Comité Départemental du Tourisme de la Vendée (☎ 02 51 47 88 20, fax 02 51 05 37 01), 8 place Napoléon, in **La Roche-sur-Yon**.

North of La Roche-sur-Yon, homage is paid to the thousands of Vendéens who died during the Vendée War (1793–6), a bitter civil war fought in this region between Protestant Republicans and pro-Royalist Catholics. On 28 February 1794 'blue' Republicans massacred 564 'white' royalists

euro currency converter 10FF = €1.52

in a forest just east of Les Lucs-sur-Boulogne, 21km north of La Roche-sur-Yon. The site today is marked by a cold concrete bunker, known as the **Mémorial de Vendée** (☎ 02 51 42 81 00). It houses a museum recounting the bloody history of the war. From the bunker, a wooded path leads to the **Chapelle du Petit Lac**, built in 1867 on the site of the former church which was destroyed – along with scores of peasants sheltering inside – by Republicans on 5 March 1794.

From Les Lucs-sur-Boulogne, the northeastbound D18 towards St-Sulpice le Verdon leads to the **Logis de la Chabotterie** (☎ 02 51 42 81 00), 2km south-east of St-Sulpice. La Chabotterie is a *logis clos*, an architectural construction comprising a cluster of manorial dwellings within a walled courtyard and typical to Vendée from 1560 to the end of the 18th century. Built in red bricks, the rural dwelling is surrounded by *bocage*, fields crossed by a grid of hedges and equally typical to this marshy region. It was in the woods surrounding La Chabotterie that the infamous pro-Royalist peasant leader Charette (1763–96) was captured by Republican troops on 23 March 1796. Six days later the Vendéen leader was executed on place Viarme in Nantes, marking the end of the three-year war. From La Chabotterie a walking trail (30 minutes) leads to the **Croix de Charette**, a granite cross marking the spot where the elusive peasant hero was finally seized.

The Renaissance **Château du Puy du Fou**, 40km north-east of La Roche-sur-Yon in eastern Vendée, houses the excellent **Écomusée de la Vendée** (☎ 02 51 57 60 60), dedicated to Vendée's history and ethnography. The museum opens 10 am to noon and 2 to 6 or 7 pm (no lunchbreak from June to October). Admission costs 15FF. To get here from Les Herbiers, bear 10km east on the D11 to Les Epesses, turning left (north) just before the village onto the D27. If you pass through Les Epesses, pop into the prize-winning boulangerie ***Boissonnot*** (☎ 02 51 57 31 32), at 4 rue Jeanne in the village, and buy a buttery loaf of *brioche vendéenne*, the regional sweet treat.

The humble **tomb of Georges Clemenceau** (for information on his life see The Coast earlier in this Vendée section) lies in the small hamlet of La Potrie, off the D48. The French politician gave the land here to its inhabitants in 1922 (prior to his death) on condition that the plants, trees and scrub were allowed to grow freely. Clemenceau's simple grave (so simple it has no grave stone) lies next to that of his father beneath a cedar tree (the tree of liberty in Greek mythology). The graves are guarded by a sculpture of Athena, the Greek goddess of wisdom and knowledge.

Getting There & Away

The coast is easily accessible by train and bus; inland you have to rely on your own wheels or two feet.

Air There are scheduled helicopter flights between Fromentine, on mainland France, and Port Joinville (☎ 02 51 58 78 72) or Aérodrome Yeu (☎ 02 51 58 38 22) on Île d'Yeu. Arrivals/departures are timed to connect with buses to/from Nantes. See Air in the Getting Around chapter for more details.

Bus SNCF operates buses from Nantes train station to Noirmoutier-en-l'Île (90FF, 1¾ hours, three or four daily) on Île de Noirmoutier. Buses stop en route at Fromentine (for boats to Île d'Yeu). SNCF buses also run from Nantes to Pornic (53FF, 1¼ hours, three daily), St-Gilles Croix de Vie (71FF, 1¾ hours, seven daily) and Les Sables d'Olonne (89FF, 3¾ hours, three daily).

From Noirmoutier bus station, there are hourly SNCF buses to/from La Fosse (91FF, 40 minutes) and Fromentine (91FF, 45 minutes). There are also a couple of daily buses to Challans train station to connect with trains to/from Paris.

Train There are five to seven trains daily between La Roche-sur-Yon (65FF, 45 minutes) and Nantes, from where there are connecting trains to a great many more destinations. On the coast, Les Sables d'Olonne has train links with La Roche-sur-Yon (38FF, 30 minutes, about five trains daily) and Nantes (89FF, 1½ hours, five daily). Trains also run between Nantes and Pornic, and Nantes and St-Gilles Croix de Vie.

Boat Île d'Yeu is accessible by boat year round; tickets should be bought or reserved in advance in July and August, when seats get taken fast. Sailing time is between 45 minutes and one hour.

Vedettes Inter Îles Vendéennes (VIIV; ☎ 02 51 39 00 00, 02 51 39 15 15) operates hydrojets (three daily in each direction in July and August) between April and October. Its boats plough between Port Joinville on Île d'Yeu and Gare Maritime de Fromentine, on mainland France. In addition, there are boats to/from the port on ave Jean Cristau in St-Gilles Croix de Vie (☎ 02 51 54 15 15), farther south along the coast; and

to/from the port at La Fosse on Île de Noirmoutier. A return fare, valid for one day, between Île d'Yeu and mainland France is 160FF (children 110FF).

Compagnie Yeu-Continent (☎ 02 51 58 36 66, 02 51 49 59 69) operates regular daily boats between Île d'Yeu's Port des Vieilles, on its southern coast, and Gare Maritime de Fromentine (at least four daily crossings in each direction in summer, and fewer in winter). A return ticket costs 157FF (seniors and students 124FF, children 106FF). In addition, it costs 110/190/46FF return to transport a bicycle/surf board/cat or dog. Compagnie Yeu-Continent publishes its updated fares and schedules on its Web site at www.compagnie-yeu-continent.fr.

Vedette Taxis Amarilys (☎ 02 51 54 09 88) runs taxi boats to/from Île d'Yeu and St-Gilles Croix de Vie year round.

Poitou

The ancient world of prehistoric man is juxtapositioned with futuristic prisms and state-of-the-art glass-cube edifices in Poitou, a relatively unknown province blessed with a rich historical heritage.

In 732 Frankish ruler Charles Martel stopped invading Saracens dead in their tracks at the Battle of Poitiers, preventing France from coming under Muslim rule. The region later succumbed to English rule, under Henri Plantagenêt II in the 12th century, and again during the Hundred Years' War, when King John II of France (ruled 1350–64) was defeated by the English at the Battle of Poitiers (1356) and taken prisoner by Edward the Black Prince (1330–76), son of England's Plantagenêt King Edward III. Poitou consequently became a duchy of the English Crown, headed by John II's son, Jean de Berry, who became count of Poitiers in 1356. The captured French king resumed control of his lost territory following his release by the English in 1360.

The Renaissance showered a wealth of cultural treasures on Poitou, including a university in Poitiers whose alumni includes a clutch of French literary greats: Rabelais, Ronsard, Descartes and du Bellay.

Poitou falls into the modern-day administrative *départements* (departments) of Vienne and Deux-Sèvres (both part of the Poitou-Charentes *région*). On the outskirts of Poitiers, the capital, is Futuroscope, Europe's leading theme park of the moving image. Heading west, the great divide between the flat, agricultural plain (*plainaud*) and the soggy marshes (*maraîchin*) becomes evident. The Marais Poitevin, a green labyrinth of canals and dikes shaded by ash trees, is protected by a nature park and can be explored by flat-bottomed boat.

POITIERS

postcode 86000 • pop 107,600

Poitou's capital contains some of France's most remarkable Romanesque churches.

Highlights

- Trace biblical tales from the New and Old Testaments on the western facade of Poitier's stunning Église Notre Dame la Grande.
- Step into the future at Futuroscope.
- Discover the world's oldest funeraria and see how prehistoric man was buried at the Musée des Tumulus de Bougon.
- Punt through a green labyrinth of duckweed-coated waters in the hypnotic Marais Poitevin.

Sitting tightly on a small hilltop, its medieval streets buzz with activity, thanks to the university of Poitiers, which has lured students to the city since 1431. It is one of France's oldest universities.

Charles VII (ruled 1422–61) was proclaimed king here. In March 1429, his champion, Joan of Arc (Jeanne d'Arc), was interrogated in Poitiers by scholars and clergy who, at the end of the six-week inquiry, declared that the 19-year-old peasant girl was not mad and was a virgin. See the boxed text 'Joan of Arc' in the Facts about the Loire chapter for more about the story.

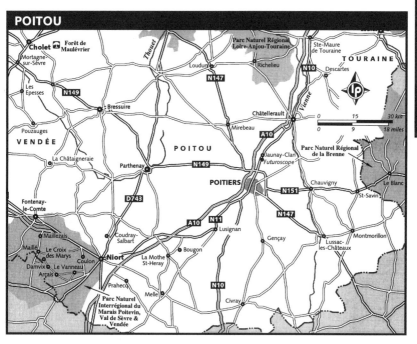

Orientation

The train station is about 600m west – and down the slope – from the partly pedestrianised old city and commercial centre, which begins just north of Poitiers' main square, place du Maréchal Leclerc, and stretches north-east to Église Notre Dame la Grande.

Maps City maps cost 3FF at the tourist office. Alternatively, invest in Blay-Foldex's *Poitiers et son Agglomération* (21.50FF), which includes a Futuroscope map and is sold at Gilbert Joseph Papeterie, on the corner of rue Gambetta and place Le Petit.

Information

Tourist Offices At the time of writing, the tourist office (☎ 05 49 41 21 24, fax 05 49 88 65 84) was at 8 rue des Grandes Écoles, but it is scheduled to move in mid-2000 to the former university building on place Charles de Gaulle. Check its Web site at www.pcl.fr/poitiers. Opening hours should remain the same: 9 am to noon and 1.30 (2 on Saturday) to 6 pm (closed Sunday between September and mid-June).

For hotel reservations and tickets for cultural events – including organ concerts in Église Notre Dame la Grande and the cathedral – head to the Centrale de Réservation Vienne Loisirs (☎ 05 49 37 48 58, fax 05 49 37 48 61, ☻ vienne-loisirs@cg86.org), 33 place Charles de Gaulle, open 10 am to 1 pm and 2 to 7 pm Monday to Saturday. It also has a Web site at www.vienne.org.

Tourist information on Vienne is available from the Comité Départemental du Tourisme (☎ 05 49 37 48 48, fax 05 49 37 48 49, ☻ cdt@vienne.org), 15–17 rue Carnot. Gîtes de France (☎ 05 49 37 48 54, fax 05 49 37 48 61) has its reservation office here too.

The Centre Régional Information de Jeunesse (CRIJ; ☎ 05 49 60 68 68) sells Eurolines bus tickets and SNCF train tickets. It opens 10 am to 6.30 pm on weekdays.

Money Banque de France, 1 rue Henri Oudin, opens 1.45 to 3.30 pm on weekdays. Commercial banks dot place du Maréchal Leclerc.

Post The central post office, housed in a historic edifice at 21 rue des Écossais, opens 8.30 am to 7 pm on weekdays, and 8.30 am to noon on Saturday. There is another on place Charles de Gaulle.

Email & Internet Access Internet access costs 35FF per hour at @DN Games (☎ 05 49 39 06 52), 14 rue des Vieilles Boucheries, open 10 to 2 am Monday to Saturday.

Cybercafé Poitiers (☎ 05 49 39 51 87, @ cybercafe.poitier@interpc.fr), 171 Grand Rue, charges 55FF per hour. It opens 10 am to 7.30 pm Monday to Saturday.

Laundry Lav 86, on the corner of rue Riffault and Grand Rue, opens 8 am to 9 pm daily.

Churches

The superb **Église Notre Dame la Grande** dominates place Charles de Gaulle in the pedestrianised old city. The 57m-long Romanesque church, which has no transept arms, dates from the 11th and 12th centuries – except for three of the five choir chapels (added in the 15th century) and all six chapels along the northern wall of the nave (added in the 16th century). The atrociously painted decoration in the nave is from the mid-19th century; the only original frescoes are the faint 12th- or 13th-century works that adorn the U-shaped dome above the choir. The modern organ, erected in 1996, is occasionally used for concerts.

The celebrated **western facade** is decorated with three tiers of stone carvings based on the Old and New Testaments. The lowest tier represents the prophets and the birth of Christ; the middle tier represents spreading the word of Christ; and the upper tier represents Christ in majesty. The lowest tier shows, left to right, Adam and Eve; the prophets Daniel, Jeremiah, Isaiah and Moses; the Annunciation; the tree of Jesse;

the Visitation; the Nativity; the washing of baby Jesus in what looks like a baptismal font; and the meditation of St Joseph. Above these carvings are the twelve apostles beneath richly ornamented archwork, and above these are St Hilaire, on the left, and St Martin, on the right. The highest carving shows Christ in majesty flanked by symbols of the evangelists and eternity. The Romanesque belfry above the choir has a steep, pinecone-like roof. The church can be visited from 8 am to 7 pm.

At the bottom of rue de la Cathédrale and 500m east of Église Notre Dame la Grande, the vast Angevin (or Plantagenêt) Gothic **Cathédrale St-Pierre** was built between 1162 and 1271. The western facade and the towers date from the 14th and 15th centuries. The stained-glass window at the far end of the choir, which illustrates the Crucifixion and the Ascension, is among France's oldest. The choir stalls are mid-13th century; the magnificent, angel-topped organ dates from 1791. The church can be visited from 8 am to 7.30 pm (6 pm in winter).

The 11th- and 12th-century **Église St-Hilaire**, across the street from 20 rue St-Hilaire (600m south-west of place du Maréchal Leclerc), was named after the city's first known bishop, who lived in the 4th century and over whose tomb it was built. The transept, the choir (decorated with late-11th-century frescoes) and the five apsidal chapels are 3m higher than the nave (mostly rebuilt in the 19th century), which is covered by three cupolas and has three rows of columns on each side. Earlier churches on this site were burned by the Arab general Abd ar-Rahman shortly before his defeat by the cavalry of Charles Martel in 732, and again during the Norman invasions of the 9th century. The church opens 9 am to 7 pm Monday to Saturday, and 10 am to 7 pm on Sunday.

The 12th-century **Église St-Germain**, rue St-Germain, houses the auditorium of the Conservatoire Nationale de Région (National Music School of the Region; ☎ 05 49 01 83 67). Attending a concert here is a must.

POITIERS

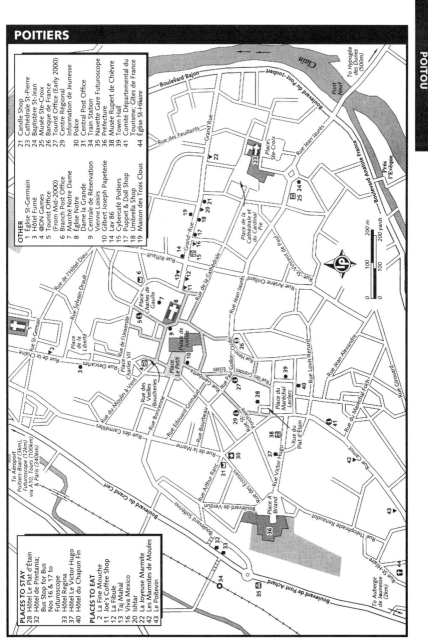

OTHER
1 Église St-Germain
3 Hôtel Fumé
4 @DN Games
5 Tourist Office (From Mid-2000)
6 Branch Post Office
7 Marché Notre Dame
8 Église Notre Dame la Grande
9 Centrale de Réservation Viennel Loisirs
10 Gilbert Joseph Papeterie
14 Lav 86
15 Cybercafé Poitiers
17 Puppet & Doll Shop
18 Umbrella Shop
19 Maison des Trois Clous
21 Candle Shop
23 Cathédrale St-Pierre
24 Baptistère St-Jean
25 Musée Ste-Croix
26 Banque de France
27 Tourist Office (Early 2000)
29 Centre Régional Information de Jeunesse
30 Police
31 Central Post Office
34 Train Station
35 Navette Gare Futuroscope
36 Préfecture
38 Musée Rupert de Chièvre
39 Town Hall
41 Comité Départemental du Tourisme; Gîtes de France
44 Église St-Hilaire

PLACES TO STAY
28 Hôtel Le Plat d'Étain
32 Hôtel de Printania; Bus Stop for Bus Nos 16 & 17 to Futuroscope
33 Hôtel Regina
37 Hôtel Le Victor Hugo
40 Hôtel du Chapon Fin

PLACES TO EAT
2 La Fine Mouche
11 Joe's Coffee Shop
12 La Fibule
13 Taj Mahal
16 Viva Mexico
20 Ishtar
22 La Joyeuse Marmite
42 Les Marmites de Moules
43 Le Poitevin

Museums

Constructed in the 4th and 6th centuries on the foundations of earlier Roman buildings, **Baptistère St-Jean**, rue Jean Jaurès, is one of the oldest Christian structures in France. Rebuilt in the 10th century and used as a parish church, it is now a museum of Merovingian (6th to 8th centuries) sarcophagi. The octagonal hole under the 11th- and 12th-century frescoes was used for total-immersion baptisms, practised by the Church until the 7th century. It opens 10.30 am to 12.30 pm and 3 (2.30 in July and August) to 6 pm daily, April to October; and 2.30 to 4.30 pm Wednesday to Monday, the rest of the year. Admission costs 4FF.

Across the lawn, the worthwhile **Musée Ste-Croix** (☎ 05 49 41 07 53), 3 rue Jean Jaurès, built atop Gallo-Roman walls that were excavated and left *in situ*, has exhibits on the history of Poitou from prehistoric times through the Roman period and the Middle Ages to the 19th century. The collection of 19th- and 20th-century paintings and sculptures includes three works by Camille Claudel (1864–1943), a gifted pupil and lover of Auguste Rodin. The museum opens 10 am to noon and 1.15 to 6 pm Tuesday to Sunday, and 1.15 to 6 pm on Monday, June to September; and 10 am to noon and 1.15 to 5 pm Tuesday to Friday, and 1.15 to 5 pm Monday, Saturday and Sunday, the rest of the year. Admission costs 15FF and affords access to the **Musée Rupert de Chièvre**, 9 rue Victor Hugo, which houses a collection of bric-a-brac assembled in the late 19th century, and the **Hypogée des Dunes**, a Merovingian funerary chapel at 101 rue du Père de la Croix (farther out along rue Jean Jaurès from the city centre).

Other Things to See

Grand Rue is sprinkled with 15th-century half-timbered houses, including **Maison des Trois Clous** at No 120. It is named after three giant nails which stick out of its facade, from which gargoyles glare down on passers-by. Old-fashioned **specialist stores** dot the street: shop for umbrellas at No 137, dolls and puppets at No 151 and candles at No 113.

More medieval houses tumble down the slope of **rue de la Chaîne** (north of place Charles VII), at the southern end of which sits **Hôtel Fumé**, 8 rue Descartes. Poitiers University was officially founded here in 1431 by Pope Eugène IV.

Special Events

In summer, during Les Polychromies, a *son et lumière* (sound and light) show is projected onto the ornate western facade of Église Notre Dame la Grande. Organ concerts are likewise hosted in all the historic churches. The tourist office has details.

Places to Stay

Hostel Poitiers' *auberge de jeunesse* (☎ 05 49 30 09 70, 1 allée Roger Tagault), 3km from the centre, opens year round. A bed in a four-bed room costs 51FF (68FF with breakfast), and a set of sheets can be hired for 17FF. Reception opens 7.30 am to 1.30 pm and 6 to 11 pm daily. To get here from the town centre, take bus No 3 from in front of the train station or town hall to the Pierre Loti stop.

Hotels Around the train station, there are several budget choices, including **Hôtel de Printania** *(145 blvd du Grand Cerf)*, above a brasserie, which offers doubles costing upwards of 110FF (140FF with shower). Two-star **Hôtel Regina** (☎ 05 49 58 20 38, fax 05 49 37 28 83, 149 blvd du Grand Cerf) has comfortable doubles costing 240FF.

In town, seven-room **Hôtel Le Victor Hugo** (☎ 05 49 41 12 16, 5 rue Victor Hugo), above a busy cafe, has doubles for 130FF (160FF with shower and toilet). Reception is the cafe-bar.

Half a block north of place du Maréchal Leclerc, two-star **Hôtel Le Plat d'Étain** (☎ 05 49 41 04 80, fax 05 49 52 25 84, 7–9 rue du Plat d'Étain) has pleasant doubles costing 145FF (150FF with washbasin and 260FF with shower and toilet). Nearby **Hôtel du Chapon Fin** (☎ 05 49 88 02 97, fax 05 49 88 91 63, ✉ chaponfinhotel@ minitel.net, 11 rue Lebascle) offers doubles with shower costing 195FF (240FF with shower and toilet).

Places to Eat

In summer, a sun-flooded *outdoor cafe* spills across place Charles de Gaulle. *Joe's Coffee Shop* (☎ *05 49 41 23 94, 191 Grand Rue*) has an interior littered with fascinating knick-knacks and entices a bohemian student set; its old-fashioned hot chocolate, stirred all day, is delicious. *La Joyeuse Marmite* (☎ *05 49 88 14 59*), at the eastern end of Grand Rue, is a cheap local bistro which serves a hearty 61FF meal, including wine and coffee.

Mussels (*moules*) swimming in a choice of sauces are the house speciality of *Les Marmites de Moules* (☎ *05 49 37 01 37, 40 rue Carnot*). Another cosy choice is *La Fine Mouche* (☎ *05 49 50 73 26, 3 rue de la Chaîne*), in the university quarter of town. Fine regional cuisine is served with a flourish at *Le Poitevin* (☎ *05 49 88 35 04, 76 rue Carnot*); *menus* start at 100FF.

Charming spots touting other ethnic cuisines include Indian *Taj Mahal* (☎ *05 49 60 26 03, 178 Grand Rue*), which has main courses costing upwards of 47FF and *menus* from 99FF; Moroccan *La Fibule*, almost opposite, which has a fabulous ceramic-tiled interior and scrumptious couscous and tajines; Lebanese *Ishtar* (☎ *05 49 50 64 64, 121 Grand Rue*); and *Viva Mexico* (*163 Grand Rue*), a cheap Tex-Mex canteen.

For self-caterers, the indoor *Marché Notre Dame*, next to Église Notre Dame la Grande on place Charles de Gaulle, opens 7 am to 1 pm (2 pm on Saturday) Tuesday to Saturday.

Getting There & Away

For information on getting to/from Futuroscope, see that section under Around Poitiers.

Air For details on flights to/from Aéroport Poitiers-Biard (☎ 05 49 30 04 40), 3km west of the city in Biard, see the introductory Getting There & Away and Getting Around chapters.

Bus SNCF buses run between Poitiers and Nantes (141FF, 3½ hours, one daily).

Train Poitiers train station, on blvd du Grand Cerf, has direct links with Niort

(77FF, 45 minutes to one hour, nine or 10 daily), St-Pierre des Corps (116FF, 40 minutes, eight daily), Tours (116FF, one hour, about 10 daily) and Aubrais-Orléans (88FF, 40 minutes, 12 to 16 daily). Poitiers is also on the TGV Atlantique train line, which runs from Paris to Bordeaux and beyond.

AROUND POITIERS

Both an ancient past and a technologically inspired future come to life around Poitiers.

Musée des Tumulus de Bougon

Megalithic tumuli built 2000 years before the pyramids in Egypt, making them the oldest funeraria in the world, are the focus of the fascinating Musée des Tumulus de Bougon (☎ 05 49 05 12 13), about 35km south-west of Poitiers, in Bougon, signposted off the N11. First uncovered in 1840, the archaeological site comprises five tumuli, dating from around 4500 BC and sheltering eight burial chambers. During excavations, several skeletons were found inside.

The museum opens 10 am to 7 pm (8 pm at the weekend) daily, July and August; and 10 am to 6 pm Thursday to Tuesday, and 2 to 7 pm on Wednesday, September to December and February to June. Admission costs 25FF (students and children 10FF, families 60FF). Guided tours are extra (10FF).

Futuroscope

Futuroscope (☎ 05 49 49 30 80), just over 10km north of Poitiers, in Jaunay-Clan, is a unique cinema theme park in which 20 innovative and visually striking pavilions (more are being added every year) display the latest technologies for making on-screen action seem more immediate.

Tapis Magique (Magic Carpet) shows action underfoot – from a bird's-eye perspective – as well as in front of you. At **Le Solido**, the 180° images appear in 3D thanks to special liquid-crystal glasses. **Le 360°** is a round projection hall in which nine screens give you a 360° view from the centre of the action. At the **Cinéma Dynamique**, the seats shake and tilt to create a virtual-reality roller-coaster ride that lasts just three minutes but seems like an eternity.

The specially made films – mostly documentaries, many of them with nature themes – are in French, but an infrared headset (available free at the tourist office at the entrance) lets you pick up a parallel soundtrack in English, German or Spanish.

Futuroscope opens 9 am to 6 pm daily. On Saturday, Sunday and holidays from March to mid-November, and throughout July and August, closing time is after the laser and fireworks show, ie some time between 10.30 pm and midnight. One- or two-day tickets are available. In the high season (weekends year round and every day during school holidays), a one/two-day ticket which includes admission to the evening laser show costs 210/360FF for adults and 145/250FF for children aged five to 12. The rest of the year, low-season rates are 145/250FF for a one/two-day ticket for adults and 100/180FF for children aged five to 12.

Year round, students are entitled to a 20% discount upon presentation of a valid student card. Ticket holders can exit and re-enter the park so long as they get their hand stamped upon exiting. When the park is open at night, the admission charge is 100FF (children 70FF) if you arrive after 6 pm.

Tickets are also sold at the Futuroscope office (☎ 05 49 37 04 18) inside Poitiers train station. It opens 8.45 am to 6.30 pm (7.30 pm in summer) daily.

Getting There & Away If you're driving from Poitiers, take the A10 northbound; signposts for Futuroscope are plentiful.

Local bus Nos 16 and 17 (one way 8FF) link Poitiers train station and place du Maréchal Leclerc with the Parc de Loisirs bus stop at Futuroscope. One or the other bus runs once or twice an hour, except Sunday and holidays, until 7.30 or 8 pm. Buses depart from the stop outside 129 blvd du Grand Cerf; buy your ticket from the bus driver.

Futuroscope's *taxis-navettes* (shuttle taxis; return per person 45FF) link Poitiers train station with the park every 30 to 60 minutes from 8.30 am to 6 pm (and at 6.45 pm when the park is open at night).

Navettes use the stop outside Poitiers train station on blvd de Pont Achard (signposted 'Navette Gare Futuroscope'). There is a Futuroscope information desk (☎ 05 49 44 77 00) inside the station.

MARAIS POITEVIN

The green, duckweed-coated waters of enchanting *Venise Verte* (Green Venice) spill across the south-western corner of Vienne and into neighbouring Vendée. In this marvellous wetland, canoe or rowing boat is the primary form of transport.

A rich and varied bird life – including large colonies of black-winged stilt, terns and shanks – nests on its soggy shores, while shoals of slippery European eels (which are caught and cooked up into a fishy *bouilliture d'anguilles*) snake about in its waters.

Protected by the 200,000-hectare **Parc Naturel Interrégional du Marais Poitevin, Val de Sèvre et Vendée** (☎ 05 49 35 86 77), the Marais Poitevin covers a sprawling area of 80,000 hectares. Its unusual terrain is split between *marais mouillé* (a wet marsh drained by canals to create dry pastures in summer) and *marais desséché* (drained marsh interspersed with villages and woods).

Niort, 76km south-west of Poitiers, and **Fontenay-le-Comte**, 25km farther west and home to the handsome **Château de Terre Neuve** (1580), are the main stepping stones into the marais. The impressive ruins of the 11th- to 16th-century **Abbaye St-Pierre** (☎ 02 51 00 70 11) pierce the heart of **Maillezais**, the largest village in the middle of the Poitevin marsh. Heading west, the marais meets the Atlantic Ocean at Anse de l'Aiguillon (Aiguillon Cove).

Information

In Niort, the tourist office (☎ 05 49 24 18 79, fax 05 49 24 98 96), rue Ernest Pérochon, opens 9.30 am to 6 pm on weekdays, and 9.30 am to noon on Saturday. It stocks comprehensive details on accommodation and activities available in and around Niort. For regional information, head to the comité départemental du tourisme (☎ 05 49 77 19 70,

Boating & Cycling in Green Venice

Venise Verte (Green Venice), with its summertime tunnels of green trees, is a delight to explore afloat. Scores of outlets in the marsh (*marais*) rent boats with or without a boatman. The Syndicat des Bateliers Marais Poitevin (SBMP; Boatmen's Association; ☎ 05 46 35 02 29), Mairie d'Arçais, 79210 Arçais, publishes an annual boating guide. Those keen to row it alone should ask for a map before sailing into the green labyrinth. Tourist trails are well marked and it is hard to get lost providing you stick to these signposted waterways.

In **Maillezais**, behind Abbaye St-Pierre, the **Embarcadère de l'Abbaye** hires out boats in summer to row through the pea-green duckweed. A boat plus boatman in July or August costs 22FF per person per hour. The riverside cabin opens 10 am to noon and 2 pm to dusk.

From Maillezais, head south along the D15 to La Croix des Marys. Continue south on the D116 (La Ronde direction) and turn left (east) after crossing the bridge. This takes you along the river bank to the **Embarcadère du Marais Bazoin** (☎ 05 46 27 87 60), in Bazoin. Self-driven boats here cost 175/200FF per hour for up to two/four people, or 115FF per person for a boat with a boatman. There are also mountain bikes to rent for 25/100/300FF per hour/day/week. A cycling path snakes along the canal.

In **Arçais**, at the western end of the village, is the **Embarcadère Bardet-Huttiers** (☎ 05 49 35 39 18, @ embarcadere-bardet@marais-arcais.com), next to the municipal camp site on route de Damvix. A boat for up to four people costs 140FF per hour with a boatman, or 90FF per hour without.

Boats abound in pretty **Coulon**, one of France's loveliest villages, which sports particularly picturesque waters. The riverside D23 linking Coulon with Arçais makes for a beautiful cycling trip. There is a bicycle hire outlet in Coulon on place de l'Église, the central village square. Signposted off the square at 52 quai Louis Tardy is the **Embarcadère La Pigouille** (☎ 05 49 35 80 99), which charges 145/175FF for a boatman-driven boat for up to two/eight people, and 180/230FF per hour/day for a self-driven canoe for up to three people. It can supply you with a picnic for 48FF.

---

fax 04 59 24 90 29, @ tourisme.2.sevres@ wanadoo.fr), 15 rue Thiers.

For details of boat and bike trips, try the tourist office in Coulon (☎ 05 49 35 99 29, fax 05 49 35 84 31, @ ot@ville-coulon.fr), 8 place de l'Église, which has a useful Web site at www.ville-coulon.fr; or in Maillezais (☎ 02 51 87 23 01, fax 02 51 00 72 51), opposite the village church on rue du Docteur Daroux. The latter sells some excellent booklets which map out cycling (7FF) and walking (9FF) routes.

The flora, fauna, history and traditions of the Marais Poitevin are explained in the Maison des Marais Mouillés (House of Wet Marshes; ☎ 05 49 35 81 04, fax 05 49 35 83 26, @ mmm@wanadoo.fr), place de la Coutume, Coulon. It opens 10 am to noon and 2 to 7 pm Tuesday to Sunday, February to June and September to November; and 10 am to 8 pm daily, July and August. Admission costs 28FF (children aged six to 16 12FF).

Places to Stay

Niort has numerous accommodation possibilities. Two-star *France Hôtel* (☎ *05 49 24 01 35, rue des Cordeliers*) offers cheap singles/doubles costing upwards of 125/ 140FF (from 190FF with shower). In Fontenay-le-Comte, *Hôtel Le Fontarabie* (☎ *02 51 69 17 24, fax 02 51 51 02 73, @ font arabie@aol.com, 57 rue de la République*), on the main street in town, has very spacious singles/doubles costing 230/260FF; night arrivals can check in and retrieve a room key by paying with credit card at the machine outside. Coulon has several hotels on place de l'Église and quai Louis Tardy.

Idyllic, secluded spots in the marsh include *Hôtel du Marais* (☎ *05 49 35 37 08, fax 05 49 35 45 18, 1 place de l'Église, Arçais*), which has doubles costing 150FF (250FF with shower and toilet); and *Le Paradis* (☎ *05 49 35 33 95*), 4km west of Le Vanneau and signposted off the D102, which is a charming, waterside *chambre d'hôte* with rooms and boats to rent.

Places to Eat

Auberge du Vieux Batelier (☎ 02 51 87 02 11), on the banks of a canal in La Croix des Marys, 3km south of Maillé, is well worth a visit. Frogs legs, eel and *préfou* (garlic bread) are among the local specialities served. In Coulon, head for *Auberge La Pigouille* (☎ 05 49 35 80 99, 52 quai Louis Tardy).

Getting There & Away

Niort train station, on place Pierre Sémard, is well connected with Poitiers (77FF, 45 minutes to one hour, nine or 10 daily), from where there are connecting trains to St-Pierre des Corps, Tours, Aubrais-Orléans and Paris.

Getting Around

The area is impossible to explore by public transport; see the boxed text 'Boating & Cycling in Green Venice' for information on boat and bicycle rentals.

The Niort bus company Casa (☎ 05 49 24 93 47), 11–13 chemin du Fief Binard, operates a daily bus service between Niort and Coulon (20 minutes, eight or nine daily; three daily during school holidays). Between Niort or Coulon and Arçais, there is one daily bus. SNCF buses connect Niort train station with Fontenay-le-Comte (45 minutes, eight daily).

Europcar (☎ 05 49 24 66 04) has an office outside Niort train station, at 90 rue de la Gare. National Citer (☎ 05 49 77 57 00) is at No 74 on the same street. Budget and Avis have offices here too.

Language

Modern French developed from the *langue d'oïl*, a group of dialects spoken north of the River Loire that grew out of the vernacular Latin used during the late Gallo-Roman period. The langue d'oïl – particularly the Francien dialect spoken in the Île de France – eventually displaced the *langue d'oc*, the dialects spoken in the south of the country and from which the Mediterranean region of Languedoc got its name.

Around 122 million people worldwide speak French as their first language. The French, rightly or wrongly, have a reputation for assuming that all human beings should speak French – until WWI it was *the* international language of culture and diplomacy – and you'll find that any attempt to communicate in French will be much appreciated. Probably your best bet is always to approach people politely in French, even if the only sentence you know is '*Pardon, madame/monsieur/mademoiselle, parlez-vous anglais?*' (Excuse me, madam/sir/miss, do you speak English?).

For a more comprehensive guide to the French language, get hold of Lonely Planet's *French phrasebook*.

Grammar

An important distinction is made in French between *tu* and *vous*, which both mean 'you'. *Tu* is used only when addressing people you know well, children or animals. When addressing an adult who is not a personal friend, *vous* should be used unless the person invites you to use *tu*. In general, younger people insist less on this distinction, and they may use *tu* from the beginning of an acquaintance.

All nouns in French are either masculine or feminine and adjectives reflect the gender of the noun they modify. The feminine form of many nouns and adjectives is indicated by a silent *e* added to the masculine form, as in *étudiant* and *étudiante*, the masculine and feminine for 'student'. In the

following phrases we have indicated both masculine and feminine forms where necessary. The masculine form comes first, separated from the feminine by a slash. The gender of a noun is often indicated by a preceding article – 'the/a/some', *le/un/du* (m), *la/une/de la* (f) – or a possessive adjective – 'my/your/his/her', *mon/ton/son* (m), *ma/ta/sa* (f). With French, unlike English, the possessive adjective agrees in number and gender with the thing possessed: 'his/her mother' is always *sa mère*.

Pronunciation

Most letters in French are pronounced more or less the same as their English equivalents. A few which may cause confusion are:

j   as the 's' in 'leisure', eg *jour* (day)
c   before **e** and **i**, as the 's' in 'sit'; before **a**, **o** and **u** it's pronounced as English 'k'. When underscored with a 'cedilla' (ç) it's always pronounced as the 's' in 'sit'.

French has a number of sounds that are difficult for Anglophones to produce. These include:

- The distinction between the 'u' sound (as in *tu*) and 'oo' sound (as in *tout*). For both sounds, the lips are rounded and projected forward, but for the 'u' the tongue is towards the front of the mouth, its tip against the lower front teeth, whereas for the 'oo' the tongue is towards the back of the mouth, its tip behind the gums of the lower front teeth.

- The nasal vowels. With nasal vowels, the breath escapes partly through the nose and partly through the mouth. There are no nasal vowels in English; in French there are three, as in *bon vin blanc* (good white wine). These sounds occur where a syllable ends in a single **n** or **m**; the **n** or **m** is silent but indicates the nasalisation of the preceding vowel.

- The **r**. The standard **r** of Parisian French is produced by moving the bulk of the tongue backwards to constrict the air flow in the pharynx, while the tip of the tongue rests behind the lower front teeth. It's similar to the noise made by some people before spitting, but with much less friction.

Basics

Yes.	*Oui.*
No.	*Non.*
Maybe.	*Peut-être.*
Please.	*S'il vous plaît.*
Thank you.	*Merci.*
You're welcome.	*Je vous en prie.*
Excuse me.	*Excusez-moi.*
Sorry/Forgive me.	*Pardon.*

Greetings

Hello/Good morning.	*Bonjour.*
Good evening.	*Bonsoir.*
Good night.	*Bonne nuit.*
Goodbye.	*Au revoir.*

Small Talk

How are you?	*Comment allez-vous?* (polite)
	Comment vas-tu?/ Comment ça va? (informal)
Fine, thanks.	*Bien, merci.*
What's your name?	*Comment vous appelez-vous?*
My name is ...	*Je m'appelle ...*
I'm pleased to meet you.	*Enchanté/ Enchantée.* (m/f)
How old are you?	*Quel âge avez-vous?*
I'm ... years old.	*J'ai ... ans.*
Do you like ...?	*Aimez-vous ...?*
Where are you from?	*De quel pays êtes-vous?*

I'm from ...	*Je viens ...*
Australia	*d'Australie*
Canada	*du Canada*
England	*d'Angleterre*
Germany	*d'Allemagne*
Ireland	*d'Irlande*
New Zealand	*de Nouvelle Zélande*
Scotland	*d'Écosse*

the USA	*des États-Unis*
Wales	*du Pays de Galle*

Language Difficulties

I understand.	*Je comprends.*
I don't understand.	*Je ne comprends pas.*
Do you speak English?	*Parlez-vous anglais?*
Could you please write it down?	*Est-ce que vous pouvez l'écrire?*

Getting Around

I want to go to ...	*Je voudrais aller à ...*
I'd like to book a seat to ...	*Je voudrais réserver une place pour ...*

What time does the ... leave/arrive?	*À quelle heure part/arrive ...?*
(next)	*(prochain/e)*
aeroplane	*l'avion*
bus (city)	*l'autobus*
bus (intercity)	*l'autocar*
ferry	*le ferry(-boat)*
train	*le train*
tram	*le tramway*

Where is (the) ...?	*Où est ...?*
bus stop	*l'arrêt d'autobus*
metro station	*la station de métro*
train station	*la gare*
tram stop	*l'arrêt de tramway*
ticket office	*le guichet*

I'd like a ... ticket.	*Je voudrais un billet ...*
one-way	*aller-simple*
return	*aller-retour*
1st-class	*première classe*
2nd-class	*deuxième classe*

How long does the trip take?	*Combien de temps dure le trajet?*

The train is ...	*Le train est ...*
delayed	*en retard*
early	*en avance*
on time	*à l'heure*

Do I need to ...?	*Est-ce que je dois ...?*
change trains	*changer de train*
change platform	*changer de quai*

left-luggage locker	*consigne automatique*
platform	*quai*
timetable	*horaire*
I'd like to hire ...	*Je voudrais louer ...*
a bicycle	*un vélo*
a car	*une voiture*
a guide	*un guide*

Around Town

I'm looking for ...	*Je cherche ...*
a bank/	*une banque/*
an exchange	*un bureau de*
office	*change*
the city centre	*le centre-ville*
the ... embassy	*l'ambassade de ...*
the hospital	*l'hôpital*
my hotel	*mon hôtel*
the market	*le marché*
the police	*la police*
the post office	*le bureau de poste/*
	la poste
a public phone	*une cabine*
	téléphonique
a public toilet	*les toilettes*
the tourist office	*l'office du tourisme*
Where is (the) ...?	*Où est ...?*
beach	*la plage*
bridge	*le pont*
castle	*le château*
cathedral	*la cathédrale*
church	*l'église*

Signs

ENTRÉE	**ENTRANCE**
SORTIE	**EXIT**
RENSEIGNEMENTS	**INFORMATION**
OUVERT/FERMÉ	**OPEN/CLOSED**
INTERDIT	**PROHIBITED**
(COMMISSARIAT	**POLICE STATION**
DE) POLICE	
CHAMBRES	**ROOMS**
LIBRES	**AVAILABLE**
COMPLET	**NO VACANCIES**
TOILETTES, WC	**TOILETS**
HOMMES	**MEN**
FEMMES	**WOMEN**

island	*l'île*
lake	*le lac*
main square	*la place centrale*
mansion	*le manoir*
mosque	*la mosquée*
old city (town)	*la vieille ville*
the palace	*le palais*
quay/bank	*le quai/la rive*
ruins	*les ruines*
sea	*la mer*
square	*la place*
tower	*la tour*
What time does it open/close?	*Quelle est l'heure d'ouverture/ de fermeture?*
I'd like to make a telephone call.	*Je voudrais téléphoner.*
I'd like to change ...	*Je voudrais changer ...*
some money	*de l'argent*
travellers cheques	*des chèques de voyage*

Directions

How do I get to ...?	*Comment dois-je faire pour arriver à ...?*
Is it near/far?	*Est-ce près/loin?*
Can you show me on the map/ city map?	*Est-ce que vous pouvez me le montrer sur la carte/le plan?*
Go straight ahead.	*Continuez tout droit.*
Turn left.	*Tournez à gauche.*
Turn right.	*Tournez à droite.*
at the traffic lights	*aux feux*
at the next corner	*au prochain coin*
behind	*derrière*
in front of	*devant*
opposite	*en face de*
north	*nord*
south	*sud*
east	*est*
west	*ouest*

Accommodation

I'm looking for ...	*Je cherche ...*
the youth hostel	*l'auberge de jeunesse*

the camp site	*le camping*
a hotel	*un hôtel*

Where can I find a cheap hotel?	*Où est-ce que je peux trouver un hôtel bon marché?*
What's the address?	*Quelle est l'adresse?*
Could you write it down, please?	*Est-ce que vous pourriez l'écrire, s'il vous plaît?*
Do you have any rooms available?	*Est-ce que vous avez des chambres libres?*

I'd like to book ...	*Je voudrais réserver ...*
a bed	*un lit*
a single room	*une chambre pour une personne*
a double room	*une chambre double*
a room with a shower and toilet	*une chambre avec douche et WC*

I'd like to stay in a dormitory.	*Je voudrais dormir dans un dortoir.*

How much is it ...?	*Quel est le prix ...?*
per night	*par nuit*
per person	*par personne*
Is breakfast included?	*Est-ce que le petit dé-jeuner est compris?*
Can I see the room?	*Est-ce que je peux voir la chambre?*

Where is ...?	*Où est ...?*
the bathroom	*la salle de bains*
the shower	*la douche*

Where is the toilet?	*Où sont les toilettes?*

I'm going to stay ...	*Je resterai ...*
one day	*un jour*
a week	*une semaine*

Shopping

How much is it?	*C'est combien?*
It's too expensive for me.	*C'est trop cher pour moi.*
Can I look at it?	*Est-ce que je peux le/la voir?* (m/f)

I'm just looking.	*Je ne fais que regarder.*

Do you accept credit cards?	*Est-ce que je peux payer avec ma carte de crédit?*
Do you accept travellers cheques?	*Est-ce que je peux payer avec des chèques de voyage?*
It's too big/small.	*C'est trop grand/petit.*

more/less	*plus/moins*
cheap	*bon marché*
cheaper	*moins cher*

bookshop	*la librairie*
chemist/pharmacy	*la pharmacie*
laundry/laundrette	*la laverie*
market	*le marché*
newsagent's	*la maison de presse*
stationer's	*la papeterie*
supermarket	*le supermarché*

Time & Dates

What time is it?	*Quelle heure est-il?*
It's (two) o'clock.	*Il est (deux) heures.*
When?	*Quand?*
today	*aujourd'hui*
tonight	*ce soir*
tomorrow	*demain*
day after tomorrow	*après-demain*
yesterday	*hier*
all day	*toute la journée*
in the morning	*du matin*
in the afternoon	*de l'après-midi*
in the evening	*du soir*

Monday	*lundi*
Tuesday	*mardi*
Wednesday	*mercredi*
Thursday	*jeudi*
Friday	*vendredi*
Saturday	*samedi*
Sunday	*dimanche*

January	*janvier*
February	*février*
March	*mars*
April	*avril*
May	*mai*
June	*juin*

July	*juillet*
August	*août*
September	*septembre*
October	*octobre*
November	*novembre*
December	*décembre*

Numbers

1	*un*
2	*deux*
3	*trois*
4	*quatre*
5	*cinq*
6	*six*
7	*sept*
8	*huit*
9	*neuf*
10	*dix*
11	*onze*
12	*douze*
13	*treize*
14	*quatorze*
15	*quinze*
16	*seize*
17	*dix-sept*
20	*vingt*
100	*cent*
1000	*mille*
one million	*un million*

Health

I'm sick.	*Je suis malade.*
I need a doctor.	*Il me faut un médecin.*
Where is the hospital?	*Où est l'hôpital?*
I have diarrhoea.	*J'ai la diarrhée.*

I'm ...	*Je suis ...*
anaemic	*anémique*
asthmatic	*asthmatique*
diabetic	*diabétique*
epileptic	*épileptique*
pregnant	*enceinte*

I'm allergic ...	*Je suis allergique ...*
to antibiotics	*aux antibiotiques*
to penicillin	*à la pénicilline*
to bees	*aux abeilles*

antiseptic	*antiseptique*
aspirin	*aspirine*

Emergencies

Help!	*Au secours!*
Call a doctor!	*Appelez un médecin!*
Call the police!	*Appelez la police!*
Leave me alone!	*Fichez-moi la paix!*
I've been robbed.	*On m'a volé.*
I've been raped.	*On m'a violée.*
I'm lost.	*Je me suis égaré/ égarée.* (m/f)

condoms	*préservatifs*
contraceptive	*contraceptif*
medicine	*médicament*
nausea	*nausée*
sunblock cream	*crème solaire haute protection*
tampons	*tampons hygiéniques*

FOOD

breakfast	*le petit déjeuner*
lunch	*le déjeuner*
dinner	*le dîner*
grocery store	*l'épicerie*

I'd like the set menu.	*Je prends le menu.*
I'm a vegetarian.	*Je suis végétarien/ végétarienne.* (m/f)
I don't eat meat.	*Je ne mange pas de viande.*

Starters (Appetisers)

assiette anglaise
  plate of cold mixed meats and sausages
assiette de crudités
  plate of raw vegetables with dressings
entrée
  starter
fromage de tête
  pâté made with pig's head set in jelly
soufflé
  a light, fluffy dish made with egg yolks, stiffly beaten egg whites, flour and cheese or other ingredients

Soup

bouillon
  broth or stock

bourride
  fish stew; often eaten as a main course
croûtons
  fried or roasted bread cubes, often added
  to soups
potage
  thick soup made with pureed vegetables
soupe de poisson
  fish soup
soupe du jour
  soup of the day

Meat, Chicken & Poultry

agneau	lamb
aiguillette	thin slice of duck fillet
andouille or	sausage made from
andouillette	pork or veal tripe
bifteck	steak
bœuf	beef
bœuf haché	minced beef
boudin blanc	white-meat sausage
boudin noir	blood sausage
	(black pudding)
brochette	kebab
canard	duck
caneton	duckling
cervelle	brains
charcuterie	cooked or prepared
	meats (usually pork)
cheval	horse meat
chèvre	goat
chevreau	kid (goat)
chevreuil	venison
côte	chop of pork, lamb or
	mutton
côtelette	cutlet
cuisses de	frogs legs
grenouilles	
entrecôte	rib steak
dinde	turkey
épaule d'agneau	shoulder of lamb
escargot	snail
faisan	pheasant
faux-filet	sirloin steak
filet	tenderloin
foie	liver
foie gras de canard	duck liver pâté
gibier	game
gigot d'agneau	leg of lamb
jambon	ham
langue	tongue
lapin	rabbit

lard	bacon
lardon	pieces of chopped
	bacon
lièvre	hare
mouton	mutton
oie	goose
pieds de porc	pig's trotters
pigeonneau	squab (young pigeon)
pintade	guinea fowl
porc	pork
poulet	chicken
rillon	minced pork fried in
	cubes
rillette	minced pork paste
rognons	kidneys
sanglier	wild boar
saucisson	large sausage
saucisson fumé	smoked sausage
steak	steak
tournedos	thick slices of fillet
tripes	tripe
veau	veal
venaison	venison
viande	meat
volaille	poultry

Common Meat & Poultry Dishes

blanquette de veau or *d'agneau*
  veal or lamb stew with white sauce
bœuf bourguignon
  beef and vegetable stew cooked in red
  wine (usually burgundy)
chapon
  capon
chou farci
  stuffed cabbage
choucroute
  sauerkraut with sausage and other prepared meats
confit de canard or *d'oie*
  duck or goose preserved and cooked in
  its own fat
coq au vin
  chicken cooked in wine
civet
  game stew
fricassée
  stew made with meat that has first been
  fried
grillade
  grilled meats

marcassin
  young wild boar
quenelles
  dumplings made of a finely sieved mixture of cooked fish or (rarely) meat
steak tartare
  raw ground meat mixed with onion, raw egg yolk and herbs

Ordering a Steak

bleu
  nearly raw
saignant
  very rare (literally, 'bleeding')
à point
  medium rare but still pink
bien cuit
  literally, 'well cooked', but usually like medium rare

Fish & Seafood

anchois	anchovy
anguille	eel
bigorneau	periwinkle
brème	bream
brochet	pike
bulot	whelk
cabillaud	cod
calmar	squid
carpe	carp
carrelet	plaice
chaudrée	fish stew
colin	hake
coquillage	shell fish
coquille St-Jacques	scallop
crabe	crab
crevette grise	shrimp
crevette rose	prawn
écrevisse	small, freshwater crayfish
fruits de mer	seafood
gambas	king prawns
goujon	gudgeon (small fresh water fish)
hareng	herring
homard	lobster
huître	oyster
langouste	crayfish
langoustine	very small, saltwater 'lobster' (Dublin Bay prawn)

lotte	monkfish
loup	sea bass
maquereau	mackerel
merlan	whiting
morue	cod
moules	mussels
mulet	grey mullet
oursin	sea urchin
palourde	clam
perche	perch
poisson	fish
raie	ray
rouget	red mullet
sandre	pike perch
sardine	sardine
saumon	salmon
sole	sole
thon	tuna
truite	trout

Vegetables, Herbs & Spices

ail	garlic
aïoli or *ailloli*	garlic mayonnaise
aneth	dill
anis	aniseed
artichaut	artichoke
asperge	asparagus
aubergine	aubergine (eggplant)
avocat	avocado
basilic	basil
betterave	beetroot
cannelle	cinnamon
cardon	artichoke from Touraine
carotte	carrot
céleri	celery
cèpe	cepe (boletus mushroom)
champignon	mushroom
champignon de Paris	button mushroom
chou	cabbage
citrouille	pumpkin
concombre	cucumber
cornichon	gherkin (pickle)
courgette	courgette (zucchini)
crudités	small pieces of raw vegetables
échalotte	shallot
épice	spice
épinards	spinach

estragon	tarragon
fenouil	fennel
fève	broad bean
genièvre	juniper
gingembre	ginger
haricots	beans
haricots blancs	white beans
haricots rouge	kidney beans
haricots verts	French (string) beans
herbe	herb
laitue	lettuce
légume	vegetable
lentilles	lentils
mâche	lamb's lettuce
maïs	sweet corn
menthe	mint
mojette	flat bean from Vendée
navet	turnip
oignon	onion
olive	olive
origan	oregano
panais	parsnip
persil	parsley
petit pois	pea
pissenlit	dandelion leaf
poireau	leek
poivron	green pepper
pomme de terre	potato
ratatouille	casserole of aubergines, tomatoes, peppers and garlic
riz	rice
salade	salad or lettuce
salicorne	marsh samphire
sarrasin	buckwheat
seigle	rye
tomate	tomato
truffe	truffle

Cooking Methods

à la broche	spit-roasted
à la vapeur	steamed
au feu de bois	cooked over a wood-burning stove
au four	baked
en croûte	in pastry
farci	stuffed
fumé	smoked
gratiné	browned on top with cheese
grillé	grilled

pané	coated in breadcrumbs
rôti	roasted
sauté	sauteed (shallow fried)

Sauces & Accompaniments

béchamel
  basic white sauce
beurre blanc
  white sauce from Nantes, traditionally served with fish
huile d'olive
  olive oil
mornay
  cheesy bechamel sauce
moutarde
  mustard
tartare
  mayonnaise with herbs
vinaigrette
  salad dressing made with oil, vinegar, mustard and garlic

Fruit & Nuts

abricot	apricot
amande	almond
ananas	pineapple
arachide	peanut
banane	banana
cacahuète	peanut
cassis	blackcurrant
cerise	cherry
citron	lemon
datte	date
figue	fig
fraise	strawberry
framboise	raspberry
grenade	pomegranate
groseille	red currant/gooseberry
mangue	mango
marron	chestnut
melon	melon
mirabelle	type of plum
myrtille	bilberry (blueberry)
noisette	hazelnut
noix de cajou	cashew
orange	orange
pamplemousse	grapefruit
pastèque	watermelon
pêche	peach
pistache	pistachio
poire	pear
pomme	apple

prune	plum
pruneau	prune
raisin	grape
reine claude	greengage

Desserts & Sweets

bergamotes
  orange-flavoured confectionary
crêpe
  thin pancake
crêpes suzettes
  orange-flavoured crepes flambeed in liqueur
dragée
  sugared almond
éclair
  pastry filled with cream
far
  flan with prunes (a Breton speciality)
farine de semoule
  semolina flour
flan
  egg-custard dessert
frangipane
  pastry filled with cream and flavoured with almonds or a cake mixture containing ground almonds
galette
  wholemeal or buckwheat pancake; also a type of biscuit
gâteau
  cake
gaufre
  waffle
gelée
  jelly
glace
  ice cream
glace au chocolat
  chocolate ice cream
île flottante
  literally 'floating island'; beaten egg white lightly cooked, floating on a creamy sauce
macarons
  macaroons (sweet biscuit made of ground almonds, sugar and egg whites)
sablé
  shortbread biscuit

tarte
  tart (pie)
tarte tatin
  upside-down, caramelised apple tart
yaourt
  yogurt

Snacks

croque-monsieur
  a grilled ham and cheese sandwich
croque-madame
  a croque-monsieur with a fried egg
frites
  chips (French fries)
quiche
  quiche; savoury egg, bacon and cream tart

Basics

beurre	butter
chocolat	chocolate
confiture	jam
crème fraîche	thickened cream
farine	flour
huile	oil
lait	milk
miel	honey
œufs	eggs
pain	bread
poivre	pepper
sel	salt
sucre	sugar
vinaigre	vinegar

Drinks

bière	beer
eau	water
vin	wine

Utensils

bouteille	bottle
carafe	carafe
pichet	jug
verre	glass
couteau	knife
cuillère	spoon
fourchette	fork
serviette	serviette (napkin)

Glossary

Masculine gender is indicated as (m), feminine gender (f) and plural (pl).

abbaye (f) – abbey
accueil (m) – reception
affinage (m) – maturing of cheese
aire de vision de la faune (f) wildlife observation tower
alimentation (f) – general store
allée (f) – pedestrian lane or path (Nantes)
AOC (appellation d'origine contrôlée) (f) – label guaranteeing the origin and quality of wine and cheese
à pans de bois – half-timbered
atelier (m) – artisan's workshop
auberge (f) – inn
auberge de jeunesse (f) – youth hostel

baie (f) – bay
basilique (f) – basilica
basse mer (f) – low tide
batelier (m) – boatman
biche (f) – doe
billetterie (f) – ticket office
billet jumelé (m) – combination ticket, valid for more than one attraction
bouchon (m) – brasserie typical to Lyon
boulangerie (f) – bread shop
boule de fort (f) – Loire version of French *boules*, not unlike lawn bowls, played with heavy wooden and metal balls on an indoor court
brasserie (f) – restaurant usually serving food all day

carnet (m) – book of tickets
carte (f) – card, menu, map
cave (f) – wine or cheese cellar
cerf (m) – red deer or stag
chambre d'hôte (f) – B&B accommodation/guesthouse
charcuterie (f) – delicatessen
chasse (f) – the hunt
château (m) – castle
château fort (m) – fortified medieval castle
coffre (m) – hotel safe

comité régional/départemental du tourisme (m) – regional/departmental tourist board
commune (f) – municipality
consigne (f) – left-luggage office
corniche (f) – cornice
corps de logis (m) – main chateau building
couchette (f) – sleeping berth on a train or ferry
cour (f) – courtyard
cour d'honneur (f) – main or central courtyard; literally 'courtyard of honour'
crêperie (f) – pancake house
cru (m) – wine of recognised superior quality; literally 'great growth'
Cyberposte (f) – the post office's Internet access service
cyclisme (m) – cycling

daim (m) – fallow deer
dégustation (f) – tasting
département (m) – administrative division of France, smaller than a *région*
domaine (m) – estate
donjon (m) – castle keep
douve (f) – moat

écluse (f) – lock
église (f) – church
elevage (m) – breeding
embarcadère (m) – pier or jetty
en corbellement – corbelled
épicerie (f) – small grocery store
escalier (m) – staircase
étang (m) – lagoon, pond or lake

faubourg (m) – suburb, street
fête (f) – party or festival
fleur de lys (f) – lily; symbol of French royalty
forêt (f) – forest
formule (f) – set menu, allowing a choice of courses
fromagerie (f) – cheese shop

gare (f) – train station
gare routière (f) – bus station

gentilhommière (f) – rural manor house
gîte d'étape (m) – hikers' accommodation
gîte rural (m) – country cottage
GR (grande randonnée) (f) – long-distance walking trail
grands châteaux (pl) – major chateaux

halles (pl) – covered market
haute noblesse (f) – nobility
hôtel de ville (m) – town hall
hôtel particulier (m) – private mansion
hôte payant (m) – paying guest

jardin (m) – garden
jardin botanique (m) – botanical garden
jardin de France (m) – garden of France; Loire Valley
jours feriés (pl) – public holidays

lentilles d'eau (f) – duckweed
levée (f) – embankment
locature (f) – 16th-century dwelling in La Sologne where chateau workers lived
lucarne (f) – dormer window

mail (m) – promenade or tree-lined avenue
mairie (f) – town hall
maison de la presse (f) – large newsagent's shop
marais (m) – marsh or swamp
marais salant (m) – salt pan
marché (m) – market
marinier (m) – bargeman, boatman
menu (m) – meal at a fixed price comprising two or more courses
millésime (m) – exceptional wine produced in a year of optimum climatic conditions
moulin (m) – mill
musée (m) – museum

négociant en vins (m) – wine merchant

œuvre (f) – work (of art, literature)
office du tourisme (m) – tourist office
orangeaie (f) – orange grove
orangerie (f) – orangery
oratoire (m) – oratory

paludier (m) – salt worker
parvis (m) – square in front of a church
pâtisserie (f) – cake and pastry shop

pavillon (m) – pavilion or lodge
petite noblesse (f) – gentry
pont (m) – bridge
poste (f) – post office
préfecture (f) – prefecture, capital of an administrative département
presqu'île (f) – peninsula
prieuré (m) – priory
producteur de vins (m) – wine producer or grower, also known as a *vigneron*
produits du terroir (pl) – local food products

région (f) – the largest French administrative division, composed of smaller *départements*
reine (f) – queen
roi (m) – king

salin (m) – salt marsh
salle de garde (f) – guards' hall
sentier (m) – trail
service des urgences (m) – hospital accident and emergency ward
SNCF (Société Nationale des Chemins de Fer) (f) – French state-owned railways
son et lumière (m) – sound and light show
spectacle (m) – show, spectacle
supplément (m) – supplement, additional cost
sur rendez-vous (SRV) – by appointment
syndicat d'initiative (m) – municipal tourist office

tabac (m) – tobacconist's (also sells stamps and phonecards)
taxe de séjour (f) – municipal tourist tax
TGV (train à grande vitesse) (m) – high-speed train
toiture (f) – roof

Val de Loire (m) – Loire Valley
vallée (f) – valley
Vallée des Rois (f) – Valley of Kings; Loire Valley
vendanges (pl) – grape harvest
verrière (f) – stained-glass window
VF (version française) (f) – film dubbed into French

vigneron (m) – wine grower
vin de garde (m) – wine best drunk after several years in storage
vin de pays (m) – literally 'country wine'

voie (f) – train platform
voûte (f) – vault
VTT (vélo tout terrain) (m) – mountain bike

Lonely Planet On-line

Whether you've just begun planning your next trip, or you're chasing down specific info on currency regulations or visa requirements, check out Lonely Planet On-line for up-to-the minute travel information.

As well as mini guides to more than 250 destinations, you'll find maps, photos, travel news, health and visa updates, travel advisories, and discussion of the ecological and political issues you need to be aware of as you travel. You'll also find timely upgrades to popular guidebooks which you can print out and stick in the back of your book.

There's also an on-line travellers' forum where you can share your experience of life on the road, meet travel companions and ask other travellers for their recommendations and advice.

And of course we have a complete and up-to-date list of all Lonely Planet travel products including travel guides, diving and snorkeling guides, phrasebooks, atlases, travel literature and videos, and a simple on-line ordering facility if you can't find the book you want elsewhere.

Lonely Planet Diving & Snorkeling Guides

Beautifully illustrated with full-colour photos throughout, Lonely Planet's Pisces Books explore the world's best diving and snorkelling areas and prepare divers for what to expect when they get there, both topside and underwater.

Dive sites are described in detail with specifics on depths, visibility, level of difficulty, special conditions, underwater photography tips, and common and unusual marine life present. You'll also find practical logistical information and coverage on topside activities and attractions, sections on diving health and safety, plus listings for diving services, live-aboards, dive resorts and tourist offices.

Guides by Region

L onely Planet is known worldwide for publishing practical, reliable and no-nonsense travel information in our guides and on our Web site. The Lonely Planet list covers just about every accessible part of the world. Currently there are thirteen series: travel guides, shoestring guides, walking guides, city guides, phrasebooks, audio packs, city maps, travel atlases, diving and snorkeling guides, restaurant guides, first-time travel guides, healthy travel and travel literature.

AFRICA Africa – the South ● Africa on a shoestring ● Arabic (Egyptian) phrasebook ● Arabic (Moroccan) phrasebook ● Cairo ● Cape Town ● Cape Town city map● Central Africa ● East Africa ● Egypt ● Egypt travel atlas ● Ethiopian (Amharic) phrasebook ● The Gambia & Senegal ● Healthy Travel Africa ● Kenya ● Kenya travel atlas ● Malawi, Mozambique & Zambia ● Morocco ● North Africa ● South Africa, Lesotho & Swaziland ● South Africa, Lesotho & Swaziland travel atlas ● Swahili phrasebook ● Tanzania, Zanzibar & Pemba ● Trekking in East Africa ● Tunisia ● West Africa ● Zimbabwe, Botswana & Namibia ● Zimbabwe, Botswana & Namibia travel atlas
Travel Literature: The Rainbird: A Central African Journey ● Songs to an African Sunset: A Zimbabwean Story ● Mali Blues: Traveling to an African Beat

AUSTRALIA & THE PACIFIC Auckland ● Australia ● Australian phrasebook ● Bushwalking in Australia ● Bushwalking in Papua New Guinea ● Fiji ● Fijian phrasebook ● Islands of Australia's Great Barrier Reef ● Melbourne ● Melbourne city map ● Micronesia ● New Caledonia ● New South Wales & the ACT ● New Zealand ● Northern Territory ● Outback Australia ● Out To Eat – Melbourne ● Papua New Guinea ● Papua New Guinea (Pidgin) phrasebook ● Queensland ● Rarotonga & the Cook Islands ● Samoa ● Solomon Islands ● South Australia ● South Pacific Languages phrasebook ● Sydney ● Sydney city map ● Tahiti & French Polynesia ● Tasmania ● Tonga ● Tramping in New Zealand ● Vanuatu ● Victoria ● Western Australia
Travel Literature: Islands in the Clouds ● Kiwi Tracks ● Sean & David's Long Drive

CENTRAL AMERICA & THE CARIBBEAN Bahamas, Turks & Caicos ● Bermuda ● Central America on a shoestring ● Costa Rica ● Cuba ● Dominican Republic & Haiti ● Eastern Caribbean ● Guatemala, Belize & Yucatán: La Ruta Maya ● Jamaica ● Mexico ● Mexico City ● Panama ● Puerto Rico
Travel Literature: Green Dreams: Travels in Central America

EUROPE Amsterdam ● Amsterdam city map ● Andalucía ● Austria ● Baltic States phrasebook ● Barcelona ● Berlin ● Berlin city map ● Britain ● British phrasebook ● Brussels, Bruges & Antwerp ● Budapest city map ● Canary Islands ● Central Europe ● Central Europe phrasebook ● Corsica ● Croatia ● Czech & Slovak Republics ● Denmark ● Dublin ● Eastern Europe ● Eastern Europe phrasebook ● Edinburgh ● Estonia, Latvia & Lithuania ● Europe ● Finland ● France ● French phrasebook ● Germany ● German phrasebook ● Greece ● Greek phrasebook ● Hungary ● Iceland, Greenland & the Faroe Islands ● Ireland ● Italian phrasebook ● Italy ● Lisbon ● London ● London city map ● Mediterranean Europe ● Mediterranean Europe phrasebook ● Norway ● Paris ● Paris city map ● Poland ● Portugal ● Portugal travel atlas ● Prague ● Prague city map ● Provence & the Côte d'Azur ● Romania & Moldova ● Rome ● Russia, Ukraine & Belarus ● Russian phrasebook ● Scandinavian & Baltic Europe ● Scandinavian Europe phrasebook ● Scotland ● Slovenia ● Spain ● Spanish phrasebook ● St Petersburg ● Switzerland ● Trekking in Spain ● Ukrainian phrasebook ● Vienna ● Walking in Britain ● Walking in Ireland ● Walking in Italy ● Walking in Switzerland ● Western Europe ● Western Europe phrasebook
Travel Literature: The Olive Grove: Travels in Greece

INDIAN SUBCONTINENT Bangladesh ● Bengali phrasebook ● Bhutan ● Delhi ● Goa ● Hindi/Urdu phrasebook ● India ● India & Bangladesh travel atlas ● Indian Himalaya ● Karakoram Highway ● Kerala ● Mumbai ● Nepal ● Nepali phrasebook ● Pakistan ● Rajasthan ● Read This First: Asia & India ● South India ● Sri Lanka ● Sri Lanka phrasebook ● Trekking in the Indian Himalaya ● Trekking in the Karakoram & Hindukush ● Trekking in the Nepal Himalaya
Travel Literature: In Rajasthan ● Shopping for Buddhas

LONELY PLANET

Mail Order

L onely Planet products are distributed worldwide. They are also available by mail order from Lonely Planet, so if you have difficulty finding a title please write to us. North and South American residents should write to 150 Linden St, Oakland, CA 94607, USA; European and African residents should write to 10a Spring Place, London NW5 3BH, UK; and residents of other countries to PO Box 617, Hawthorn, Victoria 3122, Australia.

ISLANDS OF THE INDIAN OCEAN Madagascar & Comoros • Maldives • Mauritius, Réunion & Seychelles

MIDDLE EAST & CENTRAL ASIA Arab Gulf States • Central Asia • Central Asia phrasebook • Hebrew phrasebook • Iran • Israel & the Palestinian Territories • Israel & the Palestinian Territories travel atlas • Istanbul • Istanbul to Cairo • Jerusalem • Jordan & Syria • Jordan, Syria & Lebanon travel atlas • Lebanon • Middle East on a shoestring • Syria • Turkey • Turkish phrasebook • Turkey travel atlas • Yemen
Travel Literature: The Gates of Damascus • Kingdom of the Film Stars: Journey into Jordan

NORTH AMERICA Alaska • Backpacking in Alaska • Baja California • California & Nevada • Canada • Chicago • Chicago city map • Deep South • Florida • Hawaii • Honolulu • Las Vegas • Los Angeles • Miami • New England • New Orleans • New York City • New York city map • New York, New Jersey & Pennsylvania • Pacific Northwest USA • Puerto Rico • Rocky Mountain States • San Francisco • San Francisco city map • Seattle • Southwest USA • Texas • USA • USA phrasebook • Vancouver • Washington, DC & the Capital Region • Washington DC city map
Travel Literature: Drive Thru America

NORTH-EAST ASIA Beijing • Cantonese phrasebook • China • Hong Kong • Hong Kong city map • Hong Kong, Macau & Guangzhou • Japan • Japanese phrasebook • Japanese audio pack • Korea • Korean phrasebook • Kyoto • Mandarin phrasebook • Mongolia • Mongolian phrasebook • North-East Asia on a shoestring • Seoul • South-West China • Taiwan • Tibet • Tibetan phrasebook • Tokyo
Travel Literature: Lost Japan

SOUTH AMERICA Argentina, Uruguay & Paraguay • Bolivia • Brazil • Brazilian phrasebook • Buenos Aires • Chile & Easter Island • Chile & Easter Island travel atlas • Colombia • Ecuador & the Galapagos Islands • Latin American Spanish phrasebook • Peru • Quechua phrasebook • Rio de Janeiro • Rio de Janeiro city map • South America on a shoestring • Trekking in the Patagonian Andes • Venezuela
Travel Literature: Full Circle: A South American Journey

SOUTH-EAST ASIA Bali & Lombok • Bangkok • Bangkok city map • Burmese phrasebook • Cambodia • Hanoi • Healthy Travel Asia & India • Hill Tribes phrasebook • Ho Chi Minh City • Indonesia • Indonesia's Eastern Islands • Indonesian phrasebook • Indonesian audio pack • Jakarta • Java • Laos • Lao phrasebook • Laos travel atlas • Malay phrasebook • Malaysia, Singapore & Brunei • Myanmar (Burma) • Philippines • Pilipino (Tagalog) phrasebook • Singapore • South-East Asia on a shoestring • South-East Asia phrasebook • Thailand • Thailand's Islands & Beaches • Thailand travel atlas • Thai phrasebook • Thai audio pack • Vietnam • Vietnamese phrasebook • Vietnam travel atlas

ALSO AVAILABLE: Antarctica • The Arctic • Brief Encounters: Stories of Love, Sex & Travel • Chasing Rickshaws • Lonely Planet Unpacked • Not the Only Planet: Travel Stories from Science Fiction • Sacred India • Travel with Children • Traveller's Tales

Index

Text

Boxed Text

Bold indicates maps.

MAP LEGEND

BOUNDARIES

━··━··━··━ ....Regional

HYDROGRAPHY

..........................Coastline
.....................River, Creek
.............................Lake
━·━·━·━·━ ....Canal

.........................Building
.............................Hotel
..................Urban Area

ROUTES & TRANSPORT

.....................Autoroute
................Primary Road
.............Secondary Road
.....................Tertiary Road
─ ─ ─ ─ ─ ....Unsealed Road
..............City Freeway
..............City Highway

......................City Road
...........City Street, Lane
............Pedestrian Mall
⇒═══:........................Tunnel
┝─┼─┼─O─┼....Train Route & Station
▰▰▰▰▰▰.....................Tramway
············...........Walking Tour

AREA FEATURES

...........Park, Gardens
.................Cemetery
..........................Market

.......................Forest
...........................Beach
...........................Rocks

MAP SYMBOLS

🐾 **NANTES** ....City
◉ **Blois** ....Large Town
◉ **Bressuire** ....Town
◉ Chalans ....Village

● ....Point of Interest

🏠 ....Place to Stay
▲ ....Camp Site
⌂ ....Caravan Park
⌂ .... Hut or Chalet

▼ .... Place to Eat
🍴 .... Pub, Cafe or Bar

🔶 ......Ancient or City Wall
⊖ .... Bank or
                      Bureau de Change
🔺 ....Beach
🚌 🚏 ....Bus Station, Bus Stop
🏰 ....Castle or Chateau
⛪ ☷ ......Church or Cathedral
🎬 .... Cinema
🏛 ... Embassy or Consulate
🌲 .... Forest
⛲ ....Fountain
✚ .... Hospital or Clinic
ℹ .... Information
📱 ....Internet Cafe

⛩ ....Lighthouse
🗼 ....Monument
🏛 ....Museum
Ⓟ ....Parking Area
⭐ ....Police Station
✉ .... Post Office
🔲 .... Ruins or
                      Archaeological Site
⊗ ....Shopping Centre
🏊 ....Swimming Pool
✡ ....Synagogue
🚕 .... Taxi Rank
🎭 ....Theatre
🚐 .... Transport

Note: not all symbols displayed above appear in this book

LONELY PLANET OFFICES

Australia
PO Box 617, Hawthorn, Victoria 3122
☎ 03 9819 1877 fax 03 9819 6459
email: talk2us@lonelyplanet.com.au

USA
150 Linden St, Oakland, CA 94607
☎ 510 893 8555 TOLL FREE: 800 275 8555
fax 510 893 8572
email: info@lonelyplanet.com

UK
10a Spring Place, London NW5 3BH
☎ 020 7428 4800 fax 020 7428 4828
email: go@lonelyplanet.co.uk

France
1 rue du Dahomey, 75011 Paris
☎ 01 55 25 33 00 fax 01 55 25 33 01
email: bip@lonelyplanet.fr
www.lonelyplanet.fr

World Wide Web: www.lonelyplanet.com *or* AOL keyword: lp
Lonely Planet Images: lpi@lonelyplanet.com.au